RELATIONAL
HORIZONS

RELATIONAL HORIZONS

Mediterranean Voices Bring Passion and Reason
to Relational Psychoanalysis

Edited by
ALEJANDRO ÁVILA

IPBOOKS.net
International Psychoanalytic Books

International Psychoanalytic Books (IPBooks)
New York • http://www.IPBooks.net

International Psychoanalytic Books (IPBooks),
Astoria, New York
Online at: http://www.IPBooks.net

ISBN: 978-0-9995965-7-9

Table of Contents

Foreword

A funny thing happened to me when I was preparing the scientific program for the 2007 Athens conference for the International Association for Relational Psychoanalysis and Psychotherapy (IARPP). A computer malfunction caused the loss of information about the panel submissions of the Spaniards who were planning to travel to Greece and participate in the event. I was upset because I had no way to communicate with them. Not knowing even their names, I felt devastation and walked around for days murmuring, "What happened to the Spaniards?" Finally, the Spaniards sent an email message and we resolved matters. They came to the conference armed with dazzling theoretical and clinical presentations for an eager international audience. The Andalusian-Athens connection was saved. Years later in 2011, Alejandro Avila of Madrid and Ramon Riera of Barcelona co-chaired the Madrid conference of IARPP, the very year I was president of IARPP. Thus, continued the scholarly contributions of today's Spaniards to the expansion and dissemination of relational ideas and practice. If it can be said that relational thinking has been part of the global age of psychoanalysis, and I believe there is clear evidence for this, then the Spaniards have played a crucial role.

Relationality as a concept has evolved over time to become an entity of its own, on which theoretical, social, and educational enterprises have been built. In the development of relational psychoanalysis and psychotherapy, a book emerging from a specific country or geographical region is a natural addition. The creation of this edited volume by Avila is a major achievement. By composing it, Avila and his colleagues allow us to consider the vast archipelago of relational thinking with Spanish eyes.

It is of historical interest that the first translation of Freud's collected works was in Spanish by the philosopher Ortega y Gasset. But as Avila explains while relational thinking took formal hold in Spain in the early part of the 21st century, it has its roots in the 1960s when the intrapsychic began to lose its grip on the clinical psychological world of Spain. The contributors to this volume have been influenced by the early developments of the relational school in the United States and even before that by the pioneering interpersonal and cultural schools of psychoanalysis as exemplified by H. S. Sullivan and Erich Fromm. Yet, the contributors in this book travel with their own Mediterranean sensibilities about theory construction, and ways of uniting the humanities and sciences.

Culture and context have always been said to be important in modern psychology but those who practice relational psychoanalysis actually mean it. Moreover, one of the major clinical principles of relational perspective is that every psychoanalytic dyad has its unique features and from this we know that the participants have to invent their own therapeutic process of change. This process has bidirectional elements. It is rooted in each participant's psychological core and the manner in which he or she is influenced by the other. But because they were not directly educated in psychoanalysis by Anglo-American traditions, what we find in these pages is a particular passion for relational thinking that incorporates a Mediterranean sensibility with a particular Spanish coloring.

This does not mean that they use the post-Romantic European imaginary that is treated critically by many contemporary thinkers within Spain and elsewhere in the Mediterranean. The reader of this book will not find the most frequent romanticizing tendency that the Spanish culture is the expression of a tragic, primitive, and folkloric Spain. There are no references to *Don Quixote*, the poet Federico García Lorca, the painter Salvador Dalí, the filmmaker Luis Buñuel, the composer Manuel de Falla, medieval Iberia, the Franco dictatorship, *Guernica*, economic austerity, the political leftist party *Podemos*, or soccer.

The thinking and values that are at the root of these assembled essays go beyond stereotypes. They bring us to a wide breadth of coverage of contemporary relational thinking and what strategies and methods are viable and effective in best serving others. The Spanish sensibility in these pages is a modern one.

Like other nations of the Mediterranean (i.e., Greece, Italy, and Israel), Spain's cultural heritage has often been turned into a commodity for craving tourists seeking exoticism. In the volume, you the reader hold in your hands, this is highly resisted. These studies have an insightful sensitivity to globalization and its means of communication across nations and generations. In fact, it may be an underlying premise of all the chapters in this book that understanding our relationality in a global age and its pathologies allows us to brave our vulnerable, common humanity-that of our patients and our own. The pathologies, according to Florentine philosopher Elena Pulcini, can be our sense of unlimited individualism and fearful, closed communities.

Deep down what the writers know in their blood and bones is that the relational approach is neither comforting for the patient nor the therapist, but it can be healing. What is clear is that the Spaniards are not relationalists because they lack discipline. They are relationalists because they think deeply and feel deeply and therefore honor their humanity, their social consciousness and that of their patients. Lastly, they help us understand, to paraphrase the American artist Robert Rauschenberg, that relational ideas are not real estate.

We have reasons to be grateful to Alejandro Avila and the contributors to this anthology and the English language version of their essays. They remind us that some recent and sparkling thinking about relational horizons can be accomplished from across the Atlantic. We should not be surprised. We might even be influenced if we have the good fortune.

I have always been fond of a delicious story told by the playful Chilean Pablo Neruda. It was about being with the enchanting enchanter - Federico García Lorca. Neruda was reading one of the poems he was working on to his friend. Neruda says that halfway through his Andalusian friend would stop, raise his arms, shake his head, cover his ears, and cry, "Stop! Stop! That's enough, don't read any more, you'll influence me!" I believe the reader of this book may be delighted with such an influence.

Spyros D Orfanos, Ph.D., ABPP
New York City, USA

Presentation

Psychoanalysis in Spain has a plural history, rooted in Freudian and Kleinian traditions but evolved to a variety of developments linked to contemporary psychoanalysis. The impact of socio-political factors forced several migratory movements, that came back to Spain under the form of criticism to classical psychoanalysis, following emerging ideas from Latin America (e.g. Pichon Rivière) and North America (Cultural and Interpersonal Psychoanalysis, Self Psychology, Intersubjective System theories, and specially Steve Mitchell's relational perspective) that enriched psychoanalytic thinking, and promote new psychoanalytic institutions. These lines of evolution converge in the first decades of the 21st century, drawing a horizon full of advances that from the south of Europe look towards the rest of the world, in dialogue with the different psychoanalytic traditions.

Psychoanalysis began to establish its roots in Spain in 1922 when the Spanish philosopher José Ortega y Gasset recommended publishing Freud's writings. This task was completed in 1934 with the publication of a 17-volume edition in Spanish that receiving Freud compliments. In 1928 Sándor Ferenczi came to Spain to give lectures, and by this time a small number of psychiatrists already had a positive view of psychoanalysis, such as Gonzalo Rodriguez Lafora, Emilio Mira i López, and especially Angel Garma, who was analyzed by Theodor Reik in Berlin between 1927 and 1930, and became the first psychoanalyst in Spain to belong to the International Association of Psychoanalysis (IPA). Garma would have been the promoter of psychoanalytic training in Spain, but when the Spanish Civil War broke out in 1936 he was forced to leave the country and seek refuge in Argentina, where he was among the founders of the Argentine Psychoanalytic Association. A decade later, under the auspices of the Switzerland and Paris Psychoanalytic Societies, a small group of people began to develop a psychoanalytic movement in Barcelona and Madrid, and in 1959 this movement was formally accepted by the IPA under the name of the Spanish Society of Psychoanalysis (Sociedad Española de Psicoanálisis or SEP). The Spanish Society anchored its thinking on Kleinian theory, especially the Kleinian group of London. By 1973 the members of the Madrid branch of the Society began a new group that was formally recognized in 1981 under the name of the Madrid Psychoanalytic Association (Asociación Psicoanalítica de Madrid or APM) and it was in Madrid that the IPA celebrated its 33th Congress under the presidency of Adam Limentani.

In order to have a better understanding of the development of psycho-analysis in Spain, it is important to highlight the cultural context that made that development possible. By this time, the Spanish psychoanalytic arena was more complex than what was represented by the institutes that belonged to the IPA. Some phenomena that can be summarized as highlights that defined the relations between psychoanalysis and Spanish society are the following:

1. At the end of the 1960s Spain slowly emerged from a deep cultural and economic deprivation that had made it difficult to have access to psychoanalytic training. Until then, psychoanalytic training was reserved for people with a high socio-economic status.

2. During the 1970s psychoanalysis was severely criticized for its lack of social and cultural interest. Those were the times of the Antipsychiatry and the Freudian-Marxist movements, and strong political involvement of many people in culture and the sciences, but less so among Spanish psychoanalysts associated with the IPA. At that time also many psycho-analysts from Argentina, Uruguay and Chile came to Spain fleeing the military dictatorships in those countries. Many of them remained in Spain as practitioners, supervisors and training analysts, and became prominent figures who contributed not only to psychoanalytic thinking but also to the renewal of mental health programs in Spain.

3. Finally, from the end of the 1970s until now, different psychoanalytic theoretical trends began to flourish in Spain that went beyond classical Freudian and Kleinian perspectives, such as the Lacanian and cultural and social-interpersonal psychoanalysis (mainly in its group version). In addition, the writings of Ferenczi, Fairbairn, Winnicott, Bion, Pichon Rivière and others were translated to Spanish and began to have a greater influence. By the 1990s, self psychology and intersubjective theories enriched psychoanalytic thinking, as well as Steve Mitchell's relational perspective.

Until recently, psychoanalytic training and practice in Spain had been mainly a private affair. The presence of psychoanalysis in the universities as a part of the curricula in psychology, psychiatry, and social work had been minimal, and decreased strongly in the last decades. This has been in part due to the lack of interest of many IPA psychoanalysts to expand psychoanalytic thought to other arenas, persuaded by the notion that analytic training must occur far from the universities and must be confined to psychoanalytic institutes. And concerning psychoanalytic practice, there is a widespread notion that psychoanalysis cannot be provided under the public health system. Thus, without public health programs that support psychoanalysis, and with a psychoanalytic training that is framed outside the universities, the Spanish scenario is very different from that existing in countries such as Germany, Italy or France.

Given that psychoanalytic institutes in Spain were primarily under the auspices of the IPA and, therefore, ruled by more traditional psychoanalytic values, the winds of change have blown in groups that exist outside the IPA. During the 1970s many training and clinical psychoanalytic institutions were created outside the IPA, some of them under the Cultural-Interpersonal tradition and affiliated to the International Federation of Psychoanalytical Societies (IFPS). Some of the psychoanalysts who came from Argentina created their own societies, more open to the views of contemporary psychoanalysis.

From the second half of the 1990s until now there has been in Spain a greater openness to contemporary psychoanalytic trends of thought: Self Psychology, Motivational Systems Theory (from J. Lichtenberg, F. Lachmann, and J. Fosshage); Intersubjective Systems Theory (from R. Stolorow, G. Atwood, D. Orange), Relational Psychoanalysis (from S.A. Mitchell, L. Aron and others) all of them have exerted a deep influence and some of the more classically oriented practitioners have shifted their theoretical views to new ones. Increasingly, too, new candidates are choosing to train outside IPA societies, and even some societies, such as SEP, are widening their scope to include contemporary psychoanalysis in their training curricula.

In the last three decades a group of Spanish university professors involved in psychoanalysis have come together each year to share interests and to promote psychoanalytic training and research within the Spanish universities, developing some publications (Ávila & Poch, 1994; Poch & Ávila, 1998, among others)[1]. By this time, Spanish researchers have been also accepted to

---

1 See: Ávila Espada, A. & Poch Bullich, J. (1994). *Manual de Técnicas de Psicoterapia. Un enfoque psicoanalítico.* Madrid: Siglo XXI Eds; and Poch Bullich, J. & Ávila Espada, A. (1998). *Investigación en psicoterapia. La contribución psicoanalítica.* Barcelona: Paidos.

join the Research Training Program of the IPA in London so that some research programs in psychoanalysis and psychoanalytic psychotherapy have been conducted in Spain, even if without much support from other public or private institutions. In the clinical and training arena some themes, activities, groups of interest and leaderships must be highlighted. Relational psychoanalysis, along with contemporary Self Psychology and Intersubjective Systems Theory, were introduced in Spain since 2000, and the first Spanish conference on Relational Psychoanalysis was held in Almagro in 2002, with the participation of Robert Stolorow and Gianni Nebbiosi. In 2005 the Spanish Chapter of the International Association for Relational Psychoanalysis and Psychotherapy (IARPP) was founded by A. Avila, and in 2006 the Institute of Relational Psychotherapy and its *Agora Relacional Center* (Madrid) were also founded, an institute that organizes annual conferences and a variety of lectures given by prominent figures of contemporary psychoanalysis, such as Joseph Lichtenberg, Robert Stolorow, Donna Orange, Steven Knoblauch, Frank Summers, Michael Eigen, Hazel Ipp, Margaret Crastnopol, Sandra Buechler, James Fosshage, Howard Bacal, Horst Kächele, among many others. The institute also hosted the IX International Conference of IARPP in Madrid in 2011, and started a book series on relational thought (Relational Thinking Series)[2], now with 20 titles, and an e-journal (CeIR, since 2007)[3], both in Spanish open to worldwide Spanish speaking community.

This book emerges from these efforts and joins three last decades of efforts developing relational psychoanalysis from the perspective of Spanish authors. We consider our conceptual roots and the special influence of Ferenczi, Balint, Winnicott and Mitchell, between others. Relational thought is anti-Cartesian and involves a fundamental questioning of the classic division of the two substances – thought and matter – inherited from the theological separation between body and soul, and the subsequent focus on intra-psychic phenomena. In this way, we try to overcome extreme therapist/patient asymmetry and static terms – such as transference– that convey the idea of a difficult communication between two independent minds or self-contained compartments.

---

2 "Pensamiento Relacional" Series (www.psicoterapiarelacional.es/Publicaciones.aspx) under the direction of Alejandro Ávila. Since 2010 until now 20 volumes have been published or in progress, including Spanish authors originals plus translations of main works of S.A. Mitchell, R. Stolorow, G. Atwood & D. Orange, M. Eigen, S. Buechler, D. Ehrenberg, P. Bromberg and more.

3 ISSN 1988-2939. DOI: 10.21110/19882939 www.psicoterapiarelacional.es/CeIRRE-VISTAOnline/CEIRPortada.aspx

A fully explanation of main relational concepts and the evolving trends of relational thinking is summarized, with special attention paid to reconsidering diagnostics and psychopathology in a way that allow us to re-think our clinical practice and experience, identifying the relational basis of excessive mental suffering. The relational perspective in psychoanalysis transcends the classic dichotomy "unconscious fantasy" versus "real trauma" and allows to integrate in the therapeutic space the irreconcilable states that fragment the historical sense of the self and that constitute the adaptation to the trauma. It also allows us to structure models that explain vulnerability and resilience, as well as psychopathological itineraries based on early trauma.

Clinical psychotherapeutic technique is also revised as a balance between relational providing and frustration in a context of involvement and mutuality between clinician and person, with special attention paid to setting role in the change process, and the specificity of clinical work in contexts like couple relationships and sexuality and the work with children and adolescents. Along the book the useful of research findings (Neuroscience, Infant research) to relational clinical work is considered as a way to face our challenges as psychotherapists in a changing world.

The chapters included in this book contribute to contemporary psycho-analysis with new horizons that dialogue with current worldwide developments, writen from our Mediterranean shores, a sea that has always been the source of Western culture, the cradle of explorers, thinkers, clinicians and scientists.

Alejandro Ávila
Madrid, April 2017

1

Relational Psychoanalysis In Evolution: Roots, Concepts, Trends And Challenges[1]

Alejandro Ávila Espada

Our Roots

Relational thinking in the area of clinical and community mental health work has a long history. In Spain this formally began during the Conference on Intersubjectivity held in Almagro (Ciudad Real, Spain) in 2002, with the participation of prominent figures in relational thinking, such as Robert Stolorow (one

---

1 This text is based on the opening speech at the IV *Conference for Relational Psychoanalysis*, Salamanca, Hospedería Fonseca of the University of Salamanca, 28 October 2016, whose central focus was "Mentalization". This text is based on the review and updating of concepts in various previous papers (Ávila, 2002, 2005, 2013a, 2013b, 2015a, 2015b, 2016). I thank my colleagues Joan Coderch, Carlos Rodríguez Sutil and Juan José Martínez Ibáñez for the ideas we have shared and their valued opinions.

the main developers of Intersubjective Systems Theory in North America) and Gianni Nebbiosi (an exponent of Contemporary Self Psychology in Europe). Amongst those of us present at that inaugural meeting in Almagro were those seeing it as being the way forward for clinical work in our context: people who represented and were interested in the relational perspective, which, in its many facets has brought together diverse traditions of renovation in psychoanalysis, humanist thinking, and socially-committed clinical psychology.

Those of us in Spain who have held these ideas right back since the 1960's, a journey of more than 40 years, hailed from different traditions: social, group and link psychoanalysis, which took up the thoughts, and clinical and psycho-social studies of E. Pichon Rivière (1985), and which put the social before the intrapsychic[2] (also present in the work of E. Fromm[3]); J. Bleger's (1959) and the Baranger´s (1969) dialectic ideas and the theory of the analytic field; the recognition of Sullivan's[4] interpersonal approach; F. Fromm-Reichman and H. Searles' focus on working with severe mental illness. Others came from the Kleinian tradition, but have gone beyond it, relinquishing the sphere of unconscious fantasy and embracing the social and interpersonal reality found in the patient-therapist relationship (such as Coderch, 2001). Also present were avid readers identifying with Winnicott (such as Abello and Liberman, 2011; Sainz, 2017), as well as those who vindicate Ferenczi's clinical thought and that of the followers of the Hungarian school, such as M. Balint (Balint, 1967; Daurella, 2013). We also came together in our interest for contemporary Self Psychology arising from the second period of Kohut's work (such as Riera, 2002). And many of us read, debated and incorporated into our clinical work the ideas of authors such as Mitchell (1988), Stolorow, Brandchaft & Atwood (1987), and Stolorow, Atwood & Orange (2002), amongst others, references for our thinking at the turn of the 21st century.

This renaissance in social and intersubjective thinking was inherent to psychoanalysis from early times, with Ferenczi, Rank, Adler and Jung disputing the rigid interpretation of Freud's thinking; although it has always

---

2 See the book by F. Fabris (2007) for a more in-depth knowledge of the contributions and influence of Enrique Pichon-Rivière's thinking. See also the recent book: R. Losso, L.S. de Setton & D.E. Scharff: *The Linked Self in Psychoanalysis. The pioneering work of Enrique Pichon Riviere* (London: Karnac, 2017).

3 For an introduction to the relevance of E. Fromm's work, see the chapter by R. Castaño in the compilation by A. Ávila (2013c).

4 For an introduction to the relevance H.S. Sullivan's work, see my chapter in *La tradición interpersonal. Perspectiva social y cultural en Psicoanálisis.* (Ávila, A. (Ed.), 2013c).

been disavowed in Freudian psychoanalysis, it was never fully set aside, and was resurrected time and time again. What we today term 'relational' cannot be understood without vindicating the trauma theory against the fantasy theory, as well as Ferenczi's freedom of technique; nor without Adler's social questioning or Jung's anthropological-cultural principles in understanding the construction of subjectivity.

These seeds were able to grow in the space made by these authors and their followers, particularly in the interpersonal approach developed by Sullivan from the 30's onwards. Without this interpersonal sensitivity, the crisis of Freud's drive theory (as a core explanation of psychic dynamics) or Kleinian endogenism would have become entrenched. North American Ego Psychology had already indirectly led towards a relational scenario by focussing on the reorganisation of defences through transference. All reflections on object relations led to highlighting the importance of the (relational) object in constructing subjectivity, and when Greenberg & Mitchell (1983) reviewed these concepts, it was the prelude to the conceptual formulation of relational clinical work (S.A. Mitchell, *Relational Concepts in Psychoanalysis*, 1988).

The growth of the relational perspective was unremitting during the 1990's, and since then it has taken its rightful place among the principle forces of change in contemporary psychoanalysis, providing a common roof to the different traditions re-examining psychoanalysis. There was a slowly growing interest in recovering Ferenczi's work and thinking (which had been eschewed for years) after the publication of his 1932 Clinical Diary[5] and the debunking of the falsehoods about him disseminated by E. Jones. Winnicott's work was re-read and understood beyond his clinical work with children, and his ideas were reviewed alongside Kohut's Self Psychology. Jungian psychology and relational thinking converge on many points. Attachment theory began to be considered as central in understanding child development and clinical psychotherapy. Infant research has continued to contribute proof of the fundamental role of the processes of early intersubjectivity in psychological development (see Beebe & Lachmann, 2013), and neuroscience has confirmed the active role of the relational context in the shaping of neural networks that pick up emotional experiences in connection with their meanings, which can be modified by relational experience.

At the same time, relational sensitivity was intrinsic to questioning gender bias (Benjamin, 2004), as well as other social, racial and ideological

---

5 It should be noted that it was not published until 1988, when J. Dupont, his legatee, was able to distribute translations of the text.

inequalities, and discord among different cultural traditions (Altman, 2011). All this as well as looking to philosophy to review the ethics involved in clinical practice (Orange, 2010).

Summarising this historical development[6] of the roots of relational clinical thinking on mental health: the psychoanalytic tradition's focus on the intrapsychic is being progressively influenced by numerous theoretical developments coming from both classic and contemporary analysts who are allowing themselves to think more freely. At the same time, advances in knowledge contribute to a better understanding of the nature and functioning of the processes that intervene in the differentiation of subjectivity. This complex dialectic between opposing conceptual standpoints, evidence from research, and epistemological perspectives is crystallising around two crucial developments, mentioned above: intersubjectivity theory (emerging from the framework of contemporary Self Psychology, mainly developed by R. Stolorow and D. Orange), and what would be termed 'relational psychoanalysis', an expression coined by Stephen Mitchell, a melting pot of a wide range of thinking which has not ceased to grow since the end of the 90's. Beyond institutional issues and debates over historicism, the variety and quality of positions that converge in this new perspective are remarkable, and are proof of transformation of a thinking begun by Freud's prodigious work, which was already under review by Ferenczi, in the counterpoint brought by Jung, and then continued by so many restless seekers of the origins of subjectivity.

The different lines of thought coming together in relational thinking share the following points:

a) They have been developed by clinicians with a genuine interest in their patients' needs without sacrificing them to the demands of research, inflexible theories or 'orthodox' interpretations of those theories.

b) Observing (and intervening from) the co-created relationship; a scene that is shared and participated in by both patient and clinician is considered fundamental. Thus, both participants 'bring' their own personalities and relational matrices, mutually influencing one another, albeit with a certain asymmetry regarding ethical responsibility (the clinician's care for the patient).

c) They have recognised that patient and clinician come from and belong to social contexts that define them, thus accepting a questioning of the

---

6 In my 2015(a) paper, I include diagrams illustrating this development (figure 1), and the integration of different lines of thinking into the relational perspective (figure 2).

social and ideological meanings of clinical intervention, the meaning and function it fulfils in a given society, and the values it promotes and those it rejects.

Dialogue in the relational space is based on these premises and along these lines of transformation. Rather than a prescriptive theoretical focus, it has become a place of meeting where, in the U.S., the U.K., Italy, Canada (among other cultural areas)[7], there have been continual systematic contributions and development of ideas and experiences which have transformed clinical practice, as well as our way of understanding the world, both as people and clinicians; this is a *world* whose references are being undergoing profound examination.

In this appraisal of trends in relational clinical work and identifying the challenges facing it, having now described its historical bases, I should like to examine the conceptual framework. I will define some concepts regarding diagnosis and psychopathology, and then address issues of method, all seen in the light of the concepts and results from research in neuroscience, human development, and change processes in psychotherapy.

The Relational World

By 'relational' we understand a *perspective* from which to understand the nature of human and social processes which are manifest both in the expression of each person's subjectivity (an innate intersubjectivity, humans come to the world geared for social connection), as well as the social formations resulting from human action. These derive from structures of relationship within a constituent socio-subjective matrix. Individuals, starting out with the disposition their biological legacy provides, grow and adjust in the only world possible – the relational world (Tronick et al, 1978; Stern, 1985; Trevarthen, 1993), through networks of social and emotional bonds (from primary caregivers to a later social complexity), and they participate in their development and change[8].

Human beings emerge from and are agents in their relational weave; we are in constant construction, a construction comprising the impressions made by experience, and which is in constant potential transformation with every new experience (which is unavoidably relational), whatever its quality. Every look, every bodily contact, every potential attunement or breakdown with significant

---

7 Since the year 2000, and since 2002 in Spain.
8 See the book by our colleague Ramon Riera (2011) on the role of emotional connection in the construction and development of subjectivity and the influence of evolutionary factors. Also the *Boston Change Process Study Group* contributions (2010) and D.N. Stern work (2004).

others in our contexts – all these, filtered by our temperament, contribute to us being who we are: capable of action and meaningful experience in every relationship, be they 'real' interactions, or those contained within a subjective mental world, fantasies or memory traces. Both afford object constancy, allowing ourselves to remain fairly integrated and to be expressed in and with their multiplicities.

Thinking about others, mentally representing them, feeling with others, the assimilation and experience of empathy, imitating others and feeling imitated, inferring others' intentions and feeling recognised, recognising others and ourselves in our differences and also our links and ruptures. This task is procedurally consolidated in relational patterns that make up our systems of implicit relational knowing; *it is both ourselves and others*. For this reason, "mentalising" the relational matrix to which we belong and in which we exist (Fonagy, 1989; Coderch, 2010) is a core process in structuring subjectivity, thinking of ourselves in relation to others, our similarities and differences. At the same time we build representations of ourselves and others – not through identification, projection and introjection with already differentiated subjects. The meanings of who/what we are, and who/what others are, are the result of an essentially group process.

Three conceptual clarifications need to be made in regard to the relational perspective's[9] theoretical premises and the core ideas already mentioned:

- the break with the Cartesian distinction between mind and body that trapped us into viewing the individual as an "isolated mind" (what classic psychoanalysis described as a psychological structure based on an unconscious interaction among the drives in conflict with the social context), a container of traces of traumatic memories, fantasies and defences. The relational paradigm represents a profound shift that can be summarized as ceasing to consider subjectivity as a containing 'mental apparatus', to instead deeming it to *be the result of a relational matrix or weave of bonds* integrated by a history of experiences of meaningful relationships occurring in contexts experienced, together with the psychic and neural memory traces that connect it. Thus psychic experience and mental processes are now considered to result from the reciprocal influence between an individual and others in a bidirectional intersubjective

---

9 I follow Coderch's conceptualisation (2011), giving my own explanations in order to illustrate my point of view, and integrating the wealth of ideas that help constitute it (Mitchell, Stolorow-Atwood-Orange, Bromberg, Lachmann, Aron, and many others), as well as my own earlier revisions (Ávila, 2015a).

context (formed in the intercommunication of reciprocally interacting worlds of experience), connected by *unconscious organising principles* and in intersubjective, inter-fantasmatic weaves.

- The main focus in the study of relational clinical work is *intersubjectivity*, the phenomenal level where the intersubjective exchange takes place, which is decisive in the construction of subjective experience and the development of the self. 'Intersubjective' refers to when at least two subjectivities establish the same field with the intention of mutual recognition and where all subjectivity is known through recognition of the other. Psychic activity expands as *patterns and contents* of relational experience that can be represented and emerge from an evolution of basic human needs (attachment and recognition among them) and the difficulties in their expression and development. Intersubjectivity in mutual recognition is a central aspect in the developing self in which gratification of primary narcissism plays a crucial role until it can be substituted by a healthier narcissism, transformed through social interplay. Subjective and interpersonal realms are reciprocally determined, but we assume that the *subjective realm is constituted via the registering-internalisation of intersubjective experience*. Such internalised intersubjective experience is biologically influenced and articulated within a subjectivity that is unavoidably intra-, inter- and trans-subjective.

- It is necessary to reformulate the concept of the unconscious, differentiating its processes into discrete dimensions that consist of at least three levels of phenomena: 1) The *pre-reflective unconscious*. Pre-reflective structures of experience derived from early interactions operating as *schemata*[10] – what Lyons-Ruth (1999) has termed the *implicit-procedural level*; 2) The *dynamic unconscious*, the classic object of psychoanalysis, repressed drives[11], but also emotional states that are concealed by the defences for protection from re-traumatisation when they are not empathically validated by the context; 3) The *invalidated unconscious* (experiences that cannot be articulated as they never evoked a response from the context that granted word or meaning; for example,

---

10 Organising principles operating outside of consciousness that give form to and organise a person's experiences.

11 Experiences that were mentally represented but were denied conscious articulation as they were perceived as posing a threat to relationships that are physically and psychologically necessary for a person's survival.

the *unthought known* (Bollas, 1987)). These processes, which are inaccessible to consciousness, can and must be understood in respect of relational contexts of early life and meaning-making.

We shall now go on to identify the concepts of psychopathology, the diagnostic methods, and types of intervention that characterise our perspective.

Reconsidering Diagnostics and Psychopathology

Any diagnosis implies some kind of categorisation along a normal-pathology continuum. For this reason, I shall first revise what psychopathology is and then reconsider the value of diagnosis, both from a relational perspective.

Psychopathology has become established both as an attempt at system-izing clinical observation and as the generation of semiotics and a language that allows us to bring the complexity of human suffering under systematic observation and within a dialogue that is commonly accepted by clinicians. Burdened from the very start by a dependence on a medical model of illness, psychopathology is bound to arouse controversy as the uniqueness of experi-ence expressed in mental illness (an individual who suffers and/or makes others suffer, where those around cannot understand, look after or tolerate the suffering) cannot be reduced to the classification of an illness except for the purpose of comparison, a language shared by observers. However, no categorisation can account for what is really important for people: *I sense that you sense that I sense...* in an interminable sequence where all levels of intersubjectivity cross one another, from intrasubjective figuring (the individual interpreting his or her world of experience), the intersubjectivity we have described in interpersonal relationships and the fantasies concerning them, to trans-subjectivity (where the subjective is transcended and is manifested in phenomena that elude our understanding).

Even though it may not be possible to completely break with all the terminology of *psychopathology*, what we experience in clinical work is not reducible to the symptoms a diagnosis of mental illness has helped to recognise and define; even less will it help to identify the "clinical conditions" that can bring more confusion than clarity in connecting with and understanding another person's world of experience. If we only rely on symptoms, we fail to recognise the *person* by how they express themselves and where they acquire meaning. If we assume we have identified a personality structure and organisation, and we represent a person's dynamic and clinical traits by assigning a diagnostic category which is beyond what we feel comfortable with conceptually, we might lose sight of the person, who will never be a particular syndrome or classification however many criteria are satisfied. Ultimately, as I shall point out below, the usefulness of diagnosis–nosology is in assigning the most appropriate treatment, and as we know, if conventional psychological treatment can be characterised by anything, it is its lack of specificity.

Focusing our clinical enquiry on symptoms or clinical profiles distances us from our basic task: living the experience of an encounter that can become transformative – precisely because there is no reification, but the opening of an opportunity to allow subjectivity to surface and, in some measure, be known and shared. This is because humans are involved in a constant process of individuation arising from their fundamental intersubjectivity. It is what Rodríguez Sutil (2014) has termed "the relational person and his problems". This is a good starting point to think about psychopathology from the perspective of relational clinical work, which is understood as a "human and social science" of subjective experience. We start out by knowing a language (that of clinical diagnosis and the accepted classifications of mental disorders) to then *not* be submitted to restrictions, but move beyond their pursuit of reductionism and simplification. This can be seen in the use of labels such as "hysteria" or "borderline personality disorder" – we stop dialoguing and sharing with the person to gratify ourselves with the discovery of reified clinical work.

If we aim to connect with, understand, recognise others in their uniqueness, to leave space for transformation in the encounter with the other, clinicians must find a balance (an unstable one between their own need to recognise themselves and recognise the other in what is known) and receptiveness to an experience which could turn up surprises at any moment. In this task, relational clinicians accept the discomfort of not reifying the other through the use of diagnostic labels, and of relaxing our tendency to understand from internalised schemata as much as possible. Once beyond the demands of everyday clinical work, where we have to use our ethics and our resources to help others (see further on), a space is opened in which we will successively need to deconstruct the filters of theoretical understanding until an intersubjective encounter arises and begins its own journey.

Having become involved in this de-construction, relational clinicians:

- Set up a space of containment, then (once necessary attention has been given to the most pressing clinical needs) a holding bond where a set of measures operating in the realm of reality have been put into place considering the patient's requirements and limitations.

- Formulate our experiential understanding from the quality and characteristics of the *conflicts* expressed by people, principally their interpersonal communication, as well as their intrapsychic experience (we consider dysfunctional schemata operating outside of consciousness to be within the compass of *conflicts*, while a *disorder* derives from neural limitations - traumatic or biogenetic – in processing schemata).
- Consider that basic conflict is shaped by early environmental shortcomings that are re-edited in later relational matrices. Psychic fabric is woven on implicit relational knowing derived from the matrix of early relationships, including progressively conflictive nodes originating from contexts where there have been failings or requiring a compensatory over-adaptation to failings. This implicit relational knowing is what comes together in *unconscious organising patterns* (or specific neural networks) which are repeated in relational situations that are instrumental in activating them. These "conflicts" are re-created outside of consciousness in a person's biography through and in his present relationships, and the therapeutic relationship provides an opportunity to access the person's experience and possibly modify the conflicts. Thus we need to pay special attention to the conditions of deficit and traumatic experience, something all humans share.
- As Coderch highlights (in Coderch & Plaza, 2016), from the standpoint of relational psychoanalysis, the main source of people's emotional disorders stems from a failure in satisfying their emotional needs (love, attention, care, communication, having their love accepted, comprehension, etc) during infancy. For this reason relational clinicians take part in an optimal balance between provision and frustration, with a bias towards a provision that restores basic relational failures.
- After observing the dynamics of the most conspicuous defences in the clinical encounter, we avoid focusing on them, although we do promote resources for activating more mature, flexible defences.
- We take into account characteristics of the structural organisation of the observable personality and its clinical expressions, accepting that any categorisation is instrumental so far as unclearly defined prototypes are concerned. As clinicians, we use these to provisionally reduce our limitations of knowledge, not as representations of a person's "reality".
- We recognise the presence of determinants of character in the multifaceted expression of personality. The basic multiplicity of experience individuals build of themselves occurs as integration between socio-cultural factors and the biophysical individuality that is expressed within them.

- During our possible encounter with the other, we take note of the relational matrix formed by the constant evolution of attachment patterns experienced by a person from birth onwards, in which a *person* has developed narcissistically, and has to some extent shaped a predominant attachment pattern and has progressed from dependence to independence, while establishing (and recovering) meanings.

Thus, rather than psychopathology, relational clinicians need to re-think our clinical practice and experience in order to identify the relational bases of *excessive mental suffering* and the multiple ways it can be expressed in humans, in fantasy, bodily, and in relationships – both intimate ones and in those in which the individual acts as either agent or victim, influenced by patterns of social relationships. This is the aim of our diagnostic approach.

If we do not need to identify precise diagnostic categories to guide our practice, what diagnostic approaches and techniques will prove useful, and why do we need them?

Diagnostic procedures that consider the individual as an object to be observed as objectively as possible are misleading, although not without their use.

It is essential to observe, if we keep observer bias in check as much as possible and bearing in mind that it is an observation in which both parts are involved. We observe and bring together all the contents of what we observe, of the object of observation, the subject, and the link between both. Sullivan (1963, 1964) helped us to understand the incalculable value of detailed enquiry as a strategy to reaching a more complex, in-depth knowledge of the interpersonal reality that gives meaning to all experience; it is of utmost importance when estimating any positioning on the normal-abnormal, healthy-pathological continuum. For this reason we recognise the indisputable status of the clinical interview, which takes place precisely through detailed enquiry in an interpersonal field. This allows the subtleties of interpersonal connection to be appreciated as it glides across different languages, verbal and non-verbal.

Dialogue is explicit and implicit, and allows narratives to be registered. These narratives are essentially interpersonal and give insight into auto-biographical, contextual and historical-subjective aspects, and the complex matrix of meanings that are present in any encounter. The patient, the supposed subject of observation, tells us stories which we multiply and replicate in the different possible weaves of interaction.

Thus, the unstructured interview is the indispensable diagnostic technique, where supposed subjects of observation recount their experiences and memories, offering their narratives as participant-observers who are involved in what is experienced. The observer, gathering the information in which he is a participant (the stories are told to him or her), lets the experience reverberate while trying to keep the balance of someone who is observing facts, despite it being impossible not to be part of them. Any tactic that helps narrative flow is useful, e.g. prompting interpersonal narratives (RAP: The relationship anecdotes paradigm[12]); or enquiring into the capacity for mentalisation (The Situations Test for Mentalisation Evaluation (TESEM)[13]. And that is without mentioning the resources for expression brought by patients themselves (personal and autobiographical documents), drawings, doodles, or play, all rich sources of potential narrative which might not yet be expressed verbally, but is present all the same.

All nomothetic approaches, all quantitative or psychometric objectification have attempted to reduce the ambiguity of the data gathered, especially the inconsistency of observers' criteria -this has been necessary to be clear of ideological interpretations. However, the wealth contained within the data lies within its ideographical character, and so qualitative techniques open the door to dialogue with subjectivity. Our aim is not to categorise but to know, to open the door to self- and shared knowledge.

Obtaining *precise* details about categories of structural organisation, attachment patterns, intervening motivational systems or levels of defences is not a good strategy in relational clinical work. The same applies in respect to criteria concerning symptoms and syndromes. This valuable backdrop allows a clinician to balance his theory-based systematic knowledge with what can be observed. Relational clinicians refuse to reduce what they observe to categories of observation, instead they build the weave of shared experience where the supposed subjects of observation become *agents of self-knowledge through the reflective function that develops in the encounter with the clinician*, where both parts get to know one another and change.

The strategy for diagnosis consists in recreating patients' capacity for (self) observation in an interpersonal setting, letting themselves be accompanied in this observation. The technique is dialogue on all levels of language. Clinicians' strategies help them not to let up in their intersubjective enquiry. The goal is to re-arouse the agency the supposed subjects of observation have alienated in

12 Lester Luborsky: The Relationship Anecdotes Paradigm (RAP) Interview as a versatile source of narratives. Chapter 7 in Luborsky, LesterCrits-Christoph, Paul. (1998). *Understanding transference: The Core Conflictual Relationship Theme method*, 2nd ed. (pp. 109-120). Washington, DC, US: American Psychological Association, xxi, 379 pp.
13 The *Test de Situaciones para la Evaluación de la Mentalización*, an assessment tool developed in Spanish (G. Lanza: Revista de la Asociación de Psicoterapia de la República Argentina, noviembre de 2011. http://www.revistadeapra.org.ar/ultimo.htm)

order to mitigate the anxiety caused in interpersonal encounters, thus discovering themselves in this sort of role-reversal or pathological accommodation (Brandchaft, Doctors & Sorter, 2010), which will lessen the suffering caused by deficits, trauma or conflict.

Is There A Theory of Relational Technique?

The reflections we have just made on diagnostics clearly show the direction and sense of the answer to this question. We should agree to draw up a core idea of technique for clinical work built around the ability to gain interpersonal knowledge of the intersubjective processes making up mental life. Our principal, fundamental "technique" is participant observation mediated by an ethical questioning of the sense of our participation, the limit being our capacity for attunement with the suffering other (Orange, 2011). However, we are not speaking of a technique that can be described in a manual (although in professional training we do use certain "manuals" to build better skills for observing complex human phenomena, while avoiding norms and rules a clinician should follow).

What clinicians generally term "technique" is, in the relational paradigm, a particular way of reflecting and experiencing that takes place in the subjective participation between therapist and patient within the clinical encounter, where the shared experience of discovery will guide the process.

Together, a colleague[14] and I identified a series of relational premises regarding what we term "technique", but which are elements of the relational strategy of the clinician's intersubjective listening to and observation of the supposed subject of observation:

1. In first place, the focus of observation is the relationship between the people termed patient and therapist; it is the field shared by both and to which we have direct access.
2. We prefer to think about phenomena from their (at least) bi-personal structure, cause and manifestation – never as belonging to just one person.
3. We centre our attention (together with the patient) on "real events" in which the patient participates without substituting them with fantasies (but without relegating their role in a patient's identity).

14 J.J. Martínez Ibáñez

4. Thinking about thoughts, or mentalisation, becomes the linchpin of the therapeutic task in connection with the emotions evoked and organised[15]. Together with the other, we construct emotionally-charged language and thought for "unformulated experience" (D.B. Stern, 1997).
5. We use complex systems, not lineal, theory to understand mental functioning (with both observer and observed included).
6. We recognise anxiety in all its forms, from pathological accommodation (which reduces interpersonal anxiety), to growth-related anxiety; we are not limited to separation or loss.
7. We define the direction of human behaviour, taking into account the drive for survival, the positioning in regards to growth and to life.

Among the progressive approaches to therapeutic method, we should highlight how decades ago Kohut described accessing the *intersubjective field* (the object of study in intersubjectivity), which he called the *empathic-introspective* method (1971, 1977, 1984). This method examines a patient's principles for organising experience (through our ability to know them in empathic resonance), the therapist's organising principles (through introspection), and the intersubjective field created between them both (the bonds) and while including them both at the same time. All the different levels of communication (verbal, para-verbal, non-verbal, empathic resonance) are present in the encounter and constant evolution of subjectivities.

The therapeutic context[16] is bi-personal and ethically equalitarian, though the roles are moderately asymmetrical. It revolves around experience and the exploration of the mutual influence between the two participants, how this permanent influence and co-determination occurs, without a hierarchy of values associated to the roles. *Mutuality* is the principal characteristic, this being understood as the reciprocal recognition of experience shared by the clinician and the person seeking help, as well as the mutual influence one has on the other (Aron, 1996, 2013). The recent debate on the role of the setting in therapy (Coderch & Codosero, 2015; Ávila, 2015b)[17] has contributed valuable core reflections on the balance between the limits necessary to protect both participants and the flexibility favouring the full use of what is experienced in the clinical work.

---

15 See also J.J. Martínez Ibáñez's book (2012)
16 Formed by therapist and patient in a framework-setting that is principally ethical and which gives form and limits it.
17 See as chapter 6 of this book in a revised version.

The process of change (when it is structural we call it "analytical") can be seen when there are changes in the participants' implicit relational knowing, fundamentally through the interaction of their different "worlds of experience", or intersubjectivity. This requires constancy in the links formed and sufficient continuity, which cannot be quantified in advance. That is, we will know experientially if we are changing – the patient with the therapist and the therapist with the patient.

The traditional resources of rationally-based psychotherapeutic technique (formulated interpretations and their possible effects; insight) might contribute to this goal, but continued empathic connection between both, what is known as empathic-introspective enquiry[18] and is felt as a process of mutual influence, is the mainspring of the process of psychic change. It is ultimately the process of human help taking place in psychotherapy. As Stolorow and Atwood (1997) stated, the idea of the neutral analyst is a myth, there can only be implication and mutuality regulated by ethics.

As we suggested two decades ago now when we brought together years of experience of studying "technique" and reflection on the role of clinicians' subjectivity in their work (Aburto, Ávila et al, 1999), clinicians play a major role in treatment through their personal implication (ethics and a theoretical-technical base). It evolves via *processes of mutuality and recognition* that do not negate either the difference in roles or the asymmetrical function in the basic ethics of the encounter with the other, which means *yielding*[19] *(own space) to others in order to recognise them.* Mutuality is a dynamic process in which patient and therapist mutually regulate or mutually influence one another, both consciously and unconsciously. This mutual regulation triggers feelings, thoughts and actions which are integrated into experience of each participant.

After decades of observation and research into the therapeutic process and the phenomena involved in change (see below), the usual themes re-examined in all theories of therapeutic action need their basic relational character revising, in essence as well as expression: therapeutic alliance, transference, counter-transference, role response, enactment, resistance, impasse, negative therapeutic reaction, termination anxiety. This task has partly been done by relational authors (Orange, Atwood & Stolorow, 2012; Coderch, 2010, 2012, 2014; Buechler, 2008; Ehrenberg, 1992; amongst others). Compared with the classic concept of the neutral, asymmetrical position of the analyst who

---

18 The method described by H. Kohut (1971, 1977, 1984), and to which reference has already been made.

19 In the sense made by E. Ghent (1990, Spanish version, 2014)

goes through all those experiences just mentioned, the relational perspective transforms each phenomenon in the clinical encounter into a respectful exploration of joint reality, which gives rise to mutual meanings that therapist and patient have built as a therapeutic dyad and with the occasion to re-enact their relational matrices.

Some evidence from the examination of clinical work shows:

1. There is no transference or counter-transference, but bi-directional mutual influence between therapist and patient at all levels of connection and interaction. Meaning is made through the contexts acting at different levels of phenomena (intra-, inter- and trans-subjective).

2. In an analytic context favouring (together with other subjective and environmental factors) the evolution of the change process, a new context of experience is created that can be described as an *optimal balance* (see Bacal, 1998) between "relational providing" (however much is needed, but no more, to restore self-object deficits and gratify basic need on that level), and "relational frustration" (the necessary minimum that allows a perception of want which enables active exploration of the surroundings and the encouragement of spontaneous play and creativity). Relational providing and frustration are not deliberately employed strategies, but inevitable consequences of the encounter between the two differently organised worlds of experience of so-called patient and therapist. The therapist does not "decide" to gratify or frustrate – they simply arise. As a result, they can be observed, shared and thought about during the therapy.

In summary, relational clinicians define their *strategy for change* as anything that allows the relational dimension to become the area of therapeutic action; techniques and tactics facilitate this but are not agents of change. Enquiry into technique demands we take a stance on the value of research.

Is Research Useful For Relational Clinical Work?

The need to provide scientific evidence is in vogue; we are trapped in the "politically correct" argument that for scientific and socio-economic reasons, clinical interventions and treatment undertaken to relieve people's suffering and cure illness must be based on available scientific evidence. In consequence, we should only use those interventions whose effectiveness has been proven by criteria accepted by the scientific community. This leads us to the situation where "randomised clinical trials, e.g. double blind studies" are extrapolated from the field of medicine to psychological and psychosocial treatment, and when the rigour of such trials cannot be applied, correlational and other levels of acceptable evidence can be employed. However, if we accept this stand, we neglect certain basic characteristics of psychological intervention, whatever the theoretical frame of reference. We would, for example, overlook the following:

1. Psychological intervention cannot be reduced to the application of a technique, but falls within a strategy of interpersonal influence that one person effects on another (or others), and in which use can be made of apparently structured techniques but which are suggestive of an intersubjective quality of action and the multiple contexts present in its meanings.

2. Mental and behavioural problems, disorders, are not specific patho-logical entities. We have already stated that the narrow model for infectious diseases cannot be applied to clinical psychology since there is no pathogen which once controlled and eradicated will lead to good health. Not even an apparently repeated pattern of features and dynamics of certain behavioural disorders (such as phobias, more specifically, fear of flying) reduces subjective and contextual differ-ences. This is a good example of how we can help people manage their difficulties better through a progressive exposure to the feared object, building up alternative mental schemata and acquiring skills to control anxiety. But it has limitations: technical procedures aid adaptation but they do not help the person to develop as a person. We understand, though, that to be a starting point for a clinicians' true work: as human beings they use the knowledge available to reduce suffering or attend to the management of what is necessary for survival. Clinicians begin to develop their true therapeutic task when they participate in unblocking a person's growth.

3. The "technical" agent of the above-mentioned intervention interacts with the subject at various levels that cannot be limited to the variables that the technique supposedly operates on. The "technician" might seem to be using an objective procedure, but the processes mobilised are not under the technician's control. For example, the "technician" desensitised the patient, being with him during the exposure. However, there are subtleties that are not part of the technique which play a part in the personal interaction with the patient, and in systems of mean-ings that are mobilised in the link; these make a difference which is

23

embodied in the experience the person takes with him or her and cannot be described nor evaluated.

4. All research demands replication, whether intra- or inter-subject. But two treatments are never really comparable. Every intervention is unique, every therapeutic dyad is unique, no patient is the same as another, each moment in life brings its own sensitivities. Every intervention occurs in a distinct context and moment in time. There is no replication, only the illusion of similarity.

5. In consequence, any available evidence is artefactual. Even though it brings descriptions and comparisons under a certain control, however exhaustive, systematic, and randomised it may be, there is no evidence of causality, only co-variation and probability. All this indicates trends of phenomena that may be repeated but nothing that is relevant to the real level of any specific future interaction.

These reflections have led epistemologists and clinicians, such as Hoffman (2009), to reject a heuristic approach and defend a contextual, constructivist hermeneutics for clinicians in which every clinical interaction is idiosyncratic.

So, is research irrelevant for clinicians? Evidently not: clinicians have learnt much from advances in many fields of scientific research. As regards to clinicians' understanding of a clinical event, choice of approach and reinterpretation of their practice, at least three areas of research have been crucial: a) neuroscience; b) research into human development; c) research into the change process (in psychotherapy). There have been extensive evaluations for each of these areas of study that offer an enormous number of advances that help us understand why our clinical work should be relational. They bring invaluable ideas to recover human beings as agents of their own change, and they teach us that the therapeutic relationship is the decisive place in which change is promoted and constructed so patients can become the force of their own transformation.

However, learning from research does not mean clinicians need only use the techniques "validated" by it. They need to listen and construct their dialogue with what research based on a specific circumstance describes. They should not generalise the results from a particular technique but learn from the wealth of possibilities that systematic observation offers for hypothetical situations. Clinicians occupy an idiographic position, marked by their sensitivity for the subtle, complex processes that might be symbolised. Research aspires to a nomothetic, descriptive ideal related to its explicative-predictive potential. At the same time, like researchers, clinicians should have ethical commitments to the suffering other and not be subjected to the demands of clinical ideology (theory). A good clinician is essentially an observer who is committed to the truth of the experience (the patient's, the clinician's), and as such is an exacting observer who makes science out of subjective experience.

Patients change, extending their resources for mentalisation and/or using them to develop their subjectivity. In their therapists they seek allies for change. The ways in which clinicians participate in these processes are varied, while patients use their clinicians – consciously or not – to progress. When research into the psychotherapeutic process looks at individual cases in depth, it detects these processes at a detailed level (micro), and when conclusions are drawn from generalisations of clinical groups and comparison procedures (macro level), it offers results; clinicians will need to consider whether these results are applicable or not to the specific context of each intervention.

Lingiardi, Holmqvist & Safran (2016) have recently contributed an excellent review regarding the possible dialogue between psychotherapy research and the relational turn in clinical work. They highlight how decades of research into the therapeutic alliance has progressively brought a clinically useful understanding of just how vital the role of relational processes in change are.

This is the relational paradox: the relational processes inherent to the basic human intersubjectivity can be observed under conditions of controlled, systematic observation; with that we gain vast knowledge of numerous characteristics of human beings (early intersubjectivity, attachment, intentional inference, mentalisation, emotional connection, extra-verbal communication, etc.). This knowledge, however, is not applicable prescriptively as a technique or tactic; it is knowledge that mobilises our aptitude for observation and self-observation, but does not provide us with universally-applicable tools. If clinicians do not take advantage of the contributions research brings, they devalue their abilities; if they do take advantage, clinicians grow, but they neither make their practice more technical nor do they impoverish it in a technology-oriented world. We cannot surrender to this demand, although we may need what research brings (communicated in "acceptable" terms by our representatives) to allow us to sustain our relational practice. Subjectivity - a product of intersubjective quality - needs to make itself heard and so avoid the alienation of what is subjective in the social control delineated by the macro-trend that drives us toward a stage where information technology decides what and who we are.

In conclusion, I highlight the main challenges we face as relational clinicians.

The Challenges We Face

Knowing how to convey basic human relationality in our practice: once again we state that what sets humans apart is that we are fundamentally social, both in our origins and as a consequence of our nature. Specifically, human characteristics (language, complex memory, a theory of mind –and as a result, education – play, and institutions) all converge both as causes and consequences of our specificity. Among our systems of needs (those related to our bodies, social, of knowledge), social needs are significant as a context of provision, and in shaping our actions and experience.

Embodying the relational essence of change: subjectivity is what permanently provides the basis of a sense of *identity*. It is distinct in each and every person and is subject to the radical unforeseeable nature of one's own evolution; it changes with us. It has been constructed in the inter-determination among our genetic and biological potentials, and the different intersubjective and socio-natural contexts in which our existence has occurred. Our genetic determination is open to all the epigenetic factors that influence an extremely complex and progressive neural organisation, which will become intensely differentiated in the early years of life, and in a less decisive way throughout our life cycle. Our neural plasticity, the contributions from early and later intersubjective contexts in whose co-construction we permanently participate, the differentiation of a subjective psychic reality, all shape one another in an elemental dialectic between synaptic and psychic traces. We are inescapably parties to our history and evolution and this is what distinguishes us as human beings.

Recovering agency and social-subjective sense in our clinical practice: the relational perspective, through its analysis of phenomena related to the links (intra-, inter- and trans-subjective) that make up the relational matrix, has opened new doors for clinicians as well as transforming clinical psychology, particularly contemporary psychoanalysis. Going beyond clinicians' conceptual affiliations, the relational paradigm has allowed them to recover a meaningful aspiration for clinical work with patients thanks to being able to appreciate the significance of their involvement and agency in the change process, a process in which all those present are co-participants.

Thinking critically about the theories we have built ourselves into: the relational perspective provides the bases with which we can think about a conceptual renovation of all the theories and methods of clinical work. The suggestions set out here are not intended to be dogmatic proposals but central ideas from which to think. All clinical theories must face the continued presence of the intersubjective factor, the nature by which phenomena observed in clinical work are linked – they are not only properties of a patient's psyche and behaviour but phenomena of a more extensive system that is represented in clinical work by the complexity of the system made up of patient-therapist-institution-society.

Establishing our conceptual roots, in order to recognise ourselves in their growth: the tradition of link psychoanalysis, the basis of our interest in transforming our theory and clinical practice, has led us to this dialogue in which we have reflected on theoretical and technical proposals that help us understand our task. We highlight the legacy of Interpersonal Psychoanalysis, Link Theory, Winnicottian thought, two-person psychology and Self-Psychology, early Relational Psychoanalysis and Intersubjectivity Theory. All have been approaches that are in accord with the concern shared by many of us: learning from our patients and our own experience with them, keeping the hope of change alive and defending the encounter between theoretical and clinical contributions from different traditions.

We accept the fact that the relational perspective is in constant change with contributions from numerous disciplines and levels of analysis that enrich and question: among these (as Coderch has highlighted) are the Theory of Knowledge, Phenomenology and Hermeneutics, Anthropology and Culturology, as well as the clinical disciplines and contributions from research. All share an ethos in which a better and greater social conscience of the value of subjectivity (faced with the alienation resulting from the expansion of the technological society) has contributed to vindicating an individual's relational nature as fundamental to human evolution. This is richly expressed in culture, literature, art, where new forms of relating, in particular the primacy of the values of personal encounter over the dangers of an emptying of self-objects behind the pseudo-communicative socio-technological disguise in which we are trapped. Modern day clinicians are called upon to become involved in attending to a person's current contextualised needs since there can be no lasting change that is not connected to the vectors of transformation of contemporary society.

We learn with research, but without forsaking our own spirit: evidence from neuroscience research over the few decades upholds a psychic causality that is capable of modelling the organic (Kandel, 2007a, 2007b; Damasio, 2006) with the concepts of plasticity and somatic markers. This essentially means that experience can be registered on the neural network, thus bringing about psychic change and the embodiment of emotional experience. However, experience in general, and transformative experience, is relational, as has been confirmed by research into human development. It shows how subjectivity is constructed in early intersubjectivity, and processes of attachment and mutual regulation, which are present from the very first experiences, are essentially the same as those that play a part in modifying implicit relational knowing in an adult's therapeutic and life experience.

Our challenge is to go about our clinical work without yielding to the pressures of technologisation[20]; conscious that we are relationally involved, we are present in the registers of the processes of mutuality, and being clinicians means being open to the surprises of otherness and the wealth of human *thirdness*[21]. This deserves all our efforts, a dialectic between emotions and reflexivity that is shared in the clinical encounter. We become people, all of us, by traversing the pathway of change together with others.

Summary

Relational Psychoanalysis in Spain has a long history begining with the echoes of many developments in contemporary psychoanalysis (Social and Interpersonal and Psychoanalysis of the link traditions between others) that meets Intersubjective Systems Theory, contemporary Self Psychology and Stephen Mitchell′s thinking by the nineties. This introductory chapter explores our conceptual roots, delineates the main concepts and evolving trends, reconsidering diagnostics and psychopathology in a way that allow us to re-think our clinical practice and experience, identifying the relational basis of excessive mental suffering. Clinical psychotherapeutic technique is also revised as a balance between relational providing and frustration in a context of involvement and mutuality between clinician and person. Finally, the useful of research findings to relational clinical work is considered as a way to face our challenges as psychotherapists in a changing world.

---

20 This subject is developed by J. Coderch in his paper 'Comprendiendo a una sociedad en cambio para comprender a los pacientes' (Understanding a changing society to understand patients), *Clínica e Investigación Relacional*, 11(1) (2017).
21 See Aburto, Ávila et al (2007) for a review of this concept.

2
Relational Psychoanalysis. A New Psychoanalytic Epistemology

Carlos Rodríguez Sutil

Cassius
... Tell me, good Brutus, can you see your face?
Brutus
No, Cassius, for the eye sees not itself
But by reflection, by some other things.
(Original text: Shakespeare)[1]

Introduction: What Is Relational Psychoanalysis? Reasons And Causes

Relational psychoanalysis is a contemporary trend within psychoanalysis that confers essential value to both real and internalized interpersonal relations that are part of the constitution of identity, genesis of mental disorders and the

---

1 http://nfs.sparknotes.com/juliuscaesar/page_12.html

dynamics of psychotherapy. Relational psychoanalysis is anti-Cartesian because it proposes that the world, understood as a constellation of interpersonal relations, is prior to and enables the construction of the individual human being. Undoubtedly, a child is not only influenced by his/her environment, but also develops through interaction bringing his/her own spontaneity and tendencies into the relational dialectic.

Classic psychoanalysis describes humans as dominated by innate and biologically determined sexual drives and aggression. On the other hand, the primary motivation that underpins this new perspective is the search for relationships with others, that is, attachment in its different forms and nuances, as early relational patterns tend to be recreated in future situations, in interaction with new relational partners.

Relational psychoanalysis is characterized by its environmental point of view, as well as the reduction in the asymmetry between the therapist and patient roles. It is centered on the relationship that is established in the here and now in the therapeutic session, and product of the history and spontaneity of both participants. The patient is not always mistaken when manifesting his/her disagreement with something said or done by the therapist and also at times, it is necessary for the therapist to adopt a position of self-disclosure. For example, under certain circumstances, the therapist may communicate to the patient how he/she may have felt at a certain moment due to something said or done by the patient or how he/she would have felt in the position of the other person in the scene described. This may allow the patient to capture the effects that his/her conduct produces on others and the significance of this effect. Interpretation is no longer the fundamental therapeutic instrument, while the actual changes produced in the presence of the empathic therapist are more relevant as is the therapist's attitude of taking care of or *holding* as advocated by Winnicott (1956, 1979).

Some critics reject self-disclosure considering that it weakens our role, making us appear fragile and impressionable beings. However, to show we have feelings has positive effects. It is recommendable to not be flooded by these feelings, to conceal and deny them should they occur is never the best response, and even less so to make an "interpretation" in a pure aggressive/defensive style. Kernberg (1992), an author quite removed from relational tendencies, does not declare his feelings when he feels threatened by an aggressive patient, however he does establish limits and expresses his conditions explicitly so that the patient can interpret them at least as adequate precaution.

To say that relational psychoanalysis is a change in paradigm from classic Freudian and Kleinian psychoanalysis is to affirm that there has been a change in epistemic perspective, in other words the way truth is understood and achieved. There are two ways in which the truth has been defined historically:

1) Truth as correspondence: since the tradition of scholasticism coined the term "adeaquatio", which continues to pervade Western thinking: *veritias est adaequatio intellectus ad rem*, truth is the adequacy/correspondence between intellect and the thing. During the past century positivism and logical atomism have reigned, in which the truth of a proposition has been its correspondence with reality (*verificationism*).

2) Truth as discovery: the current conception in Greek antiquity brought to the present by Heidegger's thought: truth as that something arising and coming to our encounter, that something revealing itself.

Relational psychoanalysis tries to overcome static terms – such as transference, counter-transference, and resistance – that transmit the idea of a difficult communication between two independent minds or self-contained compartments. Instead relational psychoanalysis uses terms that describe the analytic session as a field of interaction, a transitional space, of thirdness, something that is "co-created" by the analyst and the analysand in a mutual process. In accordance with that scene, truth as a discovery should be applied: something new is discovered and appears between two people in a relationship. In fact, the productive or mutative interpretation not only corresponds with the patient's mental reality (*Wirklichkeit*) but also allows his/her discovery although it may not have been initially adequate.

The truth discovered in a therapeutic relationship is also something constructed – truth as something constructed is another of the many possible forms of truth. Constructed or co-created by patient and therapist; something valid and durable only to the extent that the discovery is something coherent with the narrative truth of the present and past relationships, or – in some special cases – something that completely changes that coherence creating a new order. Relational psychoanalysis has a constructivist inspiration (Vygotsky, Piaget). These considerations lead us to the truth as the consistency of the system: the affirmation is true if it coincides with the group or mode of representation of reality, and ultimately with a form of life. A narrative reconstruction is globally correct because it is not possible to attribute meaning to an isolated sign or proposition – the "this is a 'dog'" of ostensive definitions. It is the group of propositions – the system – that makes sense as a way of adaptation to a complex reality, a *form of life*, the style of our way of being in a world characterized by integrity, or lack of it. This does not mean that all contradictions automatically disappear. This form of truth as a form of life and integrity that is not qualitatively different from discovery, self-disclosure or self-revelation: a sentence will be true when it unveils something about our mode of insertion into reality.

During the *Zollikon Seminars*, Heidegger (1987) presented a detailed and well-informed critique of Freudian psychoanalysis before an audience of Swiss psychiatrists. Meta-psychology is considered unacceptable because it transfers the Kantian theory of objects to the study of humans – converting humans into objects. Once this objectification takes place it subjects research to the paradigm of natural sciences. Freud in his first movement generated the inacceptable objectification of human historicity, transforming man into something simply seen or present – *Vorhaden*, as an effective reality, an object or *Wirklichkeit*. In fact, the theory of the three parts of the psychic apparatus (Id, ego and superego) only offers other names for Kant's three central concepts of subjectivity: sensibility, understanding and reason (or moral law). In a second movement, Freud naturalizes human beings as if they were inscribed in a causal process, and instead of providing the history of the concrete human being, offers a chain of natural causes.

Heidegger insisted that knowledge produced by natural science is not conducive to a better future or to human's liberation, at least not for the moment. Instead, it is conducive to man's unlimited auto-destruction. Freud's findings, which the German philosopher recognized, such as: projection, introjection, identification, regression and repression, should be reinterpreted in the light of existential analytic (*Daseinanalysis*) corresponding to regional ontology. Freud is credited with having discovered that human beings become ill due to traumatic relationships with other human beings. Additionally he demonstrated that disorders can be cured through the relationship of patients with other human beings – the therapists – however this must be considered as a particular way of being with others, as pointed out by Heidegger, and not due to concepts such as "transference" that infers the idea of separate and self-contained minds. The existential analytic (*Daseinanalysis*) he proposed should be a descriptive science, neither constructive nor hypothetical. As the individual's life is essentially a historical phenomenon, and existential time is circular, comprehension should also be described in a circular movement.

Karl Jaspers (1946) applied the classical distinction between "explanation" and "comprehension". Some disorders such as neurosis and other vital reactions can be "comprehended", while others can only be "explained" as in the case of delirium. On the other hand, this dichotomy did not exist in practice for the creator of psychoanalysis. As the only science was natural science (*Naturwissenschaft*), of an explanatory kind, psychoanalysis being one of its branches (Cf. Assoun, 1981, pg. 41 and ss.). However, both reasons and cause are intended to respond to the "why" of behavior, but in an essentially different way. From a logical point of view, cause is the antecedent that provokes a given event in material form, totally or partially, blindly; while reasons introduce the expectation of a result, reasons lead to action, an action directed to an end. Lastly, "teleological explanations" consider objectives and reasons.

The truth of an interpretation or any other clinical intervention is based on a coherent narrative, that is, of its consistency with the patient's vital history, therefore giving rise to different forms of narrative coherence. A purely hermeneutic version of psychoanalysis entails its risks, such as the possibility that diverse, and hardly compatible, perspectives or versions of the same reality may be offered. We find ourselves before the abysm of the "everything is valid", a common trend in "postmodern" times, of which we cannot escape by the mere recourse of asserting that an interpretation is a construction. If there is no material base to serve as anchor, an interpretation will be just as valid as any other and in sum, will not led to anything. The constructivist perspective – Orange (2010) warns us – tends to distance us, as therapists, from the atrocities that our patients have experienced, and protects us from relieving these atrocities with them. It turns us into a moderate version of the invalidating parents, and our distant attitude can serve to re-traumatize patients. However, constructivism – and "perspectivism" – should not be understood as resignation, rather as a critical philosophy with the objective to reject claims of knowledge that cannot be demonstrated.

Freud faced this delicate matter most emphatically in one of his later works, *Constructions in Psychoanalysis* (1937 b) proposing an answer, as usual, worthy of consideration: Any interpretation is not valid, because some produce the expected effects and others do not, some fit with the psychic reality of the patient and others fail; nor is it enough for us that the patient confirm or reject the interpretation. It is necessary to wait and see if there are changes. A correct interpretation is, therefore, a fertile interpretation that strengthens the "narrative identity" as described by Ricœur (1999). This narrative identity, where the self seeks its identity, may match with the truth as a system, but the unexpected always remains in the background, as a type of surprising discovery. Narrative coherence cannot be achieved only through historical reconstruction but must arise from the experience of the here and now of the relationship, of the therapeutic dyad.

If hermeneutics were the simple unilateral interpretation of the other (the text produced by the other) from an observer perspective, even in the attempt to observe oneself - we would avoid biological explanations but we would incur another risk. In that case we would slip into the idealism of mental interiorities. It is a dialogue because it is made up of questions and answers; one asks oneself how to ask the other. In consequence, language is not practiced as statements, rather as questions and answers that, surely, do not arise from a logical field but from an experiential one, that of the relationship between two or more people in which therapist and patient take care of each other. At times, it has been stated that relational psychoanalysis offers special attention and respect to the other's subjectivity. I agree with this on the condition that "subjectivity" refers to the person as a whole, not only what he or she says explicitly, nor their "mental contents", but what patient and therapist say (and do not say) within the total context, past, present and future, and in the interpersonal field of the analytic therapy.

Marcia Cavell (1993) suggests the need for a psychoanalytic hermeneutic, for it is a softer science than physics. Nevertheless, she maintains the idea that interpretations discover attachments that are causal in nature, and states that reasons are causes. Perhaps this way she avoids the risk of departing from Freud more than what would be desirable, but we fear that the cost would be leaving the epistemic problems unresolved. For Ricoeur (1965, pp. 455-456), Freud, notwithstanding his hermeneutic construction, could not decide to abandon energetic explanations. He concludes the psychoanalytic method is inapplicable if the naturalist model imposed by the Freudian economic principle is not accepted. A purely linguistic transcription eludes the fundamental difficulty: psychoanalysis' naturalism is well founded in the almost natural aspect of the forces that underlay psyches, in other words, the drives (*Triebs*). Otherwise - he continues to state using an argument similar to that one used by Jon Mills (2005), among others, against the relational perspective – the immediate consciousness is once again prioritized. However, it is not mandatory to recur to the elements of Freudian biology of the psyche and its metapsychology, if we want to avoid the analytic method becoming lost in the byways of the mere consciousness.

If human contact is the first necessity, as Bowlby's attachment theory postulates (Bowlby 1969), the "biological" concept to which we must turn is the form of life as the total narrative of the human being in his/her context, and also to the totality of the analytic context. The principle of this hermeneutic psychoanalytic method is the integration of experiences as a whole. On the other hand, it isn't necessary to maintain the drive theory to concede that early trauma produces a deterioration or deficit in the inter-personal functioning of the individual. Recuperation of the trauma theory frees us in some way from intra-psychic metapsychological energetism and avoids the risks of pure hermeneutics. Trauma occurs when the infant cannot resolve a situation of frustration and contradiction, in which he is abused and not recognized. It is not a mere subjective interpretation, rather it is objective harm.

According to Heidegger (1927), when we choose to interpret our being in a general way, adapted to the public, living in the world of "one", doing "what one does", behaving as "one should behave", because it is "correct" or more comfortable, we fall into a manner of being that is not authentic (1927, § 37). It is a refuge in generality that avoids the often-painful self-searching. A refuge because it provides protection from angst (1927, § 40). This Heideggerian concept of an inauthentic mode is without doubt very similar to the false self, proposed by Winnicott (1965). The false self is a protective shell that is developed during infancy when the infant has not been adequately held or sustained, as protection from the helplessness provoked by primary, that is to say, catastrophic failure. The real self and the possibilities for adequate organization remain hidden, for fear of massive frustrations and in this way the infant is somewhat capable of continuing with his evolution. Expanding on this, Fairbairn's (1940) schizoid can only feel love and be loved from a distance, a method that simultaneously protects internal and external objects. The subject represents roles without believing them, or through exhibitionism gives without giving. Infant trauma splits or dissociates our mind into two spaces, an interior, isolated and protected space and another exterior space that becomes a shield, protecting against daily events.

The Isolated Mind

It is popularly believed that images are "stored", as if they were scraps of cloth to be able to compare them. So, to be able to confirm the image of "red" stored in our memory, we need a third image of comparison, and so on indefinitely (Wittgenstein, 1945-49, § 380, 381, 386). However, we need the concept "red" in our minds, rather than its image. What we need, to know you are experiencing "pain", is not to prick oneself with a needle, instead to understand the sense of the concept "pain", which has been transmitted through language in pragmatic contexts (1945-49 pp. 547-8). We ask ourselves how an idea is related to the details it is composed of. It has been said that a particular man is human, because he participates in the form of "man", but this comparison requires the resource of the "third man" who can assure what the first two have in common, and so on in an infinite regression.

Internal representations, in reality, are dependent on what occurs externally (Wittgenstein, 1949-51, II, p.30)[2].

If we discover that a representation is false, we rapidly search within certain limits, for an alternative representation that better fits with reality, coherent with a system of representations, even if this means changing the entire system, as no representation is completely isolated. But both truth and falseness are forms of representation in the world, and representations do not come from the so-called internal mind of the individual, rather from the exterior, from social communication. All existence in the world is a priori. It wouldn't be necessary to prove the existence of an "external" world and "other minds", however we have the tendency to bury the world under many theories of knowledge, we later need to prove:

Our task is not to prove that an 'external world' is present-at-hand or to show how it is present-at-hand, but to put out how *Dasein*, as Being-in-the-world, has the tendency to bury the 'external world' in nullity 'epistemologically' before going on to prove it. (Heidegger, 1927, § 43, p. 250).

We are an active part of the world before separating from it and adopting the position of theoretic isolation, of radical externality. We are not separate from the world in its perception. From the beginning, human beings (*Dasein*) are beings among other beings (*Mitsein*), and it is not a matter of subjectivity, rather of care (*Sorge*), caring for others from the beginning. The human being is never totally isolated in primitive narcissism or in a pleasure principle. Indeed the pleasure principle only could operate in a closed system, as an essentially psychopathological phenomenon (Cf. Fairbairn, 1958, p. 84).

The Cartesian conceptualization of the subject thinking about himself is a steppingstone towards the modern concept of reflexive subject, the allegedly flawless fundament of philosophy to date. Descartes in his *Metaphysical Meditations* argued that he could doubt everything except the fact that he was thinking, concluding therefore that he was in essence a thinking substance. Gassendi rebutted, arguing that to know one is thinking, doubting, feeling etc. is not enough to know the substance one is made of:

You are aware of this operation ·of thinking·, but the most important

---

2 The germ of this Wittgensteinian reasoning was first offered by Plato in his dialogue Parmenides (132a–b). It is a philosophical criticism of Plato's own theory of Forms, also used by Aristotle (Metaphysics) who introduced the example of a man to explain his objection to Forms theory. If a man is a man because he shares or participates in the form of man, then a third form would be required to explain how man and the form of man are both man, and so on, *ad infinitum*.

element is still hidden from you, namely the substance that does the thinking. This prompts the thought that you're like a blind man who, on feeling heat and being told that it comes from the sun, thinks he has a vivid and clear idea of the sun because if he is asked what the sun is he can reply 'It is a thing that heats'. (Descartes, 1641, p. 141)

Hegel came up with the idea that the object of self-awareness is another self-awareness, both as an internal reflection and an external dialogue (Cf. Hyppolite, 1974). Inasmuch the individual is self-awareness, living in a situation of reciprocity with another self-awareness, the other is incorporated as the internal other.

All things considered, Descartes offered a scheme that is mainly a secular version of the Christian (body-soul) dualism in fact using arguments similar to those used by Saint Augustine. The acquisition of the concept of soul, as an entity different to the body and that resides within it, takes place in Ancient Greece, switching simultaneously from a culture centered on shame to a culture centered on guilt (Dodds, 1951). Even in the Old Testament, Yaveh promised his followers prosperity and longevity for their families and livestock, not eternity. For the Homeric man, maximum wealth was to enjoy public admiration. According to Orpheus, Plato and Christian tradition, the soul becomes exiled from the heaven of pure forms, and is soiled and corrupted upon contact with the body. According to Saint Augustine, an infant learns the meaning of words observing objects adults point to and pronouncing the name of each object; as if born with an innate "language" of objects and concepts, simply transferring this innate language onto the words of the natural language he/she is born into. Wittgenstein confronts the assumption of a private language from the very beginning of his *Philosophical Investigations* (1945-49), finally proving that the mind is not innate, rather a product of human interaction, within a particular form of life (*Lebensform*).

From Kant onwards, self-consciousness is not so much a representation, but the form of all representations in general, that is, in order to be able to represent things, I need a representation of myself. The "I think" is the form of the apperception that precedes and follows all possible experience. Although the soul's existence cannot be demonstrated, its permanence is evident for Kant, as the thinking being, the human being, is an object perceived by external senses. This object perceived by an external observer is the appearance of a non-spatial object in itself. As of Descartes and Kant, reflexivity as structure conforms the essence of all philosophy (Gadamer, 1975; Heidegger, 1987).

On the other hand, consciousness, the 'I', in its complete magnitude, becomes an non-extensive point (Wittgenstein, 1918), the self shrinks to a point without extension, a point on which almost an infinite variety of "internal objects" representations of the self or the Id can be placed – determined by cultural trends and the Zeitgeist or spirit of the times. The thinking being does not exist; rather thought exists, as nothing in the visual field allows the inference that it can be seen by the eye (Wittgenstein, 1918, 5.633, 5.6331, 5.64). The ego that supports Western identity, the pure ego, is in reality the shifter of linguistics, a mere formal index, empty of substance. If we used Heidegger's terms (1927, chap. 4) we would say that in reality, the self does not have a way of being present, it is not a visible object, instead existence is the substance of human being. The "be oneself" of *Dasein* is a mode of existence, not a present entity, or "before the eyes", the being of *Dasein* is not regularly "myself", rather it is "oneself". As proposed by Wittgenstein in *Philosophical Investigations* (1945-49, §398 y §399), think in a painted scene with a farm. Someone asks "Whom does the house belong to?" and we answer, "To the farmer seated in front of it". But this farmer cannot enter his own house. Subjectivity is neither interiority nor exteriority, rather life in the world. Shame, for example, is not a solitary experience it is social, resulting from humiliation and contempt. We are imbued with the concept of the subject as something internal that directs our behavior (the ghost in the machine), but this subject is a representation, and representations cannot do anything themselves – in reality we do things with representations (and with words).

My self is either engrossed in the world and not easily differentiated from others, or dissolved in its isolation. According to the English school of psychoanalysis, all subjects have a fragmented background and the basic stage in personality development is the schizoid position, the "splitting" background (*Spaltung*) that appeared in Freud's latter writings.

The only original concept we have of the self is the total person (P.F Strawson, 1959), including his/her actions and verbal expressions. From our perspective the key concepts are "person", "relation" and "interpersonal" or "intersubjective" (Lothane, 2003, p. 611). All construction of the self is nothing other than a more or less deformed transposition of that primary object. A person does not have a body, rather is a body, that is, a body in movement and full of meaning, in interaction with its human environment. However, a representation cannot do anything; the farmer cannot enter his farm. The person is not composed of a soul and a body: "...body am I entirely, and nothing else; and soul is only a word for something about the body" (Nietzsche, 1883/1954, 146). The agent is the person as a whole. In sum we consider that the unconscious is relational and the self is external, the person in action and interaction.

The Construction of the Subject

Current psychological theories do not only attempt to explain the role of behavior in the environment, but also seek the key to explain this behavior inside the person. For example, if emotions work inside the person, in both the body and the mind, we should first analyze them physiologically or cognitively. From the very moment we imagine emotions, affects and passions as something private, we automatically suppose that their expression is derived from some type of internal sensation. However, even acknowledging that the emotional process comprises cognitive processing and physiological responses, social interaction is the genuine organizing factor. When someone describes their own emotions, these are almost always located in an interpersonal scenario. Now we know emotions can be produced by perceptive contagion, as has been proved in recent studies about mirror neurons (Gallese, 2009). Many times emotional expressions are automatically imitated, without cognitive interpretation of signals. Rather than an internal feeling that is later manifested, there is a permanent emotional reaction to the other's attitude and of the other to me, therefore a relationship. For example, when we attempt to voluntarily control our emotional expressions we obtain a false smile, the "Duchenne smile". Psychological functions should be explained in external terms, not based on internal organic relations (regulation): there are no natural structures rather constructs (Vygotsky, 1989, p.59).

In the mid-seventies Andrew Meltzoff carried out a series of important experiments (Meltzoff y Moore, 1977). They discovered that babies between 12 and 21 days old were capable of imitating both facial and manual gestures they observed. Previously it was believed that this capacity for facial imitation was impossible at that age as it implies different perceptive modes (the baby observes other faces but not his own, and feels his facial movements but not those of others). This conduct is neither reflex nor conditioned, it assumes that newborn babies can equate, without seeing them, their own gestures with those they see in others. Thirty years later Meltzoff (2007) elaborated the "like me" hypothesis about infant development, by which the baby experiences a regular association between his own actions and the corresponding mental states, drawing on daily experience, and at a second stage, projects his internal experience onto others when they display similar actions. These are the building blocks of commonsense psychology, and the comprehension that others are similar to myself, "There is something that is like me". In this way, according to Meltzoff, the infant acquires the comprehension of "other minds" and their mental states, emotions, desires etc. The capacity to imitate is innate and the comprehension of mental states of others derives from this.

Meltzoff's hypothesis to prove the existence of other minds is in debt with John Stuart Mill, a well-known English positivist philosopher and economist who used the *argument by analogy* (*argument per analogiam*). The affirmation that other human beings also have consciousness is the conclusion deduced on the basis of their actions and perceptible manifestations, in order to understand their behavior. Hence, the acceptance of a consciousness in others is based on a deduction and not on our irrefutable direct experience, as is the case of our own consciousness. We can only rely on the knowledge of our own existence, or to be more precise, of our internal mind – it is easier to know the spirit than the body.

I cannot help replying that my belief that I have a mind is a concept learned in human context and does not correspond to any tangible object, in other words my mind comes from the other. Many times the error resides in using expressions such as "mental states" that suggest the existence of an internal private perception. What is essential to private experience is not that we each have our own example rather that we do not know if the same is true in the other or not. For example is our sensation of the color "red" the same as that of our neighbor? (Cf. Wittgenstein, 1945-49). I propose that a baby does not compare an internal state with a visual stimulus, rather that we are simply "programmed" – and mirror neurons support this idea – to have an emotional reaction to a smile we are faced with, and to share the "mental state", which does not belong to only one rather to at least two.

Psychoanalytic thought is still dominated by the concept of the isolated Cartesian mind even today. Freud postulated a subject (unconscious) isolated from the environment, a primarily narcissistic solipsist self. Additionally, there are numerous aspects of Freud's theories and texts that point towards a Cartesian-Kantian model of mind, conceived as an isolated entity. Jon Mills (2005, p. 176) proclaimed that Freud never supported the thesis of an isolated or solipsistic mind contrary to what the "relational propaganda" allegedly affirms and according to Mills circulates uncritically in psychoanalytic publications for more than two decades. Mills adds that the Relational school has created their own straw man and has never made the effort to read the original German texts. However, if we look carefully, it is usually not necessary to openly support the isolated mind thesis, as it is an unintended assumption that underlies most psychological theories, even those apparently relational. Egocentric vision permeates our language and the metaphors we use. Of course, language is important in psychoanalysis (Orange, 2003).

Neither Freud nor his followers have directly defended solipsism, however it is an assumption implicit in his meta-psychology, coherent with the epistemology of his times. The metaphysical counterpart to the isolated mind, that has always accompanied it, is the "problem of the other minds". "How can we be sure of the existence of other minds, based on mine?" This is a reiterated theme in contemporary philosophy, especially in English language. Freud "resolves" this in his work *The Unconscious* (1915 c), resorting to the thought of John Stuart Mill whose works he translated to German in his youth, and the argument *per analogiam* aforementioned. Freud cites the argument *per analogiam* with approval not only in the English translation, but also in the original German text. We can interpret the others' behavior well giving it coherence, while this interpretation, he affirms, is resistant to ourselves therefore we must consider our actions as if "belonging to another person", as if the investigation were diverted by a "special obstacle". One of the outcomes of the myth of the isolated mind is the belief in telepathy – something Freud was ambiguous about – first we separate minds into airtight containers, and after we imagine that they can communicate without intermediaries.

Freud states that the human being has two archaic sexual objects: himself and the nurturing mother (1914b), but there is no clinical data that supports this idea of "himself" as a primary sexual object, except for the "theoretic need" that he himself alludes to and is only understandable within a dualist scheme of reality. Therefore the newborn comes into the world possessing an already formed, although imperfect, ego. This is the starting point of the assumption of primary narcissism. This is "self" narcissism in a Hegelian sense, an original ego, which is difficult to reconcile with the dyadic system formed between the infant and the mother (Laplanche, 1970, p. 100 and ss.). Narcissism is the libidinal cathexis of oneself, which necessarily means the cathexis of the ego, as an instance, in the inseparable process of the constitution of the self. The lesson we can extract from this sequence is the existence of a possible confusion in Freudian texts between the ego and the person, between the instance and the object. This confusion can be resolved if we discover that we never possessed our real person, rather the fragile ego is constructed, narcissistically, on a representation. In consequence, the real ego (Freud, 1923 a) should be a representation, however privileged, but also the ego ideal, the ideal-ego, although they are expressions that we could confer some meaning and use to. Therefore we affirm that the self is also a construction, a useful narration that we construct throughout our existence and always includes a part that is inauthentic.

Well understood, Freud's "ego" is different from the "ego" of other thinkers because it is mainly unconscious (1923 a), an ego that speaks in parapraxias: *slips of the tongue (lapsus linguae)*, memory malfunctions, failed actions, symptoms and, in general, almost all forms of conduct. Psychoanalysis, according to Ricoeur (1965, P. 441), is the discourse on the subject, but a discourse that discovers that the subject never is where it is thought to be. In this sense, we can sustain that Freud among others, inspired the postmodern dissolution of identity. On the other hand the term "ego" (*Ich*), is polysemic in Freud's texts: The ego, the mental structure, the psychic instance, as well as the most personal and experiential self, which comprises the whole person. This state of things resulted in more confusion but also in more open-mindedness. This allowed, for example, to indicate its systemic properties, and as part of these properties, the ego as the site for consciousness and self-consciousness, the self as a person. For Freud, the ego is a differentiation and stemming from the Id, a defensive psychopathological structure, or the result of the identification processes.

Notwithstanding, "my whole person" is a reality that escapes me; at most I can obtain a representation of "my whole person" or more than one, as a self or various selves. Apparently we run into a *Noumenic* reality, in Kantian sense, an analogy Freud (1915 c) must have had in mind when he expected that the unconscious be easier to understand than the external world. However, the aporia we deal with now must be resolved, so to speak, from the inside out. An aporia is an unsolvable paradox, but I propose that we take the following affirmation to its last consequences: *the person is an open reality and constructed from outside in.* An acceptable cohesive image of oneself, conscious and unconscious, should be an essential condition for the process of integration of my ego (as instance) and of course of my person as a whole; of my peculiar form of being in my world. But I will never have a definite representation of my whole person because it is the others who have given me, and continue to do so, fragments of this reality in their eyes – and in how they treat me – simultaneously with the view I have of them. Totality is never limited to the individual person, not even to the reduced group; instead totality can only be searched for in the world, and probably will never be found, because it is that mystic thing, which cannot be spoken about according to the first Wittgenstein (1918).

With great insight, Mitchell (1993) grouped psychoanalytic thinking as far as the self is concerned – "self" a concept that has as many definitions as authors - into two main groups; a group that leans on a spatial metaphor, and another group proposing a temporal metaphor. According to the first group, the self is stable and resides in a mental space, while for the latter it is something changing, multiple and discontinuous. Mitchell synthesizes both positions and defines the self as the subjective organization of significants that the subject elaborates throughout time and through actions, feelings and thoughts about oneself. At times we behave in a continuous way and at others we change greatly from one situation to the next. Well considered, I feel that the defenders of the spatial metaphor in reality defend an ego with a permanent temporal dimension, something that is stable over time, while those who defend the temporal metaphor reject consistency or substantiality and speak about a pure but empty ego.

The concept of ego – specially if we refer to the empiric, metonymic and (although it may seem paradoxical) temporal ego – is sustained in the body, the body-ego Freud wrote about (1923 a) as a projection of a surface, a changing surface and that does not always provide the same sensations and feelings, nor does it always reflect in the same way. The formation of the self depends on the separation process and the limits between one's body and the external object. We can also think about the importance of the body for the experience of oneself, characteristic of the feeling of shame (Morrison, 2008). In our culture the separation, the differentiation of our bodies in relation to others and therefore of our ego with respect to others, is approached mainly through feelings of sexual shame and guilt. The person as a whole is implied in both shame and guilt (as well as all other emotions), as complex reactions that can only be understood in the context of past and present relationships.

Donna Orange (2010, p. 23) paraphrasing Martin Buber comments, that the *We*, the community living the past and the present, depend on language. Language is always ontologically present. This *We* cannot be reduced to a third person nor a group nor an objectified multitude, it is not a collection of elements. It is the personal *I* and *You* embedded in the *We* of tradition and language. While the being of man is defined and located in the mind, separate from the body, it is possible to maintain the illusion that a circle of internal immunity exists in the face of death and the limitations of animal life (Stolorow & Atwood, 1992 p.37). My conclusion is: *We have achieved immortality, but the price is guilt and psychic pain, that is, foregoing life.*

The Unconscious, Language And Memory

Freud introduced the use of the "unconscious" as a noun, opposed to the pre-psychoanalytic use as an adjective (MacIntyre, 1958, p. 76). In his 1894 work *The Neuro-psychoses of Defense*, Freud clearly explains that ideas are repressed and once affect splits from the idea, assumes other form of expression. However years later, this clear explanation became complicated with cathexis and counter-cathexis, as in Freud's article *The Unconscious* itself (nonetheless see the III part of this last article, about *unconscious emotions*) or in his the article dedicated to *Repression*, both in 1915 (b and c). People are constantly expressing unconscious motives through their words and actions that are shown as ideas or representations (*Vorstellungen*), separate from their affect ("it's only an idea"), denied or rejected ("it's a repulsive idea", "it's not mine"). The unconscious is what I do not consider or what I reject separate from affect that follows its own path.

Freudian unconscious could be equated to the concealing and revealing of the being, as is perhaps suggested by the concept of *conscious record* of the unconscious (*Fixierung, Niederschrift*) (1940 a, chapter 4). The task proposed by Freudian psychoanalysis is based on making the two "versions" or "registers" coincide, to make the unconscious, conscious. This established a complementary conscious register for the psychic unconscious. The instrument for this inquiry, as we know, is interpretation and its subjective counterpart that is looking within (*Einsicht*) thanks to free association. He argued that as conscious processes are discontinuous, consciousness cannot be the primary phenomenon. The concomitant somatic processes are more complete, therefore it is necessary to postulate the existence of the unconscious.

Freud (1915c) clearly distances himself from Descartes and Introspectionism by denying that consciousness is the privileged access to our psyche, but returns to introspectionism in the way the unconscious is characterized. Freud finished the introduction to this article showing how the concept "unconscious" has a double genealogy, in one sense as a continuation of primitive animism, and on another as a derivation of Kant's external perception theory:

Just as Kant warned us not to overlook the fact that our perception is subjectively conditioned and must not be regarded as identical with the phenomena perceived but never really discerned, so psychoanalysis bids us not to set conscious perception in the place of the unconscious mental process which is its object. The mental, like the physical, is not necessarily in reality just what it appears to be. It is, however, satisfactory to find that the correction of inner perception does not present difficulties so great as that of outer perception – that the inner object is less hard to discern truly than is the outside world (1915c, p. 171).

I suppose that some of the conditions for these internal objects to be increasingly more discernable is that they are, paradoxically, "less internal", are no longer noumenic, and we can analyze them in a more "phenomenological" manner which, in my understanding is the same as saying "relational".

Otherwise, as is pointed out further into this same text, the noumenic aspect reappears with the notion of "drives" which we can never be aware of.

Sartre (1943, p. 602 and ss.) denied the unconscious with the following argument: If by definition, psychic occurs consciously, there is no reason to speak of an unconscious psychic. However, some critics also argued against Freud's first psychoanalytical works stating that since "hysteria" is derived from "hyster" that is, uterus, then masculine hysteria is impossible. Although it is a question of convention or nomenclature and therefore undeniable, it is probably an error to assimilate everything psychic to consciousness. Again, it is an error because it disregards a large part of observable reality, although perhaps more easily observable in others than in oneself. The existence of an unconscious psyche is justified because as shown in clinical practice we cannot explain our own behavior with the data present in our consciousness, due to the emergence of symptoms that symbolize conflict, and in daily life due to the appearance of lapses and failed actions, dreams and other phenomena termed "formations of the unconscious" by Lacan (1957-1958).

The introduction of the unconscious was not so much a discovery as a change in nomenclature – as also occurs with the great theories in physics – a new way of representing events, so that our attitude should be pragmatic and not a matter of faith. But this change in perspective also implies radical conceptual confusion. Psychoanalysts are mistaken, according to Wittgenstein (1933-35, 1969), when unconscious desires are interpreted as a type of desire etc. transferring part of grammatical 'desire' to 'unconscious desire'. Confused by their own and new representative convention they think that in some way they have discovered "conscious thoughts that were unconscious before". They think that the subject is separate from his own unconscious states, and that consciousness is a screen before the unconscious. These ideas, with the concomitant aura of paradox and mystery, indicate that psychoanalysts do not understand their own discourse regarding the unconscious mind. In the long run, the unconscious is endowed with the same quality of being interior and hidden, that in our culture is usually attributed to the concept of 'mind'. MacIntyre (1958) portrays this idea clearly: "… And to fall into this way of talking is half-way to reduplicate the Cartesian substantial conscious mind by a substantial unconscious mind" (p. 98). He adds, "The unconscious is the ghost of the Cartesian consciousness." (Ibid.). With this I conclude that the Freudian unconscious must be revised not as an entity, but instead as a permanent characteristic of psychological processes, in some cases more pronounced than in others. By this same operation, consciousness should no longer be a space or entity to become a quality of the psychological act and internal traits and structures should also disappear.

However it does not seem simple that we give these metaphors up, in psychoanalysis nor in psychology in general. What we should establish is that behavior is in our interest and that the "formations of the unconscious" deserve our interest as significant behaviors within the human context. In other words, the psyche is relational before any difference is made between conscious and unconscious.

Although during the past fifty years it has no longer been uncommon to cite similarities between Freudian models and cognitive psychology (Cf. Erdelyi, 1985, 2010; Glymour, 1991; Epstein, 1994), it is surprising that Freud is rarely recognized as the predecessor. As stated by Glymour (1991, p. 44), a large part of contemporary cognitive science would be what we could have expected from Freud had he had a computer. From a relational point of view, the most important part of the coincidence is indebted to the Cartesian isolated mind. Shevrin and Dickman (1980) published an article in the *American Psychologist*, titled "The psychological unconscious: A necessary assumption for all psychological theory?" During the last decades of academic psychology we have witnessed the recuperation of the mind and of consciousness, and almost immediately after of the possibility of unconscious processes. In this way many Freudian ideas are at the core of psychological debates today, explicit or implicitly, not only regarding the role and nature of the unconscious, but also about irrational conduct, cognitive biases and styles, etc. This return to Freudian themes and concepts has ironically been named, "the Return of the Repressed" by Gail A. Hornstein (1992).

It has always been acknowledged that we ignore many things about ourselves, but until an internal world populated by mental representations was conceived it was not possible to think about the "corrosive" doubt of whether a representation could exist without the subject or person perceiving it, or at least some of the mechanisms that produce it (Chacón, 1994). Consequently, consciousness and the unconscious lie together. The unconscious structures that regulate the psyche are postulated by Piaget and by Chomsky (Cf. Piattelli-Palmarini, 1979) among others, without the need to recur to introspective experience. These two authors played an important role in the so-called "cognitive revolution" in the mid-century (Baars, 1986). While Piaget considered himself Kantian and Chomsky affirmed his Cartesian vocation, both agreed that structures are innate. They also agreed that we are aware of the results but unconscious of the mediating mechanisms. Piaget rejected the representation of the unconscious while, if I have understood Chomsky's (1980) chapter about language and unconscious thought correctly, he accepts unconscious representations although his work is centered on grammatical rules. However, not all authors within cognitive development agree to the scene just described. Vygotsky (1989) and his followers (Leontiev, Luria) proposed that psychological functions should not be explained on the basis of internal organic relationships (regulation), instead on external terms: there are constructs rather than natural structures. From an externalist perspective, processes are developed in the public scene rather than in the cranial box, despite the fact that the brain is a necessary organ in this process. For Vygotsky any superior psychological function is external, social, before becoming internal, before becoming a function in the social relationship between two or more people. Development does not mean greater socialization, in reality it is an individualization of social functions.

Jerrol A. Fodor (1975, 1980) infers that representational systems in animals and people must be similar, as they both present similar difficulties in for example learning disjunctive concepts. He states that the existence of internal mechanisms is primitive, something innately given. On the other hand, there is an analogy between learning a second language and learning the first language from an innate capacity. For Fodor, the language the organism is born with is the computer "machine language" (1975). He even speculates with the possibility that an organism be born speaking its own machine language. If a person already has an innate language, how can it acquire a new one through costly years of learning? This reminds us of the Augustinian version of how language is learned – Fodor (1975) in fact defends it – as if the infant arrives at a new country and does not understand that country's language. That is, it is like already having a language that is the language of the proposed thought. To consider that thought is developed inside our heads is a fast-held concept in our western culture, integrated for centuries into our form of life. Fodor assumes, for example, that even when the psychological terms denote a disposition to behave in a certain way, to be prepared in the corresponding mental state would be a necessary causal condition. And he uses expressions like "What's running through Alfred's head", "What's running through Misha's head", are the same thing (Fodor, 1975).

Therefore we can object that thought as internalized language is a relatively late developmental acquisition, conditioned by social learning, and is a "higher mental function" in Vygotsky's (1977) sense. Internal speech is an ability that once learned conditions all our vision of the world and makes us think that internal language is original – something primary. Of course it is a matter of the perspective we adopt about the origin of psychological life, starting from the inside or from the outside. In psychoanalysis, schools can loosely be divided into those who believe that projection is the origin and those who on the contrary, state that introjection is the only origin possible. According to the relational and externalist model, interpersonal communication exists before any other system of representation. The internal image is subsidiary to the authentic external image, and lastly to language (Wittgenstein, 1945-49, II, p.196).

A fallacy is an argument that begins with a true premise but reaches erroneous conclusions. Clark Glymour (1991) introduced the expression "Freud's androids". In order to overcome the isolated mind it is necessary to remove the *Homunculus Fallacy*, as expressed by Anthony Kenny (1991), which is the senseless application of human adjectives to entities that are not human enough. These "explanations", frequently used in psychoanalysis and cognitive psychology, populate the mind's interior like an army of little men (*Pandemonia*) undertaking tasks, reacting, giving orders, etc. It is a temptation to say that the eye produces a photograph in the mind, but this photograph must be seen by another eye in the mind, and so on, indefinitely.

The psychoanalytic unconscious suffered a formalization process in order for it to be assimilated by cognitive psychology, eliminating semantic content, since otherwise it would not be accessible to the computer. However the unconscious is actually useful in understanding human behavior as it includes a network of social meanings (that arise in free association), although not as a formal intra-psychic structure. If the network of meaning is erroneously understood as an intra-psychic structure the collective unconscious will be conceived at something internal, intimate (similar to Chomsky's structures) in an environment that runs the risk of being colonized by mysticism or dominated by inferences taken from biology. Free association and the therapeutic relationship develop a new narrative from the known material and the new contents that arise in sessions. A narrative that is different from what the subject is used to, implicit in his narrative, but that until that moment was unconscious! Unconsciousness is not what we observe, or do not want to observe; it is what we do 'unintentionally'. It is never hidden, like Poe's "purloined letter" in Lacan's (1956) seminar. The unconscious is what is not attended to, or is rejected, and the affect remaining disconnected, like that unknown bad aftertaste. Heidegger, in a paragraph of "Being and Time" refers to what is hidden in relation to the unconscious, with what I consider an instructive explanation:

There are various ways phenomena can be covered up. In the first place, a phenomenon can be covered up in the sense that it is still completely *undiscovered*. There is neither knowledge nor lack of knowledge about it. In the second place, a phenomenon can be *buried over*. This covering up can be total, but more commonly, what was once discovered by still be visible, though only as a semblance. However, where there is semblance there is "being". This kind of covering up "distortion", is the most frequent and dangerous kind because here the possibilities of being deceived and misled are especially pernicious. (1927, p. 32)

All forms of unconscious derive from specific relational developmental contexts. It can be said that the unconscious, is created within a relationship and is bi-personal, established between two or more people. It can also be legitimate to speak of group, family and even social unconscious. The functioning of the individual unconscious psyche is social by nature (Cf. Mitchell, 1988, 1993; Lyons-Ruth, 1999; Gerson, 2004). What Mitchel suggests (1988, p.15) when he depicts the mind in general can be applied to the unconscious psyche: The mind does not arise from internal pressure rather it is dyadic (two or more people) and interactive, seeking contact, engaging with other minds. I suggest that the mind is the same as the interpersonal pragmatic context itself. The relationship with the other that constructs the psyche is dialectic, in the sense of the opposition of contraries and the radical battle for recognition (Benjamin, 1995), or the supposedly calm acceptance by the other part, as in the concept of "self-object" (Kohut, 1966, 1971, 1984). The self-object refers to all the objects that provide the experience of the cohesive self (or the feeling of oneself) and continuity over time.

Regarding the many different existing theories related to memory, I consider that Maurice Halbwachs' is most consistent with a relational paradigm. Halbwachs was a sociology and pedagogy professor at University of Strasbourg and at Sorbonne University, working in collaboration with Marcel Mauss until he received a chair in Social Psychology at the Collège de France, in 1944, a year before dying in the Buchenwald concentration camp. Halbwachs (1950/1997) provided the following example: When I encounter a schoolmate he can make me remember other old schoolmates, the classrooms, the teachers, etc. However, these memories are not stored in my interior, instead, what we recuperate is a scheme made up of incomplete impressions, fragmented elements of the past. Memory is a reconstructive activity in the present, rather than a resurrection of the past. "Individual memory" implied in Cartesian thought assumes a paradoxal formulation: memory doesn't work when we are in isolation. Individual memory is not possible outside the frame of reference of collective memory. Individuals, as members of groups, are what they remember, but their memories are only the point of view of collective memory, a point of view that can change when the individual relates to other groups.

It is frequently said that representations are unconscious, not due to defensive processes, rather because they have been acquired by non-verbal modes at the beginning of life. Primitive representations are collected at a level denominated *procedural memory*. Eagle (2011, p. 170) compares them to the habits or motor abilities recorded in body processes. This type of register in the body is similar to the concept of "character" from the time of Reich (1933-1976), or more recent concepts such as "deficit" pathology (Killingmo, 1989), that imply incorporated action schemes. However action schemes do not require the existence of images or representations. Representations, of all types, appear much later.

Conclusions: Change of Paradigm?

Can the reader imagine what our theories could be like if we began to construct metaphysics from the perspective that my identity is at stake, that it's a risky business, and I try to continuously convince myself that I am the same as others, rather than the assumption that others are similar to me. However, this option has a schizoid tinge and is also in debt to our western metaphysics, specialized in favoring the isolated individual. Relational thought is anti-Cartesian, and I will add that it questions the classical division of the two substances – thought and matter – inherited from the theological separation between body and soul, and the subsequent focus on intra-psychic phenomena, within them, reason and intellect, over and above the purest and spiritual passion and emotions. Therefore the mind is a private space and in consequence, the process of becoming ill is considered something mainly individual and internal. I think that the metaphysical/epistemological position that is most coherent with the relational paradigm consists in affirming that there is no essence previous to existence – as with the platonic idea – rather that essence is present in existence - an existentialist position. Therefore there is no ego isolated from others, a subject without a world. We are part of this world, at this time, from the very beginning.

Freud's article *The History of the Psychoanalytic Movement* (1914 d) states certain criteria to delimit what psychoanalysis is and is not. According to Freud, psychoanalysis is an attempt to make two things comprehensible: transference and resistance. All investigation that recognizes these two aspects, he adds, will be psychoanalysis even if different results are achieved. From the classic perspective, "transference" is the phenomenon that consists of shifting past images or representations and their associated emotions, to the current relationship. In practice this phenomenon has been understood more or less explicitly, as a production on behalf of the patient of an erroneous representa-tion of reality, especially as a mistake in the 'female' patient contrasting with the correct representation of the male analyst. Analyst and patient, as "floating entities", that influence each other, without becoming a relationship. When the underlying Cartesian model is substituted by the idea that what the person in effect acts are (external) functioning schemes and not (internal) images, hence schemes become activated rather than transferred.

The analytic space is an intermediate area between the reality of whom the therapist is and the patient's fantasies and projections, and vice-versa, but it is also a field co-created by both. This field can be used as a space to play in and construct a new relationship (Bromberg, 1995). A step that was probably decisive in order to reach this relational concept was the recuperation of the "counter-transference" concept that took place after the fifties. Transference is a way to organize the present according to past experience, in the interaction field between therapist and patient, not excluding relationships external to the analytic session. It's probable that when faced with a patient with a rigid relational style we will continue to use the term "transference": The external object is not treated like an internal object. However it would be better to say that the person whom we are relating to is treated following the patterns we used in the past with others, not considering ostensible variations. Therefore, the interpretation of transference in the analytic situation is not enough to produce change. The relationship with the therapist must evolve until it becomes a real relationship between two people (Fairbairn). The therapist's task is a paradox. It does not consist in accepting or rejecting being an object, rather in learning from the patient how to become an object that is useful for the patient (Winnicott). As therapists we are included in all attempts to understand, but understanding is always the continuation of a dialogue that began even before we arrived.

Relational psychoanalysis is still psychoanalysis, also because it maintains the concept of the unconscious – even expanding on it – and continues the attempt to make transference and resistance comprehensible, although these concepts have changed and have been re-interpreted. In fact, it has become possible to complete these phenomena by observing the important part that the analyst adds to the process, from his/her own unconscious, overcoming the limits of what is understood as counter-transference. Transference is not simply completed with counter-transference instead the analytic situation is a common construction between analyst and patient. The relational or intersubjective perspective pays particular attention to the unconscious but is not limited to the classic dynamic repressed unconscious. We maintain and discard terms that are traditional to psychoanalysis, such as transference and counter-transference, however relational psychoanalysis is coining new concepts that as theoretic tools, allow us to have access to and develop the therapist-patient relationship. Concepts such as "enactment", "now moments", "responsiveness", "mutuality", "thirdness" are part of this new technical panoply that at this time I am merely naming (Benjamin, 1995; Cf. Espinosa et al., 2005).

It is not infrequent to read and hear that relational psychoanalysis is so removed from psychoanalytic principles that it should be seen with distrust. It is has been categorically affirmed that it is not even psychoanalysis, as it simply belongs to the field of psychology. On my part, the consideration that psychoanalysis belongs to a field of knowledge separate from psychology has never been satisfactory, according to the attitude manifested by its founder whom, as is known to all, read a lot of psychology and literature, and few psychoanalytical texts, among other reasons because he was inventing it himself. We also look forward to the undeniable opening of current psychoanalysis to other fields of science and psychology: the systemic model, neuroscience, cognitivism, developmental psychology, etc. Purism only favors a not so golden isolation. However, if we finally discover that we have abandoned the psychoanalytic dwelling – official or theoretically – something which does not seem probable nor is it our intention, we would have to take it in stride.

Whether we accept Forms of Life, then the structures of the unconscious, or, for us, the form of reality, depends on the particular way a particular human society adapts to the world. Perhaps the forms of life are another mode of biology, perhaps we are biologically conditioned to be born and live in a society that makes us individuals and endows us with language, like chatting termites. Language is a way in which society adapts to the environment. However – and I would like to be very clear about this – the rules of this language, this network of symbols, have to be found outside, not from within.

Existential analytics cannot be mere hermeneutics. Since the forties with the object-relations theory, the relational paradigm has given great relevance to negative early experiences that came from the environment and that produced the pathology, which is a partial recovery of the traumatic theory. This recuperation began with Sándor Ferenczi (1933), and there is growing interest today in the investigation of early infant development, in connection with the research undertaken by Daniel Stern (1985). The narration that therapy aspires to is not a mere intrapsychic creation of the patient, instead it must significantly integrate these traumatic situations and those initial influences – developmental traumas - which intervene not only as repressed or dissociated contents but also in the constitution of our bodily self and our habits.

Summary

Relational thought is anti-Cartesian and entails a fundamental questioning of the classic division between two substances – thought and matter – inherited from the theological separation between body and soul, and the subsequent focus on intra-psychic phenomena. In this way we try to overcome extreme therapist/patient asymmetry and static terms – such as transference– that convey the idea of a difficult communication between two independent minds or self-contained compartments. Relational psychoanalysis changes the way truth is understood and attained: Truth is a discovery, something that is constructed or co-created by patient and therapist, therefore a paradigmatic change from classic psychoanalysis.

The recuperation of trauma theory frees us in some way from intra-psychic metapsychological energetism and avoids the risks of pure hermeneutics. Trauma occurs when the infant cannot resolve a situation of frustration and contradiction, in which he is abused and not recognized. It is not a mere subjective interpretation, rather it is objective harm. We are imbued with the concept of the subject as something internal that directs our behavior (the ghost in the machine), but this subject is a representation, and representations cannot do anything by themselves – in reality we do things with representations (and with words). In sum we consider that the unconscious is relational and the self is external, the person in action and interaction. As the essence of human being is located in the mind, separate from the body, this makes it possible to maintain the illusion that a circle of internal immunity exists in the face of death and physical limitations: We have achieved immortality, but the price is guilt and psychic pain, renouncing to life.

On the other hand, relational psychoanalysis is still psychoanalysis, because it maintains the concept of the unconscious – even expanding on it – and continues in the attempt to make transference and resistance comprehensible, although these concepts have changed and have been re-interpreted.

3

Ferenczi and Balint In the Origins of Relational Psychoanalysis

Neri Daurella

We know that "the school of Relational psychoanalysis was not born of a single seminal theorist or homogeneous group of theorists from which it then evolved, diverged, or remained loyal, and it is thereby not subject to evaluation by its degree of deviation from orthodoxy", as Philip M. Bromberg wrote in the *International Journal of Psychoanalysis* some years ago (Bromberg, 2009). But there is no doubt that, to contextualize the emergence of this upward trend in the current psychoanalytic landscape, most notably in USA but increasingly so in the rest of America, Europe and other countries, we have to go back to the Freud-Ferenczi conflict which became evident at the IPA Congress held in Wiesbaden (Germany) in 1932.

Wiesbaden 1932: Confusion of Tongues Between Ferenczi and Freud

A few days before the Congress, Ferenczi went to visit Freud in Vienna to make him know his work *Confusion of tongues between Adults and the Child.*

The language of Tenderness and of Passion, which he intended to present at the Congress. Freud had considered Ferenczi (the founder of the Budapest School of Psychoanalysis) his favourite pupil, and now he had been seeing for some time he was moving away from him in the theoretical and technical field, and he felt very disappointed. He had tried to get him back on the right track with interpretations, he had even tried to recover him through the institutional way, offering him the presidency of the IPA, but Ferenczi had not accepted this position, claiming that he was at a critical and self-critical time on theoretical and technical aspects of psychoanalysis, and this critical state of mind was unlikely to make him a good president, whose function, according to him, was rather to preserve what existed. The opinion/interpretation of Freud on this decision is known thanks to the letter he wrote to his daughter Anna on August 24th, 1932:

"The renunciation of Ferenczi represents a neurotic action of hostility against the father and the brothers in order to preserve the regressive pleasure of representing the role of mother with his patients."

Judith Dupont, the publisher of Ferenczi´s Clinical Diary (not published until 1985, 52 years after his death) says in her prologue: "It was a painful encounter, where the misunderstanding between the two men reached its climax. Freud, very upset by the content of the article, asked Ferenczi to abstain from any publication until he retracted the positions he expressed in that text. The next day, Freud wrote to his daughter Anna: "Ferenczi has totally returned to the etiological perspective in which I believed and abandoned 35 years ago: that the most common cause of neurosis are sexual trauma in childhood. He uses almost the same words I used then." In spite of everything, Ferenczi presented his paper at the Congress of Wiesbaden and generated a great controversy that would close in false the following year due to Ferenczi´s death and to a phenomenon of massive repression of his thought in the official psychoanalytic world. Balint, the main disciple of Ferenczi and keeper of his legacy, wrote (1968) that the conflict between Freud and Ferenczi was an authentic trauma for the psychoanalytic world.

From our current perspective, we can understand a little more what happened: 35 years before, Freud had written his famous letter to Fliess (September 1897) in which he abandoned his theory of trauma and seduction as an etiological explanation of neuroses and introduced his theory of child psychosexuality and Oedipal fantasies as an alternative explanation. He was very pleased with his ability to recognize his mistakes and his undoubted seren- dipity, but could not accept that the same ability to recognize his mistakes and the same serendipity of his pupil had led him to take a step further in the path initiated by his master. He considered a regression what Ferenczi considered a progress. "I no longer believe that you correct yourself as I corrected myself one generation ago", wrote Freud to Ferenczi after the Congress of Wiesbaden.

At the same time, Ferenczi was writing in his Clinical Diary (which, as I said before, was not published until 1985) his interpretation of Freud's attitude:

"I think that Freud originally believed really in the analysis, followed Breuer with enthusiasm, and applied with passion and dedication to the healing of neurotics (if necessary, he would spend hours with a patient suffering from a hysterical crisis), but certain experiences surely shook him first and then appeased him, surely as happened to Breuer with the relapse of his patient and the problem of a countertransference that suddenly opened before him like an abyss. In Freud, the equivalent was perhaps to discover that the hysterics were lying. After that discovery, Freud doesn't love his patients. He loves his ordered, cultivated superego (another proof of this is his antipathy and his expressions of censure towards the psychotic, the perverse, and in general "everything that is too abnormal"). After this shock, this disappointment, very little is said about trauma. The constitution begins to occupy the main place. This, of course, involves a bit of fatalism."

Freud reproaches Ferenczi his *"furor sanandi"* and Ferenczi reproaches Freud that he has stopped believing in the therapeutic function of psychoanalysis. He criticizes the drift increasingly impersonal of the treatment method, that becomes a more intellectual enterprise than interested in therapeutic change.

But let's leave the history of Freud's relationship with Ferenczi and see if the recovery of trauma theory represented a step back or a step forward in the history of psychoanalysis.

The Theory of Trauma In Ferenczi

Your daddy is rich
and your ma is good-looking
So, hush, little baby,
Don't you cry
(Summertime)

When Ferenczi recovers trauma theory as an important etiological factor in mental pathology, he is speaking in a much broader sense than that of the early Freudian theory of seduction. First, he is not just talking about trauma linked to sexuality, but also to the hostility of adults in relation to children, and he's not ignoring the role of fantasy and oedipal conflict of the child in the genesis of pathology, but considers that children´s eroticism is tender and adult eroticism is passionate, and trauma occurs when the adult doesn´t fulfill his protective function, but uses the child for his passionate purposes, not necessarily in the form of explicit sexual abuse, but in many different ways, which have in common the fact that they ignore the true needs of the child.

The misunderstanding of Freud was to think that Ferenczi had left aside the role of the oedipal fantasy of the child to return to the traumatic role of adult seduction, but what Ferenczi actually did was to give a different version of the Oedipus conflict, on the basis of the obvious asimetry of the actors in conflict. The language that Ferenczi uses when speaking about the child is far from Freud´s when he speaks of the "polymorph perverse". Ferenczi doesn´t deny that the erotic tendencies of the children are shown much earlier than what was believed before Freud´s discoveries, but he says that, even in regard to sexual matters, what the child wishes is just play and tenderness, not the violent manifestation of passion, and when the adult prematurely forces his feelings, the child is very afraid.

However, as much or more pathogen than this trauma by excess of passion of the adult considers Ferenczi the trauma by default, due to lack of desire, in the case of a child who is not a welcome guest in the family. In *The Unwelcome Child and his Death Drive* (1929), referring to the Freudian theory that divides the drives into *Eros* and *Tanatos*, he highlights how the unwelcome child may prematurely lose the taste for life and be viewed from the outside as a being lacking in capacity to adapt, with a congenital weakness of his ability to live, when maybe the explanation has to do with a not so obvious trauma, or rather a succession of microtraumas that occur when the child captures consciously or inconsciously many signs of aversion, impatience or disgust of his mother. With regard to children raised in this traumatizing environment that may go unnoticed, says Ferenczi:

"I wanted to indicate the probability that children received with coldness and without affection die easily by their own will. Or use one of the numerous organic means to disappear quickly or, if they escape to this destination, they always have some pessimism and a certain dislike for life."

Another variant of trauma in the relationship between adults and the child is what he calls "the terrorism of suffering", which he describes very well in *Confusion of tongues between adults and the child* (1932):

"Children are forced to endure all kinds of family conflicts and carry on their weak shoulders the heavy burden of the other family members. They don´t do it out of selflessness, but to enjoy again of the peace disappeared and of the tenderness associated with it. A mother who continually laments her sufferings can turn her child into a careful help, that is, turn him into a true maternal substitute, regardless of her child´s interests."

Ferenczi subscribes to the Freudian theory of complementary series, but gives a warning about the possibility of not sufficiently taking into account the traumatic factor in pathogenesis and supposing the presence of a constitutional factor of great weight when the traumas are not very evident in the history reported by the patient, when, as the song says, there is a rich father and a beautiful mother, and, despite all, the child has reasons to cry, perhaps because the parents narcissism doesn´t allow them to know the true needs of his son.

Michael Balint, the direct heir of Ferenczi´s legacy, explains very clearly the central idea of his teacher regarding what he considered traumatic: the essential disproportion between the child´s limited ability o manage excitement and the stimulation of adults, excessive or insufficient, unconscious and therefore uncontrolled, full of passion and therefore burdened with guilt. The child doesn´t care if adults call this careless stimulation hygienic regime, funny play, education for freedom, being an exemplary model, strict morality, reward or punishment, or whatever you want" (Balint, 1949). Ferenczi´s main message was to emphasize the discrepancy that often occurs between the authentic needs of the child and the uncontrolled (for being unconscious) gratifications that allow themselves the adults responsible for their upbringing.

Identification with the Aggressor

So far we´ve seen how Ferenczi, referring to traumatized children, speaks of fear, disgust for life, failure to adapt, which, in a terminology currently in vogue, would be called "resilience reduction". But the most interesting contribution of Ferenczi in 1932, in the Congress of Wiesbaden, would be what happens when traumatized children are able to use defense mechanisms and especially what he called "identification with the aggressor". Due to the phenomenon of of massive repression of the thought of Ferenczi that occurred in the psychoanalytic world , most psychoanalysts link the concept of "identification with the aggressor" with Anna Freud, when it´s evident that he attended the Congress of Wiesbaden and there had the opportunity to listen to Ferenczi when, talking about the effects of incestuous seductions on children, said:

"It´s difficult to guess the behaviour and feelings of children after these events. Their first reaction will be rejection, hate, dislike, and will oppose a violent resistance: "No! I don´t want! You hurt me! Leave me!" This, or another similar, would be the immediate reaction if it were not inhibited by intense fear. Children feel physically and morally defenseless, their personality is still weak to protest, even mentally, the strength and overwhelming authority of adults leaves them dumb, and may even make them lose consciousness. But when this fear reaches its culminating point, it forces them to automatically submit to the aggressor's will, to guess his least desire, to obey totally forgetting themselves, identifying completely with the aggressor."

An author belonging to the current of the relational psychoanalysis, Jay Frankel (2002), explores the Ferenczian concept of identification with the aggressor and says it refers to our defensive response when we feel over-whelmed by the threat, when we have lost the sense that the world will protect us, when we are in danger with no possibility of escape. Then we make our self disappear. We dissociate the present experience: like chameleons, we mimic ourselves with the world around us, exactly with what scares us, to protect ourselves. We stop being ourselves and we become the image someone has of us. And all this, automatically.

Biologists say that the phenomenon of adaptation by which the chameleon becomes hardly visible in its usual environment adopting its color is called *crypsis* (from the Greek word *kriptós* (hidden). Some animals use cryptic mechanisms as camouflage and defense to protect themselves from predators, so we might think of the identification with the aggressor as a psychological defense mechanism that has very clear instinctual roots in the service of survival.

The meaning that would later give Anna Freud (1936) to this mechanism would be would be more limited. She refers to the phenomenon of how the child, personifying the aggressor, assuming his attributes or imitating his aggression, is transformed from being threatened to becoming a threat.

But Ferenczi gives a broader scope to the mechanism. He describes three virtually simultaneous actions: the child

a) mentally submits to the aggressor
b) this subjugation allows him to guess the aggressor's desires. It could be said (and this doesn't say Ferenczi, but it's my idea) that an authentic cryptesthesia occurs, that is, a state of sensitivity above normal that is in the base of phenomena like premonitions and prophecies
c) makes a kind of traumatic pseudo-progress or pathological prematura-tion that allows him to do what he feels will save him.

Here Ferenczi refers to a typical dream, that of the wise baby, in which a baby suddenly begins to talk very wisely to his family from his cradle:

" His fear of exalted, in a sense crazy adults, transforms the child into a kind of psychiatrist. To guard himself against the danger of uncontrolled adults, he must be fully identified with them. It's incredible what we can learn from our wise babies, the neurotics."

What a vivid description of what we now call parentificated children! We see how Ferenczi´s concept of identification with the aggressor isn´t merely an imitation of the aggressor´s behaviour in a later scenario, victimizing another as he was a victim before, but a substantial alteration of the process of development and maturation of the child´s self, which also includes the introjection of the adult´s feeling of guilt. The traumatized child feels much confusion, feels at the same time innocent and guilty of what is happening (be it an active seduction, an abandonment, or the climate of "terrorism of suffering" in which he lives immersed), and the trust in the testimony of his senses is broken.

But the traumatic effect is just consolidated in a second moment, is a consequence of the denial. As Luis Martín Cabré says, "when the child goes to another adult to clarify and find a meaning to what has happened, he receives from this adult, who cannot stand the child´s speech, a denial that interrupts any introjective process and paralyzes thinking. The adult, who behaves almost always as if nothing had happened, forbids the child not only the words but the possibility of representation and phantasmatization. Words are buried alive." (1966) We could say that the version of adults drowns the child´s experience. It´s a true phenomenon of what is popularly known as "gas-lighting".

The Re-Traumatization

What was most controversial at the Wiesbaden Congress was not so much the recovery of the importance of trauma in the pathogenesis, nor the presentation in society of the concept of the identification with the aggressor, but the fact that Ferenczi dared to make a public self-criticism and used this concept to refer to the risks that psychoanalytic therapy may be not only ineffective but also re-traumatizing.

He began by explaining how he had met with patients who weren´t advancing in their therapeutic process and how he consoled himself attributing this impasse to their great resistances. From time to time, these patients accused him of being insensitive, cold and even cruel, but these explicit complaints only manifested exceptionally, and he was often baffled when he saw that, at the end of sessions, the patients eventually accepted his interpretations with a docility that appealed to him. He examined his conscience, he suspected that these docile patients secretly experienced impulses of hatred and anger that they didn´t dare to manifest (in fact, one of his reproaches to Freud was that in his personal analysis he had not let him work through his negative transference). And this is how he links the concept of identification with the aggressor with the analytic relationship:

"I came gradually to the conclusion that the patients perceived very finely the tendencies, sympathies and antipathies, and the humor of the analyst, even when the analyst was unaware of them. Instead of contradicting and accusing him of weaknesses and errors, patients identified with him.".....True Usually they don't allow themselves any criticism of us, it doesn't cross their minds, unless they receive from us express permission or direct encouragement." ..... "They fall into extreme submission as a result of their inability or their fear of displeasing us in criticizing us."

So far he speaks about patient's identification with the analyst, but then he speaks of the analyst as a subtle aggressor:

"Much of the criticism rejected refers to what we might call professional hypocrisy. We politely welcome the patient when he enters, we ask him to communicate his associations, and we promise to listen attentively and put the maximum interest in his well-being and in the task of clarifying his condition. In fact, it may happen that some internal or external features of the patient are difficult for us to bear, or even that we feel that the analytic session brings an unpleasant disturbance to a more important professional concern or an intimate problem. Here I see no other way than to become aware of our own problem and discuss it with the patient, admitting it not only as a possibility but also as a real fact."

The indication of what today is called self-disclosure was, therefore, not to repeat in the analytical situation what was once traumatizing for the patient as a child in his relationship with adults, and which made him lose confidence in them and in his own perceptions: the lack of sincerity and authenticity of adults when, in relation to the child, let themselves, consciously or unconsciously, be carried by what Ferenczi calls their passions: they traumatize the child, and when he complains, are not capable of recognizing what has happened, they deny it, make the child doubt his own perception, or even accuse him of being exaggerated, or a liar, or too grouchy, or ungrateful, or say they have done it for his sake.

On July 27, 1932, Ferenczi writes in his *Clinical Diary:*

"What is traumatic? An attack or its consequences? Children's ability to respond in an adaptive way to sexual attacks and other passionate attacks is much greater than we imagine. Traumatic confusion is only reached, most of the time, when attack and response are denied by the adult charged with guilt, and treated as if they were something punishable."

This traumatizing confusion of tongues can occur again in the analytic situation if, when the patient shows in a thousand ways his suffering, meets with an analyst who responds with an attitude of extreme distance and emotional coldness, with interpretations that the patient feels persecutory or distant from his vital interests , which respond more to the analyst´s interest in his theories than to what the patient needs. This can leave to a real re-traumatization and that, instead of being the relation with the analyst the occasion of a corrective emotional experience (as said another Hungarian analyst, Franz Alexander), would become a re-traumatizing experience, in which the patient has to be submissive once more, identifying once again with an aggressor who transmits to him the message that he does it "for his own good". This makes it very clear Ferenczi in *Confusion of tongues*:

"The analytical situation, this cold reserve, the professional hypocrisy and the antipathy towards the patient that is hidden behind it, and that the patient captures with all his being, don´t differ much of what made him sick earlier, that is, in his childhood. ..... If we push the patient to reproduce his trauma, his condition becomes unbearable. ..... But the ability to recognize our mistakes and correct them as well as the authorization of criticisms, make us gain the trust of the patient. *This trust is what establishes the contrast between the present and an unbearable and traumatic past.*"

To finish this section on re-traumatization, I wish to reproduce here some fragments of the annotation made in his *Clinical Diary* on August 13, 1932:

"Record of the sins of psychoanalysis"

(Reproaches of a patient)

1) The psychoanalyst tempts the patient to transference: the deepest understanding, the keen interest in the finer details of biography, and the movements of the soul, are naturally perceived by the patient as signs of a deep personal friendship, even tenderness.

2) As most patients are living among the wreckage of their soul, clinging to a float, they will be blind and deaf to the facts that can show them the low personal interest that analysts feel for their patients.

3) Meanwhile, the patient´s unconscious perceives all the negative feelings I the analyst (boredom, irritation, feelings of hatred when the patient says something unpleasant or that touches the complexes of the doctor.

4) The analysis is a convenient opportunity to put into practice without feeling guilty unconscious actions purely selfish, inconsiderate, immoral, we could even say criminal, for instance: a feeling of power over a series of devout, helpless patients who admire him uncondi-tionally; a sadistic content for their suffering and their helplessness; unconcern for the duration of the analysis and even tending to extend it for purely financial reasons; if one wants, he makes the patients contributors for life."

"The transference, which we see how it generates in excess in the analysis, and which the ignorance of the analyst doesn't succeed in solving (in order to do that, he would have to know himself better and to know his behaviour), ultimately plays in the analysis the same role as the egoism of parents in the education."

"Without sympathy there is no cure (at the most intellections on the genesis of suffering."

The Ferenczi Case: Innovation and Repression

Ferenczi, consistent with his clinical experience, had come to the conclusion that the classical analytic technique (inducing the patient, lying on the couch, to recall or relive the original trauma while the analyst was keeping a pasive, objectifying, supposedly neutral attitude) created a climate not essentially different from which in the patient's childhood had led to illness, and this conclusion led him to try to introduce changes in classical technique. But the psychoanalytic community at that time couldn't tolerate Ferenczi talking so directly and openly about what analysts feel and do in their office, in the intimacy of the relationship with the patient, alluding very directly to the analyst's emotional commitment.

He valued above all the experience of the patient-analyst relationship and warned against overvaluation of interpretative work not linked to the patient's experience. And he considered that empathy, the capacity to feel with the patient, was the basis of the psychoanalytic technique. In *Elasticity of the psychoanalytic technique* (1928) he raised the importance that the psychoanalyst doesn't appear before the patient as an idealized and infallible object. He radically reversed the Freudian metaphor of the analyst as a surgeon and laid the foundation for a theory of countertransference as a maternal disposition. For Ferenczi, the patient in the course of the analysis must have access to a reparative experience, as far as possible, of that which has been denied to him during childhood, rather than to the benefits of the lifting of repression.

If we try to understand why the contribution of Ferenczi was ignored after his death, in 1933, one year after the congress of Wiesbaden, during at least 50 years, we have to situate ourselves in that historical moment. We know that Freud had the freedom to learn by trial and error and the serendipity that allowed him to discover psychoanalysis. But we also know how Freud himself, "fearing the abuses to which psychoanalysis would be subject as soon as it became popular" (1914), not only created the IPA, but also adopted a position of control of psychoanalytic orthodoxy through the creation of a secret committee, supporting the formation of an autocratic structure to watch over the psychoanalytic essences and declare what was and was not psychoanalysis. Moreover, he used the interpretation of the unconscious motivations of discrepants to disqualify them, and this recourse to the *ad hominem* attack became common among psychoanalysts.

It's not a matter of entering here to examine the complexities of the relation Freud-Ferenczi. What interests me is to point out how the abusive use of personal interpretation outside the context in which I only consider it's ethical to use it (that of the intimacy of the psychoanalytic session) became a widespread practice among psychoanalysts (not just the wild ones, but members of the IPA). Thus, for instance, to deny validity to the ideas and methods of Ferenczi it has often been said that they were a consequence of the failures of his analysis with Freud, a kind of acting out or the result of his unresolved transference neurosis.

This climate may perhaps partly explain why when Ernest Jones, in his biography of Freud, moved from the psychoanalytic interpretation of Ferenczi to a pure and hard psychiatric *post mortem* diagnosis, he found virtually no resistance. Jones literally wrote that "Ferenczi, to the end of his life, developed psychotic manifestations which were revealed, among other things, in a distancing of Freud and his doctrines (1957). So Jones *presented as one of the psychotic symptoms of Ferenczi his distancing of Freud and his doctrines.* What psychiatrist would consider a colleague's critical thinking a symptom of psychosis? In what scientific society would a statement of this kind be taken seriously?

When the third volume of Jones' work was published, Balint, disciple and depositary of Ferenczi's legacy, wrote a letter to the *International Journal of Psychoanalysis* stating that, despite the progressive physical weakness of Ferenczi due to the disease that led him to death, he had always mantained lucidity and had discussed with him in detail the controversy with Freud. The letter was published after convincing Jones to Balint to remove from it a reference to the fact that Ferenczi had been the analyst of both of them, and together to it appeared a commentary of Jones insisting on his diagnosis. Carlo Bonomi (1999) comments that Balint's letter today could be considered too cautious and diplomatic, but he adds that "Balint shrewdly intended to record his disagreement and to entrust to the next generation the task of ascertaining the truth, thereby communicating the idea that his generation had no great liking for truth."

The less diplomatic responses, logically, came from analysts who were already outside the IPA, such as Erich Fromm, who would compare Jones´ pseudodiagnosis of Ferenczi with the Stalinist practice of discrediting opponents by calling them spies or traitors. Fromm (1958) would argue that psychoanalysis was not only a therapy and a scientific theory, but also a "movement" that "at times and in some of its representatives manifests a fanaticism that is only found in religions and political bureaucracies".

But, what elements were there in the thought of Ferenczi so disquieting to generate such a defensive movement? I´ve the impression that Ferenczi aroused much fear because he was a professional more commited to the pursuit of therapeutic efficacy than to the defense of the purity of the method, and this, in the eyes of the holders of institutionalized psychoanalytic knowledge became a model dangerous for many inexperienced therapists loaded with good intentions. He was a psychoanalyst who, when he found the results attained with the standard technique unsatisfactory, was self-critical, rehearsed technical variations, published his results and learned from his mistakes. More or less the same as the young Freud did when he made his journey from hypnosis, through the cathartic technique, to the discovery of psychoanalysis. It´s not surprising that for twenty-five years Freud had Ferenczi as his privileged interlocutor. Both had the courage and critical ability of the most creative scientists to question the given and go a little further. Although there came a time when Freud, and more than Freud himself, his heirs adopted a more defensive attitude focused on conserving the heritage than to continue in the line of research.

Ferenczi, unlike many of his IPA colleagues, more concerned with defining what psychoanalysis was or was not, or whether it was to be categorized as a form of psychotherapy, or to differentiate pure gold of ignoble alloys, was dedicated to adjusting the technique to the needs of each patient. Ferenczi, unlike Freud, didn´t consider it important to establish analyzability criteria. For him, there were no intractable patients, but inadequate or insufficient technique. He was not resigned when impasses occurred in a treatment and criticized the option of analysts who took refuge in allusions to the patient´s insurmountable resistance or narcissism.

Balint (1968) summarized very well how Ferenczi understood the analyst´s function:

"If the original trauma of the patient in his childhood consisted of excessive or insufficient stimulation by the environment, with the subsequent lack of understanding or indifference of the same environment, the objective of the therapy should be: a) to help the patient return to the traumatic situation, b) to observe carefully what degree of tension the patient can endure in that state, and c) to ensure that the tension is maintained at that level by responding positively to the patient's wishes and needs, while the patient is in state of regression. Byproduct of this research was the first in-depth study of the therapist-patient relationship and the discovery of what we now call the technique of interpreting countertransference ".

At this point the Ferenczi-Freud divergence occurred. Freud criticized Ferenczi's technique by stating the dangers involved: the impossibility of satisfying all the needs of a patient in a state of regression and the difficulty for the patient, even in the event of an improvement, to become independent really of the analyst.

The controversy between master and disciple was not settled. And this would be the starting point for the later elaboration of Balint.

Balint: Basic Fault and Therapeutic Relationship

In 1937, in a symposium held in Budapest, Balint appears as heir to Ferenczi and begins to publicly expose his own theory as the fruit of the work of a Hungarian school of Psychoanalysis, differentiated from the schools of Vienna and London.

He disagrees with Freud's concept of primary narcissism and proposes as an alternative the concept of primary love as the first moment of child development. It is based on the fact that the child is born in a state of intense relationship with his environment, both biologically and libidinally. The fetus is literally like a fish in the water. It's a pattern of relationship similar to the one we maintain after birth with the air around us: it's indispensable and we use it without realizing it. But if it suddenly lacks, we are aware of its enormous importance. And above all, that is not the same as us. In the intrauterine life individual and environment are related in a state of total harmony. But birth involves a traumatic change and forces a process of adaptation, of separation of the individual from the environment. The harmony is broken and the others begin to appear, not so unconditional, with clear contours and limits that the child will have to recognize and respect.

At first most of those others will be indifferent or frustrating, but some will show that they can provide gratification. These will be called "primary objects" (Balint uses the word "objects" but refers to people), with which the individual establishes a peculiar relationship.

"A common feature of all these primitive forms of relationship is that in them the other is taken for granted, the idea that a»work of conquest" may be required to get it to collaborate has not yet arisen. In this harmonious relationship of two, only one can have desires, interests and demands of his own; it is of course assumed, without exception, that the other, the object or the benefactor substance, will automatically have the same desires, interests and expectations." (Balint, 1968)

Here Balint detaches as much from Freud's concept of *primary narcissism* as from the concept of Ferenczi's infant *omnipotence*: he replaces omnipotence for *harmony* and primary narcissism for *primary love*.

Recovering this initial harmony will be our permanent aspiration, and almost never satisfied. However, on some occasions we do have the impression of recovering this harmony. Balint cites several: orgasm, religious ecstasy, the most sublime moments of artistic creation, and some special moments in analytical treatment. These states, which may seem narcissistic, are just the opposite: states in which the individual has the impression of being in a fully good relation with his world, states of total harmony.

Balint's primary love is very different from what we might call "mature" or "adult." It is a pre-Oedipal love, exclusively of two persons, in which one absolutely depends on the other, to which it uses and demands that it maintain the state of harmony. It is a love doomed to frustration, because it does not take reality into account. And this inevitable frustration will mean breaking the basic trust the child initially had in their environment. And the imprint of this rupture will mark the later relations of the individual. So the situation of every newborn child is high risk. Very immature, and intensely dependent on the environment to be able to develop, it is very likely that the discrepancy between its real needs and what it receives from outside, as Ferenczi said, will occur.

Balint goes one step further in the theorization of these first constitutive moments of the human being when coining the concept of *basic fault*:

"A basic fault in the biological structure of the individual, involving both spirit and body, in varying proportions. The origin of this basic fault lies in the past, in a considerable discrepancy between the individual›s needs during his early years (or even its first months) of life and the care received at this time. This discrepancy creates a deficiency whose consequences are only partially reversible. Although the individual can make a good and even an excellent adaptation, the vestiges of his early experiences subsist and intervene in what we call his constitution, his individuality, or the formation of his character, both psychologically and biologically. The cause of this early discrepancy may be found in the congenital factor - that is, the baby›s needs may be excessive - or in the environment, which provides him with care which may be insufficient, negligent, irregular, hyper-anxious, hyperprotective or simply lacking understanding " (Balint, 1968).

Balint takes the term *basic fault* of geology and crystallography, to refer to "an unforeseen irregularity in the global structure, an irregularity that in normal circumstances may remain hidden, but, if tensions occur, it can lead to a rupture, a deep breakdown of the global structure ". He uses this term because it is the one used by many of its patients to describe what they felt was the source of their problems: they were not talking about complex, or conflict, or situatio, but fault, "a fault in the basic structure of the personality, something like a defect or a scar".

He argues that we all have a basic fault, although its severity will depend on the circumstances of our early childhood. According to the experience of our basic fault, we may have some compulsive patterns of relationship: these are the so-called character traits. Balint cites the original meaning of the Greek word *character*: chisel, sign or mark made with a chisel. Thus, character is a set of signs or marks that make the person who carries them recognizable.

The more traumatic the experience of the basic fault has been, the more rigid will be the protective structure that the individual will have set up to continue living. Is there any chance of breaking the rigidity of this defensive structure that makes us relate to the environment always in the same way? Can we learn again to relate innocently to the environment, to love without conditions and enjoy without anxiety? We can start again? To this Balint responds that in order to start something new we must return to the point where it was interrupted. A new beginning means not only changing a person's behavior but its libidinal structure.

Obviously one cannot do it alone. If the trauma occurred in a relationship, healing will only occur in a relationship. It takes two people: the one who suffers from the consequences of the primitive failure of the environment (the patient) and the one who is willing to become a new environment and not fail (the psychotherapist). Thus, the therapeutic enterprise is an attempt to restore the patient's basic trust.

The therapist's job, according to him, is to help the patient to develop a primitive relationship in the analytic situation, which corresponds to his compulsive pattern of relation, and to maintain it without interference, quietly, until the patient can discover the possibility of new forms of relationship and can experiment with them.

For this process to take place, the psychoanalyst must avoid three dangers in which it would be easy for him to fall:

1. Although it is logical for the analyst to become important for the patient, he should not be rigidly clinging to a form of relationship only because it has been useful in other cases, or in previous phases of the treatment, but must be willing to accompany the patient in his evolution.
2. Sometimes the analyst must avoid behaving like an independent object with well-defined contours and must be willing to act as one of the primary substances, to be there like earth or water, indestructible and ready to be used.
3. The analyst, however, must avoid looking omnipotent, because if he gives this impression the patient will never be able to escape from his regression and instead of a therapeutic progress a regression state will occur.

From this enumeration we can deduce a couple of conclusions:

- To be therapeutic progress regression is indispensable, although we cannot forget it implies serious risks.
- The way the regression manifests depends only in part on the patient, on the characteristics of his personality and his illness; on the other hand it depends on how the therapist responds. Regression has much to do with the quality of the relationship between both of them.

This brings us to the distinction that makes Balint between ,alignant and benign forms of regression. The fundamental difference between the two is as follows:

"In one of these ways regression is directed toward the gratification of instinctive longings; what the patient seeks is an external event, an action of its object. In the other form, what the patient expects is not so much a gratification by external action as a tacit consent to use the external world in a way that allows him to deal with his internal problems."

In both forms of regression, the participation of the environment, the therapist, is essential. But in each case it is a very different participation. In malignant regression, the patient does not return beyond the narcissistic level, and the therapist is a partial object to which he feels unsafe, and therefore he is avidly demanded of acts that, instead of calming the patient's needs, intensify them more and more, turning him into a true "addict" of the therapist. To this malignant regression called Balint also *regression directed towards gratification.*

Instead, in benign regression, the patient returns to the level of primary love, and the therapist plays the role of those primitive substances prior to the appearance of the objects. Therefore, it does not act, but creates an atmosphere in which the patient feels content, as in a supporting liquid from which will end up coming back to be born again. In this form of regression, the patient does not seek gratification through acts of the therapist; he only pretends that the existence of its individuality and of its internal life is recognized to him. To this benign regression Balint calls *regression aimed at recognition.*

Primary Love
And Psychoanalytic Technique

In the book bearing this title, published in 1952, are collected Balint's writings on technical proposals derived from his theoretical conceptions. Here we already see an analyst who describes how he works at that time unlike how he did it twenty years earlier. The relational shift has already occurred clearly.

In the article *Changing Therapeutical Aims and Techniques in Psychoanalysis* (1949) he already says that from the recognition of the importance of the relation, the most important field of investigation will be to consider what is the contribution the analyst to what happens in the psychoanalytic situation, thus showing its Ferenczian imprint. The psychoanalyst is no longer going to confine himself to interpreting the internal world nor the transference of the patient, but is going to consider how he is influencing the creation of a climate that allows the patient to open up, or, conversely, how to avoid creating a climate which causes the patient to close in band. Balint emphasizes how this strange relationship we call the psychoanalytic situation is influenced by the frustrations and satisfactions, demands and conscious and unconscious gratifications of both participants.

In *The Hazards Inherent in Consistent Interpretation* (1968) he formulates his clearest criticism to the Kleinian analysts of his day. It should be borne in mind that Balint, who emigrated to Great Britain in 1939, and witnessed in London the Controversial Discussions between Kleinian and Annafreudian analysts of the 1940s, would be part of the independent group of the British Psychoanalysis Society, where there were also Winnicott, Fairbairn and Bowlby, to which we can also consider precursors of the current relational psychoanalysis.

Balint criticizes the language and the interpretive technique characteristic of the Kleinian, which interpret in terms of "breasts", "milk", "attacks on the contents of the mother's body", "persecution", etc., The patient feels that he is being forced to accept a crazy language, and ends up introjecting and idealizing his analyst and his technique, without ever recognizing a therapeutic failure. In this way you can enter an endless spiral: the patient shows his discomfort and the analyst interprets, but there is no change, and both analyst and patient feel increasingly guilty. All this leads to more manifestations of discomfort on the part of the patient and on the part of the analyst to a frenzy of interpretations still more intelligent and deep than the previous ones, as it indicates Balint with evident irony.

And in *The Unobtrusive Analyst* (1968) he proposes that the attitude of the analyst has to be unobtrusive, not intrusive, not fond of being noticed. The more omniscient and omnipotent the analyst shows, the greater the danger of a malignant form of regression. The more it reduces the asymmetry between the patient and him, the more discreet and natural the patient can be seen, the more likely that the effusion will take a benign form.

The analyst has to ask the question with each patient: what type of technique is most appropriate for this particular patient? Which will have the best therapeutic effects? He stresses that one must accept the patient's regression and acting out experiences without hurrying to interpret. The interpretation must not come until the patient has left his regressive state. And to value it, you must take into account non-verbal communication.

As to how the analyst can provide the climate that the patient needs to allow the psychoanalytic process to take place, Balint says that the analyst is not obliged to "give primary love" to the patient, but he offers him his time, his atmosphere, his attitude. It does not mean that he is obliged to compensate the patient for the privations he has suffered by giving him more love, more affection and more care than his parents gave him. He should give enough time free of external interferences and stimuli so that the patient can find his own way, not showing him the "right" way based on correct or deep interpretations. And in addition to recognizing the patient's needs and perhaps even satisfying them, the analyst must show that he understands those needs and is able to communicate his understanding to the patient.

Conclusion

I have tried to show why Ferenczi and Balint can be considered pioneers of relational psychoanalysis. This influence is increasingly recognized. I was just finishing writing this article and received the latest issue of Psychoanalytic Dialogues where Robert Grossmarkt (2016) openly recognizes it in his article *Psychoanalytic Companionship*. It is not the first time he mentions it, if we consider his previous article, *The unobtrusive relational analyst* (2012).

Returning to the article of Bromberg (2009) to which I referred at the beginning, if we consider that "the source of therapeutic action in psychoanalysis is the interpenetration of affectively alive interpersonal engagement and the shifting self-states that organize the internal object worlds of both patient and analyst", I think we can consider Ferenczi and Balint our older brothers. Bromberg mentions Ferenczi as one of the parental figures of the relational psychoanalysis, but he says that none of them carries parental authority. That's why I prefer to talk about older brothers.

At this point it is already commonly accepted that the clinical work of the psychoanalyst involves the use of his most personal resources, beginning with the observation of his countertransference and the recognition of the emotions and feelings that the patient awakens in him as an indispensable instrument for treatment. We know that the neutrality of the analyst is a myth. And we recognize that the analyst cannot be equal emotionally with all patients, but tries to regulate his affects according to the patient being treated and the moment of treatment.

The advantage we have over the time of Freud, Ferenczi and Balint, is that the current development of neurosciences gives us a more solid basis for relational thinking: we now know more about the importance of the implicit unconscious and procedural memory, about the results of direct observation of the interaction of parents and children, and the contributions of cognitive psychology. And we are better able to tolerate what we do not know and to value more what the other disciplines contribute us. From our present moment, more favorable, it is fair to recognize the contributions of the pioneers who opened the way to the relational perspective in psychoanalysis.

Summary

This chapter aims to show how relational psychoanalysis is not a recent discovery, but has its origin in the Freud-Ferenczi conflict on the traumatic origin of psychopathology that was openly shown with the publication of Ferenczi's paper *Confusion of tongues between adults and the child* in 1932. Ferenczi's evolution from classical psychoanalysis, whose aim was to make the unconscious conscious through interpretation, to a critical position that considered yatrogenic an analysis very based on the intellectual capacity of a supposedly neutral analyst, was very difficult to be assumed by the psychoanalytic community of his time . The innovation that meant Ferenczi's attitude, his empathy with patients and his revision of the technique to avoid retraumatizing them was an innovation that was the object of a defensive repression for many years after his death. Balint, the custodian of his legacy, was the main guide to continue his work, and provided crucial concepts such as basic failure and therapeutic relationship, primary love and psychoanalytic technique. Increasingly, current relational psychoanalysts recognize in these two pioneers two important parental figures, or, as I prefer to say, two older brothers, who paved the way for the current development of relational psychoanalysis.

4

Winnicott's Contributions to the Relational Perspective In Psychoanalysis

Francesc Sáinz Bermejo

Identity is built through interaction with others. The baby needs a stable adult figure that guarantees existential continuity. This is how Winnicott understands the processes of maturity in the child. For this British paediatrician and psychoanalyst, the baby does not exist if it is not in relation to someone who takes care of him. In the same way, the mother exists because she has a baby to take care of. The American intersubjective authors add that the analyst does not exist if there is no patient to treat, and the patient does not exist as such if he does not have a caring analyst. In the same way as a book does not make sense if there is not a reader who goes out it. There is no author without a reader. This inspired the Italian playwright Luigi Pirandello in his play "Six Characters in Search of an Author." For this reason the Winnicottian idea of 'go out to' is an essential element in the identity construction of the growing child.

The adult caregiver shares with the baby his own subjective experience, lends him his capacity to be and to do, goes out to him and at the same time he is the recipient of the spontaneous gesture that the child performs with his action, his rudimentary babbling and his whole being. The common space is a shared and co-constructed space, and the experiences that are developed within belong to a common field that exists because the two members make it exist. Transitional experiences, which include the objects and the transitional phenomena, evidence the existence of an intersubjective space. The two members are authors, senders and recipients. We can say that we are co-authors of our identity at most. The human being is born in an unknown world, with a life to live without knowing the meaning or objective to carry out. The only possible reality is represented by the person/s responsible for their upbringing. For Winnicott, the child must be the creator of his own reality, in this way he will come to feel that he can partly own his own life or, in Winnicott's words; he can live life in first person. The creator of his own life needs someone to bring him what shapes life, in order to be created. The child discovers what he finds and encounters, what he seeks without searching for it. The adult caregiver knows what he wants to achieve through taking care of the baby, but at the same time he becomes a discoverer of him and himself as the shared experience moves forward.

Transitional experiences allow the child to move from what Winnicott calls non-integration towards integration, a path in which its members are not exempt from difficulties. The most important feature of transitional phenomena is flexibility; the rules are made by walking, just as the poet Antonio Machado says in his verses "You make the path by walking". Child and mother figure walk a path together and make the path as they go. For this reason, Winnicott locates the game in the transitional phenomena, and calls the transitional space potential space. Creativity has nothing to do with being able to create works recognized by humanity but with the capacity to generate one's own life. That arduous mission can only be carried out with someone who also has his own mission. The needs, although different, occur in the parenting players. Adults have children to meet personal needs; children need their parents, or caregivers, to satisfy their own. We count on the needs of the former being as close as possible to what we consider a good enough mental health. Adults bring the child to the world so that he can create it and feel that he is the main character of his own life. But adults approach the world biased by their own subjectivity, so two subjectivities meet united by a common and intersubjective space.

Winnicott tried to show to the psychoanalytic community of his time the importance of not studying the subject in isolation. For the construction of a personal identity the environmental provision is necessary, that is the ability of the environment to promote transitional experiences which include respect for the child's spontaneity. The environment must allow the baby's natural idiosyncrasy to emerge, and its role is to support and go out to it. The individuality of the child must be accepted, one must allow him his solitude, but not leave him alone with his suffering; He must be given space, but one must be close enough to assist when needed. The idea of the individual and the isolated mind has been refuted by one of the most important currents of psychoanalysis nowadays, and which forms the basis of relational psychoanalysis. It is the intersubjective approach initiated in the United States by Stolorow and Atwood (1992), and by these and Orange (1997), and developed by many other authors from different latitudes.

A Critique of the Idea of Drives Being Independent of Relational Experiences

Winnicott defined his views in continuous dialogue and discussion with Freud's ideas, and especially with his supervisor, Melanie Klein. He was very interested and needed to express the concepts in a personal way. He tried to avoid closed doctrines and theories that did not accept possible discussion. In Winnicott, his independence based on freedom of thought prevailed.

He was convinced that what he called the constitutional had a specific weight in the construction of identity, yet the complexity of identity could not be reduced to biological endowment or genetics. In accordance with the psychoanalysts of his time, he considers that the child is endowed with the capacity to love and to hate, sexuality and aggressiveness is part of the innate biological set up, but what we call drives, are for Winnicott a potential that will develop according to the experiences that the child will live over his relationships with others. For Winnicott, there is nothing in the baby that cannot be understood in terms of need. The need for destruction, derived from the death drive, makes no sense to this author. Klein's primary envy, as an expression of the deadly drive, even less so.

The pulsional theories served to psychoanalysis to establish bonds between the biology, the constitutional thing, and the psychology and human relations. Freud's definition of the term drive: "trieb", refers to an innate, biological force that pushes us towards the relationship with others. The problem is that Freud understands that the drive needs to be discharged into the other who becomes a recipient of the subject's sexual and aggressive impulses, including the incestuous impulse, more aggressive than loving. What Winnicott contributes to what we, years later, call the relational perspective in psychoanalysis, is that the child is related to their caregivers in a loving and aggressive way, but it depends on the way how they understand everything that the child presents to them, and of course on what their experiences provide to the child. The future of impulses depends on the relational dynamics in which the child is both recipient and sender at the same time, depending on the ability of the caregivers to collect what the child sends. Bion describes it in an excellent way in its container-content model. Container figures perform the role of receiving, tolerating and returning the child's anxieties so that he can metabolize them in a more appropriate healthier way. For Bion, the beta elements, disintegrated and without meaning, become alpha elements, meaning and sustainable, all thanks to the container adult's skills. The important thing for Winnicott is that the difficulties the child has to assimilate this process depend partly on his own abilities, but above all, they depend on the adult's real abilities to adapt to the child's needs. Adult caregivers not only contain and return meaning, they also bring their sufficiency and inadequacy, and they are able to return love, but also frustration and hatred. In some cases, the child can only adapt to his reality sacrificing his own mental health. Self-drive alone, regardless of the relational experience and relationship styles of the caring figures, explain little of the child's mental functioning.

In any case, from a relational and, therefore, Winnicottian point of view, there is only one drive, which can be called the "life drive" and which includes aggressiveness and its different forms of expression. The environment must collect, contain and give emotional meaning to aggressiveness, love and sexuality. Only through the interaction and affective bonding, the different behaviours and mental representations will be established on the capacity to love and to hate. Bowlby taught us that the only basic drive was the need to relate to the other, just as Fairbairn (1941) had raised it. When the environment cannot adequately sustain the aggressiveness, this tends to dissociate from the capacity to love, and this is when the split between love and aggression occurs. Dissociated aggressiveness can be corrupted and become destructive. Love can also be dissociated. In this way, one can only love or hate; the whole object becomes partial.

There are people whose love part works well, they can develop love towards others and bond in a healthy way, and however, their hostile part is not integrated and works independently. When it is activated, it can sweep away any kind of love. There are men who love their wives and take care of them "properly", the problem is that when their self is damaged, frustration and hostility colonize the full self, their main emergent is destruction.

Winnicott shows us that:

It is true that the child has an enormous capacity for destruction, but he also has it to protect what he loves from its own destruction. (1939, p.108[1])

Aggression has two meanings: on the one hand, it is directly or indirectly a reaction to frustration; on the other, it is one of the two main energy sources that the person possesses. (1964a, p.114)

For Winnicott, it is important the emotional response of the child's immediate environment to his spontaneous expressions. The interpretation that adults do, how they collect it, understand it and how they react, is of vital importance for the child to give meaning to his experiences with the others. The way caregivers understand children's reactions depends on their psychological characteristics and their mental health. There are also other factors related to theories or ideologies they have about upbringing, cultural variables and social pressures.

When caregivers are unable to tolerate natural aggression, because of excessive weakness or excessive aggressiveness, the child cannot make healthy use of it. It has to be insanely inhibited or it can become destructive. The child may need to destroy or attack the "object", but the most important thing is the object's ability to survive. For this reason, Winnicott affirms that when the object survives the destruction of the child, he can begin to use it naturally (Winnicott, 1968). At this moment the authentic differentiated affective relationship begins. Natural aggression cannot kill the caregiver, because he is out of the omnipotent reach. The baby may live within the initial omnipotence, but in the eyes of an empathic adult, the child is helpless, dependent and full of needs waiting to be satisfied.

For Benjamin (1999), Winnicott, in his work on the use of the object (1968), "it refers to that zone of experience or theory in which the other "other" is not merely the ego's need / drive or of the cognition / perception, but has separate and equivalent centre of self". We agree with Benjamin that instead of talking about object relations, it is more appropriate to do it about relationships between subjects, what we call "intersubjectivity." When the drive is picked up by the environment, little by little the self will become in charge of the aggressiveness.

We can answer Winnicott's question posed in 1939:

Is aggression given by anger aroused by frustration or does it have its own root?

We consider that there is a biologically programmed potential for aggression, so it can be considered as drive. However, we believe that aggressiveness

---

1 In this paper, quotes have been translated from the Spanish edition.

is part of the same vital drive. However, aggression, like the capacity for love, will be modulated according to the bonds established with external reality, where the external objects qualities are of cardinal importance for the construction of the child's identity.

In order for the child to feel that his ability to love and hate are part of life, he needs adults who do not frustrate beyond the possibilities of the child to bear the pain, and who can interpret their expressions in a concordant and not malignant way. There is nothing worse for a child to feel bad about himself than an adult who attributes malice to his actions and does not know how to understand them in a different way.

People who have had in their childhood parents with inadequate mental health are less likely to manage well their abilities to love and hate. There are parents who are deprived, and damage their children with their own aggression or they abandon them in their necessary child care. Despite their regret, they hurt children, even if they love them and their intentions are good. When parents or paternal figures are people with narcissist pathology, psychopathy or perversion, they leave little room for their children to develop an adequate mental health. The child may feel that the abuse received is because he does not deserve better, at times he may feel that he is himself the generator of his parents' upset or even their evil. Some fill with hatred towards themselves or towards others, distrust of their ability to give love, others perhaps engage in ruthless conduct with others identified with their aggressor. It may lead them as they grow old to pair off with sick people in order to take care of them, even let them abuse them. Children of perverse parents may have felt that they have been treated as lifeless objects and for their own parents' inappropriate purposes. Each human being organizes his inner world in terms of what he has felt in the relationship with others, how he has been felt, how he has been thought and how he has been treated. The construction of the identity is a very complex subject, and for this reason it cannot be reduced to the drive, neither to any of the biological, psychological or sociocultural components involved. The factors, as I pointed out another time, combine, transform and work in a multidirectional way.

The Transition From Non-Integration to Integration Is Not Possible Alone

In early childhood, relational and interactive events occur, and they are much more sophisticated than they might seem on the surface. The difference between this winnicottian conception and the Kleinian view is that what happens in the mental or internal world of the child, for Winnicott is totally related to what happens in the mental or internal world of the caregiver figure. The one depends on the other. The external world is thus a shared and co-created experience between the two. Similarly, for Sullivan, anxiety is not transmitted only by the mother, but emerges in the interaction between them. The subjective needs the objective support to develop properly. The external reality generates frustration, but, at the same time, it establishes the fantasy in a reality. In order to develop an integrative subjectivity it is necessary that it is sustained by objectivity.

The human being is heir to biology and son of his circumstances. By nature we are relational beings, and our relationship depends on our way of being, feeling and doing. The main impulse of the new-born is the adaptation to the environment and, to achieve it; he has the biological potential and assistance of his caregivers. For this reason, Winnicott, in his expression of "good enough mother" and its derivatives, what stands out is the ability to adapt to the baby's needs. If adults adapt adequately to the idiosyncratic needs of the child, the child will have to make less effort and less sacrifices, so that his personal spontaneity will be preserved.

People who take care of their child lend their ability to feel and think, put words to the emotions of the child so that they can become feelings; they also lend the guardian of the self that Winnicott calls the "False Self."

The path from non-integration to integration requires childcare. The arduous path to go requires what Winnicott calls the transitional.

The processes of maturity in the child need a facilitating environment, which means that the child must find a small group of humans willing to escort him and provide for him, and the tendency to integrate is supported by two series of experiences: the technique of childcare in which the child is protected from the cold, bathed, cradled, named, and, in addition, the acute instinctive experiences that bring together the personality in a whole from within (Winnicott, 1945).

When the child is assisted and cared for by the environment, the state of non-integration does not mean excessive suffering; On the contrary, it must happen. In order for the fragments of the self to be gathered and integrated, they must first be dissociated. This initial dissociation is not a defensive or unhealthy state.

In the normal child's life there are long periods of time in which he does not mind being a series of numerous fragments or a global being, or if he lives in the face of his mother or in his own body, Provided that the fragments gather and he feel that he is something (Winnicott, 1945, p. 206)

With the "care that the child receives from his mother" each infant is able to have a personal existence, and thus begin to establish what could be called a "continuity of the being." On the basis of this continuity of the being, the inherited potential is developed little by little until the individual infant is constituted. If the maternal care is not good enough, the child really does not reach existence, since there is no continuity of the being; instead, personality is established on the basis of reactions to environmental intrusion (Winnicott, 1960b).

The state of non-integration, when sustained and escorted by the caregivers, will develop in the child's capacity to take charge of his own emotions, feelings and thoughts. However, the failures experienced in those moments in which the child's self is not differentiated, can be installed in the procedural memory (as Coderch raises, 2010). For Winnicott (1963) the subject cannot refer to something that has lived but was not there to be experienced, or registered. The person will experience a fear of breaking down something that paradoxically had already happened. To avoid this, defensive strategies will appear. Winnicott calls them stages of disintegration. The disintegration is seen as a way of defending oneself from some primitive experiences in which the subject did not have the caretakers to sustain him and therefore it is as if they had let him fall into the abyss. Again, catastrophic anxieties do not depend on any mortal instinct but on the relational experiences maintained from the beginning of life. We will return to the subject later.

The False Self Allows Adaptation to the Environment And Human Relations

The true self is essentially related to the genuine, spontaneous and natural aspects that belong to the child. It interacts with the mother figure's true self, and if this figure is spontaneous, genuine and flexible, it adapts without too much difficulty to the child's needs. This role is exactly what Winnicott defines as the role of a good enough mother. The False Self protects the real one; it is activated by the protection that caregivers give to the child. It is as if the environment lends the child a false self to defend the most precious part of him.

Winnicott understood that the natural fragility of the child requires protection; the adult caregivers perform an assistance role. In the depths of the self we find the true self, the most childish, emotional and needy in us, the most authentic and at the same time the most fragile. The adults protect the child by lending him a false self, which is, at first, external to the child, it becomes a part of the self through relational experience. The false self protects the child from the external and potentially harmful, and also does not let the most authentic part to be exposed to external dangers unnecessarily.

Winnicott, as a precursor of relational psychoanalytic thinking, appreciates that the patient must understand not only his mental functioning, stimulate insight or reflexive function through thought, but also what is the most important in psychotherapy, which is the relational experience with the therapist; in the terms we are discussing now: the psychotherapist can, together with his patient, create a bond and trust where the true self can emerge and to which it can be legitimized as it is. It would be like allowing a child to express himself freely without censoring him. Connecting the false self with the true self, recognizing the need of every human being to defend himself from suffering, allows the patient to evolve in his emotional growth. It must be considered that trust in the other sets in when the relational experience allows the possibility of distrust.

As for the aetiology of the dynamic functioning between the false and the true self, we can say that we find the relational essence of Winnicott. The construction of the false self does not arise from the individual psyche, but from the interaction of the child self with the parent in charge of his care.

The environment must protect the child by helping him build the false self, but it has the commendable task of facilitating the true self to express itself and to relate to reality. Only a few people with a certain personal capacity are able to facilitate this complex process in their children. The result of this relational experience is that the subject can be adapted to society without sacrificing his personal spontaneity. A truly protected and cared self can develop its capabilities with itself and with others. The process we call mentalization today (Fonagy, Bateman) will be possible from these experiences.

Adapting to realities and emotional experiences requires flexibility and emotional permeability, which is acquired in the interrelation with adult figures that are flexible and permeable to their children's needs.

Look to Be Seen And Look Inside the Other to Find the Own Interior

In the work on the mirror's role in the face of the mother and the family, Winnicott (1971) studies the idea that the baby is reflected in the face of his mother. When he looks at himself he sees him, but for things to work out well, the mother should be able to empathize with her child's emotions. The child looks and knows that he is looked at and recognized. The mother tries not to impose too much her own mood, but lets the child's perception mould her. The child then receives what he himself has given and it is returned so that he can verify it.

In the same way the patient needs our perception. Sometimes we make very correct and "complete" interpretations that do not have a beneficial effect on the patient. If he does not feel understood in his emotional pain, the interpretation may seem appropriate, but it is untimely. Legitimizing and validating the patient's feelings is more important than discovering hidden material and revealing the unconscious. The second may be possible, but the former must happen first.

Winnicott expresses the child's need to receive what he gives. The baby's search for eyes that look at him allows him to find himself. If the child does not receive what he gives, and the adult figure returns his own projections and distortions, the child stunts his creative capacity and continues looking for someone to return something confirming his existence. That is why many children "prefer" being treated badly rather than being abandoned and ignored. They even tend to behave badly to be told off by someone. To exist for no one is a terrifying experience. The other consequence of not receiving what they give, that is, not having anyone going out to them, is that the mirror function is damaged and perception takes the place of apperception (Winnicott, 1971a). The perception is pure sensoriality, information that is received through the senses. The apperception involves sensoriality, sensations perceived, but connected to the affections and the emotions concerned. Apperceiving is much more complex because it includes emotions. The mother looks at her baby, returning her understanding and, at the same time, giving her affection. "To look after» comes from the idea of looking and being watched with love and affection. The ability to live events accompanied by their mental, symbolic and emotional representations is the basis for the construction of an integrated personality. In Winnicott's words:

At one point, the baby looks around. It is possible that when he is in front of the breasts he does not look at them. Most likely, a characteristic feature is looking at the face. What does he see in it? In order to get to the right answer we must base ourselves on our experience with psychoanalytic patients who can remember the first phenomena and verbalize (when they feel it is possible to do so) without offending the delicacy of what is preverbal, nonverbal and non-verbalisable, except perhaps poetry.

What does the baby see when he looks at his mother's face? I suggest that he usually sees himself. In other words, the mother looks at him and what she seems is related to what she sees in him. All this is taken for granted too easily.

I request that what mothers who care for their babies do well naturally it is not taken for granted. (Winnicott, 1971a, 148)

Identity is constructed through the eyes of the other; it is not a passive process: the look allows to articulate very complex phenomena, looking to be seen and to be recognized. Looking within the other allows one to explore the emotions of the other and, therefore, his own. It is likely that the child knows the inner self of the other before his own; to achieve this it is necessary that the caring figure allows the child to look inside her; so she will not become an opaque mirror that only returns a flat image. The concept of mentalization has to do with the ability to perceive that the other, who we are in relation with, has an inner self. If I see the inner world of my caregiver, I can look into my own. Once again we find the relational Winnicott, there is no isolated mind or intrapsychic relationship as an autonomous entity, but the child can discover his own mind because someone who looks inside his own allows him to discover it.

When the caregiver is sunk in psychopathology, his mirror role will be distorted, and then it may happen that:

Many babies have a long experience of not getting back what they give. They look and do not see themselves. Consequences arise. First, their creative capacity begins to atrophy, and in one way or another they seek other ways to get the environment to give them something of their own. They may do so by other methods. (1971a, pp. 148-149).

The baby reacts looking for ways that can lead to psychopathology:

... It forces the baby to strive to the limit of his ability to anticipate events. This causes a threat of chaos, and the child organizes his withdrawal, or does not look (except to perceive) as a defence. The one that is treated this way will grow with confusion as far as the mirrors and what they can offer is concerned. If the mother's face does not respond, a mirror will then be something to be looked at, not something within which one looks (1971a, p. 149).

This important Winnicott's work on the mirror has technical implications for clinical work.

The therapist, too, must not be a sphinx, but someone who looks into his patient and allows him to look into him. The patient, then, has the impression that he is dealing with someone similar to him. If the mother figure is a mirror for the child, the child is also a mirror for her. Hence Winnicott's cross-identifications, two beings that recognise themselves in each other's eyes and that are verified as people capable of mutual influence. That is to wake up emotions and feelings in a bidirectional way. The interpersonal relationship has to do with the mutual recognition of both as subjects capable of feeling and making the other feel.

A patient treated by Winnicott asked him, a few years after the completion of their therapy, for a picture of him. She had seen this picture on the back cover of a book written by her analyst and asked him if he could provide an enlarged and clearer picture. This patient had a very stiff and cold mother who gave her an also stiff and little empathic nanny (Winnicott believed it was to avoid being replaced by a better "mother").

The patient had little regard for herself, which resulted in low self - esteem and a certain chronic sadness. She had showed Winnicott some pictures of her mother and her nanny, and now she would ask for one of him that she saw in his book. The patient's request was that she wanted to see those lines extended and all the features of "that old landscape", meaning the face of his analyst (an elderly man at that time).

Winnicott sent the picture and offered an interpretation: "The patient thought that she was merely acquiring the portrait of that man who had done so much for her (and I did). But she needed to be told that my wrinkled face had certain traits that she linked to the stiffness of her mother and her nanny" (1971, p.153).

To find the stiffness of her mother and her nurse in the analyst who had done so much for her. To find the faults of her childhood environment in the present. The analyst believes that the stiffness of his face is not the result of the patient's transference distortion, but the patient may be able to find in the analyst stiffness features that refer to her childhood experience. The corrective aspect of the transference experience is that now the patient can feel it and think it along with the analyst. Children tend to believe that they have built the stiffness of their parents or have generated environmental failures. Now, the analyst represents the adult able to take his own responsibility and that is when the patient can take care of hers.

The Union Between Mind-Psyche-Soma Depends On Childcare

Too much mind prevents mentalization and transitional phenomena. In a masterful job, Winnicott (1949) speaks of the differences between the mind and psyche-soma. The mind, so necessary to think and understand the feelings, can become a problem for emotions, feelings and spontaneity. If the child develops the ability to trust his caregivers, body (soma) care joins felt and recognized emotions (psyche). The environment provides emotional sense to bodily sensations, it is a simultaneous process. While mom takes care of her child attending to his physiological needs, she gives acceptance and love, giving it an emotional sense. Feelings and fantasies arise from the union of these experiences. The confident mind lets go with the body and emotionality, is what Winnicott calls a psychosomatic experience. Actually, it is a harmonious combination between the mind, the psyche and the soma.

The concept of mentalizing arises from the French School of Psychosomatic (Marty, 1995) related to alexithymia, the inability to express emotions through words. But what is really significant is not the inability to express, but the inability to make connections between events and emotions, that is everything that has to do with feelings. For the French school, the operative or concrete thinking is related to the inactivity of the preconscious. Meaning that something remains in the unconscious and something is recorded in the conscious, but there are no links between them. The person lives "ignorant" of the impact events have in his emotional world. The "insight" cannot be activated, missing the necessary bridges that allow us to feel and then to think.

For Winnicott (1963) the person is afraid to live something that actually already happened but was not there to record it in his consciousness. This paradox, Winnicott's very own, brings us to the idea of being able to remember something that actually did not happen. One is aware of the traumas that occurred if the person could consciously remember. Grief, mistreatment, abuse of any kind; but no one can record something that should have happened and did not happen, for example everything that has to do with the emotional resonance from the environment.

"The trauma of what did not happen" (Winnicott, 1963). When one can become aware of it, the person may say, "Now I see that my mother never treated me with affection, like I meant nothing to her. It is possible that she could not feel her own emotions. I thought she loved me, but I had never experienced that feeling of being loved by her". Winnicott thinks we should help the patient understand that the fear she has to experience certain emotions comes from the past. What she really fears it will happen, already took place. The return to a state of non-integration when the experience is to not have been held is very difficult to bear. For Winnicott, the patient will defend herself from this fear through disintegration.

Another paradox, the disintegration is a defence to not live again an unthinkable experience. If you are offered the patient a suitable frame to provide the experience of being held and understood, he can get carried away and feel the emotions that can then be designed and carried to the consciousness. In severe cases, we shouldn't be carried away by the idealization of our capabilities as therapists, as our work provides foundation for containment and fixing childhood experiences, but no damage once caused and installed in the person's insides, cannot be modified by a new experience, however adequate that is. In his work on the fear of collapse, published posthumously, Winnicott argues that the patient is afraid of a lived but not experienced collapse. The possibility of daring to collapse is offered, but this time he will be sustained and especially recognized. The patient may feel that now he has both a good enough and not good enough analyst, who is able to help and also to recognize his own faults. If the analyst recognizes his involvement in the welfare and in the patient's discomfort, he gives him room to his own emotional involvement. Very different from the classical approach in which the analyst shows the patient projections for him to take over its proper functioning with others. Not that we think is wrong, but it is insufficient.

For Winnicott, when the child feels in danger of not being supported by his adults, he develops a false self that sometimes becomes a mind separated from the psyche-soma (1949). The mind not included in the psyche-soma operations tends to atrophy, staying inactive, or to hypertrophy. The two circumstances serve to protect the subject, but also keep him from minding and symbolizing his own suffering. Epistemic trust has to do with confidence in bonding. If the child investigates the world without a foundation of emotional security, the epistemic can become an unhealthy pursuit of knowledge or inhibition in his desire to know.

When there is an environment of trust, what Bowlby calls a bond and a secure base (1969), the creature can let go without fear. Ghent (1990) suggests that the opposite of love is fear, inspired by Winnicott when he says that the child allows his spontaneous gesture when the mother responds to him, not imposing her own difficulties.

Mistreated and abused children are not recognized in their emotional needs so they are not entitled to feel their own emotions. In such cases the child cannot discern whether the difficulties in his environment and the adults in it have been caused by him or, on the contrary, are part of the natural character-istics of it. Not knowing if it was the child himself who caused his mother's depression or the abuse to which he is exposed, or being able to understand it is the depressed mother who can-not or does not know or does not want to properly treat her child, changes overnight the perception that one has of him and others.

Psychoanalytic interpretations, if given, should be especially careful and contribute to the establishment and maintenance of an optimal frame, as Armengol and Hernandez said some years ago (1991). If reliability is spoiled, the process of restoring the self is damaged, to use an expression of Kohut (1980).

Giving oneself up to another or submitting, are two different ways of under-standing the concept of "surrender". In his 1949 work, Winnicott shows that the mind must be close to the psyche-soma, in order to have a proper psychophysical functioning. The psyche represents the emotional, linked to the body. Affective expressions and the spontaneity of human reactions become a whole. Being able to think about the experiences when it is not detached from the emotional, allows an understanding of feelings and fantasy. This is all part of what we call subjectivity. The child's caregivers offer it a safe environment where he can display his spontaneity. As we said, the environment, although "perfect" at an initial stage, is becoming good enough and is not error-free, that is why we added the idea of not good enough. Kohut expresses it in the concept of "optimal frustration", Winnicott, similar to Balint, refers to environmental failures. Today, it is undeniable that damage during the upbringing has some consequences on the developing person; therefore they affect the individual mental and brain processes. The current neuroscience, or what Talarn, A., Sáinz, F. Rigat, A. (2013) called relational neurobiology allows us to understand that environmental processes and specifically relational experiences from childhood, are installed in the mind and in the brain. The influence is always bidirectional: biology influences the psychology and vice versa. It is also necessary to remember that although the individual and his experiences can be modified; there are structures that remain despite the efforts of the bio-psycho-social treatments. We must also remember that the difficulty of knowing the aetiology of mental disorders lies in the factors involved, that combined together are very difficult to isolate and to study. Empirical studies that are well built from a methodological point of view provide us with data that may be relevant to the progress in science. But we must be aware that they often represent parts of a whole difficult to split, because the whole is never the sum of its parts. The protective environment offers the child the possibility to be himself, provided it is careful not to drown him with excessive protection and not to leave with excessive absences. The continuous care produces the experience of existential continuity and of being oneself despite the changes. Letting go confidently is close to the idea of giving oneself up. The environment gives the mind, wisdom, even the false self for the child to express himself freely. The identity is built slowly and one of the basic experiences is to belong to someone. We have all been someone. "Surrender" can mean giving oneself up and submission (Ghent, 1990). Our hypothesis is that the right environment that protects the child, allows the experience of belonging to someone, on the condition that he is gradually able to come off that dependence, to feel real. You can exist for yourself because you have first existed for others. For Winnicott, dependency at the early stages of human development is absolute and it is gradually becoming relative (1963b). If the child is not protected and well treated, he can continue looking for people who provide the experience of belonging. The need of becoming someone, to be someone, at the price of sacrificing the true self that has had few and unfortunate conditions to develop in freedom, is the foundation of submission. Submission can be a form of masochism (Ghent, 1990) that has been built from the perversion of the need to exist for others. Some women, primarily conditioned by a sexist culture, grew up with the idea to exist for the other (husband and children) as if they had no right to existence. It is different to live for someone as a way of annihilating one's identity, than belonging to someone and still be yourself. The family has the responsibility to provide this experience to the children "you are ours to become yourselves." It is necessary that the parents or substitutes have good mental health and their emotional needs are satisfied enough not to use their children for their psychopathology.

When the natural process of belonging fails, the sickening need to belong to someone appears, whoever that someone is and at any price.

Transitionality As Relational Exchange
—A Two-Way Experience

The conceptualization of Winnicott on transitional phenomena (1951, 1971) space and objects, allows us to include in them human phenomena as the very paradox of our existence.

The dream of creating something that already exists, to accept the dependency to become less dependent, found on the outside and the inside, being alone in the presence of someone, or escorted in the absence, using the false self to give the true self. This also allows us to accept the idea that we propose, to be someone to be oneself. Therapeutic experience understood as an instrument of possible change.

As Coderch expressed (2010, 2012) therapeutic change is possible through the relational experience and interaction between analyst and patient. The interactive model between parents and children is the prototype of the experiential world where personal identities are built. The human being is helpless at birth and if we look closely throughout his life, he keeps this first continuous helplessness in some way. Living is a difficult lonely way that can only be carried out accompanied. We join and are joined throughout life. As we stated above, we are therefore interdependent beings who move from absolute dependence to relative dependence, as Winnicott wrote (1960).

Psychoanalysis offers the patient the possibility of recreating a relational experience. We tell him that we will help him try to understand, we will think together, he must provide all that is within reach and we'll escort him on the road. That is true, but we are also going to live a relational experience together, and if it works well, both parties will benefit. Although responsibilities are shared, they are different for each one of the members involved. Therapy cannot provide what the upbringing did not provide at the time, nor can correct mistakes. It can offer an opportunity to somehow return to a new beginning (Balint, 1968), that is, a new experience with new contributions and limitations. The patient is asked to let go as much as possible, to dare leaving his usual defence systems and to let go to this new experience. The analyst in return offers his ability to hold him and understand him in order that beneficial changes occur to the patient. Trust is built with experience, it cannot be a priori. If the analyst cannot play, he cannot let go. His mind also takes up too much space and will not help the patient to move from one state where no game is played to another where it will be possible to play, as Winnicott (1971) suggests. What Winnicott proposes is that the therapeutic experience is a shared one. The field work represents the transitional space, which accommodates the subjectivity of the two participants. Unidirectional interpretations have to give room for the search for a meaning co-built by the patient and the analyst. The relationship has a sense of mutuality, but it has to stay asymmetrical, so the patient can project and transfer his emotional experiences in the analyst. The analyst must collect and return experiences as the analytic tradition dictates, but he must also assume its involvement in the process and recognize his ability to fail. This phenomenon gives the patient the experience of having a good and not good enough analyst and time, and this dismisses any hint of shared omnipotence.

The therapeutic work should be aware that the patient needs to repeat his personal drama in the therapeutic relationship that it needs to be sufficiently new, good and different to allow him to leave the loop he is in, as Hirsch stated (1994), relational theory has highlighted that the patient looks for two things: repeating the old experience and having new experiences (Cooper and Levit, 1998).

Relational Psychoanalysis, as already pointed out by Ferenczi and Winn-icott, is when the therapist acknowledges that the patient has been treated in a similar way to the subjects of his childhood, and it produces a reaction. It also opens the way to understand the phenomenon. The new experience has to do with the therapist recognising his fault and responsibility on the possible damage caused to the patient, he can react in any possible way, but the fact that the therapist recognises his mistake can cause the patient to understand what happened in his childhood in a different way. Orthodox analysts can recognise, at best, a mistake and apologize to the patient, but we are not talking about this level of basic friendliness, but the patient's need for his therapist to fail him, he will do it even reluctantly, then we will admit it and gather emotionality that awakes in the patient. In our experience, therapists who practice orthodox psychoanalysis are very reluctant to admit mistakes or failures in their interventions, as expected. What we are trying to address is recognising failures as the way for the therapist to show that the psychotherapeutic process is a dialogue between two people with limitations and fallibility.

Two simultaneous processes occur: One of experiential order and the other is a new way to understand, feel and think a little differently. Emotion, cognition and experience are three inseparable and fundamental elements in the way we understand the therapeutic objective from the perspective we defend.

We know that people may want to change, but often do not know how to do it, as the change produces fear of leaving old defences and collapsing. When the disease has achieved a high level of homeostasis with oneself and with others, it is very difficult to change. Pathological personality structures are less ductile and less likely to change.

If new objects (subjects) are radically different from the old ones, the higher the psychopathology, the greater the difficulties for the person are to accept the new experience. Psychotherapists should notice this important statement; the new is well received when the need for the old is respected, as Greenberg noted (1986).

The therapeutic process as we are defining has to do with the human phenomenon studied through constructivism. Reality is always a construction by the observer, and the observer notes, in one way or another, part of what is observed.

Thus it is clear that the psychotherapeutic process is an intersubjective experience, in which the two participants are observers and observed, and at the same time the main characters of the relationship and bonding that is taking place, each according to their subjectivity, and the difference implied between their roles of therapist and patient.

The Good And Not Good Enough Analyst–Transference And Countertransference

It is thought that the patient will tend to distort the relationship with the analyst based on his childhood transference. The analyst's framing and proceedings will act as a stable work field, so if the patient feels abandoned, injured or not understood, will be the consequence of his transference distortion. The analyst will remain immune and neutral. The Kleinian psychoanalysis tends to understand that the analyst collects projections or transfers and returns them in the form of understanding, through the instrument of interpretation. Taking the patient to the transference refers to the analyst explaining the patient that what he feels or felt about someone in the present or past revives in the figure of the analyst. It is very rare that the analyst gets involved as a subject capable of producing both positive and negative feelings in the patient. If he got involved, he would lose the supposed neutrality and his role as an observing objective analyst. For the current relational psychoanalysis, the psychoanalyst is not objective, since as a subject, he has subjectivity, though it must be monitored and controlled to be used positively by his patient. From our point of view, for relational and intersubjective psychoanalysis authors, the idea of the analyst as a subject is basic, and we believe it comes from Ferenczi and Winnicott tradition.

The analyst, as a full member of the therapeutic process, is involved as a subject. If the analyst recognises his subjectivity with the patient, he can no longer be considered a neutral observer. In the best case it will be a participant observer, as Sullivan (1953) noted and therefore recognizing his involvement he loses immunity and he will be offered in the analytical work as an active participating subject. Interpretations will not be only directed to the patient in a unidirectional manner, but to the relationship between them. Clearly the degree of involvement will be different and, although the mutuality between the two is given, the relationship will not be symmetrical (Aron, 1996). Winnicott, following the tradition begun by Ferenczi and at risk of being considered little psychoanalytical by the "establishment" of that time, conducted decisive proposals, which are part of the essential pillar of relational psychoanalysis. They are essential and distinctive from relational psychoanalysis in relation to orthodox psychoanalysis. As Mitchell (1988) notes, psychoanalysis of object relationships is not the same as of relational psychoanalysis. In the first, the base of relationality lies on the drives, especially in the death drive, and in the second one it is understood that there is nothing to be explained unidirectionally. Therefore, to relational psychoanalysis, the instinctive is the need to bond, and the quality in relational interactions.

Transference for Winnicott is an opportunity to reorganize the emotional world and experiences. The work of the psychoanalyst is not to interpret, but to facilitate the patient the development of a new relational experience. The analyst must set the conditions for this new emotional experience to occur properly.

He will offer a holding where the patient dares to breakdown without fear of falling into the abyss. If that is possible, the confidence in the therapeutic relationship will settle, and they will be able then to think together, rather than interpret. Emotionality leads to thought, feelings shape cognitions, and they hold back these feelings. The analyst is involved in this interactive process. It is no longer only a receptacle of the patient experience. The analyst will safeguard his countertransference, but will show "his cards." Winnicott says, "I think I basically interpret for the patient to know the limits of my understanding" (Winnicott, 1968, p.118). We believe that, in this way, the patient may abandon the idea of being with an omniscient oracle and, on the contrary, will reinforce the idea that both work together to achieve the therapeutic goal. From this starting point, Winnicott believed that the patient needs to meet an analyst that allows him to experience his childhood transferences, in the hope they could be understood and recognised. Thus, the experience leads to "insight" and the patient may be more aware of his past and present relationships. At the same time the patient needs to meet an analyst who offers a new experiential world. One way to do so is not responding in the same way they did in his childhood environment, rectify, as a corrective emotional experience (Alexander, 1956). If the adult caregivers in his childhood were too stiff, narcissistic or depressive; if they gave little importance to the affections or created feelings of abandonment in the child. The analytical function, within the own parameters of psychoanalysis, will try to modulate or modify those experiences. If the bonds were fragile, uncertain or ambivalent, therapeutic experience can start building the confidence to establish a more stable and secure new bond. So far, we have collected some contributions that are shared by many psychoanalysts. The corrective aspect of psychotherapy or psychoanalysis is the least valued by orthodox who think that interpretation as an instrument of change prevails. Alexander already had many difficulties when he presented his work on the corrective emotional experience. Even Kohut opposed him, when the melody of Alexander's work was not very different from what Kohut himself subsequently developed. However, what Winnicott proposes goes further, as we said above, following the tradition started by Ferenczi and little disclosed at that time, even until recently. Winnicott believed that the patient needs something else than his analyst, he needs him to fail, so those faults that happened during his childhood can be met here and now in his relationship with his analyst, he must fail and acknowledge the patient's emotional way to feel these weakness or mistakes, and also acknowledge himself as someone failed. This is the real revolution of relational psychoanalysis. The analyst fails and then becomes a not good enough psychoanalyst. In this way, he offers the patient both experiences, good and not good enough to meet his needs, like what happened in his childhood, with the difference that now he can feel, experience and think again. Acknowledging inflicted pain and being a subject able to fail is greatly constructive for any human being. It is the way the subject dares to look inward and to recognize his own shortcomings, including own projections.

To define countertransference, Wolff's idea seems very appropriate:

It is the psychological needs that are mobilized in the analyst's subjective experience, according to his participation in the analytical process with the analysand (patient). In other words, the analyst's countertransference is the counterpart and the natural complement to the patient's transference, but not necessarily a reaction to it. (Lancelle, 1999, p. 62.)

We suggest the concept of "reverse countertransference" (Sáinz, 2017), to define what the professional makes the patient feel. It is a phenomenon like countertransference but as we are suggesting it as belonging to the patient, we add the adjective reverse.

We understand the therapeutic process within an asymmetrical mutuality between patient and therapist, (Aron, 1996). Both are immersed in an interactive and binding process in which they influence and regulate each other. The subjectivity of each one of them is in a transitional space where the game is possible (following the already described Winnicott's conception). In classical psychoanalysis, countertransference is the emotional response experienced by the therapist from emotions and feelings that the patient feels and communicates to him in one way or another.

Despite the terminology, it is not necessary to understand the analyst's countertransference as a response to the patient's transference. We can think of it as the emotional and cognitive mobilization from the analyst interacting with the patient. The patient moves, awakens, and starts the therapist free associations, thoughts, feelings and cognitions.

Implicit knowledge is mutual: As the therapist thinks he knows his patient enough, that is how he understands, his psychotherapeutic work processes; how he accepts the therapist's words, how he suffers, how he love, how he gets frustrated. We can say that the patient is also in a position to know, somehow, the therapist's idiosyncratic reactions.

What we suggest is that the transference-countertransference movement is bidirectional. In the same way that the therapist may think "for now I will not tell such a thing to the patient, it would be inappropriate", the patient may think "I'll wait a little longer to talk about this topic, the analyst may not understand it now."

What we are describing as *"reverse countertransference"* does not have a pejorative sense; the patient knows his analyst because he relates and interacts with him, it would be strange that he could not realize some of his peculiarities, it would mean that the therapist maintains a robotic relationship with his patient, and then patients with normal cognitive abilities would also notice.

We are mentioning the patient cognitive and emotional abilities outside the area of conflict, a concept developed by the "ego psychology" (Hartman, 1939).

If the patient communicates his perceptions to his therapist, the therapist should refrain from interpreting them as arising from the transference or as defensive projections. Beyond transference phenomena, relational phenomena with a broader spectrum occur.

We also would like to mention another conceptual contribution on the subject: what we could call the "para-countertransference" (Echegoyen, 19). "Para" means "similar to", but not equal. We address this way a phenomenon that arises in the patient-therapist relationship and that has to do with feelings that therapists develop towards people related to the patient's past or present. They are countertransference issues that are not addressed directly to the patient, although it is through the relationship with him that the therapist experiences them. We can feel sympathies, antipathies and other emotions about the patient's parents or his wife or husband, his brother, his friend. For this reason, and out of respect for our patient, we do not take any single member of his environment for individual therapy, but we want to draw attention to how important they can be for us the subjects to which the patient relates. We feel that they help us, or interfere with us, or annoy us. We were happy about some couple separations, some parental home independence. Notice how little neutrality we have and how much memory, as Bion alerted us. Far from being a problem, recognizing these "para-countertransference" emotions allows us to work better with our patients. Feeling them and thinking them is a good way not to act them out.

In classical psychoanalysis something like that would be considered a serious resistance, even with elements of manipulation by the patient, however from today's perspective, we can study it as a phenomenon more related to the interaction between the two members of the process. It is entirely consistent with the idea that the mother cares for her child trying to understand what he feels and what he does, and the child tries to understand his mom and what she feels and does about him and about others. The analyst interprets it as patient resistance depending on his therapeutic tradition or healing ideology.

As Rodríguez Sutil (2007) suggests "resistance is a justification of the analyst point of view, so the best way to avoid a coercive influence is not to eliminate our own values and vision of reality, but to make them as explicit as possible" (p.34).

It is very different that the therapist tells the patient, "I think this feeling is very difficult for you, and therefore you prefer to avoid it, perhaps because you think that it is for the best now, but in my opinion is that being able to address it now would be beneficial, what do you think?".

If we consider the therapeutic work as a free relationship, elements of added power must be avoided, understanding that every human relationship involves implicit power. The aim cannot be to eliminate these elements, but to make them explicit to be addressed the best possible way, ultimately we must start from the basis that Gadamer shows (Rodríguez Sutil, 2007) when he states that "the possibility that the other is right is the core of hermeneutics"; and we add that this should be the compass that guides the psychotherapeutic work.

Neutrality is impossible for the therapist, because the moment we intervene in the life of another human being from any point of view, we do it from our personality and our way of doing things, therefore from our subjectivity. Some medical professionals have the hopes that medicine becomes an accurate, unambiguous science, in which a cybernetic machine diagnoses, predicts and deals with extreme precision with ill patients. This requires the patient to be reduced to his illness; the opposite of what Hippocrates taught us "There are no diseases but ill people who suffer them".

With this type of medical understanding the patient idiosyncrasies are dismissed, there are only symptoms, syndromes and measurable illnesses, bounded, measurable equally susceptible diseases therapeutic options, delimited in the maximum possible objectivity, which claims to be absolute.

Applying this cybernetic model to mental health means that behaviours, emotional meanings and relational variables must be reduced to the least operating and tangible; to behaviour with no meaning, biochemical substance, the neurological area or the specific anatomical area.

If the professional understands that in a depressive disorder there is a low level of serotonin, he will discard any other casual reason of any nature. The objectified goal will be to replace the missing serotonin in the body.

If this could be proved, as we noted, it would lack anamnesis, biography, even clinical interview or conversation; it would exclude any possibility of psychotherapy, especially psychodynamic; however, we must warn that humans would be reduced to their minimum.

Serotonin may be involved in depressive processes, but not to be confused with the etiology of those or even less with the therapeutic indication.

To avoid this great epistemological problem, we advocate science studying mental and relational phenomena accepts the etiological complexity and variables acting on the therapeutic function as fundamental premises.

Eradicate all subjectivity by the clinician; it is to reduce the human to a mass of molecules.

As said earlier, we are subjective because we are subject receivers, transmitters and reality builders. Reality is always subjective and does not belong to a single individual or to a single age of mankind.

We return to Winnicott, who felt that at times it was necessary to let the patient know some of the feelings he experienced as a therapist, in other words, to communicate some countertransference. It may appear to have similarities to the "Self disclosure" of some intersubjective authors, however there are some differences. What Winnicott raises is that the analyst can explain his countertransference with the aim that the patient becomes aware of what he can cause in another person. It also makes sense to show his limits as a psychotherapist and as a human being. Sharing countertransference feelings may result in the patient feeling that he is in therapy with an equal, not with a machine. We believe that this aspect is one of the most explicit phenomena in Winnicott's contribution to the relational and intersubjective thought. Winnicott tells one of his patients that he sees a man on his couch, but he is listening to a woman. The patient says that maybe he is going crazy, to what Winnicott replied that, if anyone, the madman is not the patient but the analyst. Winnicott assumes that in the transference relationship the patient is not the only one who brings experiences to the relationship, but so does the analyst, just as happens in family relationships. We are talking about mutuality, as today's relational authors manifested.

At the work on hate in the countertransference, Winnicott raises that in the moments when you feel real hostility towards the patient, it is preferable to tell him than to act it out. The therapeutic sense is given by the fact that it is the patient who is partly causing emotionality in therapist; he will take care of it, while communicating about the state of it. Like what a mother does when she tells her son that she is tired and that her tolerance is lower. It does not mean that the child is solely responsible for the decreased tolerance, but it is a relational issue that is generally characterized by bidirectionality, even though one of the components is always more responsible than the other.

Little does a very significant narrative in her book "Story of my analysis with Winnicott" (1985). According to the author, Winnicott told his patient Margaret Little that he thought it was necessary she knew he hated her mother. Such intervention has all the ingredients to be considered an "acting out" by the analyst. However, Winnicott used one of his feelings in a therapeutic intervention. Little's childhood is known, especially the part referring to her mother characteristics, lack of empathy and damage caused to her daughter, it is obvious that there is very little room for relationship. Winnicott wants to tell his patient that she has every reason to feel mistreated and damaged by her mother. Someone like him can see from outside that it is a fact, not a product of her fantasies, or her projections, or of her destructive drive or even her unresolved Edipo. We would not recommend to our psychotherapists in training to say such phrases to their patients, there are better ways, but the "music" that sounded in the words of Winnicott, in his own patient's words, is essential in understanding the relational perspective of psychoanalysis.

On another occasion, Winnicott was questioned by a patient who asked if after everything she had told, he saw some hope for improvement. Winnicott said that the truth is he saw little hope of change but offered his therapeutic help. The patient confessed that Winnicott's honesty made her feel hopeful for once.

In the author of this writing's example we can see the direct influence of Winnicott in his clinical work.

I recently visited a person who had seen her daughter die in front of her, while playing with other children, death came suddenly. After hearing the story full of suffering and pain, I could only say the following: "Your pain at this time is in contact with his daughter, you need to feel this pain." The patient replied that the other day her husband and son went away from home for a few hours and it was then that she could mourn and express her grief, knowing that she would not hurt them. My intention above all was to legitimize her right to feel and express the profound damage she was sunk in.

At the end of that first visit, I said I could not help her very much facing something as painful as the death of her daughter, but that I could escort her and that it was my wish to do so. No more comments were needed and we agreed for next appointment.

For all the reasons we have argued throughout this chapter, we consider that Winnicott made many efforts to treat his patients as subjects in continuous interaction with the analyst. What he could offer was a relational and bonding experience in which trust could be a fundamental element in the treatment. He saw the analyst as someone involved in the therapeutic work, not at any time as someone neutral and external to the process. The most important thing is that he offered himself as a fallible, good and not good enough subject. He left an important legacy for followers who consider ourselves within the relational and intersubjective perspective today, we help the patient from what we are to him and offer a new relational opportunity, however we encourage the patient to find in us something old attached to something new. Relational psychoanalysts know that we help the patients partly because we try not to fail in issues their caregivers failed, but we must be aware that we will indeed fail our patients, but at least we can acknowledge it and talk about it.

If the patient lacks basic emotional care, he must find them somehow in the therapeutic experience; if his suffering was not acknowledged, if there has been little concern for his person or his feelings; if he has not been allowed to look inside the other to find himself or if he has not been acknowledged the mistakes in his upbringing, somehow all this will be part of the therapeutic experience, gradually, as it emerges.

If the patient is suffering by his own memories, we must escort him so he can forget, while we help him face the guilt. If he needs to elaborate what happened in a biographical moment, our job is to be interested in his story and help him stitch together his narrative details.

Patients who have children relational experiences that established the basis for mentalizing will take advantage of the therapeutic work in an easier way. We can then carry out a relational, interactive and reciprocal mutuality experience. For people with little willingness to mentalizing, the main goal of therapy is not that they metalize their experiences, but to provide them new relational experiences in the therapeutic relationship and out of it, so they can expand their experiential world.

We must accept that there will always be many loose ends, to feel, think and understand, and that the therapist can escort the patient as a fallible good and not good enough subject, or bad enough, as Abelló and Liberman said in their excellent book (2011). All of it is necessary for new different experiences to occur. The therapist must know how to play to help his patient develop his own playing capacity.

Winnicott And Relational Perspective In Joan Manuel Serrat's Mediterranean

Serrat is a Catalan and Mediterranean songwriter. He has the ability to share profound experiences in his song lyrics, structured by exquisite melodies that have increasingly become, as often happens with other artists, collective heritage.

Winnicott said that if there was some truth in what he said poets had said before, and following that I decided to write a book called "Feel and think Serrat. Reflections on the work of the poet and musician by a contemporary psychoanalyst"(Sainz, 2014). I found a way to spread the psychoanalysis, trying to make it accessible to anyone who has an interest in poetry, songs or just in Serrat. My main goal was that potential readers realize that the knowledge psychoanalysts boast emerged from the experiences and implied observation that every human being is capable of carrying out, just by living its own life. Any psychoanalyst who wants to practise his profession must take advantage of his own experiences and think about them. He would be a very bad professional if he was only interested in psychotherapeutic or psychoanalytic theories.

Winnicott has taught us that the scope of our work as psychoanalysts or psychotherapists is limited, as is the ability to understand. The possibilities for change are in all of us, but they are not always possible or feasible. Sometimes acknowledging it and learning to live with it is better than trying to fix the unfixable.

Serrat, does not deny the pain, grief and suffering in his songs, but they also show the joy, hope and all that comes from love. Realism, undeniable feelings and acceptance of what we are. To feel, to think and therefore understand, when it is possible. We can neither explain nor fix everything. Our society partly convinces us that we can achieve all our goals, but that is wrong. Children should not be educated for success, as we can read in certain college slogans; the child must be helped to build a free identity based on emotional ties and the ability to love, including the frustrations, anxieties and grieves.

Serrat says in one of his songs: "Today can be a great day, using it or letting it go depends partly on you." It is interesting for me to note that it is important to acknowledge that there are many things in life that depend on us, but not all. So Serrat says "partly". In another song, he also teaches us that we must make the most of what life offers us. "Occasionally life kisses on our lips and colours unfold like an atlas…" "…and we are in good hands ..." We cannot expect constant happiness, but we can be aware and try to make the best out of the good, without obsession, as it comes. Revealing our own life makes us live it first hand, as Winnicott noted. Feeling true and authentic is more important than existing.

One of the most iconic Serrat albums is called "Mediterranean," a few songs lyrics and music by himself. He describes the feelings of loss of a love that was or could have been in "Lucia". Serrat says "There is nothing more beautiful than what I've never had, nothing more loved than what I lost."

How you can lose what you never had leads us to believe that loss is not only suffered from what we had in the past, but also from what we thought we might have in the future. If the character in the song loses Lucia, who he never had, it means that what he wanted for the future can no longer happen. Serrat makes us feel and think this way, as it happens with our personal relationships and with our patients.

The title song of the album is called "Mediterranean", now revived by what is happening with the Syrians and other refugees. The European governments must accept that the territories do not belong to anyone, and that no human being is illegal anywhere, despite their origin. Serrat's description of the Mediterranean Sea is linked to the experiences of his childhood, his bonds. For Serrat, the places are transitional spaces, given relational experiences.

One verse says: "I carry your light and your smell wherever I go" and that is because of what he says in the previous verse, that this is possible because "Perhaps because my childhood is still playing at your beach, and my first love sleeps hidden behind your reeds". Naturally, first love with parental figures and children's beach games are carried along in our lives, they will be transferred to any human relations that find on the way. But surely the verse that struck me the most in this beautiful song is when our singer says: "By dint of misfortunes, its soul is deep and dark" it refers to the sea. However, it made me think of the pain suffered by many children in their childhood, that by dint of misfortunes, their soul becomes deep and dark. Their experiences are recorded in their memory, often implicit, in their mind and in their brain. The only way to brighten these souls is through a new human relationship that provides them with a new way of living. It is important and essential that life gives us new opportunities, new experiences, although we know that there is damage that will remain forever.

Either way, humans are somehow like the characters of playwright Luigi Pirandello in "Six Characters in Search of an Author": we are looking for an author or authors who help us in the difficult task of developing ourselves as people.

Summary

Winnicott, a British paediatrician and psychoanalyst, practised these two professions throughout his life. He was intuitive, creative and gifted with an unusual ability to play. He has been one of the most influential psychoanalysts of the twentieth century, connected with psychosocial realities, supportive of disadvantaged children and with a special capacity for clinical work with patients of different conditions and psychopathologies.

Supervised by Melanie Klein for a few years, Winnicott did not want to be part of the Kleinian or the Anafreudian group that emerged after the so-called disputes that took place in the British Society in the early 1940s. Freedom of thought and his theoretical originality led Winnicott to be part of the "Middle group", known today as "Independent Group". In this chapter we argue that

Winnicott understood the upbringing and formation of the child's identity inseparable from relational experiences with adult caregivers. The statement that the baby does not exist independently of the care he receives from attachment figures puts Winnicott at the centre of relationality in psychoanalysis. The gaze of the other allows the child to see himself, to look into the other, allows the child to recognize his own interior. The drive is a biological potentiality that needs relational experience to acquire meaning. Destruction has to do with a relational fault, when the environment is not able to contain or give meaning to the aggressiveness inherent in life.

Emotions are part of the somatic experience; the mind must feel confident in childcare to develop in a healthy way. For Winnicott, the path from non-integration to integration is only possible through interpersonal and intersubjective relationships. The child needs to create his own reality, but he can only carry it out through the adult caregiver who facilitates and provides the transitional experiences. These experiences need the subjectivity of both the child and the caregiver, they occur within the transitional space, which we consider intersubjective space.

For Winnicott, therapeutic work is based on the relational experience between patient and therapist; the analyst not only collects the patient's transference, but he is also considered to generate it. Background faults are collected in the transference in which the analyst himself is involved as a subject.

Therefore, we think that Winnicott is an intersubjective psychoanalyst and a pioneer in the relational perspective in psychoanalysis. The chapter ends with a small contribution of the relational psychoanalysis in the Mediterranean of the Catalan singer-songwriter Joan Manuel Serrat, briefly commenting on some of his songs[2].

---

2 SONGS BY JOAN MANUEL SERRAT

Hoy puede ser un gran dia. En *En Tránsito.* Ariola (1981).
De vez en cuando la vida. En *Cada loco con su tema.* Ariola (1983)
Lucía. En *Mediterráneo.* Novola (1971).
Mediterráneo. En *Mediterráneo.* Novola (1971).

5

The *Charm* of Thinking: The Work of S. A. Mitchell and His Impact In Us

Ariel Liberman

We shall not cease from exploration
And the end of all our exploring
Will be to arrive where we started
And know the place for the first time.
(Little Gidding, part V, Four Quartets, T S Elliot)

On ne commence pas par le commencement.
On ne termine pas par la fin.
On est toujours en route, toujours en chemin.
Comme Charlot ...
(V. Jankelevitch)

It might seem politically incorrect today, in certain places dominated by everyday – clinical or personal - preoccupations, to say that if I think about SM, about that first moment of attraction, about what I 'fell in love with', what his *charm* meant to me, in Jankélévich's words, it was that *'je ne sais quoi'* and *'presque rien'*, that almost nothing that inhabited his way of thinking. If I were to put it in more concrete terms – perhaps betraying the founding moment of our encounter – I would say that what attracted me and seduced me about him was his pleasure in thinking, in the history of ideas, or that contagious pleasure in thinking which his texts convey. There is a cadence in his texts, an appeal to the reader, an inexplicable embrace, and this was the fertile ground for our encounter.

I first came across Mitchell when reading some paper of another psycho-analyst one day, in Buenos Aires, around 1997 … Something in the above held my attention and soon after I found myself reading what was then the only work translated into Spanish: ''Relational Concepts''. I remember the bar, the enthusiasm, my first debates with him and with myself.

In Mitchell, I met a thinker who was articulating ideas which echoed my own personal research, who was asking questions which were not being asked or given adequate formulation in my usual milieu. To give just one example, his text on ''The problem of Will'' (1986, 1988) echoed in a sequence of texts I had drawn upon in ''The Choice of Neurosis in Freud's Work'', ''Pascal's Wager'' or my M. Phil thesis ''On Freedom, in Sartre''. This enquiry into will, or what we today call agency, regains in my opinion its full pertinence and legitimacy in psychoanalysis. The same thing occurred for me with regard to all his work questioning the *a priori* considerations of the analytic position and his attempt to transform this into an ever renewed effort of construction, of self-reflexion always ready to consider the unconscious participation of the analyst's subjectivity. For the first time, I really understood something I had heard on several occasions and probably repeated it: that in psychoanalysis the analyst himself is the instrument at work. Even if today this technical metaphor does not seem the most appropriate for me, with Mitchell I was able to see that the analyst and his subjectivity are structurally embedded in the analytic process and that to deny this interactive dimension beneath various conceptual guises, amounts to no more than the defensive preservation of an impregnable place/bastion of blind comfort in our work.

To comprehend the impact Mitchell has on how I understand psycho-analysis, it is undoubtedly necessary to contrast it with the background of those places in which I received my psychoanalytic education-training, so to speak, meaning my "professional complementary series" –to take a Freudian concept.

I come from a city (Buenos Aires) which, from both a psychoanalytical and philosophical perspective, is strongly oriented towards French thought.

My psychoanalytic training was nourished from the outset by analysts such as Lacan, Aulagnier, Castoriadis, Green, Laplanche, to name a few. So, I grew up in this large family, with its tensions, its internal disputes, its passions and 'small differences'...

I do not at all deny this background, for many reasons; it is my personal history, it is not possible to think outside a tradition –shared and personal- and the denial of one's origins generally leads us to enact certain unconscious loyalties or blind-spots. There were also, of course, other non-French authors who informed my training from very early on and who hooked my attention: Winnicott, Kohut, Klein (to name but a few) and, undeniably, many local thinkers, my maestros/teachers, either firsthand, or those who had been an influence on them and whose clinical knowledge they transmitted to me indirectly. Among these we will find those who we now name/define as "Rioplatense Psychoanalysts[1]".

I must say that their influence mostly manifested itself outside Argentina, like a kind of nostalgic fulfillment of desire –just like the Tango, the experience of missing and being exiled from Buenos Aires, even while being present there; the experience of being there and not being there at the same time ... which is the city we long for?

Mitchell was a kind of passport for me, an enormously enriching stroke of fortune in my filiation, taking me with him to his horizons and beyond, both in the analytic context and others. I began to read English again, each foreign language being a new way of experiencing the world – as Borges said - a language I had completely foresaken, and to discover my enthusiasm for thinkers that Mitchell introduced me to, such as Isaiah Berlin, Richard Rorty or Richard Bernstein and, of course, many analysts I didn't know or whom I only knew by name or hearsay. The most striking example of this is the whole realm of interpersonal psychoanalysis – classical and contemporary.

All this I recount was what brought me back some years ago to the River Plate analysts, and I returned to them with new eyes, able to renew with this vast caudal of creative thinking from the perspective which little by little was becoming my own and in which Mitchell was and is a constant travelling companion. Renewing with these creative analysts who, like myself, are

---

1 I use sometimes the spanish expression to familiarize the reader with the word by which we identify the people who reflected upon the psychoanalysis that originated in that particular geographical area: the River Plate. It refers to the two important nations who meet at the border: Uruguay and Argentina. They are more or less represented by the inhabitants of the two most important cities of the area: Montevideo and Buenos Aires.

inalienably stamped with exile and moving freely on the outskirts of centers of power and psychoanalytic thinking, is for me today a compelling project.

In other papers, I work on Racker and Baranger. In this chapter, I would like to draw attention to another pioneer of River Plate psychoanalysis, José Bleger, whose impact on our field/profession is also of considerable importance.

Based on the classification of the "great creators" in psychoanalysis proposed by Bruno Winograd (2002, p. 16), that he and we know are schematic although illustrative, we can differentiate the following: 1) Psychoanalysts whose work present great internal cohesion – Klein, Lacan, Kohut, Ego psychology; 2) Psychoanalysts with less internal cohesion but that have allowed their ideas to be developed in several ways – Winnicott, Aulagnier, Bion, etc.; and lastly, 3) Psychoanalysts that have combined different vocabularies in their schematic constructs. Here, Winograd places, among others, psychoanalysts like Kernberg or Green and those Argentinian and Uruguayan authors that we usually refer to as classical "Rioplatense" (River Plate): Pichon-Rivière, Racker, the Baranger, Bleger, Liberman, etc. My impression is that Mitchell can be found in the last category, among those psychoanalysts that knew how to think outside of the dominant schools of thought, always opening new ways of questioning the inherited "truths".

Or, following another classification, somewhat provocative and schematic, of the dominant schools of Latin-American thought that Willy Baranger and Jorge Mom (1984) created, Mitchell and the Rioplatenses psychoanalysts are not, as differentiated by these authors, prophets nor guardians of the law, on one hand, nor are they part of the indiscriminate expansionists, on the other; nor are they "fanatics of offer" or "fanatics of demand", using another metaphor frequently used in said profession (1984, p. 606).

Drive/Intersubjectivity

We know, of course, that there are many solutions to the question of compatibility or incompatibility of drive and intersubjectivity, and these always depend on how we understand the terminology that comprise said question.

We also know that when drive theory enters the debate of ideas, it doesn't only become a theoretical problem but also one concerning "identities", "belongings", "legitimacies" or "affiliations" or, same thing, "exclusions", "anathemas" and other common varieties that we can summarized with the following affirmation: "That – what you're thinking/doing- is not psychoanalysis".

In the last decades, there have been many efforts made by the great psychoanalysts to reformulate a drive theory in accordance with the current times. As an example, we can use the proposals of two prominent authors from different geographical contexts: Jean Laplanche, in France, to whom intersubjectivity is a requirement for a de-biologized drive; or the proposals of Otto Kernberg, in the USA, in which affect theory and early mother-infant experiences serve as a primary basis for its reconsideration. These have been different strategies used to somehow preserve de Freudian "drive theory" by modifying its basics/fundaments, even as said Greenberg (1991), by contradicting many of the Freudian postulates -is the case of Kernberg.

All these revisions and questionings, including those made by Mitchell, have their origin in the debates concerning the "concept of drive" and the Freudian "metapsychology", occurred during the post- World War II era.

Mitchell comes from a tradition of thought (interpersonal psychoanalysis) that from early on opposed the metapsychological considerations by thinking that, as Habermas would say a couple of decades later, that Freud's work as well as his followers was pierced by a "scientism misunderstanding" (Habermas, 1968/1990, p. 215). Habermas believes that "Psychoanalysis in fact unites the hermeneutics to conclusions that seemed genuinely to belong to the natural sciences". Or, as Paul Ricoeur points out, "Freud's writings present themselves firstly as a mixed discourse, even ambiguous, that speaks as much of conflicts of force that make us think of an energetics as well as meanings that can be linked and give rise to hermeneutics" (1965, p. 75). Hermeneutics and energetics go hand in hand in his work and that of many psychoanalysts in complex ways, a hybrid that responds to different needs: on one hand, the clinical part, where the matter of meaning acquires privilege; on the other, the theoretical (or meta-psychological) part which, according to the scientific demands of Freud era, searches and/or postulates an energetic basis that could therefore be potentially quantifiable, as a way of legitimizing itself. Meaning and energetics seem to belong to very different kinds of demands and fields.

Epistemology And Drive: Bleger View

These contradictions were formulated very early in the Rioplatense context of Bleger's and, later, Willy Baranger's work (there were other psychoanalysts in the US who went in the same direction also during the same époque).

In Bleger's introduction to his book published in 1958, he suggests the need for psychoanalysis to make from his link with epistemology "a moment of the psychoanalytical practice" (1958, p. 17). For Bleger, this does not mean that psychoanalysis should transform into a philosophy, but that the epistemological reflection, that is, the one that examines knowledge, "is involved in the operational field of investigation and therapy of psychoanalysis" (Bleger, 1958, p. 19). It's not necessary to go outside to find it because we can discover it inside, working as assumptions. This leads him to work on the *zeitgeist* through which Freud carried out his ideas, that possess a range of implied assumptions that have been inconsiderately accepted, from categories to conceptual *a priori*'s, as Bleger affirms, that organize thought according to certain historical and social conditions. Agreeing with Pichon-Rivière, he calls them "referential frameworks". Years later, Kuhn speaks of "paradigms" and Foucault of "episteme", each trying ti identifies the "conceptual *a prioris*", historical and disciplinary, that organize, according to Bleger, "the intimate structure" of theory and with which "facts" are described.

Bleger believes that Freud's work has two fundamental referential frameworks going through it: mechanistic physics and evolutionism. We only mention these for the purpose of contextualizing as Bleger does. Willy Baranger (1967) calls "the economical discontent", that is, the difficulties that this theoretical hybrid or mixed discourse of meaning and force created for the development of psychoanalysis. Baranger suggests that "a conflict emerges between loyalty and rigor: the progress of psychoanalysis necessarily implies the reformulation of certain Freudian concepts and the abandonment of others. Doing this is being loyal to Freud whenever it is necessary and rigorous" (1967/1993, p. 52).

As we've mentioned earlier, something was scientific to Freud and his era whenever it was possible to formulate it quantitatively, that is, measurable. Freud understood dynamic psychology as the capacity to "derive all psychic processes from the interplay of forces" (Bleger, 1958, p. 74). The term dynamic has usually been used in two ways in psychoanalysis that, according to Bleger, require a distinction given certain confusions and the fact that they don't refer to the same kind of problem. On one hand, Freud talks about dynamics the way we've just used here to derive psychic processes from the interplay of (energetic) forces that he assumes are its origin – this is the concept Bleger will fundamentally argue. On the other hand, the term "dynamic" is used to address "the study of conduct in its development, in its evolution" (1958, pp. 111-112). And today, when studying Freud, we usually link the dynamic concept with the idea of conflict, although we usually release conflict from the interplay of literal forces as did Freud in Bleger perspective.

Bleger criticizes the dynamic-economic dimension in Freud's work, relying on Politzer's work and based on the idea that suggesting that "drives" are the background of psychic activity is an abstraction that materializes an inference. For Bleger this abstraction emerges because we "does not start from concrete man, but from an inference elevated to the category of *primum movens*, of entelechy" (Bleger, 1958, p. 78). To him, it is necessary to reconsider the matter of drives in psychology and this requires that analysts try to capture "the specific reality that has been assimilated, grasped, through this animistic and idealistic formulation" (1958, p. 79). It's a matter of questioning this pseudo-biology, but attempting to clear up the specific clinical reality that tries to express itself in these terms. Mitchell will agree completely with this attitude (Mitchell, 1988).

To Bleger, the idea of a "force" is a "anthropomorphism *de retour*" (1958, p. 81), a return of the anthropomorphism that is in the origine of physics, science that took the subjective sensation of muscular force to assert a mathematical function, and we reintroduced this "force" into the interior of the individual. As Bleger states: "from *force* as a mathematical function it went to *Force* as entelechy; from here it went to *drive*, then to *instinct*, ending the progressive mythologizing with *Instinct*" (1958, p. 84). So: from a lowercase force, that is, a description, to uppercase Force as an entelechy or a thing of the world; and from lowercase instinct, descriptive again, to uppercase Instinct, that is, *primum movens*: origin and final explanation of all movement and psychic activity. Mitchell will also follow in his work the road to recover the phenomenology that contains the drive model without defending its "ontological double (twin)" or, as Bleger states, its hypostasis: drive theory.

Let's take a look at another argument by Bleger that we find enormously suggestive and rich as a way of considering this matter. When it comes to drives[2] and the distinction made by Freud in his structure between charge (that we today translate as "pressure", *drang*), source, aim and object, Bleger finds this moment in Freud's work, mainly from 1905 onwards, as opening two paths. He states that: "on one hand, Freud acknowledges the object as something independent of instinct, and thus breaks away from the classical notion of instincts and *puts individual history in place of innate predetermination of instinct*; but, on the other hand, by acknowledging a charge in the instinct, he seriously compromises the significant progress achieved and, although he discovered the productive way of analysis of object relations, predominantly chooses the way of analyzing forces as primary elements" (Bleger, 1958, p. 56). This reflection by Bleger is interesting to us for two reasons: one, it

---

2 Bleger, as we've seen, following the Standard Edition, tends to use drive or instinct. But it's clear that he refers to *Trieb*, even more so in what we address next. We update his terminology so it doesn't cause even more confusion although, surely, these usages and translations can be the object of further reflections on how they've created certain kinds of confusions – not all, as it has been intended sometimes.

allows us to differentiate the breakaway by Freud from the popular notion regarding sexuality (reflected in the traditional notion of instinct), thereby, as he states, transforming psychoanalyses into an individual-historical approach; and second, the way Bleger places in that perspective a possible foundation for the analysis of object relations, that is, an overture to a notion not far from Fairbairn's ideas. So, object contingency questions the universality of the object presupposed in the idea of traditional instinct but, according to how we have understood this quote, not the primary link to the object. No natural object but historical object. Out of all the references we have read on the subject of object contingency in the Freudian drive structure, this is the one that we have found to be the most clarifying.

From this twofold way opened up by the drive structure, the accent put it in the object leads to the consideration of the person as an open system, while the accent on the charge (the economical perspective) leads us directly to a psyche that operates as a closed system. As Baranger clearly states in his criticism of the Freudian energetic perspective and of the closed system it implies, "neither emotion nor action can be conceived as a discharge of tensions" (1967/1993, p. 57). It follows, he states, that we work with the meaning of an emotion and/or an action, and not with its ability to charge and/or discharge whatever… They are expressions of the world of object relations of the individual.

Mitchell And the Rioplatense Psychoanalysis: Following Fairbairn's Steps

Our hypothesis is that Fairbairn[3] is the common ancestor of the works by Rioplatense psychoanalysis and Mitchell's ideas, which constitute – apart from the explicit recognition this author might have – many of his alignments. The critique made by Fairbairn of Freudian libido theory – its energetics –, as well

---

3 "The unconscious determination of the patient to preserve his inner world as a closed system at all costs would appear to be the phenomenon on the basis of which Freud was led to formulate the concept of the pleasure principle as the primary determinant of behavior. In my opinion, this formulation is a mistaken generalization from what is essentially a defensive phenomenon—one so highly defensive that it cannot be regarded as representing a primary principle of behavior. There can be no doubt, as it seems to me, (a) that the pleasure principle can only operate within a closed system, (b) that the maintenance of inner reality as a closed system is essentially a psychopathological phenomenon, and (c) that, in so far as inner reality is maintained as a closed system, behavior will be determined almost inevitably by the pleasure principle" (Fairbairn, 1958, p. 380).

as his emphasis on the priority of the object when it comes to comprehension/ construction of the psyche, seem essential to us.

Mitchell, unlike the River Plate authors – maybe with the exception of Bleger – places Fairbairn as a key influence in his theoretical propositions. Throughout the years, he outlined what would later be his central hypothesis about Fairbairn: this author does not suggest another contribution to the relational conception of the mind, but he proposes/suggests a "radical relational project" (2000, p. 105). Mitchell is, of course, aware that his take is also radical and goes down to the roots of what he understands as Fairbairn's central project.

In 1993, facing the criticism he received from "classical" authors of psychoanalysis for publishing his book *Relational Concepts in Psychoanalysis* (1988), Mitchell states:

Because they do not find Freud's drives in my perspective, Bachant and Richards feel I leave out motivational concepts. What they fail to grasp is that I regard object seeking, in Fairbairn's sense, or interpersonal integrating tendencies, in Sullivan's sense, as super-ordinate motivational principles that are powerfully active. I also believe that people seek pleasure, power, exercise of function, security, and all sorts of other things. I think it is more useful, however, to regard these other motives, although irreducible, as shaped and structured in the context of the relational matrix that provides a sense of self in relation to others. (p. 463)

It's clear in this quote that Mitchell is aware of the variety of reasons that can drive someone's life. What interests him, what seems to be of most use in his theoretical-clinical understanding, is to think that this ensemble of motives, organized hierarchically by different psychoanalysts and that can be amplified or reduced depending on the categories that we use, is structured and configured, formed, in the context of relational matrix that give them meaning.

This leads him to suggest, not for the first time but more clearly, if we understand better the concept of object-seeking as "drive" or as "ground" (2000, p. 104). This part of his reflection, in one of his latest texts on Fairbairn, focuses on a debate with his friend and co-author Jay Greenberg who, in his excellent book *Oedipus and Beyond* (1991), argues with Mitchell about his take on Fairbairn and about the relational model in general. Although Greenberg's take on Fairbairn captures well, according to Mitchell, an aspect of his work (probably those aspects related to Freudian models of reference[4]), he still presupposes a strong hypothesis that is highly problematic to Mitchell: that

---

4 This is why Mitchell's article is called "Fairbairn's object-seeking. Between Paradigms".

the concept of drive is necessary – in a broad sense – in order to reflect upon what the subject searches for in the other and that relational psychoanalysis pretended to create a "psychoanalysis free from drives", as Greenberg critically affirms (Greenberg, 1991, p. 70).

In the debate over the necessity or not of a concept of "drive"[5] that pushes the individual to seek interaction, Mitchell insists that approaching the matter in this way, that is, that suggesting a "drive" preexistent – and therefore pre-experiential– to the relationship that pushes the subject to interact presupposes – that is, has as an assumption – that the "individual *qua* individual" is the most appropriate unit of study. This leads us to return to the first polemic regarding the Freudian drive model and, therefore, the return to the old and continual division in the notions about the relationships between man and society.

Bleger, for his part, in the 50's, denounced a triple mythology rooted in our culture and which he saw as profoundly affecting our understanding of the psyche. The myths he underlines are: that of the 'natural man', the 'isolated man', and 'the abstract man'; three closely linked assumptions. According to him, these mythologies lead to a series of false antinomies (binary oppositions) from which psychoanalysis is not exempt: individual/society, innate/acquired, nature/society. This led him, in his day, to question certain aspects of the dynamic conception of the mind, as we see, following Fairbairn's footsteps – positing an understanding of the psyche in which impulses/drives derive from object relations and not the inverse (1956). He tried it, in a way that today might've been insufficient, to cope the problem of the relationship between internal and external realities. With his Marxist background, he emphasized the central social nature of human beings and tried to integrate it with classical kleinian thought. All these mythologies, Bleger insists, are ways in which thought has denied the primary social condition of what is human.

Contemporary biology and other disciplines agree also with the questioning of these assumptions. Therefore, Mitchell considers any understanding of a "reified" drive or a primary psychic energy to which one can attribute the totality of his activity, to be, today, an unsustainable anachronism.

When Mitchell (2000) suggests, taking Richard Hofstadter's Crazy Loop as a theoretical-conceptual model for thinking about the paradoxes of human experience, he is, quite precisely, engaged in a struggle with these antinomies (false binary oppositions) criticized by Bleger. Remember the paradigm of this type of Crazy Loop, the "drawing hands" from Escher, that illustrate the book

---

5 This time in a broad sense and not restricted to the Freudian drive theory.

"Relational Concepts". He considers that reflecting upon the problem of the relationship between internal and external realities, an all its variants, is one of our central challenge today.

In his debate with Greenberg that we refer above, Mitchell maintains that:

I believe that Fairbairn, like Sullivan (1953), was struggling toward a different way of understanding the nature of human beings as fundamentally social, not as *drawn* into interaction, but as *embedded* in an interactive matrix with others as his or her natural state. (2000, p. 105)

Thus, Mitchell continues to exhibit and appreciate the extraordinary step that Fairbairn took by defending his idea that man – libido, he said, maintaining Freudian terminology – doesn't look for pleasure (*object-pleasure*), but for objects (*object-seeking*). According to Mitchell, what Fairbairn was interested in was not to find a discreet motivation among others, as Greenberg affirms by maintaining that Fairbairn ends up with a drive-monism by postulating oral dependency as an ultimate motive of humans. Although Mitchell knows that Fairbairn sometimes is vague and not very clear in several of his texts, he doesn't doubt that Fairbairn wasn't trying to establish another drive, but to position the foundation of psychic life, the condition of its plausibility. According to Mitchell, Fairbairn understood perfectly that human beings look for pleasure and other emotional states, but this isn't a matter of debate. Referring to Fairbairn, he states:

He is suggesting that Freud stopped his investigation, his understanding of the search for pleasure, too quickly [...] For Fairbairn [...] the search for pleasure, as well as other dynamic processes, take place in the context of searching for the object, because pleasure is a powerful means for establishing and maintaining connections with others. (1988, p. 120)

Therefore, as a conceptual strategy, it doesn't seem appropriate for him to stop at the motives or needs stipulated *a priori*, according to the author's chosen frame of reference; he rather prefers (and he knows that it is a justified choice when it comes to its clinical relevance and usefulness to him, and not as something "more true") to begin with the relationship with other(s), in these encounters, as the foundation for the understanding of emotional meanings. The alternative (starting from drives determined *a priori*) seems to him to continue to maintain "the abstract man myth" as his natural state, as Bleger stated, and, therefore, isolated from the social environment. There is no "natural state" for the human other than his social being. This Platonic-Cartesian understanding has been questioned from a Aristotelic-Hegelian perspective of man as a *zoon politikon*.

Conclusions: "Il n'y a pas de dernir mot, tout mot est l'ávant-dernier"[6]

How can we assess the importance of Mitchell and of contemporary relational psychoanalysis today? In a couple of words, while I think that the contribution of the River Plate thinkers to the elaboration of relational theory is considerable, they were also marked by their time (Zeitgeist) and made vast efforts to sustain a *filiation* with certain Freudian concepts which today I consider have been questioned with some degree of conviction.

Mitchell's central reformulation of the analytic position comes to mind, in terms of the very 'fact' of interaction, and of how to draw out the clinical and theoretical consequences of this irreducible dimension of the psychoanalytic process.

So, this interaction occurring at the interface of internal and external realities - that also occurs when being and not being with another thinker, being and not being in a missed place - is at the heart of the process, and this dynamic of encounter, identification, decentering and return is one which - I hope to have shown - defines the presence of Mitchell in my own experience.

Summary

Starting with the impact of Stephen A. Mitchell's thinking on my professional career and my "professional complementary series", I will develop in this paper some of the consequences that his influence had on my current understanding of psychoanalysis and on my reencounter with psychoanalysts that emerged from the River Plate, where I come from, and especially with José Bleger. The debate that Bleger set up between drive and object relations and the epistemological question of this debate, inspired by Fairbairn but also by Politzer, are reconsidered in the light of the contributions of Mitchell's work.

I go on a journey concerning a particular subject, but during which I try to show a more general hypothesis: how relational psychoanalysis has allowed us to return to many of the authors who have been part of our background with a new point of view, recovering many of their developments that take on a new life and that derive from assumptions that haven't been analyzed to confront contemporary psychoanalysis.

---

6 Jankelevitch, V (p. 120)

6

From Attachment to Relation: A Road Across Neuroscience, Mind, and Mentalization[1]

Juan José Martínez Ibáñez

The topic that I'm about to develop in this chapter, I find it interesting, and I hope that all of you can find it interesting too, dear readers, for several reasons:

a) First of all, as humans, everything that affect us should not leave us indifferent. We, the relational psychotherapists, work "side by side" with another human being. Therefore, taking into account all the contributions that we receive from different scientific disciplines that deal with the human being, help us to have a new idea about how human beings are and, thus, the more we know about how human beings are, we can help them in a more realistic and effective way.

---

1 I appreciate the compilers of this book for inviting me to participate in it. I believe it's a good idea, in this globalized world, that the contributions we make from the Mediterranean, in Spanish language, can be recognized by the English speaking colleagues. Translated to english by N.Monserrat Gómez, reviewed by the author.

b) Secondly, and as a consequence of these new investigations, we have developed the relational model applied to the disciplines dealing with mental health, and this, for the first time, generates a definition of the mind. This definition of the mind integrates all new research into how human beings are.

c) Thirdly, through the contributions of attachment theory, along with the development of intersubjectivity, throughout communication and mentalization, are the disciplines that allow us to develop a new way of understanding the psychotherapeutic practice.

Why do I put it this way? Because we are on the 21st century, and, therefore, we have to take into account all the latest research that is being done in the different fields of knowledge, related to the human being. Next, we will see some of these important contributions to be able to know us as humans in the 21st century.

Contributions of Neuroscience And Other Scientific Disciplines

A paradigm shift is currently occurring in the basic sciences that underlie the applied medical science. Research in developmental biology and physiology now strongly supports a model of the "developmental origins of health and disease" (Gluckman & Adler, 2004). Although the role of early expressed genetic factors is an essential focus of current studies, it has become clear that genes do not specify behavior absolutely; prenatal, and postnatal environmental epigenetic factors play critical roles in these developmental origins. The social environment, particularly the one created together by the mother and infant, directly affects gene-environment interactions, and so has long-enduring effects (Suomi, 2004). The newer interdisciplinary models, therefore, detail the mechanisms by which "mother nature meets mother nurture" (Crabbe & Phillips, 2003). Complementing this conception of the nature–nurture problem, studies in neuroscience indicate that development represents an experiential shaping of genetic potential, and that early real experiences with the social environment are critical to the maturation of the brain tissue. Thus, nature´s potential, can be realized only as it is facilitated by nurture (Cicchetti & Tucker, 1994).

The updated models of attachment theory, which emphasize both emotional and social functions, and neurobiological structures, are now interacting with developmental neuroscience to generate a broad field of interdisciplinary studies. This recent information on the evolutionary origins of health and disease can be applied to clinical practice.

Neuroscientists come to the conclusion that the accelerated growth of brain structure during critical periods of childhood, is dependent on actual experience, and is influenced by social forces. They refer to the social construction of the human brain, and postulate that the cellular architecture of the cerebral cortex is sculpted by the contribution of the relations with the social environment. Allan Schore had suggested that a central concept of the disciplines of social neuroscience, and affective from development, is expressed on this principle: "the self-organization of the developing brain occurs in the context of a relationship with another self, with another brain" (Schore, 1996). In addition, now more than ever, we are more aware of the importance of the fact that "the brain" is really a system of two-brains, each one with different functional and structural properties.

The neural structure determines potential, but experience gives its specific form. As humans, we are predisposed to develop language, for example, but the specific language that we acquire depends on our environment. The specific information derived from our experiences is incorporated into the neural structures. Nature and nurture are not opposite poles of a continuum. They interact in a process of interdependence and, therefore, are inseparable.

The discussions about nature versus nurture seem to have no end, and in many aspects, meaningless, since nature and nurture can be expressed through intimate interaction. Nature and nurturing are already expressed in the moment of conception, through gestation, during childhood, youth, and adulthood. The affection of a mother, a father or other primary caregiver, impact the development of the child's regulating system of affection. Attachment processes allow the development of complex mental functions, through the complex actions of the primary caregiver. Many of these mental actions are only human (Fonagy, Gergely, Jurist y Target, 2002).

We are born with a physiological and psychobiological equipment that must be exposed to human culture in order to reach its potential. Our innate potentiality can only be realized through culture. Our life experiences are important for the differentiation of the brain tissue. The innate structure of the nervous system determines the interactions of children with their surrounding environment, and the resulting responses, in turn, affect the structure. In addition, there is no inside or outside, in relation to the nervous system, since Daniel Stern (2001) had pointed out, we are born to connect with the nervous system of others.

No one can be divorced from his/her own history and culture; we are not completely contained within our own skin. We have a biological capacity to take part in communications and social interactions, because we are born with the predisposition to form attachment bonds, and to interact with our caregivers. Humans are social beings, and our psychological functions depend on interactions and transactions with the social environment during childhood. Culture forms the human mind. It is impossible to determine how much of a child's psychological function is the child's own, and how much is product of the child's relationships. Culture consist of an infinite number of ways of being together, through language, narrative explanations, etc., in a shared life, where people depend on each other. The child comes to life, with certain innate abilities to participate in culture, and his/her actions, and resulting personality, are derived from a development process that unfolds under particular historical circumstances.

The human brain is the most complex natural system, and plastic, in the known universe. Edelman y Tononi (2000) point out that the specific environment a child has at birth, determines the connections and synapses that are formed and strengthened. In this way, genetic and environmental factors interact at each stage of brain development. The environment plays a key role in the establishment and strengthening of synaptic connections after birth. Because the human brain is relatively unfinished at birth, caregivers have a greater impact on brain structures and functions. Human contact creates neural connections.

From a basic biological perspective, the child's neural system, that is, the structure and function of the developing brain, is modeled by the progenitor's mature brain. This occurs in the context of emotional communication. The attunement of emotional states is offered by the association with the other, which is essential for the developing brain to acquire the capacity to organize itself with more autonomy as the child matures. This, in turn, also causes changes in the progenitor's brain, although the most striking changes occur in the child's brain. As we have seen, the relational experiences have a dominant influence on the brain, because the circuits responsible for social perception are the same or are very closely linked to the circuits that control the creation of meaning, regulation of organic states, modulation of emotions, organization of memory, and the capacity for interpersonal communication. The interpersonal experience, thus, plays a special role of organization, determining the development of brain structure throughout life (Siegel, 2002).

The current interpersonal neurobiological models, of perinatal and postnatal development, are changing the emphasis that has been placed so far on cognition, towards the development of communication and the regulation of affections. In a prototypical description, Walker-Andrews and Bahrick (2001) note that: "From birth, an infant is plunged into a world of other human beings, in which conversation, gestures, and faces are omnipresent during the infant's waking hours. Moreover, these harbingers of social information, are dynamic, multimodal and reciprocal". This point of view, in fact, returns to Bowlby's (1969) original description, that attachment communications, mother-child, are "accompanied by the strongest feelings and emotions", and are produced in a context of "facial expression, posture, voice tone, physiological changes, the "tempo" of the movement, and the incipient action." The psychobiologically attuned mother does more than just receiving affective communications. In addition, she regulates the arousal and affective states, which minimizes the negative states in comforting transactions, and also maximizes the baby's positive and affective states in the interactive game. The primary caregiver doesn't regulate the manifest behavior as much as the internal mental states.

Children are social beings and have a biological capacity that allows them to participate in communication and social interaction, for example, through imitation. They have an innate structure in the central nervous system for imitative behavior, which is supported by a particular category of neurons, called mirror neurons. Among primates, and also among humans, both are highly social, there seems to be specialized neurons for the visual recognition of emotions, and it is revealed through the face. These neurons are located mainly in temporal lobe cells, and, in general, they seem to focus on making visual recognition of the social environment. These neurons are called "mirror neurons", who were discovered by Rizzolatti and his research team in 1990. Mirror neurons are a type of neurons, which are activated when an animal, or person, performs the same activity that is observed to be executed by another individual, especially from a congener. The neurons of the individual imitate as "reflecting" the action of another: like that, the observer is performing the action of the observed, hence its name "mirror."

Hence, some scientists consider that mirror neurons are one of the most important discoveries of neuroscience in the last decade. These neurons detect the emotions, the movement, and even the intentions of the person with whom we speak, and re-edit in our own brain the detected state, activating in our brain the same active areas in the brain of our interlocutor, creating a "Emotional contagion", that is, one person adopts the feelings of another. Failures are linked in mirror neurons, with certain behaviors of people belonging to the autistic spectrum.

The ability to imitate emotional expressions and facial movements will help the child to discover his/her own humanity, and forms the basis for the development of identity (Gallese, 2001). The child not only imitates the expression, but also perceives that the expression corresponds to a particular sensory impression, to an emotional background, or to some vital affections. Only around the six months, children are capable to express for themselves the primary emotions that were originally defined by Darwin as: joy, anger, panic, anguish, sadness, surprise and disgust (Beebe & Lachmann, 2002; Meltzoff, 1993; Trevarthen, 1993).

The brain self-regulates and self-organizes itself through mutual communication tuned emotionally, between caregiver and child, which continues to transform the higher levels with the continued maturation of the brain. In this communication, the caregiver feels and modulates the nonverbal, motor, and affective expressions of the child, and the experiences of communication serve to fine tune the neural circuits of the child. In a proper and suitable contact, the caregiver infers the emotional state of the child, based on external behavior; The caregiver interacts with the child and, in this process, modules the capacity of the nervous system for self-organization. The diversity of interactions between the caregiver and the child are stored in the child's nervous system. Despite the changes in the relationship, during the development of the child, the caregiver remains as an external regulator for the internal affective states of the child. The active involvement of the caregiver, in the emotional interactions with the child, is the basis for the formation of the internal representations of the caregiver as a mother (Rutter, 1993; Schore, 1994; Siegel, 1999; Stern, 1985; Trevarthen, 1900).

From birth, infants are predisposed to establish attachment relationships, and to relate, in the interactions with their caregivers. They initiate and control interactive situations, and have an intuitive basis for sharing emotions with other people. Three-week infants are able to imitate other people's facial expressions, and two-day infants can imitate a smiley face (Field, Woodson, Greenberg and Cohen, 1982; Meltzoff and Moore, 1977; Stern, 1985). Studies show that learning causes growth, both in synaptic connections and in the activation of genes (Kandel, 2005). In addition, external stimulation forms the neural connectivity. The circuits are not only sensitive to the results of early experiences, but are constantly affected and modified by new experiences. External stimuli determine which connections will be strengthened, and which ones will be nullified, and the neural patterns are constantly changing.

Those connections that are activated more frequently, are maintained and developed. This process allows the brain to adapt to its environment, whether the person grows in the tropical desert or in the Artic. The richness of the nervous system rests on its plasticity, in relation to the environment. Neural circuits can develop only when they receive optimal levels of excitation and stimulation. Both, nature and moments of experiences, are important for development. Children and parents reflect the world in which they were born, and the human brain has an immense ability to develop in a simple way. The brain grows, organizes, and functions, in relation to actual experiences of life, and the actual experiences, in turn, modify all human behavior. But the complexity of the brain also makes it a fragile and vulnerable structure.

Human nature is culture, and culture is important in relation to transferring experiences from one generation to the next. Humans are born to share communication and ideas, and we depend on social exchanges. Infants enter to this world and they have to engage with human contact, adjust, and learn the systems of meanings, through constant interactions with their caregivers. Without this exchange, development would advance in biasedly, and the process of humanization would atrophy. Emotional and cognitive communication is a characteristic of our species.

Given the importance of emotions, in creating meaning, it is understandable that the biological system that helps to organize the self, is so crucial to determine the subjective experiences of our lives. Human emotions constitute the fundamental value system that the brain uses to organize its own functioning. The regulation of emotions is, therefore, the essence of self-regulation. Communication between progenitor and child, on emotions, directly shapes the child's ability to organize his or her self.

In the evolutionary mechanism of attachment, the interactive regulation of emotion, in addition, represents the regulation of biological synchrony, both intersubjectively, as well as within organisms (Bradshaw & Schore, 2007; Schore, 1994). It is currently thought, that the regulatory function of the newborn-mother interaction, may be an essential promoter to ensure the development and normal maintenance of synaptic connections during the establishment of functional brain circuits. Thus, the first brain capacities, which develop in the course of evolution, are social, and they do so in response to social exchange. For this reason, the baby, for its development, doesn't need pedagogical or cultural aids, but it is more appropriate, simply, to take him/her in arms and enjoy it. Without proper social experience with the adult, that is, in his proper relationship with the adult who cares for him/her, and a person-to-person relational exchange, it is difficult to have a good development of the orbitofrontal cortex.

Sroufe (1979, 1996), has studied children with depressed mothers who do not pay attention to the child, and found a clear connection between the degree and nature of the interaction, and a progressive deterioration of the conditions of these children. At three months, the children's responses were insignificant, unimportant, and at six months, they seemed anxious or passive. Around the year, half of the children showed insecure attachment to their mothers, and at eighteen months, all children had an insecure attachment. It has been found that the mother's personality is a more reliable predictor of future attachment patterns than the child's own temper. The child's temper, his/her receptivity, activity level, attention span, etc., influences the expression of a particular attachment pattern, but not the nature of the pattern.

Human beings are social creatures, hence, we are the source of stress of others. Stress, often, has its roots in the intimate relationships between people, and has a substantial impact on brain development. Maltreatment and neglect, in the early stages of life, combined with an innate vulnerability in the child, has been shown to increase the risk of a deterioration of the stressful state. Children who are prone to develop aggressiveness, will develop this aggressive tendency if they grow up in high-risk families. The way children process experiences, and the perceptions of the environment, has a great impact on their behaviors, including the expression of genetic disposition. Internal and external stimuli are crucial for brain development, and such factors as the hormones, stress, learning, social interaction, etc., will affect the neuronal structure.

At this point, it seems important to me to point out that all these investigations, carried out by renowned researchers, give us the empirical proof that, when relational psychotherapists emphasize the intrinsic role of the relationship as the generator of human's mental functioning, we do it based on them, and not as mere speculations, product of the mind of some enlightened. Each one of these researchers emphasizes that human mental functioning rests on the mutual interaction between actual experience in the external world, on the one hand, and the nature of each organism on the other.

If we want to incorporate some of the new research on the human being, that is taking place within the framework of scientific disciplines, we will have to accept that we shouldn't keep maintaining the concepts that correspond to another way of conceiving the human being. For example, until now, we didn't need to think about the brain, its functioning, and its participation in our lives. Or about the role of neurons and the importance of biology. We were only guided by the interpretations, with an intellectualized vision of our mind. Why? Because the starting point of thinking about all this was that our mind, like our brain, was a phylogenetic inheritance, contributed by the species. Today, we know that what is inherited phylogenetically are neurobiological processes, biological architecture, but our mind is co-created in a unique relationship with another mind, therefore, all minds are different.

For a long time, and still today for most of humans, Homo Sapiens preferred to be set apart from the animals, an orphan without family, siblings, cousins, and parents. The rhetorical questions of philosophy were: where do we come from? Where do we go? Who are we? But now we have the answers, we are members of a huge and particularly noisy family: that of the great apes. And about 6 million years ago, a single female ape, had two daughters. One became the ancestor of all chimpanzees, and the other is our own grandmother. This seems to be very basic for those of us who are committed to the human being, but is not the predominant idea in society. Still, the majority idea in the world population about how we are, belongs to the field of the phylogenetic heritage. Therefore, we have a long journey ahead if we want these new ideas to reach the population and help them to live better. That's why we have to make this mental effort to create new concepts and to leave behind the previous conceptions, because they correspond to another time, as painful as it might be to get rid of those ideas.

Michael Tomasello (2009) states that, after our ancestors understood others as intentional agents like themselves, a new world of shared intersubjective realities began to break through. It is a world full with artefacts and symbolic materials, which the members of their culture, both past and present, have created for the use of others. Karlen Lyons-Ruth (1993) states, that humans used their new consciousness about mental states, to learn from others, and to pass on knowledge to others, and this ability to conceive other minds, accounts for the explosive speed of cultural evolution, over the last 200,000 years.

Recently, epigenetic discoveries have left behind the genetic discoveries. This new science reveals that the information that regulates biology begins with "environmental signals" which, in turn, control the binding of regulatory proteins to DNA. The history of epigenetic control is the story of how environmental signals control the genetic activity. And the principles of quantum mechanics highlight the supremacy of the energy fields in their influence on matter. Consequently, the matter of the Universe is organized by certain information, represented as patterns of energy contained in the field. This approach, is a fundamental change with respect to the physical models, particularly on mechanics, which were based on the XIX century, the Newtonian theory, on which Freud based his scheme of the psychic apparatus. Others within psychoanalysis have been making a creative use of this approach as Moran (1991), Fajardo (2000), Beebe et al. (2000), Ghent (2002), Piers (2005) and Seligman (2005).

In considering the theory of non-linear dynamical systems as a potential model for the psychoanalytic theory, we have to take into account, which represents a breaking point, everything previously established between the theoretical body of psychoanalysis. Some authors consider this approach as a rupture with theories of cause and effect, based deductively. Learning is learning from patterns, from models. It is an interaction with different contexts and environments, revealing correlations, harmonies, and latent patterns. It is more about learning from a gestalt than from a mere acquisition of data. It is about learning, about what is out of control, producing underlying rules, rather than learning from information data.

With non-adaptive mental processes and patients, the last one happens. No one can say that this or that patient will adapt in a healthy way, even when the causes are very clear, because there are too many variables at stake, so many that we cannot predict the outcome in the mid-term. We also know that good health is related to change, and that the balance between chaos or disorder, and structure or homeostasis, is the recipe for good health, life, and good organization. When there is only structure or order, the system destroys itself, just as it does when the disorder is too wide or intense. Both homeostasis and disorder have the same effects, when there is a predominance of one of them over the other. It happens that the biological goes by systems, somehow unpredictable.

They are for two kinds of reasons: first, because the variables involved in the animated world form a level of complexity too large to be caught by simple laws. Second, because the relationships between these variables are too intense and imbricated, so that small variations in one of them, can amplify and make emerge at a distance, a considerable and unexpected effect (the butterfly effect).

Speaking in therapeutic terms, what most psychotherapist do is unpredictable, so Hippocrates recommendation that "the first thing is to do no harm" remains valid. What we are confirming, with this new contributions, is that psychotherapies do not cure only by their theoretical body, but that the important variable lies in the link between therapist and patient. Chaos is the set of laws governing open systems, and an open system is one that receives and exchanges energy and information with the environment. In this sense, the human being is an open system.

As a summary of some of the many researchers being conducted from neuroscience, we can say that the human brain is unfinished at the time of birth, and many of its capabilities will develop after birth. Is designed to survive in environments, in a culture, in particular languages and climates, and primary caregivers form the brain of their children in a unique way. On the other hand, parallel developments in developmental psychology, relational psychoanalysis, and attachment theory (proposed initially more than 40 years by John Bowlby (1969), as a conception of the mother-child relationship), have become the dominant model of social and human development, available to researchers and clinicians. In his attempt to integrate Psychology, Psychiatry, and Psychoanalysis with Biology, Bowlby speculated that the attachment system, an evolutionary mechanism common to humans and animals, should ultimately be found in specific areas of the brain (Schore, 2000).

Research about developmental psychology suggests that, rather than the development of complex cognitions, the achievement of an attachment bond of emotional communication, and the maturation of affect, represent the key events in childhood. The development process itself, is now thought to fundamentally represent a progression of stages, in which self-regulating, adaptive, and emerging structures, and functions allows some qualitatively new interactions between the individual and the social environment. We now know that: Emotions are of the highest order, and are direct expressions of bio-regulation in complex organisms; That the maturation of the neural mechanisms, involved in self-regulation, are dependent on actual experience; And that normal development, fundamentally, represents the improvement of self-regulation. All this researches allow us to understand the human being from a perspective different from the one which has prevailed for many years, and still present. To emphasize the human being as belonging to a complex non-linear dynamic system, allows us to reconsider all the concepts that have predominated, and to have to define new ways of conceptualizing the current reality. One of these concepts is that of the mind, and it is the one we will address in the next point.

The Definition of the Mind

Why do not we have a definition of the mind? Because as we have seen so far, we start from the mistaken idea that we all have a mind, and also with some differences, the same mind. Both, men and woman. This is a consequence of believing that the mind is a phylogenetic heritage. Therefore, it has not been necessary to define it. We all grow in the belief that it is something we all have, we do not need to have to define it, because, why defining something that we all have? What it has been are descriptions of the mind, as Freud did when he elaborated the first topical and the second topical or structural scheme of the psychic apparatus. Another description that still remains is the one that tell us that the mind is the brain. But, so far there hasn't been a definition of the mind.

The definition of the mind is something that has been absent in the scientific fields that deal with mental experience. That is why sometimes the word mind is used as a sign of something unknown, sometimes as a sign of a mysterious source of our subjective inner life, other times is equated with the brain. But, I think, it is very important to take the step of exploring a definition of the mind, to be able to achieve an understanding of what a healthy mind can really be. We must not forget that human beings are what our mind wants us to be. So, the more we know it, the better the mental resources we can use and, therefore, the better our quality of life will be.

We have already seen how recent research from a set of scientific disciplines provide us with insights that allow us to have a better understanding of how human beings are, and particularly of human mental functioning. The different scientific disciplines give us many points of view about how the mind works, bringing us knowledge in depth, and from different perspectives, of the human experience. For example, we have seen how neuroscience can inform us about how the brain gives rise to processes such as memory and perception. Developmental psychology gives us a point of view about how the mind of children grows within a family, over time. Anthropology gives us insights about how relational experiences and communication patterns, within different cultures, forms the development of the mind. Sociology can give us knowledge on how emotions have developed, throughout the social evolution of the human being. Relational psychoanalysis gives us a clinical point of view on how individuals can suffer the emotional disturbances that, in a profound way, alter the course of their lives.

These investigations talk about how the mind emerges from the brain's substance, and is mold by our communications in the interpersonal relations, from intersubjective relations. Often, these scientific disciplines function in an isolated way from one another, but always dropping insight over the field of study, which is no other than to know how human mind functions in the different stages of life.

In my book *The two ages of the mind: vicissitudes of mental functioning* (J.J. Martínez Ibáñez, 2013)[2] I have proposed, taking into account some contributions of Daniel Siegel (2012), a definition of the mind that will allow us to understand each other. The author says that: "a central aspect of the mind is that it processes in a relational way, and corporeal, the flow of energy and information". The flow of energy and information is what people share within a culture, and this flow is what we can measure in the subjects through a scanner. In this operative definition, the central idea is summarized, which would be detailed in three fundamental principles:

1. A central aspect of the human mind is that it is a relational (intersubjective) and embodied process that regulates, in a cognitive and affective

---

2 Title translated to English by the translator.

way, the flow of energy and information inside the brain, and between the brains.

2. The mind, as an emergent property of the body and relationships, is co-created through internal neurophysiological processes and real intimate experiences, both cognitive and affective, with another mind. In other words, the mind is a process that emerges from the nervous system and extends throughout the entire body, as well as from the patterns of communications that occur within intimate relationships.

3. The structure and developmental function of the mind is determined by how real cognitive and affective experiences, from real life, especially those occurring in the intimate interpersonal relationships, shape the genetically programmed maturation of the nervous system.

To put it simply, human mental connections through real experiences with another person, in an intimate relationship, shapes the nervous connections, and this relationship contributes to the co-creation of each one's mind. Together, intimate interpersonal relationships and neural networks shape the mind. The mind is more than the sum of the parts; Is the essence of the emerging. We have to accept that the mind is more than an activity that our brain does. Neuroscience reveals the connection between brain structures and its function, giving us new insights on how real experience models mental processes.

We now know that actual experience, and the activation of neurons, can alter regulatory molecules, which controls the expression of genes. This constitutes a process called epigenesis. These epigenetic changes reveal the powerful ways in which real experience modifies the way the brain develops throughout life. Recent studies in neuroplasticity of the brain have shown that the brain continues to modify its structural connections with real experience throughout life.

The mind-cognitive and affective regulatory processes, which creates patterns in the flow of energy and information can be described as emanating in part, but only in part, from the activity of neurons. To have in mind the idea that it depends only of the brain, is to limit the conception of the mind. Human beings have developed to be social beings, and mental processes are a product of both our internal neural connections and interpersonal connections with others. If we do not take this into account, it will be easy for us to slide into the lineal way of thinking, believing that the mind is only the activity of our brain.

We have to consider mind, brain, and relationships as three aspects of the flow of energy and information. The brain is the embodied neuronal mechanism that shapes that flow; Relationships are the distribution of flow; Mind is the embodied relational process that regulates the flow of energy and information.

If we ask ourselves, where is the mind? We can say that its regulating functions are embodied in the nervous system, and included in our interpersonal relationships. This emerging process, both neuronal and interpersonal, locates the mind within a physiological and relational framework of reality. The mind develops in the interaction of, at least, these two facets of human life.

As we see, the mind would be a regulatory process (for me, regulation is always cognitive and affective), of the flow of energy and information, which would be carried out through interpersonal relationships and processed at the brain level by the neural connections that would leave traces in our brain. This definition, seems, to me, to be correct, because it reflects the actual human mental functioning. This is not as it was believed at the end of the 19th and at the beginning of the 20th century, and, therefore, as Freud considered it, as a phylogenetic heritage, in which all we had to do was develop it. And that, as a consequence of this development, conflicts would appear, mainly generated by repressions. Everything was already inside our minds, and we could not be more than victims of our own drives.

Today we know that the mind is a self-organized process, which emerges from the properties of a system. This process arises from the interaction of the elements of the system (flow of energy and information within the body, and that are distributed among people), and also regulates, in a recursive way, the elements from which it emerged. This being recursive, the property of re-entry of the mind, is typical of self-organized emergent processes. It means that relationships and brain shape the mind, and that the mind shapes relationships and the brain. Mind, brain, and relationships are three aspects of a system: regulation, embodied mechanism, and distribution of energy flow and information. Of course, our mental experience is much more than a process of regulation. It implies the subjective quality of our consciousness, and the internal forms of knowledge, which enrich our capacity to feel, give meaning to things, to love, define purposes, establish connections and achieve integrity.

Intimate, interpersonal or intersubjective relationships can facilitate or inhibit this tendency to integrate coherent experiences. Early relationships in life with meaningful people can model neuronal structures that create representations of experience, and allow a coherent point of view of the world. Intersubjective experiences directly influence on how we mentally construct reality.

Learning about the regulating aspect of the mind enables us to see more deeply the ways in which the mind develops, to see changes in the brain, and to see how relationships evolve over time. When these elements act, they generate, as we said above, traces in the brain. These traces are also known as the Internal

Operational Models, a contribution of John Bowlby (1969), or as the Implicit Relational Knowledge according to the Boston Group (Lyons-Ruth, K. et al., 1998). These models or, in other words, the mind, brain and relationships, can be intentionally moved towards health. These heathy life models involve the integration of energy and information into the nervous system, and between people. Integration is the organizing principle which links the way in which the flow of energy and information is shared (relationships), modeled by the embodied mechanisms of the nervous system or, more simply, the brain, and is regulated (the mind). All this occurs in a relationship of attachment. Through a relationship of attachment, which is that unique space of intimacy that is given between the primary caregiver and the baby to ensure the protection and safety of the weakest, also allows that the inherited neurobiological mechanisms of the baby, upon entering in contact with the mind of the primary caregiver, can co-create his/her own mind.

Attachment

Attachment is a concept developed by John Bowlby (1969), a British psychoanalyst, who put the emotional aspect in the first place in the human relationship, rather than food and sexuality, characteristic of the traditional psychoanalytic model. Attachment is an innate system of the brain, which evolves by influencing and organizing the motivational and emotional processes, with respect to significant protective figures. The attachment system, motivates the baby, seeks the proximity of their parents, and establish communication with them. At the most basic evolutionary level, this system improves the chances of survival of the baby. At a mental level, attachment establishes a relationship with its caregiver, which helps the immature brain to use the mature functions of the brain of its parents, to organize its own processes. Parental help in reducing unpleasant emotions, such as fear, anguish, or sadness, allows the child to calm down and, in turn, provides a safe haven for distress. Repeated experiences are coded and stored in implicit memory as expectations and, then, as mental models or attachment schemes that serve to help the child create an inner sensation, that John Bowlby called a "safe base" to explore the world. Mario Marrone (2001) tell us: "Bowlby concluded that the child's tendency to form a strong and fundamental bond with a maternal figure, is part of an archaic inheritance whose function is the survival of the species (the protection against predators in the context of evolutionary adaptiveness), and that this tendency is relatively independent from orality or feeding" (p.23).

Attachment studies have revealed that the organization of attachment relationships during childhood is associated with the characteristic processes of emotional regulation, social relations, the access to autobiographical memory, and the development of self-reflection and narrative (M. Main, 1995). To describe the nature of attachment, qualitative terms are used: attachments are perceived as "secure" or "insecure", with a wide variety of descriptions of each one of these categories. The attachment system serves multiple functions. For a baby, activation of the attachment system involves the pursuit of closeness (Bowlby, 1973). The search for closeness allows the baby to protect himself/herself from harm, death from starvation, unfavorable changes in temperature, disasters, attacks from others, and separation from the group. Because of this, the internal experience of attachment system activation is often associated with the feeling of anguish, or fear, and can be initiated by frightening experiences of various kinds, as well as by a threat of separation from the attachment figure.

Attachment relationships serve, therefore, a vital function: to protect the baby from many varieties of danger. These relationships are crucial for organizing not only the continuous experience, but also for the neuronal growth of the developing brain. In other words, these incipient emotional relationships have a direct effect on the development of the domains of mental functioning that serve as our conceptual main points: memory, narration, emotion, representations, and mental states. In this way, attachment relationships can serve to create the central base from which the mind will develop. Insecure attachment may serve as a significant risk factor in the development of psychopathology. Secure attachment, by contrast, seems to confer a form of emotional resilience.

Although attachment behavior is contemplated primarily in childhood, it continues to manifest itself in adulthood throughout the life process. In moments of stress, in particular, an adult will "mobilize" in his/her mind, the different "attachment figures" selected and look for them as a source of protection, advise, and empowerment. For adults, such attachment figures can be their parents, close friends or sentimental partners.

When children develop secure attachments towards their parents, they allow them to go out into the world to explore and to relate to others. Initially, children seek closeness to their attachment figures, to give them a sense of security. The company of their parents, gives them a safe haven they need, especially when they are anxious, sad or distressed. As they grow, children internalize their relationships with attachment figures. They are the ones who provide them with the ability to develop a scheme or mental model of security called, as we have said, a "safe base".

An internal attachment model is a form of mental model (Bowlby, 1969). The formation of mental models constitutes a fundamental way through which implicit memory allows the mind to create generalizations and syntheses of past experiences. Subsequently, these models are used to bias present cognition, so that a quicker analysis of the perception of the instant can be made, and also so that the mind can anticipate the events that will occur next. Thus, mental models constitute an essential way through which the brain learns from the past, directly influencing over the present and shaping future actions.

Introduction to Mentalization

Some authors, from the field of psychoanalysis, have contributed with original and current ideas on the subject of thought and have developed a concept, which they had defined as Mentalization (Fonagy, Gergely, Jurist & Target, 2002; Bateman & Fonagy, 2006; Allen & Fonagy, 2006; Busch, 2008).Through many studies with mothers and children of different ages, and taking into account the contributions of Attachment Theory, Developmental Psychology, Neuroscience, Anthropology, and Relational Psychoanalysis, among others, come to the conclusion that the capacity for mentalization, along with many other socio-cognitive capacities, is developed in the experience of social interaction with the caregivers in an attachment relationship.

For the last decade, philosophers (Dennet, 1987; Fodor ,1987, 1992) and developmental psychologists (Astington, Harris, y Olson, 1988; Baron-Cohen et al., 1993; Hirschfeld y Gelman, 1994; Wellman, 1990; Whiten, 1991) have focused on the origins and development of our ability to attribute mental states to others. Dennet (1987) has argued that the application of this interpretive mentalist strategy, what he calls "intentional attitude", is an evolutionary adaptation that is successful in predicting the behavior of other subjects. These approaches explicitly reject the Cartesian assumption that mental states are apprehended by introspection.

On the contrary, mental states are incorporated through contingent interactions, reflected or mirrored, with the caregiver. Relational psychoanalysts have assumed that the child's ability to represent mental states in a symbolic way is acquired within the relationship with the primary caregiver. Thus, any disturbance during this early relationship with the caregivers will not only establish non-adaptive attachment patterns, but will also hamper the development of a wide range of capacities, vital to the child's normal social development. Understanding the mind is difficult, if one doesn't know how to understand a person with one mind. Mentalization implies centering the mental states of oneself, or on the others, particularly in the explanation of behavior. That mental state influences the behaviors that are beyond question. Beliefs, desires, feelings, and thoughts, either inside or outside our consciousness, will determine what we do.

Explanations of behavior, in terms of the mental states of others, are relatively vulnerable, compared with explanations related to aspects of the physical environment. These last ones are less ambiguous, because the physical world is less changeable. When we adopt a stance of mentalization, the mere contemplation of possible alternatives can lead to changes in beliefs. When we focus on the mind, we often come to erroneous conclusions. Many more than if we focus on the physical circumstances. This is because focusing on the mind is the same as focusing on a representation of reality, rather than on reality itself. We can act according to some erroneous beliefs about the mental states of the others. And this causes problematic situations with others, which sometimes brings terrible consequences. In the middle ages, if people believed that a person was possessed by the devil, it was enough to burn it.

Mentalization is a mental activity, predominantly unconscious and imaginative. It is imaginative because we have to imagine what the other person might be thinking, or feeling. If it lacks homogeneity, it is because each one's history is personal, and the ability to imagine can lead to them and us to different conclusions about the mental states of others. We, sometimes, need to do an imaginative leap, in order to understand our own experiences, particularly in relation to emotionally charged topics, or to irrational or unconscious impulsive reactions. Adopting an attitude of mentalization, conceiving oneself and conceiving others as having a mind, requires a representational system of mental states. Although mentalization probably involves numerous cortical systems, it is certainly associated with the activation of the middle pre-frontal area of the brain, probably with the para-cingulate area.

Focusing on mental states, it seems to be self-evident, for those who deal with treating individuals with mental disorders. But even us, psychotherapists, who are busy in our daily clinical work, we can also easily forget that our patients have a mind. For example, many biological psychiatrists feel really happy when thinking in terms of neurotransmitters that distortion expectations or self-representations. Also, parents with children who have psychological problems, often prefer to understand them in terms of genetic predispositions, rather than thinking that the cause might be due to the child's social environment. Even some psychotherapists may make unjustified assumptions about the theories about the illness their patients bring.

The basic assumption of modern development theory is that of a primary intersubjectivity, (Trevarthen, 1979). That is, knowledge about the world, is a shared knowledge. This idea, of a shared consciousness in childhood, is not new. An increasing number of researchers have emphasized the fundamental functions of such a shared attitude. Mind-sharing, established on the early stages of development, have been considered by many mind philosophers (Cavell, 1994) and relational psychoanalysts (Mitchell, 2000), as giving a stable feature to mental function. One of the ways in which we can better understand this, is that the influence of the relationship in mentalization is better explained by the assumption that the acquisition of the theory of the mind is part of an intersubjective process that is between the caregiver and child. From this point of view, the caregiver helps the child to create models for mentalizing, through linguistic and quasi linguistics processes, which involves verbal and no-verbal aspects of social interaction, within a context of attachment. This is also applicable to the psychotherapeutic task, in which the therapist, acting as a safe base to explore the world, helps the patient to develop jointly the reflexive function. This process of mentalizing also extends to other areas of life, and I have written a book called *The Enigma of Anguish: a conceptualization of anxiety from the relational vortex*, where I apply mentalization to better understand this emotion[3] (Martínez Ibáñez, J.J. 2017).

12-month-old infants are not yet involved in joint care, although, they also try to establish it by paying attention to something shared. For example, in a study (Liszkowski, Carpenter, Henning, Striano y Tomasello, 2004) they observed how 12-month-old infants behaved in front of an adult, who reacts towards the orientation behavior. The babies weren't happy when the adult simply followed their gaze, where the baby pointed, or looked at the child with positive affect, or did nothing. However, they were satisfied when the adult responded by looking back and forth at the object the baby was pointing, and made positive comments. Which implies, that this sharing attention, recognition and interest were in fact their objective. 12-month-old babies show happiness, just to inform an adult, of the location of an object that they seemed to have no interest in. Such motives, declarative and informative, are apparently purely social in their objectives.

The child assumes that this knowledge is shared by everyone. What he/she knows, is known by others and vice versa. That is, the world is shared by all, among all, and slowly, achieves the uniqueness of its own differentiated perspective. In this way, it also manages to develop its own mental self. In relation to what we know, and we understand about reality, we begin with the

---

3 Title translated to English by the translator.

assumption that knowledge is common, and that there is nothing unique about our knowledge or our feelings. In this way, children report what the other children will know, what they themselves have learned (Taylor, Esbensen & Bennet, 1994). We assume that everyone has the same knowledge as we do, because most of the beliefs we have about the world were our caregiver's beliefs, before we could make our own.

Children do not know that they are separated. That their internal worlds are something private and individual, of which they will eventually appropriate, or at least have privileged access. This configuration of development forms the unconscious fantasy, and prepares the desire for unity and fusion. They do not know that they can choose if, for example, to share their thoughts and feelings with their parents or therapist. Perhaps, one reason why children are so prone to outbursts of anger and frustration is that, as the world and individual minds are not yet clearly delimited, they expect others to know what they are thinking and feeling, and that they can see situations in the same way they do. Also, the frustration of their desires seems to be something evil, or an obtuse fact, rather than the result of a different point of view, or to prioritize some alternatives and so on.

Mentalization is developed, based on the biological predisposition of the child, that their knowledge is shared by all. The child naturally goes to the caregiver to learn from him/her about the nature of the internal and external world. Unconsciously and generalized, the caregiver attributes a mental state to the child, through his/her behavior, treating the child as a mental agent. Finally, the child concludes that the caregiver's reaction towards him/her gives sense to the inner mental states within him/her. This conclusion allows him/her to elaborate the mental models of cause and facilitates the development of a central sense of individuality, organized along these lines. We assume that that is, in general, a mundane process, and that it is unconscious, both for the child and for the parents, and is inaccessible to reflection or modification.

Parents, however, perform this natural human function in different ways. Some are alert to the early indications of intentionality, while others may need strong cues before they can perceive the child's mental state, and modify their behavior according to those cues. There are still other parents who, consistently, misinterpret their child's internal states; Their expectations, based on their past experiences, on their own internal operating models, dominate their mentalization and apply it on their children. These biases prevent the possibility of a contingent mirroring, and an emotional experience is reflected as incongruent with the child's constitutional experience. There are still other parents, who fail to mark their mirroring.

Therefore, in order for an adequate mentalizing process to be developed, it is necessary that the parent's responses to the needs of the child to adjust on a contingent manner, developing a mutual mental functioning, and reciprocal correspondence. If we take this to the professional field with the patients, it is about the therapist generating a relational space of intimacy and mutuality with the patient. Increasing cumulative evidence, both from clinical observation and form systematic research, indicate that the therapeutic relationship is one of the most powerful sources of therapeutic change, as Alejandro Ávila (2005) affirms, in the title of a very interesting paper: "To psychic change is accessed by the relationship". But we will look at it closely on the next point.

From Interaction to Relationship. The Role of Intimacy And Mutuality

In his book The first relationship: infant and mother, Daniel Stern (1985), has a chapter focused on differencing interaction from relationship. I believe that this differentiation is important, because it allows us to clearly describe two different kinds of behavior. Stern says: "We have been dealing so far with the interactions between the infant and his/her mother (or the person who acts as the mother). We must now begin to study the mother-child relationship and how it emerges from the multiple interactions that contribute to its formation. This is a difficult jump" (Ibid, p. 151).

Why does Stern stop to differentiate interaction from relationship? In my opinion, he does it because what happens between a baby and his/her mother or caregiver is a process. It is a process that begins with the interaction between both. Mother and baby need each other. But first they need know each other and that takes time. It is not immediate. The behavior of interaction is basically exploration, inquiry. The mother doesn't know the baby she has been carrying for months, and, of course, the baby doesn't know the person who is willing to let him/her live. They need to take the time to get to know each other. This first period is that of interaction.

But Daniel Stern keep telling us that: "A relationship is certainly deter-mined by the history of all separate and distinct interactions, but it implies more than the sum of past and present interactions. From a conceptual point of view, it is a different kind of organization, or a different integration of experience. One of its most important features is a persistent mental image, or scheme, or a representation of the other person". (Ibid, p. 151). Here, Stern clarifies an important difference. A relationship would be the consequence of a continuous succession of interactions in different activities, until the baby can integrate and maintain them in his/her mind, forming a representation of that person.

But let's stick with Stern: "Can we talk about an infant as someone who maintains a relationship? A categorical answer cannot be given here. However, towards the second part of the first year of life, the child shows behaviors that indicate, with great credibility, that we can begin to talk about relationships. Towards the ninth month of life, approximately, the child manifests what is designated as "reaction to the stranger". "This reaction can vary widely, from a certain prevention, to an extreme dislike of the approach or in the presence of an unknown person" (Ibid, p. 151-152). Here, Stern already clarifies that the difference between interaction and relationship would have to do with different elements of a person which, at a given moment, are integrated and form a representation of that person. Stern considers that this could occur taking into account that, in addition to the sensory and motor experiences that the child is developing, the emotional experience is added too.

Stern also tell us that: "Human behavior is almost always changing and even the inner experiences of excitement and emotion are subject to momentary variations of intensity and direction... I believe that, at least in the area of interactive human behavior, there is a unit of basic process of interactive experience which is not, necessarily, the smallest measure of perception in any mode, but rather the minimum in which a temporary and dynamic interactive event can occur, with a beginning, a middle and an end... These interpersonal procedural units may be the units of sensorimotor-emotional experience, that are initially internalized as separate representations and which, when integrated, constitutes a wider representation of another person (Ibid, p. 157-158). As we see here, Stern clarifies that to reach to the relationship we need to develop a process, which begins with successive interactions, where the sensory, motor, and emotional aspects are present, until the infant's mind can integrate them and from there, be able to generate a representation of that gesture in that person. As the infant grows in an environment that facilitates this type of interactions, the integrations that he/she will make will also have to do with a greater width of the aspects of that person that he/she will integrate.

So, the encounter between the mother and the baby, in which the intimacy predominates, begins with successive interactions where the sensorial, motor, and emotional aspects are present, which will allow, to the extent that these interactions are contingent, to be mutual, that the baby's mind integrates them in an appropriate way, allowing an adequate representation and, thus, initiate a relationship.

This means that the baby can always integrate these aspects, but some of them will be more adaptive than others, because they will depend on the emotional aspect of the successive interactions that the baby has in that environment of intimacy. And this is where I think that the aspect of mutuality, reciprocity, and intimacy take on its greatest importance. If we become aware of the successive interactions in the intimate encounters between mother and baby, whenever a "climate" of harmony, mutuality, and reciprocity develops between them, it is possible for the baby to integrate successfully that mental model.

Now, so we can talk about relationship, we will have to consider this emotional aspect of the basic processual unity of experience. If in the next interactions between the two, there isn't a mutual correspondence, a reciprocity, both minds will not be able to establish a relationship, but will continue to interact. This will cause that both minds detect deficits that later will have their consequences throughout life.

That's why I make this difference between interaction and relationship. For example, when there is a sport activity, the fans who are in the stands, interact with each other, they don't relate. This is because the factor of intimacy is not present. But usually this is defined as a relationship, the fans are relating to each other. In another example, we can think more clearly, if a child comes home from school crying, and his mother or father at that time, who are in the house, but busy with some activities, do not come close to find out what's wrong with the child, by the mere fact of being at home, they are already transmitting safety and protection, but there is no mutuality. They could tell him, "again crying", "you always come home crying", etc. So, the need for emotional support that could be given through a reflective dialogue, through mentalizing that situation, doesn't exist. Here we would say that there is interaction, but there is no relationship, because mutuality is missing.

These two factors united, intimacy and mutuality, are fundamental for me to understand the difference between interaction and relationship in the mental functioning. Our mind is developed following these processes, whether they are present or missing, in which case we would find a deficit development. This deficit development is what characterizes insecure attachment systems. Through attachment behavior, the child gets someone to protecting him/her, but he/she will not always get to feel well, comfortable and happy. It will depend on the quality of the intersubjective bond that is established between the child and his/her caregiver.

All that we have develop until here, has been to be able to affirm that, although, through attachment behavior, in that particular interaction of intimacy, it is achieved that the person in need of protection and security obtains it, but not always this behavior is going to go together to get calm and relaxation. This last one can only be achieved through a reflexive dialogue, in which the role of mutuality is fundamental. If the person who offers protection doesn't develop a reflexive dialogue, that is, if it doesn't connect in a mutual way with the needs of the other, it will only generate a process of interaction, but a relationship will not really be established. This seems superfluous, but it has its importance if we move it to the field of psychotherapeutic practice.

If during the development of a psychotherapeutic process, the therapist establishes a relationship of intimacy with the patient, the patient may feel safe in that therapeutic space, but in order to transform the contents of his/her deficit mind into more adaptive mental models to the reality that is living, he/she will need to develop a reflective dialogue between them, a mentalizing process, so communication can be mutual. We must not forget that, in order for our mind to develop, we have needed the help of another mind, but in a shared space of intimate warmth, garnished with a reflective process, a mentalizing process, that can transform hunger in satisfaction, loneliness in company, fears of a stalking death and anguish in vitality and confidence. Doing so, enables the patient to grow mentally, both emotionally and cognitively, more adaptive, healthier.

Conclusions

We have begun this journey, taking into account all the contributions we receive from the field of research in the different fields of science that study the human being. We have followed this route because our scope of work is with other human beings. And, although our field covers the area of the mental, knowing how human beings are mentally, is fundamental to be able to help them in an efficient and time-saving way.

Then, we have explored the field of the mind, managing to define it satisfactorily, always taking into account all the scientific contributions. And we have said that the mind is a process, which is always cognitive and affective and that the function it has is to regulate energy flow and information. As our mind is co-created through attachment behavior, we have walked through the theory of attachment. Subsequently for the mind to develop, it needs to communicate with another person. In order for intersubjective processes to be implemented, we need to develop them through mentalization or reflexive dialogue.

And we end our journey by stating that, in order to have an authentic relationship with the patient and to enable him/her to modify his/her deficient mental models that do not allow him/her to adapt well to his/her reality, relational psychotherapists need to develop with the patient a space of transparency to achieve the necessary intimacy and a reflexive dialogue in order to achieve mutuality. That's how we reproduce in the consultation those initial moments of human life, where, in order to grow, we need another person who can offer us a space of intimacy, and that, in many moments, also can bring us a relationship of mutuality. In this way, and not another, we were able to co-create and develop our mind.

Summary

Mind is a process, always cognitive and affective, functioning to regulate energy and information flows. Our mind is co-created through attachment behavior as an developing mind who needs to communicate with another subject. Intersubjective processes to be implemented, need to de developed through mentalization or reflexive dialogue. In order to have an authentic relationship with the patient and to enable him to modify his deficient mental models that do not allow him to adapt well to his reality, relational psychotherapists need to develop with the patient a space of transparency for Achieve the necessary intimacy and a reflexive dialogue to achieve mutuality. Thus we reproduce in the consultation those initial moments of human life, where in order to grow we need another person who offered us a space of intimacy and that in many moments also brought us a relationship of mutuality. In this way and not another, we were able to co-create and develop our mind.

7

Trauma: Discontinuity of the Sense of Self. The Relational Way to Meeting Oneself Anew

Manuel Aburto Baselga

Introduction

Some years ago at a meeting with a group of professionals interested in trauma, I commented to one of those present that I had never treated that type of patient. "That's what you think!", he replied emphatically. I realised that those colleagues did not understand psychological trauma (and its official clinical formulation, Post-Traumatic Stress Disorder) as only existing within the framework of a separate diagnostic category, but as a perspective from which to comprehend psychopathology. Including patients' actual traumatic experiences in the equation and perceiving their symptoms as attempts to adapt to unmetabolised experience changed the clinical outlook.

The year, the same group of colleagues invited the American psychiatrist Bessel van der Kolk, one of the foremost scholars of trauma, to give a seminar on the subject in Salamanca. In the discussion following one of the sessions, a Spanish psychiatrist asked the author whether PTSD was a politically-inspired American invention to deal with the problems regarding their Vietnam war veterans. Van der Kolk replied, with certain irony, that one of the countries where trauma was being most researched was Norway, where "someone has hit someone" would make the headlines. In short, in the afterglow of the anti-Yankeeism of the late 1990s, there was still some resistance to fully integrating a new diagnostic category into everyday clinical work, especially when it meant a change of perspective when looking at a patient's biography.

As van der Kolk noted (1996), recognising the role psychological trauma has played in psychopathology has gone through many vicissitudes. Symptoms persisting a "reasonable" time after a traumatic event raised suspicions they were factitious. The Protean field of hysteria gave rise to diverse hypotheses regarding its aetiology, amongst them (with Janet), trauma. However, the prevailing scientific currents also contemplated simulation or some uncertain neurological degenerative disorder, ignoring the reality of a child's traumatic past.

Also in the context of the changing history of trauma, Judith Herman (1994) refers us to the socio-political context which, depending on the particular time in history, either did or did not favour recognition of victims and therefore the existence of a violence that was hard for society to accept. The feminist perspective that Herman's work inspires emphasises gender violence and child abuse; Herman is pioneer in this area, which is so open to clinical reflection and political intervention today. We will briefly review some of those moments in history to guide us in our reflections.

I shall not go into the familiar debate that gave rise to this new diagnostic category. Its advocates ultimately aspired for "official" recognition of something that had been known about since times of old: that certain life experiences could overwhelm a person's capacity for adaptation and cause serious mental suffering with its own course of chronification. Pre-exisisting mental illness was not an indispensable factor.

Adopting the "psychotraumatological" perspective in psychotherapy was not limited, in my case, to incorporating the new diagnosis to the "clinical population" and reordering it according to defining criteria. For me it meant broadening the way of listening to patients and reflecting on what was happening between us; it was fundamental in my moving towards a relational psychoanalytic perspective. I not only became interested in the "bio-psycho-social model" of traumatic illness described in PTSD, but also I became more aware of concepts such as vulnerability and resilience, the breakdown in basic trust, and the basic assumptions that implicitly sustain our lives. Naturally, I was more interested in trauma caused by human action than "acts of God".

A very special facet in trauma is its transgenerational transmission, which has been widely studied in the children (and grandchildren) of Holocaust survivors. If the experience of those surviving the concentration camps was a paradigm for researchers of the limits of "psychological life," the effects of this experience passed on to their children made it possible to study the dynamic unconscious of fantasies and identifications that arose in order to make sense of the indescribable .

The cruelty and misery of the Spanish Civil War has been extensively documented. The war was followed by a dictatorship lasting nearly forty years which, among other things, silenced the voices of the defeated and imposed a sole perspective of the conflict. Rebuilding social cohesion was made at the expense of economic recovery under the aegis of an authoritarian state. Fear of diversity was exorcised by the imposition of unity; there was a single narrative that delegitimised other accounts, ideas or experiences. How many silences were accrued in communities and families over the following years? How were losses of all kinds, humiliation, powerlessness, surrender, and renunciation transmitted in private? Are we going too far in thinking that three generations later, we are still living with the aftermath of unresolved social trauma? A patient I treated for a short time had a distinctive medical history: a sudden disruption of consciousness that was diagnosed as Ganser Syndrome. This episode (which evolved into recurrent episodes) occurred in April 1977, shortly after the Communist Party was legalised in Spain (and represented by the same people who had already been leaders during the war). My patient told me that at the beginning of the war, when she was about 6 years old, a group of militiamen set fire to her house with her whole family still inside. She and her mother were able to escape, but not her father or other relatives. Were we looking at the delayed effects of trauma? Traumatic memory prevents historical memory from becoming fully established.

Trauma Through History

As psychotherapists we wonder about the origin of the psychological afflictions and mental suffering of the people who come to us for help. We define fields where we can use the therapeutic tools available: where genetics seems to prevail, our hermeneutic capabilities are limited. In regard to life crises, it will primarily be the misfortunes, tensions of growth, and decadence (of variable intensities) which fill human life that will set aside a special place for us and grant us our professional status. Then there is the vast area in which humans suffer and break down without really knowing why, and they come to us bringing their symptoms and uncertainties, and mobilise our already established and more recent knowledge, setting in motion inquiry that requires our full involvement. We strive to understand and explain all that psychopathology through refined models of the mind that are subject to continuous reflection. It is that fuzzy area where psychoanalytically-oriented psychotherapists before searched for out-of-tune traces of drives and their unconscious fantasies, but where now, together with the patient, we build ways to understand and change implicit relational knowing. These areas obviously overlap and merge, and they expand or contract depending on every particular epistemological position.

Before I referred to personal crises as being times in life when there is a discontinuity in the fundamental factors that underpin a person's sense of identity: gender and gender roles, body image, social status, professional identity, emotional bonds. Change, be it growth or blockages (even regression) is associated with the idea of discontinuity. What differentiates trauma from stress, or from grief?

It would seem that when we talk about stress (without the descriptor 'traumatic'), we refer to an adaptive over-exertion that can lead to exhaustion. But as Benyacar says (2005), situations become "problematic" when they "test the subject's defences, because they arise from the obstruction of a desire, expectation or prior internal need."[1]

Authors such as Horowitz liken trauma and grief, while others differentiate and distinguish between traumatic and non-traumatic grief.

Some authors emphasise the "economic" aspect of trauma, considering the "psyche as being flooded by real external factors" (Benyacar, 2005).

We could also say that trauma is, by definition, something that cannot be taken on board, it violates the basic elements of a person's relationship with his context without it being possible to reorganise these elements in a way that would allow life to continue under the same identity. These basic elements, parameters that regulate our relationships with the world from the start, are not visible, that is, they are only manifest when they break down, in the same way that the existence of air is revealed by its absence.

How have humans formulated and addressed these experiences throughout the course of history? What is the scientific history of trauma?

---

1 Unless otherwise indicated in the bibliography, quotes have been translated from texts in Spanish.

And what particularly concerns us: what place has trauma had in the history of psychoanalysis?

In terms of the general scientific community, we now have a specified field, clinically defined by the APA's bible, the DSM, in its fifth edition, as well as the WHO's counterpart, the ICD-10. These two texts gather and condense a huge amount of clinical knowledge about trauma; they instil order, establish benchmarks and milestones, criteria and time periods, and bring together the most visible parts of a confusing post-traumatic psychopathology. Every time the publication of a new edition approaches, the expectation of what this influential text will include or exclude increases: pertinent fields of research will strive to provide data and evidence to determine the results. There is no need to reiterate the powerful effects these inclusions or exclusions have on patients, therapists, industry, decisions on legal and labour issues, etc. However, neither the DSM nor the ICD are clear about - nor do they attempt to be so - the many questions relating to the subjective experience of trauma nor, naturally, the way we relate therapeutically to the traumatised person.

These classifications have recognised that people can become ill and the illness can become chronic after suffering either a one-off or a continued impact of an external threatening situation. Recognition of the countless consequences was set down with the inclusion of Post-Traumatic Stress Disorder in the 1980 publication of the DSM-III. It included a diagnostic category in which the external cause of trauma was made explicit.

Evidently, traumatic neuroses had long since been known about: clinical profiles that appeared in the wake of catastrophic events, accidents, attacks, etc. But to what extent did civil society and the scientific community in particular recognise the long-lasting effects of post-traumatic sequelae before considering them fraudulent or expressions of hysteria? To what extent were the sequelae of psychological trauma accepted as clinical symptoms and when were they viewed as cowardice or malingering? Could the sexual abuse of children be accepted a cause of trauma? What did the traumas of the twentieth century teach us?

As stated above, official recognition of PTSD has been of great importance, and this influence has been felt in many areas of life: psychiatry and psychology; in legal, social and labour spheres, etc. In the same way that the anti-Vietnam War movement fought for the recognition of the psychological effects on veterans, feminist organisations pushed for epidemiological and clinical research into domestic abuse and violence against women and children.

Memory has always been a key issue in the study of trauma. Researchers realised that traumatic memories are stored in a special way in relation to the situation, and could remain inaccessible to verbalisation for long periods of time.

After severe trauma, understanding the relationship between the event and the victim's reaction is simple. In these cases, disturbing memories seem to be the main problem. But with time, when some patients develop a secondary adaptation to trauma, the relationship between their symptoms and life events blurs. It is not easy to associate the widespread affective dysregulation and constraints on the self seen in these patients with specific events in their lives.

This is more evident in people who were traumatised as children since early trauma directly affects the maturation of the systems responsible for regulating psycho-biological processes. Disruption of these self-regulatory processes means these people are more vulnerable and tend to become more chronically emotionally unstable, engage in behaviour that is destructive to self and others, and suffer from learning disorders, dissociative problems, somatisations and distortions in their concepts of self and others.

When a child is abused by an attachment figure, a fundamental element for the development of a person in society is violated – it is an intrinsic element of relating which forms part of the relational background that accompanies the child from birth. When a woman is sexually assaulted, faith that her own bodily intimacy is in her own domain and not the will of another is shattered. When a bomb explodes on a rush-hour train, faith in the predictability of the risks of everyday life is shattered; this faith prevails in people's sociocultural contexts without them even being aware. When people are victimised by others, basic assumptions that invisibly set down the very possibility of a social environment are destroyed. How can catastrophes such as these articulate with the suffering individual's own particular context of affective bonds

Freud And Trauma

The concept of trauma in Freud's work has undergone changes and developments according to the conceptualisations that organised his thinking. In the beginning, he placed traumatic neurosis (such as train accidents and war) and neurosis of defence together. In other words, he considered a common factor of an experience from the past capable of generating pathological effects: an element invades the psychic apparatus, altering its operation, be it an acute, unexpected, life-threatening event, or an incident of a sexual nature that intrudes upon a child's development.

During World War I, some doctors opted for non-punitive methods in treating war neuroses; many of them were familiar with Freud's ideas, although not all were practising psychoanalysts. Clinicians such as Rivers, Brown and Ernst Simmel realised they could help soldiers by bringing traumatic memories into consciousness, so generating emotional abreaction and a reintegration of the patient's mind.

But many of them went no further in their use of psychoanalytic theory when treating traumatised soldiers. In his biography of Freud, Louis Breger (2001) stresses Freud and his followers' eagerness to find support for their theories in medical circles. Hence Freudians considered the reports of clinicians treating traumatised soldiers through cathartic techniques to be an endorsement of his ideas, despite the role of sexuality not being recognised in the aetiology of these afflictions. Breger is particularly critical of Karl Abraham for taking psycho-sexual interpretation of traumatic symptoms "to grotesque limits" in the soldiers he was treating.

Unlike many doctors of his time, Freud did not take under his care soldiers who were wounded or discharged for psychiatric disorders. According to Breger, this lack of hands-on experience, which might have changed his perspective, caused him to continue making errors regarding traumatic neuroses; these errors persisted over time as they were associated with the prestige of Freud's name.

Breger portrays a Freud who is unconcerned with the clinical reality offered by countless cases of affected soldiers, and who was blindly committed to the theoretical development of a sexual aetiology for psychic trauma. Thus, it was thought that after the war, soldiers would soon forget their experiences once they returned home, and so, with the war behind them, most neurotic illness caused by the war would also disappear. However, as we know, many soldiers continued to be affected by the traumas of war many years later, and were unable to reconcile the realities they had lived through in a common identity. Being committed to a theory that explained war neurosis in terms of an individual's innate forces (the sexual instinct, primitive aggression), Freud did not have the language to describe the identity disorders and social alienation that so deeply affected the former soldiers (op.cit. 339). So according to Breger's standpoint (shared with many contemporary authors), the legacy of psychoanalysis and descriptive psychiatry had a disastrous influence in the years following the First World War. The idea that crises emerging during combat were due solely to pre-existing weaknesses of the personality - that the real stress occurring in combat situations should not be taken into account - took root in military policy. Freudian assumptions regarding infantile disposition continued to dominate psychiatric thinking during the Vietnam War. So, the focus was still on the causes of disorders lying in early developmental conflicts rather than on recent traumatic experiences caused by overwhelming emotional impacts. Under the powerful influence of psychoanalysis, it was still not fully accepted that certain events in adulthood could leave such an indelible mark without resorting to the mechanism of deffered action. In Bleger's words , "the encounter between psychoanalysis and the war neuroses shows us a Freud confronting survivors of trauma and, like his hysterical patients of the 1890s, seeing then looking away from what he saw ... his need to uphold his sweeping theory of sexuality to explain everything in terms of internal- instinctual forces while ignoring the complex social conditions, to prove that psychoanalysis already knew about these conditions, blinded him to the evidence before his eyes "(p342).

The Development of Freud's Thinking About Trauma

When Freud discovered the value of the internal reality of fantasies (after ceasing to believe his neurotic patients), he termed any representational core triggering a pathogenic process as trauma, beyond its cause - whether external (a factual event) or internal (a mental event activated by desire or as a result of a failure of the defences with a consequent "return of the repressed").

This is the time of the famous letter from Freud to Fliess, dated 21st April, 1897, which is studied in detail by all students of Freud, and which is put forward as proof by those who accuse Freud of a self-serving abandonment of the seduction theory. The "awful truth" (according to Jones) that Freud confesses to his friend, and is summed up in his famous phrase: "I no longer believe in my neurotica".

Jeffrey Moussaieff Masson (1985) published a book titled "The assault on truth", which was described as "the Watergate of the psyche" and which, based on extensive, meticulous documentary research, denounced Freud's relinquishing his seduction theory, which was made public in 1905 with the publication of "Three Essays on the Theory of Sexuality".

Many authors have criticised both Masson's data and his conclusions. Despite criticising Masson's arguments, Fischer (1999) recognises that both his work, as well as that of Alice Miller (1981), led to the following epistemological question, "To what extent does psychoanalysis (and psychology in general) take into account an appropriate balance between intrapsychic factors and external contextual circumstances when considering their importance in psychological development? To what degree does it lose sight of the dialectical relationship between the constellation of subjective needs and objective situational factors to 'concentrate on what is purely intrapsychic'?" (p 35). The authors thus direct criticism towards Melanie Klein or Bion, while preserving Freud.

There can be said to be new change in theory when, based on a study of the ego and a progressive formulation of the theory of narcissism, it became necessary to conceptualise the dangers threatening an individual, the anxieties he suffers and feelings of helplessness. Freud busied himself with clinical cases which seemed to question the central hypothesis of the tendency to seek pleasure and avoid pain as a fundamental dynamic element. And *Beyond the Pleasure Principle* was published in 1920.

Most authors feel this essay is key in the Freudian development of trauma. According to Breger, Freud changed his commitment to the principle of sexuality (as far as seeking pleasure is concerned) as the main motivation of human behaviour.

Freud evidently dealt with traumatic neuroses associated with accidents and war neuroses. We should bear in mind the essay in question on was published shortly after the First World War, and Freud expressly referred to these neuroses as not being explained by direct damage to the nervous system.

The terrible war that has recently terminated has caused a huge number of such afflictions (traumatic neuroses), and put an end to the temptation to attribute them to an organic damage done to the nervous system by mechanical force (Freud, 1920, 'Beyond the Pleasure Principle').

The symptoms of traumatic neuroses were for Freud, similar to those of hysteria, but with greater subjective suffering, and the weakening and deterioration of psychological capacity.

The symptoms of traumatic neuroses resemble hysteria in the wealth of similar motor symptoms, but generally surpass the latter in clearly discernible signs of subjective suffering, hypochondria or melancholia, and more extensive signs of fragility and disorganisation of mental faculties (op. cit)

It is at this point where he established the difference between **apprehension,** (referred to as the expectation of some harm and allows an individual to be prepared for it), **fear** (requiring the presence of a definite object), and **fright** (which describes the state in which we find ourselves when we are unexpectedly endangered). What distinguished the latter, therefore, is the surprise factor, *die Überraschung.* In this sense, apprehension will not cause trauma, but protect us from it as it gives us the opportunity to "prepare" for danger. We will see how this develops further on.

Freud would go on to analyse recurring dreams in traumatic neuroses that, far from being a means to fulfilling desires, place the person back in the traumatising situation. He would also go on to address repetition of offences and narcissistic wounds suffered in childhood in the transference. He would also refer to the "destiny neuroses" in subjects who seemed to inexorably repeat the same behavioural and relational patterns that led them to frustration and misfortune time and time again, and which could not be understood from the dynamics of the principle of pleasure.

After working through various considerations regarding masochistic dynamics, repetition for the pleasure of mastery, etc., Freud concluded that "the impulse to work over in the mind some overpowering experience so as to make oneself master of it can find expression as a primary event, and independently of the pleasure principle." (Freud, 1920) Therefore, repetition compulsion would be more primitive, basic and instinctual than the pleasure principle.

Benyakar (2005) points out that this is the birth of an original theory of traumatic neuroses, based on the hypothesis of "psychic mastery" of experience as a primary need of the psyche. Thus, the phenomena of the repetition of what is unpleasurable (characteristic of the psychopathology of trauma) are due to the lack of a minimum binding of energy that is necessary to enable thought processes. Freud illustrated this idea by observing the familiar "fort-da" game, by which the child worked through his mother's absence - a situation which made him feel helpless and caused passive suffering. The child symbolically became active in this process of losing and regaining the reel, achieving a sense of mastery. Freud posed the theory of mastery at the start of *Beyond the Pleasure Principle* and offered a coherent explanation for a set of phenomena that brought together childhood play, the enjoyment of adults recreating potentially traumatising situations in theatre and fiction, dreams and nightmares, and trauma in general.

Along with the idea of a primary process for mastering psychic energy, Freud set out in his text his well-known idea of a stimulus barrier that emulates the skin covering and protecting the body, but in the psyche. The intensity of stimuli is adapted (or not) to the capacity of the barrier, which, despite the pertinence of energy metaphors, poses the idea that trauma is not linearly dependent on the intensity of the stimulus but also on the capacity of the barrier. Emphasis is thus placed on the interrelation between external and internal worlds and, ultimately, on what is subjective.

In *Inhibitions, Symptoms and Anxiety* (1926), Freud makes a distinction between *automatic* and *signal anxiety*. Automatic anxiety is triggered when it is impossible to emerge from a dangerous situation unharmed, and is associated to the subject's self-perception of helplessness. Signal anxiety is triggered by the ego through the memory of a dangerous situation which is analogous to the present one, and allows the subject to prepare for it.

The following is the summary of Freud's idea: *"Taking this sequence, anxiety—danger—helplessness (trauma), we can now summarize what has been said. A danger-situation is a recognized, remembered, expected situation of helplessness. Anxiety is the original reaction to helplessness in the trauma and is reproduced later on in the danger-situation as a signal for help. The ego, which experienced the trauma passively, now repeats it actively in a weakened version, in the hope of being able itself to direct its course.* (Freud, 1926 (pp 166-7 op. cit.)

The Exception: Sandor Ferenczi

Ferenczi insisted (and this would be his main bone of contention with Freud) that all psychological suffering is always triggered by a *real* traumatic factor. He attributed a key role to external objects structuring a child's mental apparatus, emphasizing how injurious others' psychic realities might be when they yield the power to give or impose their own meaning to all relational experience. He defended before the psychoanalysts of his day the reality of childhood trauma that adult patients relived in the consulting room, and denounced the fact that real trauma had been relegated in favour of unconscious fantasy, especially with respect to the sexual trauma: *"Even children of respected, high-minded puritanical families fall victim to real rape much more frequently than one had dared to suspect."*(Cited from Masson (2003).

Ferenczi abandoned the technique of analytic distance as he realised that with traumatized patients at times it is therapeutically necessary to be absolutely frank, admit mistakes and even reveal one's own feelings. He emphasised a breach of a child's trust when an adult distorts, denies or trivialises a situation, leading to the child questioning his or her own perception. Ferenczi foresaw many of the factors and traumatic effects that are under discussion today: fragmentation of the self; enactment through what represents the trauma in therapy; splitting of the self into an observer and an alienated body; blunted affects, and especially, the effect of an aggressor's silence on a child.

In his posthumous paper "Some thoughts on trauma" (Int. Zeits. 1934), consisting of five notes written at different times between 1931 and 1932, all on the subject of trauma, Ferenczi offers some interesting reflections on the psychic commotion inherent to trauma and the psyche's attempts to resolve the traumatic situation through dreaming. Ferenczi works in close connection to the clinical situation, as if he were constantly thinking from within his patients' skin. Psychic commotion (*Erschütterung*) is produced by surprise and induces a sudden state of helplessness where before there was confidence

When there is no possibility of acting on the environment in order to modify a threatening situation or flee from it, the alternative is self-destruction, which as a liberating factor, is preferred over passive suffering. This self-destruction acts primarily on the consciousness, prompting dissociation. In this way, the perception of the harm affecting the subject can be checked.

An unexpected, unanticipated, devastating shock can act as a kind of anaesthetic, that is, it detains psychic activity and installs a passive state of non-resistance. Perception is restrained, leaving the personality defenceless. A shock that has not been received cannot be defended against. The result of the paralysis is that while it lasts, any mechanical and psychic shock is accepted without resistance and there will be no memory trace of the impact; thus the source of the commotion will not be accessible from memory.

Subsequent Developments

From the 1950s onwards, different approaches in psychoanalysis began studying the deficits in mother-infant relationships and the traumatic effects on children. Concepts such as "strain trauma", "silent trauma", "cumulative trauma", "deprivation trauma" were coined, and the focus was put on children's relationships with their objects. The concept of trauma risked losing its specificity when it became blurred with adverse conditions or deficits in the mother-child relationship.

However, it is true that object relations theory no longer took into account a single unique event as a paradigm of trauma, with its economic idea of an unbearable quantity of arousal. What was critical about the new model was the relationship between the child and its objects: it is not the incident that is determinative in itself, but the relationship that sustains it. As is currently believed, trauma does not depend on physical injury in itself but the fact that the children are abused by those they depend on for care and protection.

As I have said, Ferenczi envisioned these views, and authors such as Balint went on to take up the torch. This way of seeing things broadened the understanding of psychic reality in traumatic situations. The more massive trauma is, the more internal object relationships deteriorate and communication between representations of the self and the good object is dissolved. Extreme examples of this can be found in the case of concentration camps, as we shall see further on.

War And Trauma

Judith Herman (1997) distinguishes three basic elements in the study of trauma:

- Hysteria, the study of which flourished under the French Republican, anticlerical political movement of the late 19th century
- War trauma or combat neurosis, beginning after World War II and reaching its peak in a context of peace movements after the Vietnam War.
- The denunciation and investigation of sexual and domestic violence, especially driven by the feminist movements in Europe and North America.

War has been of major importance in the scientific study of psychic trauma. It is a "trial ground" that satisfies one of essential conditions of research: a similar traumatic event affecting large number of people simultaneously. The basic criteria for producing traumatic disorders are clearly satisfied:

- People feel their own lives and the lives of those around them are threatened
- They witness death or injury of others
- The loss of comrades
- They commit or are victims of violence

However, the weight of the evidence of the traumatic experience in these situations has become clear in retrospect. This was not the case at the outbreak of the First World War when military doctors met with massive numbers of psychiatric casualties for which they had no diagnostic criteria nor therapeutic tools. Many soldiers started behaving like "hysterical women" (Herman, 1997). The expression of the emotional uncontrol (with terror as a backdrop), paralysis included, was no longer exclusive to the stigmatised, denigrated hysterics; what was weakness, suggestibility or the absolute expression of a "labile feminine temperament" in hysterics, could only be cowardice or neurological damage for men at war. Nevertheless, the question of psychiatric casualties rapidly stopped being an issue limited to certain individuals and situations and became a major problem affecting the troops' morale.

It is particularly interesting to analyse the First World War from the contrast between two factors: the prevailing ideology in society and the values that sustained military spirit on the one hand, and on the other, the imposing technology of war made possible by advances in science and industrial capacity that had been achieved by the beginning of the 20th century.

Historians have highlighted how the militaristic zeal associated with the underlying patriotism in politicians of the warring countries spread like

155

wildfire to the rest of society, supplanting the sentiments of brotherhood and international solidarity promoted, for example, by the Socialist International.

Stefan Zweig (2002), who bore witness to the pre-war atmosphere in Vienna in 1914, described how even the intellectuals who had stood firmly against the war were finally swept up by the torrent of patriotic euphoria imbibed by society at large, which eradicated social and cultural barriers, and which led European society towards an unimaginable catastrophe.

I shall highlight two perspectives: firstly, that the nervous crises suffered by soldiers undermined military planning and weakened military strength; they also undermined the self-gratifying visions of national greatness (Breger, 2001). Secondly, the individual was not only defenceless before instruments that did not recognise his fear, but also his own scale of values could not easily accommodate his reactions without a catastrophic loss of self-esteem. This may explain the importance of feeling integrated in a group of comrades - this was later recognised as factor in healing.

The English physician W. H. Rivers, an advocate of psychotherapy, had many soldiers affected by war neuroses under his care. He recommended a therapeutic relationship based on trust and respect and where his patients could freely express their traumatic experiences. One of his patients, the officer Siegfried Sassoon, wrote the following of his experience with Rivers. (cited from Breger):

"When I closed his office door for the last time, I left behind someone who had helped and understood me more than anyone in my life. As much as he disliked sending me back to the trenches, he realised it was my only way out. As the years pass, I knew he was right "(p333).

I include this quote precisely because it arises in an ideological and professional context in which the therapeutic relationship was still not considered to be an integral element in treatment, and is thus genuine testimony, one that is not ideologically "contaminated". Furthermore, it is difficult to resist a metaphorical reading of Sassoon's lines, which could represent psychotherapeutic work as a whole, the metonymy of "trenches" becoming a metaphor for fighting for life.

Rivers established two principles that were used in the next war: firstly, men of undoubted courage had succumbed to overwhelming fear; and secondly, the most effective motivation in overcoming that fear was not patriotism, abstract principles or hatred of the enemy, but the love the soldiers felt towards one other (Herman, 1997). Group cohesion among comrades turned out to be the most important factor in protecting against psychological breakdown.

While experience gained from the traumatic neuroses of the Great War may not have been systematically applied in civilian society, some psychiatrists did continue their work and developed a body of theory that would become the basis of modern psychotraumatology. Abram Kardiner, who began his career treating war veterans, stands out among these specialists.

In his seminal book, *The traumatic neuroses of war,* he described in great detail the hyperarousal characterising these patients, who show a low threshold for startle reactivity and a state permanent alert. He also spoke of an altered conception of the self in relation with the world, based on fixation on the trauma, an atypical dream life, chronic irritability, and explosive aggressive reactions. According to Kardiner, the ego is specifically committed to the safety of the organism and to protecting itself against the return of traumatic memories. Van der Kolk (1996) highlights a central idea of Kardiner's, shared by Freud and Janet: the traumatised individual acts as if the original traumatic situation were still present and repeats defensive mechanisms that were not useful in the original situation. This confirms that a traumatised person's concept of the external world and of himself has been permanently altered.

During World War II there was recognition that any man could break down when under fire, and that psychiatric casualties could be foreseen in direct proportion to the severity of the exposure to combat. There is no such thing as becoming accustomed to combat, and psychiatric casualties are as inevitable as gunshot or shrapnel wounds. (Herman, 1997). At one point during the World War II, psychiatric casualties were occurring at a faster rate than people joining the army. After 60 days of continuous combat, 98% of survivors had become psychiatric casualties. And the remaining 2% were considered to have aggressive psychopathic personalities (Grossman, 1996).

Psychiatrists recognised that one of the main factors protecting against psychiatric breakdown was the bond with comrades; this guided the strategy for recovery towards the soldier's speedy reintegration into his battlegroup. Group debriefing techniques were also introduced.

However, widespread, systematic research on the traumatic effects of war experience only commenced after the Vietnam War. Self-organised veterans' groups were influential, and they denounced the abandonment, if not outright rejection, which soldiers confronted on their return home. These combatants in a conflict that was massively rejected by society received no recognition or honours that might give meaning to their sacrifices and their experience as victims and executioners. Their illnesses and difficulty adapting often ended up creating profiles that were more associated with delinquency or social exclusion than with victims.

In the early 1970s, the New York psychiatrists and psychoanalysts Robert Lifton and Chaim Shatan began meeting with veterans groups to talk about their experiences. Shatan published a short article in the New York Times in 1972 titled "Post-Vietnam Syndrome" giving the tragedy experienced by those veterans its first concise, clinical-sounding name. I quote the following particularly significant paragraph from the article:

In extreme situations-death camps, active warfare- grief threatens the morale necessary for survival and combat effectiveness. Both intimacy and grief are actively discouraged in the modern military. Trainees are cautioned against forming close friendships lest a buddy should die. However, since combatants are humans too, brutalization can only suppress, but not eradicate, the normal mammalian response to bereavement.

Shatan developed the concepts of the "double social and psychic wound" clarifying what has been stated above: combatants suffer the wound of the traumatic situation of combat, and when they return to their home countries, they are wounded a second time when repudiated and misunderstood by society. That is the double social wound. In its psychological form, soldiers suffer in the contrast between the reality of the traumatic experience and the reality found when back home. The contexts are radically contradictory and inconsistent, and internal conflict is inevitable.

How can we understand this "internal conflict" from a relational perspective?

First, by playing down the concept of "internal". The internal world is a reference we use to describe a self-state. The multiple states that comprise what is called sense of self is based on the variety of modes of interaction with the environment, which involve the sense organs to varying degrees, thus defining the inner-outer dimension. This dimension is based on fundamental bodily metaphors which in turn support conceptual systems (Lakoff and Johnson, 2012). A combatant experiences mental states which are wildly different to those he had at home, to the point that once the protective mechanisms maintaining psychological integrity are overwhelmed, the sense of continuity organising the subject's life as an agent is broken. On his return home, relationships with others do not include states like those in the harrowing context and which the combatant "seeks" in every loud noise or shadow in civilian life that invokes the threat he lived through. No re-encounter is possible without finding recognition from others of him continuing to be the person he was in those extreme self-states.

Shatan (2001) notes that "a core fact in PTSD is that the wound is of human origin, i.e., directly or indirectly inflicted by other human beings; and the result is the loss of trust in other people." What is both is interesting and significant, Shatan reports, is one of the activities that most helped veterans was working with the Vietnamese in rebuilding their country.

Research Based
On the Holocaust

The end of the Second World War opened the eyes of the world to the horror of the Nazi concentration and extermination camps. The term Holocaust is used to describe the mass slaughter of citizens of Jewish descent by Hitler's regime. The DRAE[2] defines holocaust: great slaughter of human beings; act of total self-sacrifice made for love especially among the Israelites; a sacrifice in which the whole victim was burnt.

We immediately think of the widely-read testimonies written by Victor Frankl, Primo Levi and Elie Wiesel.

Shatan (2001) tells us that *"disasters of human origin are based on a relationship of cruelty, of human cruelty, of socially-sanctioned collective destructiveness that tears the fabric of human trust. One of the greatest losses in traumatic stress is the loss of the ability to trust other human beings."*

In the case of the concentration camps, people are subjected, for a time they cannot control, to treatment that radically undermines the basic assumptions that are the bases of existence among peers. This is the tragedy that Shatan refers to and which most specialists in the field describe: the loss of trust in the assumption that the other will recognise himself in us through the suffering in our faces and respect us as equals. Loss of trust is the loss of the capacity to be visible and equal to the other, to stir concern and compassion in him. We cite Jean Amery (2001), who also survived the Nazi concentration camps:

"Several assumptions mediate in trusting in the world: the irrational faith in the solid principle of causality, which is unjustifiable from a logical point of view, for example; or the similarly blind conviction in the validity of inductive inferences. But the most important assumption of this trust and the only one that is relevant in our context is the certainty that others, on the basis of written or unwritten social contracts, will care for me, or rather, respect my physical - and therefore also metaphysical - being " (p 90)

How is the gaze of the other involved in the loss of basic trust? An indifferent gaze - without the hatred, contempt or inconsiderate yearning that identifies us as being subject to desire in the other's mind - erases us. The "terrifying normality" (Arendt, H. 2013) of those who rob us of our human condition (only discernible within a relationship) violates basic relational

---

2 The Spanish language dictionary of the *Real Academia Española*. The translation of the definition is mine.

rules, which are emptied of meaning. From an object relations perspective, "the internal good object falls silent as an empathic mediator between self and environment and the trust in the continual presence of good objects and the expectability of human empathy is destroyed" (Bohleber, 2010).

Henry Krystal's stance (1978) clearly reflects his own experience in the concentration camps. He recovers Freud's concept of "defencelessness" when he points out that what is basic in traumatic experience is the subjective evaluation the individual makes of it, and his feeling of defencelessness in the face of perceived danger. Let us see how he develops the concept of traumatic situation from this idea:

The essence of recognized and admitted helplessness is the surrender to the inevitable peril. With the helpless submission to the unavoidable danger, the affective state changes from anxiety to cataleptic passivity...In the catatonoid state we are dealing with the very moment of the self being overwhelmed with a phylogenetically determined surrender pattern which is also a potential psychological "self-destruct" mechanism (pp 91-92).

The author starkly describes how in a state that he terms 'passive surrender', groups of Jews let themselves be murdered without the slightest attempt at defence: together with their children, they took off their clothes, went down into the pit, they got on top of the pile of bodies and passively waited to be machine-gunned. In these states, the condemned cooperate with their executioners. Krystal states that if the process evolves to its full potential, the executioner is not even necessary as the individual dies through his own will.

Can the death instinct be seen here? Among Freudian authors, this seems to be Dori Laub's notion (2012):

I contend that it is the traumatic loss of the (internal) good object, and the libidinal ties to it, that release the hitherto libidinally neutralized forces of the death instinct and intensifies these clinical manifestations of its derivatives in the aftermath of massive trauma (p 43).

And what of the people who survive such traumatic experiences? Many survivors of the Nazi concentration camps lived for many years in a state that Lifton (cited by Bohleber) called "psychic closing off", in which all expressions of affect seem to be suppressed, and there is a narrowing of the perception of the environment. Behaviour is robotic, reflecting the massive blocking of mental activity; people resemble the "living dead". In Krystal's opinion, this state, which is often preceded by a dissociative process as an extreme defence mechanism when confronted by reality, is the paradigm of adult trauma (Krystal, 1978).

Early Trauma

Major disasters, especially those caused by man through the twentieth century, have provided the opportunity to study the limits of psychological life. Adult humans who are constantly or systematically threatened, subjected and tortured by other humans may temporarily or permanently lose part of their human condition. The ability to establish relationships with the other is damaged, limited, distorted or definitively relinquished and lost. Because extreme threat and abuse by the other is undoubtedly an economic issue in which barriers, capabilities and opportunities to integrate "so much" are psychologically are exceeded. But this "excess" is also related to the meaning attached to it. When do we "discover" (resignify) the other's intention to annihilate? When de we cease to hold the "unthought," implicit belief' of the value of being alive? *Erschütterung* (commotion) will not only be caused by what is unexpected externally - *Überraschung* (surprise); the "sudden" understanding of what we are not (but need to be) for the other has a *nachträglich* (retroactive) quality in causing trauma.

What determines the tenacity of psychological life in extreme conditions? What makes us search our context for the last glimmer of hope that will sustain us? The object relations perspective in psychoanalysis offered answers to the question of resilience and vulnerability: the internal good object that protects against trauma. What does the internalised good object bring? The chance of finding "good objects" in the environment with whom to relate. These are the comrades whose presence protected their fellow soldiers, as observed in the world wars.

As the figure of the real mother became increasingly more important in child development theory, the importance of early relationships in normal and pathological development also became more evident. The idea of deficit, of the basic fault, of accumulated trauma changed the clinical and psychotherapeutic scenarios as the patient-analyst relationship began to take on more importance - both as a matrix of repair or provision of what was lacking, as well as a scenario for retraumatsation .

Krystal's objections (in the same vein as Anna Freud) to the indiscriminate use of the concept of trauma are understandable:

If, like Khan (1963), we accept the definition of trauma to be every unfavorable influence in childhood, or, as many authors do, assume that every event and experience in the life of an adult productive of psychopathology is also self-evidently trauma, then the usefulness of the term is lost, and it may as well be discarded. (Krystal, 1978)

He suggests differentiating between near-traumatic experiences and catastrophic trauma in order not to lose the clinical value of the concept of trauma. Krystal (2005) himself, sanctioned by his own experience as a witness and victim of the concentration camps, answers the question posed above. I quote the following paragraph:

In the winter of 1929, I developed pneumonia and puss in my right lung. Without antibiotics, this was a deadly condition. I was operated on and a rubber tube drain was inserted into my chest. I had to stay in the hospital for three months. This was my childhood trauma, which I survived only because my mother stayed with me all the time. In 1999 I wrote a paper on resilience, which won the Hayman prize of the International Psychoanalytic Association. As I write this I am reminded coincidentally that in that paper I started by discussing the essential function of "primary" childhood narcissism resulting from the "programming" of the child in a state of secure attachment to the mother that he was loved and lovable, was the most important single asset in promoting survival in Holocaust victims (p. 111).

This could be formulated as: if good self/object representations predominate "inside" us, we will be better placed to find external allies in our struggle for life or survival. We can take Fairbairn's model of an internalisation of objects further or we can radically change it and adopt Davies and Bromberg's model of dissociation.

When neuroscience, child development research and a detailed study of attachment began to converge, a relational baby was born. Being more aware of the close, subtle relational dependency (relational matrix) the baby has on its mother allows us to think about both the subtle breakdowns in connection that follow a particular pattern and will determine a certain implicit relational knowing, as well as the crude, unpredictable disruptions, intrusions and abandonments that will rupture a child's life in extreme cases, or in less extreme circumstances, severely compromise development. We can thus speak of childhood trauma, developmental trauma and attachment trauma.

When Ferenczi's Child Becomes An Adult

We will now go back to one of great debates in the evolution of psychoanalysis: what to do when a patient brings a history of child abuse or mistreatment to consultation. Should we prioritise working through the external traumatic experience? Should we analyse the impact the abuse had on the child's world of developmental fantasies? Ultimately, the paradigm of "psychic apparatus" or mind on which we base our understanding of the world will be decisive.

The multiplicity of self model is the one giving the broadest understanding - it enables us to form hypotheses about varying degrees of dissociation or to evaluate what has disintegrated. When thinking about sexual abuse suffered by patients as children, we can take all the features and dimensions of their relational life into account, without being "subject" to the imposition of a model of development consisting of instincts and primal fantasies that form the child's internal world from the outset.

Any general practitioner will have come up against the situation Bollas (1993) described when writing about the trauma of incest: at a given moment during the initial visits, the patient "reveals" the reason for coming to consult - sexual abuse in childhood. In his own particular style, Bollas dramatises the analyst's "disappointment" at what had promised to be an interesting analysis but now he will have to make do with psychotherapy, a second-best. For Bollas, this countertransferential reflection is the echo of the victim's impoverishment: "When a father rapes his daughter, she will no longer be able to play with him in her psyche. He puts an end to the imaginary" (p.205).

It is in this area of trauma especially where we re-encounter the time-honoured controversy confronting psychoanalysts amongst one another and with clinicians from other orientations. On the one hand, sexual abuse in childhood is an imposition to which there is no recourse, it overwhelms the self's capacity for integration, and destroys, as Bollas says, a potential space for play between father and daughter. Something known cannot be thought, symbolised, it is consigned to the soma and contained by dissociation. In adult life, certain situations will trigger the memory traces that have been disarticulated from the trauma; the person will become ill without knowing why.

Many will say factual reality is not limited to overwhelming an organism and harming or deforming it; reality is signified by fundamental fantasies that govern the course of life from the unconscious. The way in which the disruptive event (Benyakar, 2005) is encompassed by fantasy is what marks the direction illness will take, and therefore recovery, too.

Reality versus fantasy? I do not believe this dilemma has ever been considered in such simplistic terms. I believe it is not simply a question of positions that are more or less empathic but one of, in some respects, irreconcilable models.

Much has been written on the coexistence of different psychoanalytic schools and their impact on clinical work. It is easy to agree with the proposals of authors such as Bollas (2007) who explicitly advocate knowledge of differing psychoanalytic theories as a way of enriching clinical visions:

These theories reside in the psychoanalyst's preconscious and will be activated by the analyst's need to see certain things at certain times. So if the analyst has been schooled in Freud, Klein, Bion, Winnicott, Lacan, Kohut and others, then in my view he has more perceptual capability in his preconscious than an analyst who remains within only one vision (p 5).

However, neither should we ignore the differences that different theoretical models will ultimately have on the clinical context. The degree of personal involvement we envisage does not depend on our greater or lesser degree of empathy. Accepting that our own internal models, implicit relational knowing, self-states, ways of being with etc. influence a therapeutic relationship establishes a fundamental difference compared to other models which do not accept, implicitly or explicitly, the co-creation of the analytic setting with all that might bring.

From her relational therapeutic approach with victims of sexual abuse, Jody Messler Davies (1994) believes that, *both the reality of childhood sexual abuse and the fantasied elaborations of these traumatic events are woven into the tapestry of the adult survivor's self and object worlds; both must be accorded weight and attention in treatment ...Working with adult survivors of childhood sexual abuse within a relational model implies the cocreation of a transitional space in which therapist and patient together are free to reenact, create context and meaning, and ultimately recreate in newly configured forms the central, organizing relational matrices of the patient's early life"* (p 3).

In another article, Davies (2007) clarifies the nature of intrapsychic conflict in relational terms: *"When experience and understanding of one's self, in one self-state, is irreconcilable with another's experience and understanding of self, we have, from a relational perspective, an example of intrapsychic conflict "(p54).*

Bromberg (2011) focuses his therapeutic work on this endeavour of reconciling self-states that will allow, if successful, the experience of internal conflict without threatening the integrity of the sense of self.

A., a young, brilliant professional, recalled the scene so often repeated: when mother left for work early, father would invite A. to take her place in the marital bed; they would hug each other tightly and she could feel his arousal ... and her own. Could anything else have happened that her memory supressed? What role was the mother playing when giving up her place in the relationship? A. described her father with admiration: hard-working, caring, obliging. Her mother was warm and affectionate, although dependent on the father. When she finished her university studies, A. decided to seek work on the other side of the world, a country with a developing economy, but unsafe. Things went well, so she decided to move on to a more advanced country where would have a better chance to work in something closer to her field. She met a man there who took an interest in her and who was affectionate and tender. Something moved in her, but she didn't know why. One night she went out alone and had intercourse with the first man she met in a bar. Tobe able to stay in this new country, A. needed make a trip back to her home country and family, and this horrified her. The way she had created distance and the challenges she had taken on made her connect with parts in her that could be partially identified with the hard-working, successful father and distance her from her dependent mother. Only the relationship with a tender man in a place where she could imagine her "destiny", awake her "fate" (Bollas, 1993). Returning home, the physical closeness with her family violently took her back to states where confusion reigned, that irreconcilable mixture of love, excitement, shame and anger that disabled her to the point of illness by imagining she was "close" to them. Something she could not recognise was malfunctioning within her and this caused her great distress. The reunion with her family made her feel lost. To find herself once again, she had to return to her yearned-for country and bring an intelligent psychotherapist into her life who, without being overtly relational, took the helm from an empathic, integrative perspective.

Reflection

How do we work with trauma from a relational perspective? With the whole person, in a total relationship with the person, with the totality of our own person. I should like to explain the rhetorical nature of this answer: the people who come to us, as young A. did, bring not only their histories of trauma, but all their history (although they may not want to share it with us) - their lives are made up of achievements and failures, strengths and weaknesses, and now we will be part of those lives if we choose and commit ourselves to the task.

Quoting Davies (2007) once again:

A model of the mind of multiple self-states or a model of the based on dissociation involves a multiply-organised, associatively-linked model of networks, of sometimes conflicting coexisting systems, of meaning-making and understanding. The concept of dissociation comes into play when cognitive or emotional connections among these different subsystems of self-other organisations are damaged or broken, usually as a result of a psychological trauma, or a conflict of identification that makes the coexistence of certain self-states psychologically impossible (p55).

This multiplicity is not something akin to an archipelago of islands that are all equally flat or hilly, and more or less grouped together. The self's good objects, the self/object interiorisations, the critical mass of representations of self-other relationships that are coloured with affect, protection, creative play, recognition, etc., should all shape the "depth" of experience so the inevitable conflicts of meaningful life can exist in our mind without dividing it.

People who were abused as children cannot count on that concentration of "protective" relational representations, nor on internal models that validate their desire to exchange affection without exploiting others or being exploited, nor on an implicit relational knowing that allows genuine encounter with the other without forcibly recurring to an already-written script of victims and tormentors.

In the case of patient A., some would emphatically point to an Oedipal interpretation of events, but then we are left with a confusion of tongues.

How can the images of herself be integrated: a father concerned with the welfare of his family, a tireless worker, a self-made man who can confidently and effectively manage his work life; a demanding father who values me, and expects great things; a father who is served and looked after by a woman who only wants to devote herself to her family; a father who goes to bed with his young daughter and is aroused and arouses her for years; images of self and other that are irreconcilable.

And the silence that accompanies the abuse. What is a life of silence like over the years? There is an initial silence that aims to create complicity and grants a special status; later silence can acquire qualities of space and sound: there are places and times when there should be no words. Silence interrupts the flow of spontaneous communication, silence isolates, silence becomes independent, it is sealed by implicit denial: outside that place of relating, none of this exists. There are no signs of complicity now, there is only dissociation.

One final quote from Davies (1994):

It is our belief that it is only within a relational-psychoanalytically oriented framework, that the full complexity of the human mind and its remarkable adaptation to abuse can come to be appreciated (p 44).

The re-encounter with oneself must take place in a relational home, with someone who is able to hear all the voices that have shaped the disintegrated experiences both in the patient and in him or herself; someone who can call these voices forth in the presence of both. This undertaking is essentially a creative act, since by calling forth different voices we are encouraging a new state of self that was not lost and recovered, but may not have ever even existed.

Summary

Trauma is, by definition, something that cannot be taken on board, it violates the basic elements of a person's relationship with his context, without it being possible to reorganice these elements in a way that would allow life to continue under the same identity. When the wound is of human origin, i.e., directly or indirectly inflicted by other human beings, the result is the loss of trust in other people. Loss of trust is the loss of the capacity to be visible and equal to the other, to stir concern and compassion in him. It also means the loss of contact with ourselves.

We review the principal sources of investigation of trauma: war, holocaust, child sexual abuse; we review also the classical historical debate in psycho-analysis about fantasies versus reality related to trauma.

When neuroscience, child development research and a detailed study of attachment began to converge, a relational baby was born. Being more aware of the close, subtle relational dependency (relational matrix) the baby has on its mother allows us to think about both the subtle breakdowns in connection that follow a particular pattern and will determine a certain implicit relational knowing, as well as the crude, unpredictable disruptions, intrusions and aban-donments that will rupture a child's life in extreme cases, or in less extreme circumstances, severely compromise development. We can thus speak of childhood trauma, developmental trauma and attachment trauma.

People who were abused as children cannot count on that concentration of "protective" relational representations, nor on internal models that validate their desire to exchange affection without exploiting others or being exploited

The re-encounter with oneself must take place in a relational home, with someone who is able to hear all the voices that have shaped the disintegrated experiences both in the patient and in him or herself.

8

Between Passion and Reason– Reflections on the Spirit of the Setting in Relational Psychoanalysis[1]

Joan Coderch de Sans and Ángeles Codosero Medrano

Reviewing Concepts on Analytic Setting

The idea for this chapter came from a paper by A. Ávila Espada (2001) in the journal *Intersubjetivo,* entitled "Reglas, vectores y funciones del encuadre: su papel generador del proceso analítico"[2]. This excellent, comprehensive paper

---

1 English translation by Nick Cross from a revised version of the original paper in Spanish, published online: Coderch de Sans, J. y Codosero Medrano, A. (2015). Entre la razón y la pasión. Algunas reflexiones acerca del espíritu del encuadre en el Psicoanálisis Relacional. *Clínica e Investigación Relacional,* 9 (2): 358-393.
2 "Rules, vectors and functions of the setting: its role as a generator in psychoanalytic process"

examines in detail the parameters, theories and concepts by which the setting is governed from a generally traditional psychoanalytic standpoint. The text does contain, however, some statements and concepts that reach beyond classical theory and are suggestive of relational psychoanalysis, which the author later expands on so splendidly in his latest book, *La Tradición Interpersonal en Psicoanálisis (2013)*[3].

Ávila Espada, for example, describes the function of holding in the following words:

"A secure, comfortable environment offered by the analyst that generates a bond, at the service of the subject's need for regression and dependence, and where, however, the analyst's shortfalls will make growth possible"[4]

And similarly, when the author asks:

"Through our stance, can we activate the functions that derive from the setting and that facilitate the analytic process from a flexible, agreed-upon interpretation of the formal rules of the setting within the specific intersubjective stage of each individual analysis?" (p39)

We also detect a relational stance in Ávila Espada's article when he refers to Balint's work, when the latter warns, *"of the impossibility of applying a one-person psychoanalytic theory to the bi-personal situation of the analytic context"*. Ávila Espada continues, adding with future vision:

"We believe that this reformulation does not only apply to the study of the analytic situation, its process and technique, but psychoanalytic theory as a whole is under revision from the perspectives offered by the study of intersubjectivity, through knowing about the processes of bonding that establish intrasubjetivity"[5].

These brief examples are enough to appreciate that Ávila Espada's paper anticipates what we now understand to be relational psychoanalysis.

However, fifteen years have passed since that paper was published. We are of the opinion that the solid conceptual framework with which Ávila Espada constructs his idea of setting is still extraordinarily useful, although it is clear to anyone who has followed his publications that his way of comprehending the psychoanalytic process is now quite different from then, and so we believe this will inevitably be reflected in his concept of the setting. Furthermore, in this period of time, relational psychoanalytic thinking and its dissemination have taken giant steps forward. We therefore hope that in general terms he

---

3 *The interpersonal tradition in psychoanalysis* (Madrid: Ágora Relacional, 2013)
4 Translator's note: Translated from the original text in Spanish, p.39
5 TN: Translated from the Spanish, p. 39 in the original text

feels he could agree with reflections here on the setting in relational analytic clinical work.

Our Rationale

Like some of the many authors we could quote, prestigious researchers into infant-parent relationships and creators of *dyadic systems theory* B. Beebe and L. Lachman (2003) affirm that arguments centred on the "interpretation-relation" dichotomy have now been left behind, and the relational turn in psychoanalysis represents a total transformation of the discipline as we understood it a few decades ago. Together with an undeniable evolution, there has been an authentic revolution in psychoanalytic thought, in the sense indicated by T. Khun (1962), which has led to the emergence of a new, relational paradigm, which we consider to be incompatible with Freud's drive model, although it is not within the realm of this paper to explore the causes and reasons for this incompatibility, and it has been discussed elsewhere[6]. Thus, we agree with Beebe and Lachmann and their idea of the need for a total review of the concepts, theories, methodology etc. of what has been termed "mainstream psychoanalysis".

However, we should firstly like to state that beyond the many lengthy arguments that can be given to justify the change in theory and the practical application of the setting in relational psychoanalysis compared to the tradi-tional setting, there are six fundamental reasons for such a change, each of them justification in its own right, and which also justify this paper. The first of these reasons is the fact that the traditional setting is grounded in the belief that the human being is basically instinctual, expressed in libidinal and death drives. As such, the setting must promote the expression of these drives in the so-called *transference neurosis,* channelling them, hindering their destructive capacity and clarifying the unconscious fantasies that accompany them and which are the cause of intrapsychic conflict. In contrast, we know that relational psychoanalysis rests on the belief that human beings are essentially emotional and social, which inevitably requires the creation of another type of setting for the psychoanalytic process. This setting should be structured so that the patient-analyst relationship can allow emotions that were once inhibited or detrimental for the development of the patient's mind to be fully experienced.

The second reason justifying change in the is that the traditional setting is conceived for the study of a one-person psychology, while relational

---

6 *Realidad, Interacción y Cambio Psíquico,* Coderch. J.; (2012); *Avances en Psicoanálisis Relacional,* Coderch. J.et al.(2014a).

psychoanalysis is aimed at the study of two-person psychology, as Ávila Espada asserts in his paper; the construction of another type of setting, then, is inevitable. Nevertheless, we would like to discuss this a little further as currently our stance goes beyond conceptualising relational psychoanalysis simply as the investigation of two-person psychology as this would imply the existence two individual psychologies meeting in the analytic space. We think this concept of "individual psychology" needs to be qualified. Although what appear to us in everyday life as observable phenomena are individual psychologies, we now maintain, from the knowledge brought to us by complexity science and the theory of non-linearity, that psychological traits and an individual's behaviour are localised expressions within the system or systems to which it belongs (we can also say "contexts", to use a more common term), however much a person has given their own 'twist' leading to their own non-transferable individuality. In a strict sense there is no individual psychology because there is no isolated mind.

The third reason is that the traditional setting was conceived of following the parameters of positivist linear science, and a vision of the world, mind, and human behaviour according to a perspective of cause and effect. This has now been transcended by complexity science, which is incompatible with theories that do not take into account the reciprocal influence between patient and analyst. In the matter under discussion, such parameters are also refuted by the application of psychoanalysis of dynamic, intersubjective, non-linear systems (Stolorow R. 1997; Coderch, J. 2014a). It should be noted that there is currently a broad consensus in the scientific community that all the sciences need to be re-thought bearing in mind the contributions of complexity science, according to whose principles, in so much as human mind and behaviour are concerned, there are practically countless variables involved: For this reason the whole psychoanalytical process, the setting first and foremost, must be reconsidered from these new perspectives. However, we need to go further still, as we believe dynamic systems theory is not only a theory but an overall sensitivity and a way of being in the world.

The fourth reason concerns the goals of psychoanalysis as therapy. The traditional setting is aimed at creating the conditions for reactivating intra-psychic conflicts (always conceived of as being Oedipal in origin) in the transference and their dissolution through the analyst's interpretations. But for those of us who reject the idea of the universality of the Oedipus Complex (as has occurred in anthropology), psychoanalysis does not aim to discover the hidden to make it conscious but to help patients reconfigure their emotional worlds through interaction and a new lived experience with the analyst. In Mitchell's words (1993):

"What the patient needs is not clarification or insight, so much as a experience of being seen, personally engaged, and, basically being valued and cared about." (p.25).

Similarly, Ogden describes the goal of psychoanalysis (1992):

"I view the psychoanalytic process as one in which the analysand is created through an intersubjective process ... Analysis is not simply a method of discovering the hidden; it is, more importantly, a process of creating the psychoanalytic subject who had not previously existed" (p.619).

More recently, and now in the era of what we can consider fully contemporary psychoanalysis, Summers (2013; 2015) states that the goal of psychoanalysis is for patients to transcend themselves; for patients to emerge who were not previously there, and who feel driven and able to create something new in themselves that did not previously exist, because in the therapeutic process we should be concerned both with what the patient is and what he is not. We fully identify with these words and intentions and will return to them further on.

There are many examples of what we are referring to. We think that with what we have mentioned above it is evident that the aims of relational psychoanalysis are radically different from those of traditional psychoanalysis and, consequently, so must also be the organisation of the patient-therapist relationship that will carry this process forward.

The fifth justification for this paper is that we do not conceive that a change occurring in the patient's mind in the course of the psychoanalytic process can come from someone's - the analyst's - action outside the patient (- the starting point of the design of the traditional setting) but from a relational paradigm. Change takes place through the mutual regulation of affects by reason of the internal *feed-back* caused by *recursion* or *recurrence,* which is applicable in all systems according to general systems theory, and therefore also in the supra-system formed by the two systems of patient and analyst, that is, the dyad itself is its own source of change (Coburn, W., 2014 Coderch, J., 2015).

The sixth and last of these reasons is based on the fact that the advent of relational psychoanalysis can be explained through advances brought about by clinical experience itself and by related disciplines, such as neuroscience, anthropology, infant observation, linguistics, etc., and also by the fact that patients are not the same as in Freud's time because of changes in society and culture. In this era of post-modernity, democracy, the demand for rapid results, the loss of reliable values, and inveterate individualism, our patients are more critical, less likely to submit to an analyst's authority. They are more reluctant to agree to treatments requiring time, perseverance and patience and which are incompatible with the hectic pace of modern life and the demand for instant gratification so prevalent in our culture. A different culture and different patients require a different setting.

General Considerations

When referring to setting, we particularly wish to point out the need to avoid the reification that has taken place within psychoanalysis with concepts such as the "unconscious", "id", "ego", "superego ", etc., that is, sets of psychological, conscious and unconscious functions and processes articulated by Freud and which time and intellectual laxity have transformed, in psychoanalytic language, into things within the mind. The way in which we use the concept of setting and the term designating it is not an entity but a process, a living, dynamic means through which patient and analyst relate and interact with each other. We can say that the setting is represented by the ever-dynamic and unforeseeable intersubjective field formed by the meeting of two subjectivities.

As a large part of the psychoanalytic community continues to confide in the drive-defence model, we prefer to work on the principle of the existence of two psychoanalyses: Freudian psychoanalysis (with all its orientations and schools), and relational psychoanalysis, founded on the relational paradigm that we have set out in the publications mentioned in the footnotes. We therefore feel it is crucial to review the philosophy and spirit guiding the development of the setting in the clinical practice of relational psychoanalysis.

Considering the enormous volume of papers written from a relational perspective, opening new horizons in theory, methodology, and experimental, clinical and social areas, we were somewhat surprised by how little mention has been made of the setting. It is as if it were simply supposed that the setting not be so rigid and unchanging as in classical psychoanalysis, without the need for any further comment. This may indeed be the reason for the lack of publications on the subject.

The setting typical of mainstream psychoanalysis is solidly predetermined by unassailable rules due to the fact they have a close bearing with the drive-defence theory upholding them: But they are totally at odds with the aims of relational psychoanalysis. This may have given relational therapists the impression they need not worry too much about the setting, which should simply be fully integrated into the flexible, anti-hierarchical, democratic spirit typical of relational psychoanalysis. What also may have been part of the paucity of papers on the relational setting is the fact that in clinical practice, relational analysts are fully and personally responsible for what they do rather than merely complying with rules and norms they have been taught and that would often save them from the anxiety of having to decide for themselves.

We certainly do not intend to propose any kind of guideline or type of psychoanalytic setting that is valid for all patients and all analysts, nor do we intend to track down all the existing literature on this topic. The more limited aim of this paper is to offer some reflections on the setting, conceived of in the spirit of relational psychoanalysis, in the hope that they may be of some use to the readers, even if they only wish to contradict them and remain steadfast in their own points of view. The idea guiding us is the spirit that we believe presides, by definition, the therapeutic process in relational psychoanalysis. As in any other occupation, it is obvious that you cannot tell a patient that he or she may come and call at the office door at any time of the day or night. And taking this as given, everyone is free to think for themselves andaccept the consequences.

We should like to say a little about regression in the setting. With the exception of some more free-thinking analysts such as J. Sandler and A.M. Sandler (1994), analysts have firmly believed that a patient's *regression* is necessary for the psychoanalytic process, understanding it as the return to a level of mental functioning characteristic of an earlier stage of a subject's psychological development. Encouraging regression, and thus the appearance of the so-called *transference neurosis*, is thought to be one of the most important functions of the setting. Nonetheless, we believe, based on the idea of the human being's fundamentally social and relational nature, the setting should stimulate and facilitate the *progression* of patients' psychological functioning - this is why patients seek help, not regression. Subjects, as patients, have already "regressed" when they come to our office, i.e. there are certain immature, inhibited, pathologically dissociated etc. dimensions of their psychology. So what is the point of infantilising them, making them more dependent on the analyst? All seasoned analysts with their own and others' clinical experience have seen extreme examples of dependence. We fully agree with H. Loewald (1960, 1979), for whom good analysts, like good parents with their child, always see their patients as being more advanced than they really are. In this sense, our view is that when patients sees themselves in their analysts' minds, in a higher proximal zone than they are really at, they identify with that image in the same way that a young child one days lets go of the furniture she was holding on to and begins to walk when she sees herself walking in her mother's mind.

The Setting Stimulates, Promotes, And Shapes Different Dimensions of the Psychoanalytic Process

A setting that accommodates a patient's multiple selves.

An indisputable assertion within the relational paradigm is that every human being has not one self but multiple selves relative to the various contexts in his or her life (Mitchell, S., 1993). When people go to an analyst, it is a new and unfamiliar situation for them and all their potential selves. Depending on the analyst's attitude during the initial visits, this state of potentiality may be conserved or inhibited. Shortly after, determining the setting is critical. The new analytic patients feel they are situated in a certain position in relation to their analyst, and this position will determine, for better or worse, the course of analysis. We argue that the spirit of the setting appropriate to relational psychoanalysis is one that gives patients a feeling of being people whose demands regarding the guidelines and formalities, both external and interpersonal, governing the course of treatment are heard and taken into account. They will be treated as equals and considered able to reflect insightfully on the analyst's attitudes and words. And patients will thus be able to unfold their different selves, characters, resources and capacities for mental growth. Anything else would not be in the spirit that should prevail within relational psychoanalysis - patients would feel limited to express only fragmented aspects of their selves.

Internal setting and external setting.

Generally, when speaking of setting, more attention is given to the external setting, which is seemingly more "objective," consisting of a set of explicit rules that establish a spatial and temporal scene within which the psychoanalytic process takes place. Within this external setting, an internal setting gradually develops; an intense but ineffable relationship is built - intentionally or not - by analyst and patient. But by no means are the two settings independent of one another, quite the contrary. The long experience one of the present authors has supervising, and a study of clinical work leave no doubt that when the external setting is based on impersonal, rigid norms, if the analyst's stance does not prevent it, these characteristics tend to be passed on to the internal setting, to the point that it can be difficult to differentiate one from the other. For example, we might ask whether in the familiar situation of the psychoanalyst who only answers questions with an interpretation, this forms part of the external or internal setting. Although the analyst may not have spelt it out in the set of norms regulating the mutual relationship, if the patient perceives the analyst as systematically answering his questions as interpretations, in line with every human's innate tendency to search for coherence and categorisation, as Kant has taught us, he will categorise his analyst's posture as inherent to the set of rules that must be followed in his analysis. Naturally, the patient does not set out to differentiate the external and internal setting as we do, nor what forms part of each. In these cases, at some point the patient commonly stops asking questions because he has understood that this goes against the rules that have been imposed, and we believe that the majority of analysts who usually formulate interpretations as answers to their patients would testify to this.

The authors in the *Boston Change Process Study Group* (BCSG) do make this differentiation and describe the aim of the setting in guiding the analysis, much like the banks of a river guide the flow of water. In their 1989 paper, the BCSG speak of *moments of meeting*: they state that at these moments, patient and analyst meet at a personal level, *they come out of their transference and countertransference roles.* By being spontaneous and disregarding the roles assigned to them under the rules of the setting, they clearly break out of the setting that had been imprisoning them. But in the relational setting, we need not think that at these moments of meeting patient and analyst are jumping the rules which by definition affect them: such a setting is flexible and allows wide emotional movements in both directions without breaking barriers.

The vital links between clinical theory and setting

Every psychoanalytic school and particularly every analyst inevitably structure the setting they offer their patients according to the general theory of mind and clinical theory they follow. The human mind has a natural tendency to seek coherence and categorisation, as mentioned above, and this can even be seen when observing young children (Hobson, P., 2004). This need to find consistency in our perceptions and our way of organising any situation we find ourselves in will also naturally be expressed in clinical work. We believe the setting, as a framework analysts have traditionally offered their patients, is like a foretaste of how treatment will go, and so it should be in line with the theory of mind and clinical theory the analyst works with, i.e., one ought to be coherent with the other. At this point, we should point out that the setting followed by mainstream psychoanalysis (strict Freudian, Anna Freudian, Ego Psychology, the Kleinian school, French psychoanalysis, etc.) is perfectly consistent with its clinical theory. Let's say, for example, that a tenet of a certain clinical theory is that patients should reproduce their early objects and the fantasies, drives and emotions experienced with them in their relationship with their analysts, leading to a transference neurosis, as referred to earlier. In this case the need for a rigorous setting with strict rules that obscure the analyst's personality and promote confusion with the early objects in order to stimulate the transference in the sense mentioned is perfectly coherent. It would therefore make no sense to try to carry through an analysis along the lines of the clinical theory of Ego psychology using, say, a relational setting.

Quite another thing is the debate about whether a particular clinical theory can be upheld or is refuted by clinical practice and modern-day science, and whether the norms encouraging the reactivation of what was experienced with patients' early objects in their relationships with their analysts is really effective. And indeed if the norms do truly conceal the analyst's personality or if they make it more visible by contrasting it to more common standards of human relating. Actually, we think that the more analysts strive to conceal their personality, the more their subjectivity will become evident in the attempt, as people's mental or physical acts always come about by virtue of their subjectivity, in the same way that no-one can escape their DNA.

As such, we hold that the most logical and favourable way for analysis to proceed is for the setting to be in tune with the analyst's theoretical and practical assumptions as much as possible. It does happen that as a result of the wide-spread dissemination that relational psychoanalysis is currently enjoying, we have observed some confusion in supervisions, seminars, clinical presentations and debates. Many psychoanalysts and psychotherapists trained in traditional psychoanalysis - now they are mostly middle-aged and older - are attracted to a type of setting that is closer to the patient, more democratic and more dialogic, in line with relational psychoanalyticpractice. They try to use it with patients whom they try to help based on the classic drive-defence paradigm of intrapsychic conflict based on a supposedly universal Oedipus complex, all of which results in considerable inconsistency and is highly ambiguous, both for therapist and patient. From the point of view of teaching relational psychoanalysis and its prestige, it is important to address and clarify this oft-made confusion as it leads to a terrible vulgarization of relational psychoanalysis, which unfortunately all too often becomes a "be nice and friendly to the patient." We believe that it is more beneficial to the patient that the analyst's sympathy and warmth be given within the relational paradigm's general theory.

The weight of tradition in the setting and its role as an initiation rite.

The authors' experience is that when reflecting on the setting in psychoanalysis, we cannot keep out of mind the multitude of ideas on everything that has been written and said about the setting in the field of traditional psychoanalysis, as well as how we have both personally experienced it. But there is something that is not present amongst these ideas - because it has generally not been spoken about: what it means emotionally for the patient to become part of something that will not fail to be felt by him as a special world, a world distinct from reality, a world that is mysterious and unknown, the world of the psychoanalytic legend. If the patient knows something about psychoanalysis, especially if he or she is a mental health professional or more still, an aspiring psychoanalyst, the setting undoubtedly takes on an initiatory rite-like nature. Perhaps the fact the couch is still considered essential by most analysts is what most strongly emphasises this initiation-like quality, especially as it is physical, objective, and many suppose is common to every patient-analyst dyad. The type of relationship that the analysts impose in classical analysis with their silence, and their language limited to the formulation of interpretations, also contributes to this feeling of a gateway to a world reserved for just a few.

In clinical papers up until now, patients' emotional responses when finding themselves obliged - if they wish to be helped - to accept what we call a classical setting have not been sufficiently taken into account. That is, artificially constructed forms of relating (materially and interpersonally) which must be complied with for the long period of the analytic space. Odd situations in human relating must necessarily lead to odd adaptive responses - we call them "iatrogenic artefacts" - and therefore patients behaving differently than in their daily lives and their interpersonal relationships. We could say that when this type of setting is used, the analyst does not get to find out what patients are really like in their everyday lives. It seems as out of place as if a cardiologist when checking someone's heart only used a stress test and was uninterested in the subject's usual state of health .

Either way, we would like to point out something shared by both classical and relational settings: they are both part of a tradition. Most analytic dyads possibly do not consciously reflect on (for the fact they are beginning analysis and establishing a setting that will be the distinguishing feature of this beginning) the fact that they continue - or better still, personalise - a long tradition that began with the first analyses undertaken by Freud and that has continued down through generations of analysts. It leads to an almost reverential fear of infringing norms and overstepping the limits of something that is sacrosanct. This is confirmed when one of the factors that psychoanalytic training institutes place so much importance on is preserving the setting at all costs when young analysts take on their first supervised clinical cases.

We cannot know directly what other analysts feel in that regard other than what we hear through supervisions, but there are some general clues. The most important seems to be, from the beginnings of psychoanalysis, the reverence given to the setting consisting of a set of rules, commandments, and prohibitions. Of course it can be said that this is not a pure sentiment, but one that accompanies a technical consensus on rules based not on emotional considerations but on rationality. Even if this is so, we feel there is more to it than this, we believe that analysts facing the delicate question of the setting have always felt imprisoned and constrained by tradition, as if they felt observed and judged by hundreds of erstwhile analysts, many of them outstanding and admirable; we aspire to be their worthy successors and we fear their judgement in the form of the analytical persecutory superego. Largely because of the nature of the setting we have been taught, in our clinical practice psychoanalysts are representatives of a tradition to which we must be faithful. This can be seen in the papers and discussions presented at scientific meetings where any intervention appearing to go just a little beyond the limits of the setting is accompanied by excuses and justifications. In relation to this, J. Greenberg (1996) says, ironically, that at any psychoanalytic meeting where clinical material is presented, it seems, given the discussions arising among those present, that the most important thing is not the patient's possible improvement, but if the analyst has scrupulously followed the rules of analysis.

The attitude we are discussing here has greatly hampered the progress of psychoanalysis. Even though the setting does not constitute all of psychoanalysis, it does lay down the key lines of the process. For example, the imposition on the patient of the basic rule, "Say whatever comes to mind without holding anything back" - a custom that is disappearing - immediately means the demise of any dialogue because the sequence: association-interpretation-association-interpretation, etc. is not remotely a dialogue in the human sense of the word. The fear of being labelled as a non-analyst has inhibited the creativity of many of the leading figures of our discipline. Among those who dared challenge the psychoanalytic superego, some were completely excluded from the lessons taught in the psychoanalytic institutions for generations, analysts such as Ferenczi, Karen Horney, Clara Thompson, Frieda Fromm-Reichmann, and J. Bowlby. Others, like Balint, Winnicott and Kohut (at this juncture we prefer to refer only to analysts who are no longer with us) had to do a lot of explaining in order to not suffer exclusion from academic life. The usual way of escaping the ire of those reluctant to embrace the new has been by claiming contributions were only aimed at patients considered unanalysable by classical analysis. One of the most prominent examples of this is Balint, as he himself expresses in his

1968 book when he refers to "the classical technique and its limitations" and where he justifies making modifications in order to help "unanalysable patients."

As we have said before, it is true that things have changed considerably since relational psychoanalysis emerged with force at the end of the last century, its influence being felt in all areas of psychoanalytic thinking . But it shouldn't be said, as often happens when making reflections such as those we propose in this paper, that we are arguing with straw men. Conservative, purist attitudes continue to exist- naturally with every right - widely within the psychoanalytic community; for the benefit both of psychoanalysis and patients we believe we should continue reflecting on this as ground-breaking authors still feel they need to apologise. To give an example, an excellent, recent article by R. Grossmark (2012), which is applicable to all patients, follows the pathway Balint marked out in *The Unobtrusive Analyst"* (1968b). Grossmark persists in needing to base his contributions on the perpetual argument that they are aimed at the patients who are too ill to be treated by classical standards, as did Ferenczi, then Fairbairn, then Balint, and then Kohut, etc. each in their in way. We believe there is confusion between the severity of a patient's illness and the likelihood that the impact of the analyst-patient interaction will reach the most basic and archaic structures of the patient's mind, however severe. We are convinced that the spirit of the setting we advocate is the best for all patients, severely ill or not, if working within the relational paradigm. We will come back to this later.

Negotiating the setting and its ongoing construction.

The relational setting must be in accordance with the presiding spirit of the paradigm, and on the explicit basis that one person seeks help and another will give it. But once this agreement is established, the prevailing atmosphere in the relations between patient and analyst is not authoritarianism, nor imposition, but democratic and respectful of ideas, needs and suggestions - both the patient's as well as the analyst's. Consequently, we favour a negotiated setting that will then be built upon.

However, perhaps this is easier said than done, there will be doubts and questions once the magic word 'negotiation' has been uttered or written: what should be negotiated when establishing the setting? How should it be negotiated? How far should it be negotiated? Should everything be negotiated - is anything non-negotiable? To answer these questions, we need to differentiate between two matters. One relates to concrete facts and the other is quite distinct, referring to the main emphasis and the myriad variables involved in the exchange between patient and analyst, what we might term the internal setting. We will need to deal each of these two questions separately.

The negotiation of facts is something we believe to be indispensable and relatively feasible. It is very difficult to help anyone if they are unwillingly forced to accept certain external conditions under the premise of "take it or leave it". Before reaching this point, the analyst needs to think very seriously, because there is the danger that a patient who has reluctantly accepted certain conditions will turn the tables, explicitly or implicitly, with something like, "Well, I've already accepted your annoying, onerous demands, now it's up to you to make my problems go away. I've met my part of the deal, now let's see how you make my symptoms and problems disappear." When this situation arises, one an analyst with decades of experience under his belt has experienced on more than one occasion when supervising younger therapists, if possible, it is essential to either rebuild the setting from the start, or if not, to refer the patient to another therapist.

One important point concerns using the couch or sitting face to face. Although for years now the authors of this paper have inclined towards face to face, there have occasionally been some patients, probably due to the idea of the psychoanalytic couch in the popular imagination, who specifically ask to use the couch, even in cases of isolated problems whose treatment is far from needing psychoanalysis in the strict sense. In these cases, it is up to each therapist to proceed in the way she or he feels most appropriate, but we do think that there will be negotiation if the analyst wants to work within the relational paradigm. The same is true in regard of the frequency of sessions, always such a thorny, delicate subject where theoretical, ideological and corporatist issues meet and which cannot be dealt with in depth here (Coderch, J., 2010). We shall quote two internationally renowned German psychoanalysts, Helmut Thöma and Horst Kächele, from their treatise *Teoría y Práctica del Psicoanálisis*[7] (1989):

> *Today it seems fairly settled that the standard statement - only four hours or more a week allows the development of the transference neurosis - is a residue of an ideological conception of psychoanalysis. Where for real financial reasons the frequency of weekly hours has had to be reduced, ... it has been shown that the essence of the analytical task does not depend on this external factor* (vol.I, p.300)[8].

Joan Coderch, one of the authors of this paper, has shown what the analytical task Thöma and Kächele refer to can achieve with patients in treatment with once-weekly sessions for years (2014).

---

7 *Psychoanalytic Practice* in its English edition.
8 TN: translated from the Spanish text.

In our opinion, a totally imposed external setting, a 'one size fits all' where the future patient's demands or views are not taken into account do not connect at all with the spirit of relational psychoanalysis and cannot but lead to submission, identification with the analyst, "as if" cures , etc. We do not believe that anyone who understands what relational psychoanalysis is would work this way.

With regard to the second point focusing on negotiating the dialogic and emotional exchange between patient and analyst: the internal setting is not explicitly agreed on from the outset, but is gradually constructed during the course of analysis. This is complex. In the explicit agreement established before the beginning of a psychoanalytic therapy, analysts do often refer to some aspects of the relationship, such as the use of formal or informal address, shaking hands or not, the availability to receive phone calls, the patient requesting changes of appointment times, etc. We know that decisions taken in this respect are important in terms of what we can term the 'internal setting', as they define the type of relationship, something like channels and bounds that are either narrow and inflexible or wide and open to spontaneity. It would be easy to assert that the atmosphere, the emotional climate (cooler or warmer, closer or more distant, accompanying and experiencing with, or technical and interpretation-based, etc.) depends on the analyst and his or her theories, but this is not exactly true. We know there is an uninterrupted, mutual influence between patient and analyst, the transference and counter-transference (whatever the sense these terms are used in) are co-created, and no analyst is exactly the same with all his or her patients because each one awakens varying emotional responses (we could different self-states), some conscious and other dissociated. It is therefore fairer to say that between them they create an internal setting within which this interaction between two people takes place.

Mutual regulation of affect and the creation of intersubjectivity.

Firstly, we must warn that talking about what happens between two unique individuals, patient and analyst, is overly simple and lineal, done for the sake of clarity, nevertheless, it is necessary to go into more depth to better understand the that is appropriate to the setting in relational psychoanalysis. We now know, according to the theory of non-linearity (Thelen, E. and Smith, L., 1994), and dynamic, non-lineal intersubjective systems theory (Stolorow, R., 1997) that patient and analyst form an *interactive dyad*, a suprasystem formed by the systems that are analyst and patient (Beebe, B. and Lachmann, F., 1998, 2003, Coderch, J., 2014a). In this dyad, reciprocal changes in the self-regulation of affects of each of the two parts modify the self-regulation of affects in the other, thus effecting a change in the dyad that affects each of its parts. This occurs in uninterrupted succession under the principle of recursion or internal feedback (referred to in section 2 above) that takes place in any dynamic, intersubjective and non-linear system or suprasystem. In our view, this is the heart of the psychoanalytic process, and so worthwhile discussing in more detail. We will deal with two key points (Coderch, J., 2015).

One concerns the mutual regulation of affect mentioned above. At present, researchers such as Gallesse, Eagle, Migone, Emde, etc., hold that the system of mirror neurons is the basis for the establishment of a sense of self in the newborn, and of empathy and the development of social feeling in humans. Gallesse says in this regard (2009):

This common relational character is underpinned, at the level of the brain, by shared mirroring neural networks. These shared neural mechanisms enable the shareable character of actions, emotions, and sensations, the earliest constituents of our social life. According to my model, we-ness and intersubjectivity ontologically ground the human condition, *in which reciprocity foundationally defines human existence. This common relational character is underpinned* (p. 530, emphasis ours)

Consequently, if we apply the knowledge provided by mirror neurons to psychoanalysis, what many clinicians had warned of can be asserted: the undeniable reality of the mutual influence between analysand and analyst, whatever the intentions and fantasies that either may hold. Every shift in the mental state of each of the participants in the analytic dyad, stated verbally through the semantic content of words or the prosody of the language, or sub-verbally through gestures and facial expressions, etc., results in the same neural networks being activated in the other person. Thus the analyst, whose attention is turned to herself, can perceive not only the emotions and thoughts that are somehow triggered by her own activated neural networks and which are equivalent to those in her patient, but also the corresponding somato-sensory processes that accompany such mental states. In other words, she can share her patient's senses through his experiences of the relationship: indeed, we can say that this analyst not only understands her patient but also recognises him in the same way as a mother recognises her baby (Coderch, J., 2015). The spirit of the setting in relational psychoanalysis is driven by making possible this resonance of mental state-emotions, sensations and thoughts - in the analyst's mind and bodily sensations as well as with the patient in relation to the analyst. We should add that we do not have, nor do we wish to have, rules for shaping this type of setting, be it external or internal - this would be at odds with creativity and the reality of the uniqueness of every analyst and every analytic dyad, where the spirit of a relational psychoanalytic setting should rule.

Our second point refers to intersubjectivity. Let us recall briefly that from the relational paradigm we consider that recognising one's self is achieved after passing from intrapsychically experiencing others as omnipotent objects formed to serve one's own needs (an intrapsychic dimension) to the recognition of others with selves similar to one's own, but distinct, with their own particular needs and attributes and through which we need to be recognised to feel and recognise ourselves (an interpersonal dimension). Put another way, we sense ourselves as individuals when we sense ourselves in others' minds. Hence Benjamin's forceful axiom: "where objects were, subjects must be" (Benjamin, J., 1995). We note, however, that the fullness of thought and creativity are obtained through the right balance between one dimension and the other. But this need to recognise and be recognised is never exhausted, it persists throughout life and is a source of personal growth. Let us look at F. Summers' striking words (2013) on the matter:

Development and self-experience are closely linked to the contact and subjectivities of others who are experienced as separate. The self is born of the intersubjective world and bears the hallmark of this world in the very fibres of his being. Continued contact with others is necessary for the self's nutrition and sustenance (p.36).

We fully subscribe to these words, which we interpret in the sense that intersubjectivity is the nutriment of subjectivity (subjective experience) and the self. Clinical work and infant-parent research show that a deepening intersubjectivity with others, which, as we have seen in Gallesse's words, is the origin of sociability among humans, stimulates development of the self and the emergence of new interests, resources and abilities that previously did not exist. This is linked to what we understand the objectives of psychoanalysis to be, as mentioned in section 2, and which can be summarised by saying the aim is for a different analysand to emerge compared to what he was like before. This leads us to hold that one of the fundamental pillars of the psychoanalytic process is continuous emotional and cognitive exchange between analysand and analyst, in an endless dialectic of proximity and mutual recognition, with moments of denial, to then again strive for proximity. We thus defend the right to expect that anything that advances this intersubjective dynamic will permeate the spirit of the setting. Following from this, we should aspire to create a setting that encourages dialogue that is open to any eventuality, far beyond the one-person interpretations formulated by the analyst. This requires an analyst who is not only free from the fear of being recognised as a person but available to be recognised and interpreted by her patient by her emotions and her way of recognising him as a means to promoting the growth of both of them. Hence the analyst should keep as far away as possible from being concerned about maintaining the cool "analytical distance", unachievable neutrality, and delusory anonymity.

Accommodation or self-expansion

Thus far, we can see that the therapeutic application of relational psychoanalysis is aimed at promoting the growth and development of the *self* (or subjectivity, to express it in other words) so that new ways of *being*, of living life open up for the patient (Summers, F., 2013, 2015).This includes freeing up resources and capabilities that have been inhibited by the negative pressure of the context or contexts in which the patient has lived, as well as the creation of new attitudes and abilities , which are the result of the interaction of the two participants in the analytical dyad.

Many people seeking psychoanalytic help have built a system of *accommodation* right from infancy to adapt to the demands, requirements, and intolerances of their milieu and so avoid the trauma of being rejected, unloved, shamed, ignored, etc. (Brandchaft, B., 1993, 2007; Brandchaft, R., Doctors, S. and Sorter, D., 2010, Coderch, J., 2014a).When these individuals begin analysis, despite their conscious wish to be helped, the fear of being re-traumatized often leads to their systems of accommodation being activated and they pre-reflexively push out of their minds and behaviour anything that they fear could lead to rejection by the analyst as they identify the analytic situation with something from their past. If the analyst is not fully aware of the risk that the patient may be accommodating, the system of protection will almost unavoidably be replicated (-we will not discuss here why this is more likely to happen with some styles of analysis more than others). Only careful reflection by the analyst on the responses that her behaviour and interventions bring about in the patient can prevent a reactivation of the system of accommodation. We know that patients "read" the theories on which analysts base their work and after a time, analysands develop who will conform with them and with what we can call their attitudes in their dealings with patients. Again, we feel that it is in the spirit of relational psychoanalysis that a relationship should develop that inspires the patient to feel he contributes directly to the construction of the setting. In other words, the spirit in which the setting is based is not that of patient and setting as two separate entities, but where the patient experiences himself as co-constructor of the setting and forms an intrinsic part of it.

We do not think that relational psychoanalysts can avoid creating a relational patients as they also rely on their theories, but we do hope that if the analysis goes reasonably well, with time these relational patients in construction will be patients who do not accommodate nor who are dominated by the fear of feeling rejected, alone, not understood, but will be patients who do not submit nor are in constant struggle with their analysts. They will hopefully be patients then, whatever their afflictions and difficulties in real life, who express themselves spontaneously in analysis and can converse freely rather than simply "associating" in order to adapt to what they suppose their analysts' theories are.

Consequently, if our aim is to foster creativity and an unfolding of what patients could be but still are not, then the most appropriate course within the goals of relational psychoanalysis is to build a setting that will allow patients to gain confidence and be in a situation where they feel they can enter into an interpersonal relationship, perhaps for the first time in their lives according to their own wishes and emotional needs, through dialogue that is unconstrained by the demands of others, pressure in their milieux, or by fear of rejection or threat. It is therefore fitting to give them the occasion that what we call setting be a common construction; in the same way that today it is increasingly recognised that transference and countertransference are created, so is the intersubjective field. Otherwise, an internal setting with an analyst who zealously maintains his or her analytic abstinence, seeking anonymity, showing no kind of emotional response, and whose interventions are limited to interpretations, would favour from the very start a reactivation of the patient's system of accommodation, and his scope of experience would be limited to expressing only what he feels would be welcome.

The setting as a structure of reception and a place of hospitality.

A) Structures of reception.

The anthropologist and philosopher L. Duch (2000) has created a new concept, the *'structure of reception'*, which is tremendously helpful in defining the setting in what we understand to be relational psychoanalysis and which we will comment on briefly here.

Babies today are born with brains fully prepared - fruit of a long evolution of the species - to grow, develop and live as a human beings. However, unlike other mammals, they are helpless, totally defenceless, to the extreme that they would die if upon arrival they did not find a new 'womb' to replace the uterus and which can be termed *relational and socio-cultural matrix* (A. Plaza and J. Coderch, personal communication); it is basically formed by the parents and the baby's milieu. The baby receives the stimuli and experiences that are necessary for its brain to become the brain of the *sapiens sapiens*, which, incidentally, has only existed for some 150,000 years (Tomasello, M., Hobson, P. 2004).

When the young human later leaves this relational matrix, they will need other structures of reception, such as schools, cities or towns to live in; peers; professional teaching; and political, cultural, artistic, recreational, and sporting institutions, etc. These structures progressively mould the youngsters to be able to properly take on their roles as men or women, and we believe that a couple relationship specially performs this function of reception and emotional support, together with the question of sexuality. From the perspective of non-linearity, however, it should be noted that individuals do not passively relate or receive the influences from these structures but co-create and form part of them through their interactions.

We are discussing structures of reception here as we consider the psycho-analytic setting to be part of them - it can give patients the feeling of not only being benevolently received, as has sometimes been said, but also that they are part of these structures; these structures also can adapt to the needs of patients, who are not asked to be the only ones to have to adapt, as happens in the traditional setting.

Clinical work shows only too well that people who come in search of help have not had a sufficiently receptive, friendly context in their childhood and adolescence, and what they require when their suffering becomes too great is someone who can bring relief. When these people seek help, they anticipate they will find in the person they go to, someone who will listen and understand. And this is the nature and the spirit with which to construct the relational setting.

B) The setting as a place of hospitality.

We might ask, how could the manner of receiving and hosting someone seeking help from an analyst not be hospitable? It is essential to devote some time to this point

If we refer to hospitality, we cannot fail to mention the influence of the philosopher Emmanuel Lévinas and the impact he has made on the dynami-cally-oriented psychology, especially on our professional practice, questioning and enriching many of our ideas. His philosophy defends that openness to the unknown, the other, following the call of ethics is what can bring us freedom (Lévinas, E., 1977.1993).

In the field of psychoanalysis, D. Orange seems to us to be the highest advocate of the spirit of hospitality before the patient. In her desire to deepen the concept and process of *intersubjectivity,* this author (2011) turns to ethics and the thinking of three 20th century French humanist, spiritual philosophers: Ricoeur, Derrida and, more specially, Lévinas. Orange refers to Lévinas, among other authors, whose philosophy is characterized by ethics being understood as a radically asymmetrical relationship of infinite responsibility towards the other person (p.46). She also emphasizes that, for Lévinas, the response to the demand of the other should be, *"Me Voici" (Me here:) I am indeed my brother's keeper and there is no escape* (p.47).

In her article 'Hospitalidad clínica: Acogiendo el Rostro delOtroDevastado' (2013a), (Clinical Hospitality: Welcoming the Face of the Devastated Other) Orange warns that for Lévinas the other has the infinite right to protection and care, and therefore, there is what he called a *curvature of the intersubjective space.* For Orange, this means that an ethical relationship is not between equals, but is essentially asymmetrical; she quotes Critchley's work (2002) on Lévinas:

Inside that relation, as it takes place, at this very moment, you place an obligation on me that makes you more than me, more than my equal (2002, p.14).

Orange also highlights in Lévinas' philosophy that responsibility toward the other completely transcends one's need for comfort. With regard to treating the other as an object of study, Lévinas raises the value of the face, face to face encounter, which goes beyond the idea we have of the other.

Orange suggests that some aspects of Lévinasian ethics may seem extreme to clinicians, especially the concept of substitution. In her book *Thinking for Clinicians: Philosophical Resources for Contemporary Psychoanalysis and the Humanistic Psychotherapies* (2011), Orange elaborates on three concepts, and advocates that psychotherapists who follow in Lévinas' footsteps should be clear about three precepts: "irreducibility", "proximity" and "substitution". The patient who demands of me, is not a façade *reducible* to a nervous system or a control centre. *Proximity* is the distance in our relationship with the other, but the other is close because there is no space to evade our ethical obligation. *Substitution* is understood as the obligation to accept to endure the other's fate, even risking one's life to save him.

In her study of Lévinas (2011), Orange points out that his humanism is not a theory, not a spirit, nor a turn of expression, but is the availability of psychoanalysts and therapists working phenomenologically with our devastated neighbour, to take our vulnerability and our trauma as guests in our work (p.97 in the Spanish edition).

Through her work, Orange shows that Lévinas acknowledges a limitation in his ethics when the relationship with the other opens up to a multitude of people: *between two, my obligation to the other is infinite, but when there are three of us, it is legitimate that there are limits, agreements and laws.* Orange thinks that in Derrida there is a confluence of the ideality of Lévinas' ethics and dose of practical post-modern realism, which is necessary to apply to the norm to make it viable in the human world, particularly in psychotherapy. Orange (2013), criticises this contemporising as an "ambiguity of hospitality", although we feel it is a more fitting, more proximate ethics.

Consequently, in her study on the ethics of Lévinas and Derrida applied to psychotherapy, Orange reminds us of the Winnicottian availability of the therapist, a way of being with the other, where the setting or analytical framework could be compared to the symbolization of the mother-infant metaphor, a necessary condition to satisfy deficits from the patient's past. The therapeutic session offers a second chance for emotional development within the analytic process, this time offering the "good enough" holding environment the patient did not have in childhood.

Orange (2013) also equates empathy with hospitality, understanding it not as fusion - standing in another's skin - but as the need for separation from the other. She believes it necessary to create a space for the patient in the heart of the person offering hospitality in order that the devastated other may have a second chance to develop. However, she also understands this may be a disturbing for clinicians, especially regarding the concept of setting, given that we are human beings with limitations. Orange refers to the case of a patient who complained that in psychotherapy and psychoanalysis everything was set up to protect the therapist, not the patient's needs. Before he could come to terms with a more or less conventional therapy, Orange would see her patient taking walks along or sitting by the sea.

Thus, every analytic dyad and every intersubjective field must find its own process, its own setting, its own organizational rules and its own limits, so they gradually adjust to the rhythm of the two parts and with the sole purpose of helping the therapeutic process move forward. Stolorow(2012) notes there are no rules that fit all cases nor technical guidelines that are valid by default: each encounter between patient and analyst is a unique intersubjective field that is less accommodating to technique than practical creativity. We prefer to speak of the setting in terms of a posture of being with the other that adapts as the relationship with the patient progresses.

Orange's reflections on the idea of hospitality applied to the setting have also led us to think about the concept of *surrender* proposed by E. Ghent in a paper on masochism and submission (1990), as we believe both concepts, hospitality and surrender, are closely related. When considering this concept in Spanish, we agree with A. Liberman (2014) in that we would have preferred to keep the English term rather than translate it because all its negative connotations in Spanish. Liberman understands the concept of *surrender* as an attitude of "entrusting oneself", "letting go", "abandon", very appropriate terms. Regarding this concept, he also speaks of "great sensitivity, personal commitment, and vulnerability (p. 97).

Ghent clearly differentiates between surrender and raising the white flag of submission. Ghent's notion of surrender goes beyond the limits of individuality, it is a transcendent act so does not always necessarily need another. For this reason he says that one may surrender in *"the presence of another"* but *"not to another"*. Ghent describes nuances and features that characterise surrender, of which we quote two:

Its ultimate direction is the discovery of one's identity, one's sense of self, one's sense of wholeness, even one's sense of unity with other living beings. This is quite unlike submission in which the reverse happens: one feels one's self as a puppet in the power of another; one's sense of identity atrophies. (p.109).

In surrender there is an absence of domination and control; the reverse is true in the case of submission.(p. 109).

J.Benjamin (2004) also uses the concept of *surrender, citing Ghent, when speaking* about intersubjectivity and the idea of thirdness. We believe she makes this reference as for another to be recognised and to reach full intersubjectivity, it is first necessary to surrender to the other.

In this "letting go", "entrusting oneself", "surrendering", there is no relinquishing of one's subjectivity, but there is a renunciation to impose it on the other, a recognition of the other and a letting oneself be guided, temporarily, by the other. We believe that this is consistent with intimacy, almost on the verge of *merging limits,* which is in the spirit of the relational setting.

The "Expressivist Turn" and Romanticism

In order to further clarify the spirit of the setting as we appreciate it, it will prove useful to dedicate some discussion to the socio-cultural movement in which relational psychoanalysis is grounded even though its roots lie in a different era. It is beneficial for psychoanalysis, essential even for its survival, not to lose contact with the pulse of the world about it as this pulse is expressed both implicitly and explicitly in each and every patient coming to analysis.

The socio-cultural movement we refer to is what the philosopher Charles Taylor, in his book *Sources of the Self: The Making of the Modern Identity* (1996), has called the *Expressivist Turn,* a term that has been widely accepted by many thinkers and scholars of culture. The 'Expressivist Turn' should be understood as a reaction against the extreme idealisation of reason, against the

191

rule of rationalism in culture in all its aspects, in art (neoclassicism), in morals and in formalist customs and social conventions that neglected and disdained the emotions, imagination and fantasy. This climate had dominated European culture and society from the age of the Enlightenment, which arose in France, driven by encyclopaedists (led by Diderot and D'Alembert), and which culminated in the French Revolution, the English Enlightenment , and the rationalism that had repercussions in Germany with Kant's forceful admonition *Sapere Aude!(*Dare to think!). This European cultural and intellectual movement began early in the eighteenth century and was strong until the mid-nineteenth century (although different authors disagree on this time scale). The debate about just how far the Enlightenment endures (tremendously deformed by technology) in the post-modern era is a controversial issue of enormous depth, and its discussion requires great knowledge, (Horkheimer, M, and Adorno, T, 1947; Coderch, J., 2001; Bauman, Z., 2007).

Taylor describes the Expressivist Turn in the following words (1996):

I am speaking about views which arise with the German Strum und Drang and continue developing thereafter through the Romantic period, both English and German. Rousseau is naturally its point of departure, and its first important articulation comes perhaps in the work of Herder; thereafter it is taken up not only by Romantic writers but by Goethe and, in another way, by Hegel and becomes one of the constituent streams of modern culture.(p. 503).

In Europe this movement is better known as *Romanticism* or the *Romantic Era,* and was initiated by Herder after a sea voyage he undertook in 1769 (Safranski, 2007). Taylor cautions that the Expressivist Turn and Romanticism are not fully related, as evidenced by links of the former with Goethe and Hegel. Nonetheless, we believe that instead of considering them to be different movements but ones that influence each other, it is more correct to think of the Expressivist Turn as having a far left (represented by Romanticism, and at a personal level by authors such as Schiller, Novalis , Hölderlin, Scheleirmacher, etc. in Germany and Rousseau in France), and a far right which is less revolutionary, in which the figure of Goethe especially stands out and who, in the face of the outpourings by certain fanatical Romantics and the excesses of the French revolutionaries, exclaimed, *"I prefer committing an injustice to putting up with disorder."* It is difficult, for example, not to categorise certain of Goethe's works, such as *Faust,* or *The Sorrows of Young Werther,* as romantic, despite their moralizing and bien-pensant leaning. Relevant themes in Romanticism are the revolt against neo-classicism in art (- so formalist, so contained, so sexually demure, so far removed from passion); against the oppression of the emotions by reason; against social convention; against traditions and cold harmony on the one hand, and, the vindication of an individual's rights, imagination, emotions, freedom of expression, sexuality and free, creative, passionate spontaneity on the other. Romanticism affirms a common love of nature as a source of life that humans should feel in communion with. For romantic authors, life was like an overflowing torrent; a bubbling, roaring restlessness, and they confided in the inner voice of every man to govern his own destiny. We think that in this expansive wave in favour of emotions and against the absolute rule of rationalism, psychoanalysis resides at an intermediate position between the two ends of the Expressivist Turn.

It is well known that the Expressivist Turn had a great influence on politics and social customs, and in its facet as Romanticism, it had an enormous impact on art, literature, and love between man and woman (at that time homosexuality was covert), especially, in choice of partner. Until then, there was no concept of marriage for love, and choice of partner was always transversal, that is, between people of the same social and economic status. Romanticism broke taboos and barriers and proclaimed the universal right to happiness and to follow one's instincts. The cultural repercussions of this movement were enormous in Germany and France, but rather weak in Spain generally, although significant in literature, poetry and drama (Zorilla, Espronceda, Becquer, the Duke of Rivas, etc.).

The reader may be wondering the reason behind these digressions into expressiveness, marriage, transversality and Romanticism in a paper reflecting on the psychoanalytic setting. But hopefully this will become clear when we say we believe that Freud's psychoanalysis was born, with a lapse intime, as a part of the Expressivist Turn, as a reaction to the rigid social conventions, moral hypocrisy and rejection of passions prevalent in Freud's Vienna. Unfortunately, after the early years of the new discipline, passionate, rebellious years in its fight against hypocrisy and social conventions, and whose ultimate expression is reflected in the appearance of *Studies on Hysteria*, in collaboration with J. Breuer, and publication of his Case Studies (1895), the patriarchal model and cold rationalism once again triumphed, with Freud and his followers now attempting to convert psychoanalysis into a respectable, conventional natural science accepted by the whole scientific community. Freud and his early disciples privately spoke of the "psychoanalytic movement", which we believe is a vestige of its affinity with the Romantic "Movement".

We would like to add that after many generations of classical psychoanalysis based on the belief that psychological disorders are a mere expression of biological drives and should all be treated with the same technique, we believe that the advent of relational psychoanalysis is similar to a new proclamation or rebirth of the Expressivist Turn, at times very much in its romantic facet, claiming freedom, spontaneity, respect for every patient's individuality, as well as creativity and passion for providing help, as opposed to "analytical abstinence" and reserve against the disparagingly called *furor curandis* of traditional psychoanalysis. Ultimately, we see that even the most classical analysts, true to their technique, at the outset of a psychoanalytic treatment tell their patients to *express* themselves freely, to verbalise whatever thoughts and fantasies come to mind, to break the barriers of social conventions and prejudices. We believe this is a true, lasting memory of the origins of psychoanalysis, shyly hiding behind technique. Such a pity then, that betraying what they have just said, they try to domesticate this expressiveness with their theory-based interpretations.

Fortunately, however, we are not alone in considering what we might call the *expressivism-romanticism* so clearly seen in so much of relational psychoanalysis. What distinguishes the relational from the classical paradigm is relinquishing the drives as a *deus ex machina* that move and explain everything, and shifting to being concerned with emotions. For example, in his book *The Psychoanalytic Vision* (2013), F. Summers titled one chapter "The romantic interpretation of psychoanalysis" and places M. Eigen as one of the representatives of romanticism in psychoanalysis. And rightly so in our view: it is sufficient to read the paper he presented at the Joint Conference of IARPP-Spain and IARPP-Portugal (Cáceres 2014), *Tears of Pain and Beauty: Mixed Voices*, to remove any doubt about his affinity to romanticism in psychoanalysis. Summers shares the same stance in his above mentioned book. Stolorow also, in his 2012 paper, as well as insisting on a *shift from drives to* affects, talks of the need of love amongst all, as a last hope for salvation for this disoriented, lost, suffering humanity, in a concluding paragraph that is pure poetry.

After this series of reflections on the relationship between psychoanalysis and the Expressivist Turn, we should like to speak briefly about the kind of psychoanalysis within the relational paradigm for which we envisage the setting we have tried to define. The reader will already have formed an idea about this style of psychoanalysis and its aims. It might be useful to add that we seek (or should we say we dream of?) an analysis that spurs patients to *pursue their self-realisation in an unlimited way* and to seek their identity with passion following their inner voice, the voice of their own self rather than the voices of others, including their analyst. An analysis that goes beyond finding hidden intrapsychic conflicts that must be resolved by the analyst's interpretations, but if conflicts are found, the analyst should help the patient integrate them and turn suffering into a creative force (Atwood, G., and Stolorow, R., 1993). We believe that there is no creation without suffering, as shown both by the history of psychoanalysis as well as the history of mankind. We aspire to a psychoanalysis that trusts in patients' own transforming force while the analyst accompanies them in the unfolding of their selfness rather than trying to impose his or her own theories (Grossmark, R., 2012). An analysis that emphasises what is *new* in the current analytic relationship, which the past helps to understand and work through (Mitchell, S, 1988). An analysis that cannot be rightly accused of being solely concerned with converting analysands into good, well-adapted citizens without drive or originality (or we could say *normopaths?)*, a particularly serious matter when it comes to professionals coming to analysis who aim to become psychoanalysts themselves. All in all, a psychoanalysis whose process is driven by a setting in which patient-analyst intersubjectivity is a permanent, inexhaustible source of therapeutic experiences for both (Coderch, J., 2015).

With these last remarks on our concept of the psychoanalytic process, we hope to have drawn a clear picture of the spirit that should always be present in the relational setting. In fact, everything we have said can be summed up in a nutshell: *Recognising the other and developing a sense of self are interdependent phenomena. Intersubjectivity, recognising the other and feeling recognised by the other are nourishment for theself. Therefore, the spirit of the setting in relational psychoanalysis is to stimulate and promote a deepening intersubjectivity.*

Conclusions. Romanticism As An Attitude of the Spirit

There is no doubt that the Romanticism that formed part of the Expressivist Turn was clearly manifested in the birth of Freudian psychoanalysis, and we firmly believe that what we call the spirit of Romanticism, the vestiges of Romanticism in our time, has played an important role in the emergence and development of relational psychoanalysis. The focus on emotions, fantasy, imagination, dreaming, creativity, ambition, individuality, and self-realisation has emerged in opposition to the technical rationalism of classical psycho-analysis centred on biological drives as the explanation for all psychological events. In short, a return to the passions against the tyranny of reason. One manifestation of these embers of Romanticism can be seen, for example, in the May 1968 student protests; we can find nothing more romantic than the rallying cry *"All Power to the Imagination!"*, although in this case, Romanti-cism was enmeshed with politics, something that has frequently led the latter along perilous paths. Romanticism tends to be unruly, radical, alien to the world and, in the case in question, does not seek consensus nor welfare; it has its own agenda, sometimes acting against life, seeking suffering and even death: heroic death, romantic death. In Spain this was personified by the remarkable essayist and writer Mariano José de Larra, who standing in front of the mirror, shot himself in the head, holding a copy of Goethe's novel, *The Sorrows of Young Werther* in one hand, pistol in the other. This was not the only case. An epidemic of romantic suicides spread through Europe following Goethe's novel. Romanticism, used wisely, is good for dreaming, writing poetry and novels, for acts of heroism, for intimate friendship, for doing good to others, compassion, solidarity, love and for psychoanalysis, but not for politics or, if taken to extremes, for life.

We say all this as we do not wish to be interpreted as proposing an irrational, limitless move towards Romanticism in psychoanalysis, taking it to extremes, and neglecting reason in favour of passion. That is not our aim as passion, or Romanticism, can also be go off course, be corrupted and perverted, ending in delirium and madness, as in the most hideous, cruel cases of national socialism or fascism (which does not mean that Hitler and Mussolini were romantics, but took criminal advantage of naive and sometimes ludicrous illusions of Romanticism and the romantics). The Enlightenment became denatured in much the same way and led us to instrumental reasoning in pursuit of human superiority and dominion over nature, which is annihilating the planet Earth. It is a matter of finding the proper balance between reason and passion, in both culture and psychoanalysis. Extreme rationalism in psychoanalysis led to a metapsychology based on biological forces in which psychology is absent. This was discredited decades ago, but it lingers on owing to factors we cannot now go into (Coderch, J. 2014b), and has presided over the decline of psychoanalysis in present-day culture and society. At the same time, an excess of passion, obviating the right dose of reason, would lead to an anarchic psychoanalysis, fragmented into multiple schools and lacking any true meaning, an "anything goes" ending in its own demise, becoming pure charlatanism. In summary, it is not an irrational, disproportionate, depleted Romanticism that we, the authors of this paper, are interested in, but it is the romantic spirit that permeates the deepest roots of the relational turn which can enrich psychoanalysis and launch it to the greatest heights.

We are confident that Ávila Espada and other fellow readers will now appreciate what the psychoanalysis we (now) dream of is, at the same time as forgiving our romantic boldness.

Summary

At the outset of a psychoanalysis, the analyst explains to the patient the rules that will guide their relationship from the start through to termination. These clearly set out guidelines are known as the external setting; the internal setting is the unique, unrepeatable interpersonal configuration that the analyst-patient relationship will acquire over time. Traditionally, analysts have established the external setting - and have also attempted to do the same with the internal setting - according to Freudian drive-based metapsychology. The appearance of the relational paradigm in psychoanalysis, where human beings, given their biological nature, are considered to be fundamentally relational and social, has given rise to another perspective on emotional disorders and the way those suffering from them can be helped. It is therefore essential to formulate another type of setting to be able to practise psychoanalysis from the perspective of this new paradigm. This chapter will offer no rules or norms to define the setting; it aims to describe its nuances and style – what we could call its spirit – in an attempt to make it harmonious with the essence and objectives of relational psychoanalysis.

9

Any Port In A Storm: A Complex And Relational Focus On Addiction In Love And Relationships[1]

Luis Raimundo Guerra Cid

The way we interact —with ourselves and the others- is the most reliable instrument for measuring our mental health.

Advances In Our Perspectives of Human Relationships

One of the main pitfalls in our clinical practice resides in the fact that a high percentage of patients have relationship problems as a primary or secondary conflict. Many of them "respond to" a relationship in which there is a love addiction. Love is a concept of which little has been written in the history of

---

1 Translated by Rodolfo Pérez Sánchez and Rosanna Small.

psychoanalysis although it has seen some brilliant contributions (T. Reik, 1994; E. Fromm 1956; O. Kernberg 1995; S. Mitchell, 2002).

As clinicians, one of the best ways of understanding the dynamics of a human relationship is from its relational and intersubjective base. If to this we add: an anthropological point of reference and Nonlinear Dynamic System Theories (NDLS), we can obtain a more detailed view of such dynamics.

From an anthropological standpoint the first thing that we observe is that the concepts of a "couple" and marriage are both social and cultural constructions. This means that: neither 1) the gender of the couple members, nor 2) the way in which the couple is formed, and, least of all, 3) the supposed obligations they have towards each other, are universally accepted norms.

1) Gay marriage is now legal in many countries around the world; for example, in some parts of the United States, Canada, Spain and Portugal among others. However, this practice has been documented by anthropologists in diverse regions and tribes across the world. One example we might reference is the African Nuer Tribe, where Evans-Pritchard (1940, 1951) conducted a great field study about the institutionalisation of gay marriage between the young Azande warriors. Another case is the Nandi (Kenya) where "husband-women" marry other women and dedicate themselves to "masculine" tasks. (Jiménez, 2011 p. 201).

In addition to same-sex marriage, there is also an extensive documentation of a third gender, at times cohabiting in a couple. This phenomenon can be seen in various Native American tribes, in what is known as the "Two-Spirit" tradition. One specific case is the Navajo Tribe. They distinguish between three genders: male, female and the highly valued "Nadle"[2]. The recognition of three different, physical genders results in four types of gender status: women, men, true Nadle and false Nadle. This third gender Nadle retain privileges which the rest of the Navajo do not and have totally adapted to their culture, being able to partner with both women and men.

2) The way that a couple is formed is not universal and this is something we may observe in our own culture. In the past, religious marriage was necessary for a legitimate relationship. Nowadays, however, recognition is also social. In a classic study, Stephens (1963) indicated the impossibility of giving a global explanation for marriage that is valid for all cultures. Characteristics that were believed constant: marriage ritual, sexual legitimacy and marital duties; are not

---

2 The Nadle, with genital ambiguity, is a hermaphrodite (Bolin, 2003, p. 237). The false Nadle, therefore, masquerades as a true Nadle. By doing this, he gains privileges that the other Navajo do not have, such as the sexual election of gender.

found in many cultures studied by anthropologists. This matter leads us to the final anthropological aspect that I wish to highlight.

3) Obligations within relationships are in no way universal. As an example, I can turn to P. Bohanann, an anthropologist who spent several years with the "Tiv" tribe of Nigeria. According to his investigations, when the "Tiv" married they adopted a set of simple and rigid rules. Some of them were: for the wife to cook at least once a day for her husband, take care of the children and to sleep with him. The husband, in turn, provided clothing, prepared good farm land for her and, in the event that she fell ill, sought the help of the shaman. (1996, p. 69).

Although marital obligations exist, it is not expected from a "Tiv" marriage that the husband and wife be friends. The secret beneath a "Tiv" marriage resides in having multiple offspring without engaging in any disputes. Therefore, we must bear in mind that couples as we understand them are principally a "western invention": a socio-cultural construction.

In the "Nayar" culture -a group of Hindu castes -couples separate as soon as they are married. The wife returns to her birthplace and has the right to be visited by other men while men are permitted to see other women. Here the concept of fidelity clearly falls apart and it becomes very complicated for westerners to understand.

After this brief summary, we may observe that in our western culture the mass-media, social networks, cinema, TV, etc. are constantly dictating to us how a couple must behave, often through 'norms' that tend towards idealisation and extreme romanticism. Although marriage and other forms of cohabitation are universal institutions, their approaches are not, and demonstrate wide variety. Romantic relationships, as we understand them, are a cultural construction; not comparable to those of ages past nor to other types of society.

The importance that we place on what we expect from the other, or what the other is obliged to do (and in a certain way to be), is an intersubjective product modulated by culture, society and family.

Another fundamental concept for understanding romantic relationships is the theory of Non-Linear Dynamic System (NLDS)[3]. Just as the patient-therapist relationship or the first mother-child bond, a couple is also a complex, dynamic and nonlinear "system".

---

3 For the purposes of this essay we will only comment on the application of NLDS to relationships and relationship dynamics. For further explanation of NLDS we refer the reader to the chapter 8 of this book written by J. Coderch and A. Codosero "Between Passion and Reason. Reflections on the spirit of the setting in Relational Psychoanalysis".

What is a NLDS? It is any complex system in which multiple factors intervene, factors which reassert them selves. Frequently, the most important elements are the ones which appear in the initial conditions and give rise to complex consequences by means of a butterfly effect. These systems are chaotic but do not at all imply a lack of order: they are self-organizing and self-structuring. Examples of such system are meteorology, social organisations, human psychopathology, patient-therapist relationships, mother-child relationships and, of course, romantic relationships.

What are the basic principles of NLDS? I concur with S. Seligman (2014) with reference to the following:

1) Transactional processes are key features of non-linear systems. In my opinion it must be taken into account that moments of transition are the windows of change. It is easier to change in a transition than try to do it in a new phase. The beginning of a relationship can be understood as a transitional period in which the initial conditions and the "sensitive dependence" take special importance. But there are also different transitions in a relationship that should be acknowledged, such as the birth of children.

2) Systems can amplify tendencies that might shift them in one direction or another.

3) Sensitive dependence on initial conditions. When a system is in a sensitive state, small changes may make a dramatic difference.

4) Dynamic systems are self-organizing.

Before we move on to the application of NLDS to relationship dynamics, we will observe some of the principles regarding the human couple. These rules have different degrees of flexibility but above all, they debunk those myths, many of which are idealistic, that surround the human couple.

a) Every intense relationship is based on the *Transference Principle*. All relationships and feelings that we have towards others are modulated by our romantic relationships, by the bonds formed in the first and second infancy and by those which we maintain during adolescence and adulthood.

This *Transference Principle*, which I prefer to name *Anthropological Transference* (Guerra Cid, 2001, 2006) in order to differentiate it from the transfer which is produced in a patient-therapist framework (and usually with *Drive Theory* connotations), is universal. Furthermore, it can be conscious or unconscious and declarative or procedural (Implicit Relational Knowing). In *Transference Principle,* in addition to the importance of attachment relationships formed during infancy, we must also take into account the image of romantic relationships unconsciously generated during childhood and adolescence.

b) *A romantic relationship is a mutual co-construction of the two protago-nists*. Its creation, maintenance, progress and regression are the fruit of the interaction between two people. A relationship is something that remains independent to each partner while at the same time both participate in it. In contemporary psycho-analysis, this concept is defined as *Thirdness* (J. Benjamin, 1988).

Thirdness is not a "mine" or a "yours" but an "ours", a relational phenom-enon produced by the couple. This concept allows us to reflect on, define and treat the multiple problems that can emerge in a relationship, including sexual issues (Castaño, 2011).

c) *A relationship is an open, complex and dynamic system*. Each partner plays a role within the system. However, these functions and roles that the individuals of the couple fulfil can be transformed. The system can also undergo changes through external influence and evolve into other states.

Within this system, however, the saying "opposites attract" is untrue, given that if both characters are truly opposed, there are lower levels of connection, common spaces and empathy. A distinct concept from "opposites attract" are two poles which, although different, complement each other. Two complementing characters who generate grow thin themselves, in the other partner and in the relationship as a *thirdness*

d) A certain level of *individual intimacy* is always necessary in order not to fuse with the other, thereby creating a symbiotic relationship. The couple have to leave space for each member to be themselves, even if only in everyday tasks. Always doing everything together and having no distinction between each other does not imply a deeper relationship, a closer relationship, or greater love.

e) Likewise, when you are in a relationship, *absolute individuality becomes impossible* because of what a couple is by definition. Often, many of my patients have shared with me a desire of being able to continue with room for manoeuvre and with all their power of decision making. This is a complicated matter given that the compromise of a relationship always requires "losing" a certain amount of individuality for the other.

This is one the most complex balancing acts in a relationship: main-taining some level of intimacy but, at the same time, sharing with the other and accepting the "frustration" of having to cede (time, energy, space…). Independence is complicated further, with the necessity for camaraderie and cooperation when children enter the relationship, transforming the couple transforming into a family.

In this regard, J. Willi (1978, p. 21) proposed three functional principles for balance within a relationship:

1. Both members must have the same importance in the relationship.
2. The same member cannot always be progressive (meaning active and strong) while the other is always regressive (passive and weak).
3. Boundary Principle. Being fused or joined without limits is just as negative for a couple as living life totally apart from each other. This probably refers to the difficult task of maintaining the balance between ones intimacy and the part of that intimacy that we lose when we are in a relationship. Fromm affirmed along these lines: the hardest thing about relationships is being two while still being one.

f) During the medium or long term a relationship needs *position and definition*. That is to say, the couple, or always at least one of its members, will eventually confront the other with "*What* are we?" and "What do we conform to?" So-called "sex buddies" or "friends with benefits" exist as such due to a tacit, or sometimes explicit, agreement on "what they are", depending their own definition. However, experience has taught us that even in these situations, when it reaches long term it becomes complicated and one of the two tends to tighten the cord.

Often, one of the members has the intention to go further. This upsets the balance, generating a point of inflexion through which usually come three options: 1) the relationship breaks up, 2) it continues in some way according to its definition (committed, 'going out'); or 3) it may enter a new pathological situation in which one partner wishes to maintain his or her status and the other wants more and more emotional involvement. It is, of course, unlikely that the relationship can continue indefinitely through ambiguity or lack of definition.

The following principles can be defined as "cultural nature":

g) As mentioned, the idea of romantic love, with all of its consequences and what is expected of one partner to do for the other and vice versa, *is a cultural construction.*

h) For this reason it is incredibly difficult to try to *maintain a deep and meaningful open relationship.* The stereotypical desire of many is to be able to maintain a loving and profound relationship with their companion, their life partner; and at the same time be able to have fleeting affairs or even a lover. When faced with the fact that "it's possible to be in love with two people at the same time" it should be noted that psychologically it is negotiable and debatable. Culturally, however, it is not. Our culture openly sanctions such behaviour to greater and lesser degrees.

i) A romantic relationship is a system which *is connected to other systems;* while those other systems interact with the 'relationship system', at times surrounding and at others merging with it. Status, age, the existence - or lack of - children and the life cycle of the couple; all these factors mean different things to the 'couple system', depending on the society and culture to which it is linked.

j) For a romantic relationship to be solid and stable *it is not necessary to form a friendship* which then leads to love. Those relationships based on the "strike of Cupid's arrow" and "love at first sight" can also be strong and profound. In this regard J. Willi (2004, p. 22) undertook an interesting investigation in which it was observed that there were practically no differences between those couples who had grown into love after some time of knowing each other and those who had fallen in love suddenly.

NLDS Application to Human Couple

In order to adequately treat relationship problems, either individually or in couple therapy, we are at a greater advantage if we analyse them as NLDS. This enables us to find a set of *attractors* produced at the beginning of the relationship and which will become fundamental in the development of it (*Dependent Sensibility* - Lorenz 1972). These attractors can be found in the initial conditions of any complex system and can cause powerful and unpredictable butterfly effects within the relationship.

In addition to the *attractors*, we must pinpoint the *maintainers* of the relationship and their process of change. With these three variables we will also have the capacity to see what kind of relationship is lying underneath and if it represents a "*relational affectopathology*"[4] (Guerra Cid, 2006, 2013, 2015).

Many of the *attractors* that I will mention here also function as *maintainers* of the relationship, either in a similar way or through transformation. One example would be basic needs such as affiliation or validation.

In any case, this is not a static system, but a flexible and dynamic one. Therefore, *attractors* can also be *maintainers*, and certain *maintainers* arise with force and with the character of *attractor* in the initial conditions.

A) Initial conditions: attractors or pull factors

1) The first *attractor* or pull factor which arises during the initial conditions is related to an anthropological concept called "***radical unanchored drifting***"

---

4 I use the Word "affecto" for its relational implication. Affecto means, from its Latin etymological meaning "affectus", put someone under some state or influence the mood. The term refers to how the others affect on us and produce certain mood states and diverse feelings (anger, affection, love, etc.). Pathology: from Greek *pathos*, English *suffering*.

defined by Spanish psychoanalyst and anthropologist Luis Cencillo (1978)[5]. This concept refers to the "*un-programmed*" state in which human beings are born:

"We are born un-programmed and during our childhood we are programmed; most of the time this is done wrong (or we latch on to the wrong information) and we fail to learn how to love, not to mention to learn what we want" (Cencillo, 2000, p.25)

We seek, therefore, to "*anchor ourselves*" to others. Our attachment figures during childhood, our role models and our reference points for affection supply us with filters through which we understand and handle reality, in particular that reality related to our emotional world. We also *anchor ourselves* to our culture, its functions and its symbols.

2) **Expectations** are of at least of two types. On one hand, there is the behaviour that we expect from our partner. On the other, is the expectation that is generated due to being viewed as "in a relationship" by our social circle and by society in general (also includes socio-economic factors). For example: the social status we except to achieve for having, or not having, a romantic partner.

3) There also exist two types of **attribution** of characteristics. Firstly, what the other must be like (a saviour, unconditional, comforting, etc.); and secondly, what is gained from being in a relationship (also from a cultural and a personal perspective). These expectations and attributions are the building blocks for idealisation (Guerra Cid, 2015).

4) Referring to **idealisation**, T. Reik (1944) affirmed that it is the main driving force for falling in love. In addictive relationships, idealisation plays a central role as the members of the couple seek and pursue an unattainable ideal in order to compensate for their own personality defects. With regard to idealisation we must remember this phrase by S. Mitchell: "*Idealisation is, by definition, illusory*" (2002, p.28).

Certainly, what we attribute to and hope from the other is closely related to our fantasies and our subjective needs. Therefore, when these factors become *maintainers* of the relationship, they may transform from a dynamic of desire

---

5 Cencillo coined the concept: "*desfondamiento radical*" in Spanish, which describes the state in which we are born: totally "un-programmed" with no firm anchor or base which guides our existence. He contrasts this state to that of an animal at birth, which has an instinctive programming and anchor/base. As humans are born in this state of "radical drifting", with no predetermination or programming; we need something to anchor ourselves to "en que fondarnos", in order to face reality with purpose. We anchor ourselves to belief, religion, tradition, ritual, customs, society and relationships and use them as a base to compensate for our lack of instinctive, genetic anchor.

to one of reproach. This is produced because we desire a change in our partner which confirms our expectations of suitability: when reality imposes, it causes frustration.

At this point we want to change the other according to what we desired of them. It is at this moment in the process when desire becomes reproach towards the object of our love, who does not reach the benchmark of fantasised idealisation.

5) **The necessity for affiliation.** This is a universal human instinct concerning the need to feel attached to something or someone. Taking a broader view it helps to rescue an idea from S. Mitchell: that of *object-seeking* as an ever-present universal motivation and which leads us to search for "the object" that will help us to organise and comprehend our own subjectivity.

This construction, therefore, is the reason that falling in love happens, from one moment to the next, when we find another that complements and structures us.

6) **The necessity for validation and mirroring.** In addition to our affiliation, in order to sustain our self-esteem, we need the positive reflection that our partner holds up to us. This is general factor that intensifies in its search when narcissism is unstructured. We need the other to validate our psychological, spiritual and physical aspects in order to re-organise our own self.

This *attractor* can become an intense *maintainer* of the relationship but can also turn against it. This is especially the case if the relationship is the only cause of *"re-narcissitation"*, as it means that we might distance ourselves from other types of validating points of reference.

7) **Implicit Relational Knowing (IRK).** Automatic and unconscious, but not repressed; if we understand it from the perspective of the Boston group or from the internal operative models from Bowlby's attachment perspective. IRK is a clear example of a factor which works as an *attractor* and a *maintainer*. I have observed it on various occasions. In one case, a patient was excessively *"responsibilised"* since childhood and, at the age of 8, when she had to look after her schizophrenic brother, *"maternalised" (role reversal)*. Gradually her role became that of a carer to both her brother and her mother, who would tell her daughter her relationship problems, sexual problems and sexual intimacies that she had with her father[6].

This generates an IRK of a carer: a role reversal. During therapy sessions, she explains that she has no sexual desire whatsoever and that she feels more

---

6 "Soft incest" according to the French psychoanalyst P.C. Racamier (1995)

like a mother than a wife to her husband, whom she has known and who has been her only relationship since adolescence. In terms of the roles of both, they had effectively taken on these roles as he did not work and behaved like an adolescent: smoking, drinking and playing videogames.

8) Also, it is important to understand the influence of the **attachment system** (secure, evasive, ambivalent, etc.) that the individual has experienced and of different *imprinting* that could have affected her in the area of sexuality or emotional nature.

During couple therapy, or when a relationship problem is presented to us in an individual treatment, we must always ask the patient what they saw in their partner at the beginning of the romance. In this way, can obtain knowledge of what was motivationally explicit for the patient when they decided to enter the relationship. We should also infer from our patients which implicit motivations were present at that time. These implicit motivations are the hardest to discern, given that factors such as IRK and the dynamics of expectation and desire are often hidden, even from the patient themselves.

These initial conditions can provide us with a certain capacity for predicting the *maintainers* of the relationship and some insight into the resources that therapist and patient could use for the process of change.

B) Maintaining *factors of the relationship*

As indicated, often many of the initial condition *attractors* equally function as *maintainers*, therefore, as a therapist, we must focus on them specifically as they are highly resistant to change. The emotional and motivational factors present in *maintainers* are divided in two basic groups:

- **General maintainers:** comprise factors which are almost always needed in order to maintain healthy relationships as well as pathological and addictive ones.
- **Specific maintainers:** refer to those which predominate in some conflictive relationship structures and which help to maintain pathological relationships[7]. We have called these structures "relational affectopathologies" –RA- (Guerra Cid, 2006, 2013).

---

7 In using the term "pathological" I'm referring to the Greek etymological definition: "suffering", not to the commonly used meaning for mental illness.

General maintainers

General maintaining factors include the following:

1) **Narcissistic compensation of an 'unstructured' self.**

According to T. Reik (1944), we fall in love because we see in our partner whatever we believe to be missing in ourselves. Idealisation of what the other possesses (at a physical, psychological and material level) and our own narcissistic failures drive us to seek to complement ourselves with another. In some ways, every process of falling in love has these ingredients. However, whether a relationship is healthy or unhealthy depends on the intensity of the idealisation of the other and on the magnitude of failings and deficiencies in our own *self* with its different states.[8]

2) **Zeigarnik Effect.**

Studied in Gestalt psychology and related to memory, in particular it was discovered that we remember more clearly unfinished tasks than those we complete. Applied to psychoanalysis by Luis Cencillo (1977), this concept explains how throughout our lives we seek, in various models, those emotional attachments that were not formed or not fully formed.

3) **Fear of solitude.**

Solitude and ostracism are highly disturbing elements in our society, elements which we intensely fear. Our brain is relational and works more efficiently while interacting with others. This means that human beings are not designed, from an evolutionary point of view, for isolation. That being said, we can - in fact, we must - have solitary spaces.

Usually solitude represents a lack of protection when it is associated with survival instinct. However, as humans have evolved, our culture has managed to transform solitude into a circumstance with powerful emotional reference points far beyond our instincts.

Depending on family, social or cultural contexts, solitude or loneliness can be interpreted as failure, rejection, punishment, abandonment, torture, relief, etc.; according to the subjectivity of the individual. These are the factors, now not merely instinctive but emotional, that we have to work on with those patients who

---

8 In contemporary times our *self* is not defined as something unitary and unchanged by time, but instead understood as a framework through which we can observe different states (Slavin 1996; Bromberg, 1998; Watchel, 2008, D.B Stern 2010). Which for some, is equal to one individual having different "selves". For others, the *self* is discontinuous and has different states; which, upon being assumed, generate a sense of integration of personality within ourselves, an image of spontaneity and naivety; all of which are fundamental factors in the mental health of any individual.

demonstrate resistance to being alone. This becomes fundamental for helping them to reorganise their subjectivity. A common factor in romantic relationships, particularly those which involve addiction, is the fear of "ending up alone".

4) **Abandonment phobia.**

We could say that abandonment phobia has a certain survival instinct component. However, increasingly often in clinical practice, we observe patients with a genuine terror of being left alone and who maintain relationships which are absolutely insane and addictive.

Some of these cases fit within the classic "*Abandonment neurosis*" - G. Guex (1950) - and others correspond to personality disorders within the "Borderline personality organisation" framework of O. Kernberg (1984). In the majority of contexts, we observe that a lower level of structuration and integration of our *self* directly correlates to a higher fear of being abandoned by our partner.

Specific Maintainers: Relational Affectopathologies (RA)

Relational affectopathologies can be defined as the following:

"An extreme imbalance in the management of emotions and affections as well as a distortion in evaluating from "where" (which type of person), "why" (what aim is pursued) the energetic resources - both physical and psychic - are being employed, and "how" they are carried out: implicit and explicitly. This inadequate management has disastrous consequences for those who suffer from it intra or interpersonally in the spheres of work, social and family life". (Guerra Cid, 2006, p. 159; 2013 p 122).

With regard to relational affectpathology we must bear in mind that:

- They are not diagnostic categories but explanatory approximations of how different types of relationships can occur from predetermined personality patterns which reassert themselves.
- They are a Non-Linear Dynamic System (NLDS) with different levels of intensity depending on the personality of each member couple, and of the push and pull factors (*attractors, maintainers and repulsors*) that can alter the system.
- It is rare to find a pure pattern of affectopathology in any relationship problem, given that this phenomenon often overlaps with other common features such as co-dependence, sadism or power struggles, making it difficult to draw a line between one affectopathology and the other.

- The origin of Relational Affectopathology is multiple. We must consider the most recent relationships we have lived through and the comparison between them. Moreover, as we have seen, the family environment in which the individual was raised is highly important, given that the implicit relational knowledge (IRK), quality of attachments, imprinting, etc., are derived from this early experience.

The example set for the individual by their parent's relationship is highly important, so too are the different conflicts that have occurred in different generations and directions in the intergenerational heritage of the individual: among ancestors, grandparents, uncles and aunts, etc.

- Romantic love is a cultural construction. In our culture the basic components of love are: responsibility for the loved object, active worry for their growth, interest in knowing and learning about the other and mutual respect (E. Fromm, 1956). To these we should add: a capacity for giving up and letting the other go, altruism relative, unconditional support and affectionate giving towards the other (Guerra Cid, 2006, 2013). In RA, the above components are altered in distinct ways.

The following are the principles of RA and some of the connections between them[9]:

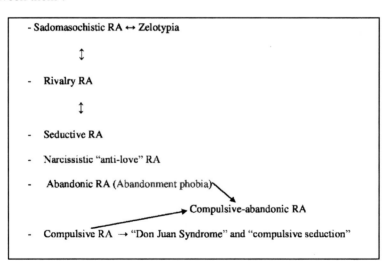

```
- Sadomasochistic RA ↔ Zelotypia

        ↕

-   Rivalry RA

        ↕

-   Seductive RA

-   Narcissistic "anti-love" RA

-   Abandonic RA (Abandonment phobia)
                                    ↘
                        ↗ Compulsive-abandonic RA

-   Compulsive RA → "Don Juan Syndrome" and "compulsive seduction"
```

---

9 For space limitation reasons, all the RA descriptions are summarised. We have selected just the main attractors and maintainers of each one. For further studies, we recommend our book "El clavo ardiendo. Claves de las adicciones amorosas y los conflictos en las relaciones sanas y patológicas" (2013). Barcelona, Octaedro. (Any port in a storm. Love addictions keys and conflicts within healthy and pathological relationships).

Sadomasochistic Relational Affectopathology (SM-RA)

A classic concept of the dynamic-systemic theory of J. Willi (1978) is one of collusion. Between both members of the couple there is a common unconsciousness which, I would add, is both declarative and procedural. Without explicitly knowing, each one of them plays a role which complements that of the other. One usually represents the progressive/active/caring pole while the other is regressive/passive/insecure. When these roles remain fixed and unchanging the couple "enters collusion".

In SM-RA this collusion is more dynamic. Freud affirmed that "A sadist is always at the same time a masochist" (1905). Equally, the sadist can often be more dependent on the masochist than the other way around. From this we determine that one of the fixed principles of this dyad is co-dependence.

In the role of masochism we can see, among the *attractors*, a great need for affiliation and attachment. In addition, at the beginning of the relationship, they see in their love interest someone with strength, security and decision. They are also usually people with a high level of responsibility in the relationship: "caring for a partner and accepting them no matter what they do is the obligation of a good spouse". This attitude is automatically, and implicitly, assumed.

The partner who occupies the sadistic role sees in the other, at the beginning of the relationship, traits such as sweetness, tenderness and capacity for self-sacrifice; qualities which give them the idea that the other is controllable and malleable for their purposes of exerting their power in order to compensate for their narcissistic deficit. In fact, these factors are the maintaining principles, or *maintainers*, in the active role.

One of the classic *maintainers* of the passive role in this relationship is "moral masochism" (Freud 1924). Nevertheless, during clinical observation many other *maintainers* are observed which are not due to the unconscious need to be punished. Rather more potent *maintainers* reveal themselves:

1) A desire to control the sadistic partner. This is especially common when a continued abuse from a punitive figure was suffered during childhood. Many individuals need to prove to themselves that they "can" face this figure, as a way of restoring their self-esteem.

2) The obsessive need for mirroring from the sadistic partner. Those who have suffered multiple humiliations by important figures during their childhood or adolescence have an urgent need to find attachment. In some cases, the search for this attachment is transformed by the

Zeigarnik Effect: through which the figure who is chosen during this search for recognition and affection is a sadistic and punitive figure of the highest level. In most cases mirroring never occurs.

3) As previously mentioned, co-dependence in this RA is fundamental. J. Willi indicated the "anal-sadistic collusion" as the root cause of sadomasochistic relationships. At the nucleus of this collusion, the sadist maintains an attitude of subduing the other in order to hide his or her own fears of separation. This overcompensation is designed to make their partner dependent so as not to admit to their own dependence (1978, p. 119). Meanwhile, their masochistic other half fears independence because it implies acting by yourself and dealing with the consequences. Therefore, they unconsciously prefer that the other take control so that they can avoid accepting their possible autonomy.

Narcissistic "anti-love" relational affectopathology (N-RA).

This RA is named "anti-love" because when narcissism is intense and deep, it moves away from everything that implies "loving another". In fact, many of the aforementioned components of love are severely compromised. There is no solidarity and ceding to the other only occurs if a benefit, greater than the effort invested, is achieved. Nor is there motivation to gain active knowledge of "who" the other is, as the necessary "*de-narcissitation*" has not occurred in order to place their attentional focus on the needs of others.

The narcissist always places their partner into a mistaken and erratic position, turning them into an object of continuous degradation in order to prove their own value. This is a powerful *maintainer* in the relationship, as the partner of the narcissist also attempts to demonstrate their worth.

At the initial conditions, the narcissist seeks a partner with physical attractiveness, among other variables, which will grant him or her with status. On other levels they search for someone who will provide mirroring and intense idealisation, due to a deficit that they usually carry since childhood (Kohut 1971, 1979). These will work later as powerful *attractors* and strong *maintainers* as the other regulates and compensates the damaged *self* of the narcissist. These *maintainers* reassert themselves continuously through the poor capacity of the narcissist for mentalisation and for understanding their own and others emotional systems.

In N-RA there is a "narcissistic-spectator" dynamic. The narcissist needs the mirroring from the spectator. As for the spectator, they *anchor them selves* through the other who they idealise. In the same way the spectator "re-narcissies" their partner through the successful unfurling of the qualities of the narcissist. This dynamic functions as a powerful *maintainer* in these relationships, where roles are static.

Seductive relational affectopathology (S-RA).

S-RA is related to hysteric personalities. A common feature of these types of dynamics is that one partner displays seductive traits. The motive for the seductive figure is to find an opportunity to feel valued and accepted: to do this they use a (more or less unconscious) mechanism based on seduction. This seduction can be erotic, intellectual or of other types, such as "being a good guy". For a RA to take place, the other partner usually exhibits controlling tendencies or has childhood experiences of role reversal.

It has been consistently observed that hysteric personalities suffer very difficult childhoods (sexual abuse, parental abuse, etc.), for this reason, the need for affiliation becomes an important *attractor* in the initial conditions of the relationship. It is partly from this need that they opt for a position of helplessness, or even sickness, whereby the partner must take on the role of carer. This circumstance provokes a dynamic of "father or mother carer" in the relationship from the very beginning. Willi (1978) stated that the hysteric couple must act as an "auxiliary self", which becomes even more intense in abandonment neurosis and the A-RA.

In the seducer-seduced dynamic the principal *maintaining* motive is the sick-carer dynamic. Another powerful *maintainer* (in addition to those *attractors* which function as such) is found in the obsessive traits of the seduced partner, who wants to control the ambivalence of the seducer.

Finally, we must take into account that in subjects who have hysteroid tendencies, mentalisation failures are present. In these individuals, as result of the traumas they have suffered, above all the sexual ones, their *self* is on stand by and has not developed effectively. A *repulsor* of the S-RA system is when the seducer experiences intense emotional encounters which act as a type of emotional correcting process: nothing heals more than feeling understood in the mind of another.

Rivalry relational affectopathology (R-RA).

The main element within the initial conditions is that one of the members starts out with a weak *self*, while the other partner appears with an active and progressive role, essentially as a carer. With time, the partner who had the passive role wants to acquire the active one, which produces a serious conflict. The consequence is a fierce power struggle within the relationship, which can be "de-eroticised"[10]. Usually, when the partner initially in the passive role breaks the idealisation and wants to become active, is the moment when R-RA is at its most intense, when both members intending to take on a permanent carer role.

This RA is directly connected to the sadomasochistic RA. However, one main difference is that in R-RA, the roles often change and we are unable to define who plays the sadistic or masochistic role. The aggressor-attacked dynamic is bidirectional, which means it becomes truly difficult to determine who is attacking and who is defending. The *attractors* explained above in SM-RA are therefore important for understanding this circumstance.

R-RA also maintains close ties with S-RA. One of the hysteric aspects that is often ignored is rivalry. Moving away from the orthodox interpretation of the Oedipus complex, I believe that the triangle generated between the parents and the child can be source of serious future problems. Especially when rivalry against one parent is incited by the other or when the parents humiliate each other. These circumstances occur because one of the parents (or both) has sought, in the child, an ally for defeating the other.

The principal motor of this RA is one of the elements of hysteria most often ignored: the desire to occupy a position of privilege and, in particular, to shine; through the rivalry with, and ultimate defeat of, the other. This is the fundamental *maintainer* motor, the issue of "power" which ends up destroying the relationship.

In addition to this, an imbalance is produced in the principle of individuality, as each partner wants to preserve their own space without ceding any territory to either their partner, or to the couple (understood as *thirdness*).

Compulsive relational affectopathology (C-RA).

If the aforementioned RAs are susceptible to becoming addictive relationships, the following are even clearer examples. What is a romantic addiction? One that implies a loss of liberty and a dependence on one another and/or the concept of being in a relationship in order to achieve self-esteem and security. Moreover, in a romantic addiction there is a marked loss of perspective of one's own and the other's qualities. Dependence can be one way: one partner heavily relying on the other; however, co-dependence is more frequent.

In C-RA the subject is an addict in the sense that he or she is unable to end a relationship, no matter how harmful; or, because they compulsively need

---

10 It has been continually observed that the members of these relationships refuse to have sexual relations because it would be like "surrendering to the other".

one relationship after another. These relationships can simply be promiscuous and based on sexuality. One example of C-RA is the "*Don Juan syndrome*"[11]. When relationships are compulsively stringed together almost without gaps, the subject has a problem "reading others", as it seems that none of their partners are good enough. We term this phenomenon "compulsive seduction".

At the beginning of their relationships, these people seek the other not as a compliment but as a basic part of their *self*. This is produced by a butterfly effect: what at the start were failures within the *self* becomes a profound dependence on being in a relationship. This *attractor* is stronger when idealisation is greater and their partner plays their part passively in order to be the perfect partner.

In other circumstances the compulsive role aims only to defeat and occasionally humiliate the other when their expectations are not fulfilled. In this way their compulsive conquest may continue. The various dehumanised internet dating apps that exist in modern times only augment the intensity of these pitiful behaviours.

In C-RA, the Zeigarnik effect functions both as an *attractor* and a *maintainer* simultaneously. These individuals lack secure attachment and an integrated *self*. They attempt to compensate for these needs through a compulsive search for the affection they never received. Therefore, it becomes difficult discern the line separating this affectopathology with the narcissistic one. Perhaps, the difference is one of degree: in C-RA the greatest deprivation has been of affection and of feeling of "being lovable" which grants a concrete sensation of "self". In N-AR, however, the deficit is due to mirroring.

Sometimes within this type of system there is a very powerful socio-cultural *maintainer*. On one hand, the compulsive personality feels valued and desirable because they are in a relationship or have multiple sexual partners. They understand that their seductive skill grant them appreciation within their environment and that having a partner gives them a successful status. Their partner might also experience a feeling of narcissistic triumph: being chosen among so many lovers feels like an achievement in front of their society. These relational circumstances ensure that each protagonist is "hooked" on the other.

Abandonic relational affectopathology (A-RA).

I have previously referred to these types of patients in order to explain abandonic phobia as a maintainer of the RA. We know that continuous failures

---

11 The "Don Juan syndrome" is not only found in C-RA, but between this one and N-RA, although it can also explain hysteric issues. Therefore, for O. Kernberg (1995, p. 261) the "Don Juan syndrome" is the prototype of masculine narcissistic pathologies, among others.

(pedagogic, emotional, attachment, mentalisation and empathetic response) during the first and second phases of infancy can cause a circumstance in which the *self* becomes fragile and unstable. In this way, the patient has a decreasing capacity to withstand the accumulative failures of the context. In this vicious circle resides the origin for most psychological disorders and imbalances. This is more pronounced in abandonic, narcissistic, dependent and masochist personalities.

In the A-RA, the passive-abandonic role exhibits an exaggerated demand for care, something impossible to accomplish. It is as if one would say, 'You should know what I need without me saying it'; demanding a safety net that is not just secure but magical. The other, often raised in an environment of hyper-responsibility and blame, will try by all means to prove their capacity for commitment. This is the abandonic-saviour pair, who make their respective IRK fit together in order to have this type of relationship.

Once again the Zeigarnik Effect is highly important from the beginning of the relationship, functioning both as an *attractor* and as a *maintainer*. The *abandonic* patient has suffered various types of abandonment (physical, emotional, etc.), or has subjectively viewed them as abandonment, throughout childhood. In this way, the patient occupying the passive role hopes that other relationships will compensate for the abandonment suffered early on.

They even fantasise about the dreaded abandonment by the other and 'test' their theory constantly. In the active role, we usually find "saviours", a phenomenon over and above *role reversal*. They feel that, not only must they care for the other, but that the well-being of their partner is wholly their responsibility.

On occasion, however, the saviour also demands recognition, at least for the labours they have undertaken for the other. This causes an angry response from the abandonic partner and an increased need to be recognised in their misfortune. In this way, the relationship enters a spiral of demand which only produces reproach. Subsequently, the previously mentioned roles break down and the relationship becomes a subtype of rivalry affectopathology: a rivalry to see who can satisfy more demands.

Compulsive-abandonic relational affectopathology (CA-RA).

In abandonic patients, while "not being abandoned" takes precedence, some of them can tolerate solitude and even seek it. In this variation of the previous RA, whoever occupies the passive role cannot tolerate either solitude or abandonment. The basic difference between the compulsive and the abandonic is that the first has a greater tendency to end relationships. Occasionally, however, there is a fusion of both problematic at a relational affectopathological level, when the active pole of the relationship exhibits characteristics both of *paternalisation* and of demonstrating a certain degree of ambiguity at the hour of commitment. At the same time, in the passive pole the characteristics are both: fear of abandonment and fear of being left alone.

Proposals For the Process of Change

One of the matters that most concerns the psychotherapist is understanding why our patients are in relationships of suffering. When we achieve understanding, the next problem is: how to help initiate change? Usually, the patient who comes into therapy has already begun the process of change, and we just have to continue along that path. However, as every case is incomparable and unique, we must work meticulously and provide a custom-made treatment (Cencillo, 1977, Mitchell, 1997).

In order to customise treatment, it is fundamental to analyse the aforementioned factors and combine them according to the singularity of each patient. Perhaps the best way of evaluating how the patient interacts socially is within the therapeutic relationship. It must be spontaneous, genuine and emotionally corrective. From this point onwards the task of interpretation will make sense; if and when the patient actively participates in the investigation of the factors that trouble them.

A change in the way one acts in a relationship can only take place from the deepest level, never from simply trying to modify behaviours. This would not be change but suggestion. Often, change is easier during the windows of transition: if an addictive relationship ends, it is easier for the therapist and patient to perform changes during the transition phase before a new relationship, than if a new one has already started.

In terms of change, it is essential to retain knowledge of the three types of unconscious: dynamic, implicit and invalidated.

The ***dynamic*** unconscious (Coderch, 2005) is related to ***declarative memory*** around the individual historicity of each person. We must bear in mind that the way we are in our diverse *self* states is the way we have been configured by the relational matrix (Mitchell, 1991; Slavin 1996), above all we must pay attention to those *selves* which are dissociated, as these will play out in the therapeutic relationship.

At the same time we should take into account the IRKs associated with the aforementioned states: all this configures the ***implicit memory***. In this last aspect, what is most important is the *enactment:* where different experiential and relational modifications in the relationship between the patient and therapist will occur. Change is therefore produced through accumulation of emotionally corrective factors and by the integration of *self* versus its dissociations.

We must also consider the ***invalidated unconscious*** or the elements of subjectivity that have never been validated by the patient's surroundings (Storolow and Atwood, 1989). The product of this invalidated unconscious is unconscious fantasy and enactment. Working with all these factors has a double effect. On one hand we can see how the patient interacts with their partner; on the other, how they bring these conflicts to the therapeutic relationship in the form of enactment. Only from this perspective are we capable of carrying out emotionally corrective experiences with them.

When change is produced, "what" was unconsciously desired and the implicit automatisms can vary. In the same way, there can be variation in "how" the objectives are pursued (ways, operations and, of course, implicit relational knowing) but also in the election of the object and the way the patient sees "being in a relationship".

We will an example of a 34 year old patient who felt like a "failure" for not having a partner. She continuously used sexual seduction as a vehicle to attract men but ultimately, this meant that they would never commit as they saw the relationship as a "fling". After some time in psychotherapy the "how" changes, in the form of "how she approaches men": abandoning seduction in order to be more genuine. Another change was her view of "being in a relationship" as a success or a failure. In this way, she felt less pressured and was able to be more selective in her choice of men.

As in every complex process or system, change is normally produced by an accumulation of micro-processes. In a similar way to fractal theory, a micro-process tends to replicate the macro-process. Focusing on psychotherapy, this explains how at the local level (BCPSG, 2002, 2005), little scenes are produced between therapist and patient, which reveal how the psychotherapy process is going. The accumulation of these small processes through a different, emotionally corrective relationship, will cause change in the long term.

Usually, a series of sequences during sessions demonstrate how the therapeutic process, as a whole, is progressing. The exact same process happens with romantic relationships, we can particularly see this when a patient comes and recounts an intense argument. We observe how that small sequence of events is a microcosm, symbolically and implicitly, of what constitutes the entire relationship, with its positive and negative parts.

To summarise, change must be produced:

- In the structure of the *self*, causing change, both in the way of seeing oneself and in the relationship with oneself; and in the deep-seated abilities for relationships with others. The change is neither valid nor total but occurs only at the superficial levels of the behaviour or conduct.
- Change is gradual and spontaneous, and is related to the reactions to what the patient says and does and to the ways in which we help them to organise their subjectivity.
- The trigger of change is often related to the *attractors* and these, to the initial conditions. Moments of transition are also highly important, in which there are "windows" through which change is possible. How we manage a transition totally depends on how we enter and behave in the next phase.
- We must attend to particular *repulsors* which exist in each pathological relationship. These *repulsors* have a tendency to destabilise the system and therefore change its pathological patterns. They are, in the end, more powerful than the *attractors*. These *repulsors* will convert to become *attractors* of a new and healthy system.
- Without a doubt, change often produces an alternative solution to that which is unconsciously pursued, either in the "way of pursuing it" (the ways, operations and of course, implicit relational knowing) or in the final objective or target that a person is looking for.

I began my discussion by highlighting the principle role that culture has over us. To finalise I will come back to it from one of its most recent facets: new technology. As therapists, it is highly important for us bear in mind its influence. Social media, dating apps and other tools are increasing our distance from the real world. We are moving from a virtual reality to a virtualisation of the reality (Guerra Cid, 2016). We increasingly observe that attractors related to idealisation (expectations and attributions) are often irrelevant; or how mentalisation, the fundamental capacity for sharing and loving, is being compromised for the sake of living exclusively within the fiction created by social media.

Modern man, hidden behind his screens, learns that his virtual interactions have hardly any consequences. However, when he translates those interactions into the real world he may continue to think in this way and therefore fail to communicate and misunderstand or become definitively inhibited and unable to communicate further in this way, transforming into an isolated individual. In this society of immediacy and through a culture of "everything in just one click", young people and adults are developing low frustration tolerance and are completely unfamiliar with the delay of gratification.

The mass-consumption of the Internet, with its limitless possibilities, the ease with which we can communicate with others and the virtual nature of these networks, lets our expectations of what the world can offer us run wild, while this in itself generates fantasies and idealisations which virtualise our reality.

When using the term virtualisation of reality I am referring to a process characterised by a continued abuse of communication through social media, the mass consumption of internet and interactive apps, and by the accompaniment of the Smartphone as an extension of ourselves (in some cases as an extension of the own self, or even as a transitional pseudo-object). All of this produces:

1. Poor capacity and/or atrophy of mental processes such as introspection, empathy and the ability to read both their own emotional states and those of others.
2. Increase in Alexithymia (the inability to recognise and/or express emotions or affection)
3. Severe lack of communicative and interactive functions in "face to face" situations
4. Reality testing becomes less and less fitting, with the incapacity to delay gratification or tolerate frustration: the need for immediacy (culture of "everything in just one click")
5. Diverse phenomena concerned with dehumanisation (misunderstandings – as consequence of the aforementioned lack of mental processes – bullying, ghosting, vamping, etc.).
6. Failures in the controlling process of the other (social awareness)
7. Problems within auto regulation of the individual (impulsive behaviour against reflexivity and evaluation of social and psychological situation).

In relational psychoanalysis we are aware that the variations of the implicit, negative, relational patterns turn into a new relationship, and within this relationship we are also aware that the change is more "how" than "what", but doing this is complicated while we sit camouflaged behind our technological devices. Technological textual communication and its continued abuse produce severe atrophy of mentalisation, especially in its interactive and emotional aspect, producing errors in reading our own and others' emotional states. In this way one's 'self' is not only disassociated but partially virtualised.

What lies beneath is a double movement of profound dehumanisation and "psychopathologisation", that is to say, the loss of our sense of reality in that which we seek, given that we are moving away from unreal and ideal situations to subsequently face a very different reality which frustrates our expectations. The individual in need of coherence resolves the situation by virtualizing reality and intending, in real life, to connect with-disconnect from or accept-not accept the other through one click.

One example we can see in the continuous bombardment of applications created to meet new people and date. Increasingly, we want to meet 'the one' over the Internet rather than in real life. 'Apps' with clear implications of market success where bodies and hopes are bought and sold. Everything here tends to be more virtual that it seems, from the photos edited with Photoshop which offer images of your ideal, yet exaggeratedly unreal, future romantic partner, to the invention of personality traits, hobbies and habits which make them more attractive. This is, ultimately, a scam.

'Ghosting', however, might be an ever greater scam. This phenomenon occurs when, usually after meeting someone from the Internet for a 'blind date' and after having sold false attributes and expectations one of them, perhaps as fruit of the disillusionment that the virtual world has created, suddenly disappears and blocks the other user, ensuring that they will not be able to make communication through any channel. This generates an annihilation of his or her "self" in those who suffer it, as they see themselves rejected by the other without explanation, even after having shared moments of physical intimacy.

This is one of the consequences of the virtualisation of reality; in this case the individual blocks the other, not in the virtual realm but the real one. They know each other, they might have even slept together in a weekend of passion. But, as if the other were an online purchase, the order is cancelled and the item is returned. This occurs because mentalisation not only comprises our understanding of mental states but also of our needs, desires, mistakes and delusions. (Bleiberg, 2013).

The problem with ghosting is that at this point the consequences have become very real and, even if reality has been virtualised, this causes significant hurt to those who suffer ostracism and incomprehension of what has happened. Recently, a patient told me:

"I don't know what's happened, we met up on Thursday and then on Friday, we went for dinner, we laughed a lot and then we slept together. On Saturday they stopped speaking to me, they blocked me on the website that we used when we met, on Whatsapp and on Facebook. I'm shocked and confused, I'm upset. Have I been used?'"

As therapists we must consider these phenomena because they are highly traumatising for our patients. These situations might become phobias and resistances within the affective interaction with others.

For every case that I know of where things have gone well on the Internet, there are dozens where it has gone horribly wrong, I imagine that many of my colleagues will confirm this. In my opinion it is the abuse, we go beyond mere 'use' into obsession and addiction, of the smartphone, social media, the Internet, etc., which alienates the individual in virtual reality. This alienation produced by the "virtualisation of reality" contains two paradoxes that influence communication with the other:

The communication paradox:

We think that currently we are more connected than ever because we can text, write to each other and maintain conversations with people anywhere in the world. However, our most human and real communication, which is the "skin on skin", often remains unused or worse still relegated to a superficial sexuality. So much communication of such terrible quality. This is the "communication paradox", despite us having more transmission channels, it is becoming more superficial and more exploited than ever. The individual seems to be well connected but is often found to be more disconnected and isolated in "real" terms than he has ever been.

The intimacy paradox:

We believe that we can more fully enjoy our solitude and that with our devices we can communicate with others without those others invading our intimate sphere. This is, of course, untrue, because of the continuous feedback and bombardment of data between individuals, we are always checking our phones, our texts, our social network profiles. It is common to see whole groups of people sat at tables consulting their Smartphone instead of interacting with those who are sat with them. This leads to increasingly common cases of people who leave their phones near to or in the bed and check their messages or even wake up in the middle of the night to respond (Vamping). Worse still is when, by using certain "dating" apps any stranger can see your location, try to 'get to know' you at any time.

From the moment in which all those who are connected with you (and sometimes those who are not) know all about your life through highly detailed exhibition on social networks, intimacy is dead. Intimacy is dead when anyone who messages you knows exactly when you have read their message and your privacy is at risk because you know that they know that you have received a message that you are impelled to reply to. You must have signal at all times, never disconnect, be constantly checking…One of the winning moves of the magnates of this industry was to create a technological and supposedly vital need where before no need had existed (Guerra Cid, 2006).

The example of the smartphone is paradigmatic in relation to everything I have mentioned. It is clear that the use of the smartphone has its pros and cons, but the abuse of it only cons. Since mobile phones begun to be used, the feeling to me was that some people used it as if they were sustained by a transitional object. Today, I am aware that it is, rather, a transitional pseudo-object. This transitional object is required to be capable of mediating between internal and external reality, of moving with ease between spaces and realities (Winnicott, 1971). However, the smartphone as a *transitional pseudo-object* is understood as moving between one virtual reality and another, increasingly virtualised and decreasingly real "reality".

The most recent great construct in contemporary sociology, has been described by S. Bauman (1999) as "liquid modernity", where our social ties and ties of affection develop less and less density and cohesion, slipping through our fingers. In museums, the visitors observe paintings through the screens of their smartphones, taking photos but without seeing the painting. At rock concerts they film the show through the screen instead of living it. As a greater percentage of the population partake in virtualising reality, our society is no longer neurotic, as Horney or Fromm argued, but increasingly borderline with disturbingly narcissistic traits.

The exaggeration and histrionics observed on social media show individuals who are always happy and enjoying life, sharing their intimacy with all of cyberspace. Zones of virtual success where positive reinforcement is obtained by way of "likes". Reality becomes hard to distinguish, under the guise of the technology that encases us and makes us more valuable than we are, perhaps the valuable, beautiful, intelligent people that we desire to be but who we never will be. The eternal clash between the 'real' and the 'ideal'.

In the face of this problem the psychotherapist can play a crucial part. The best antidote to the dehumanisation caused by a lack of mentalisation is found in a new relationship, above all if it is a therapeutic one. As Avila Espada points out: "*Mutual influence creates and transforms experience and, as a consequence, its neural imprint*" (2013, p2).

Psychotherapists must take care of this matter and return to the relational matrix with the patient. If we focus our communication with them through texts, "whatsapps" or social media; or if we produce virtual mirroring through "likes" and various comments, we will produce a re-traumatisation – through the virtual world- that will cause problems within clinical communication, the moments of meeting, mentalisation and the treatment itself.

All of these issues become even more important when dealing with relationship conflicts, romantic addictions and pathological relationships. If we do not want our patient to settle for any port in the storm, we must provide real communication. In the face of frustration throughout the emotional history of any person, social interface and social networks seem like a magical way out. The patient, however, needs the certainties and experiences of genuine and spontaneous interactions. In confronting the 'ideal' with the subjectively real, we might not find a port in which to shelter, but neither will we fear the storm.

Summary

One of the main pitfalls in our clinical practice resides in the fact that many patients have a relationship problem as a primary or secondary conflict. Many of them "respond to" a relationship in which there is a love addiction. Little has been written in the history of psychoanalysis about love, although it has seen some brilliant contributions (T. Reik, 1994; E. Fromm 1956; O. Kernberg 1995; S. Mitchell, 2002). A deeper study of the human couple and its conflicts requires a psychodynamic, intersubjective and relational perspective. But furthermore, we take into consideration the culture from two aspects: Its influence in the construction of how a couple must be and their functions, moreover the consequences of new technologies within the search and/or the continuation of romantic relationships.

On the other hand, from the non-linear dynamic system theory, we analyse the main factors that cause pathological relationships (attractors, maintainers and repulsors), as well as the different resulting structures, that we have named "affectopathologies". Finally, the text shows some guidelines for psychotherapist in order to stimulate the processes of change seeking for healthier partners and the management of addictive and conflictive relationships.

10
Sexuality in Relational Psychoanalysis

Rosario Castaño Catalá

"Sexual passion, whether concretized into repetitive compulsive scenarios or allowed free rein in a more spontaneous and authentic interpersonal context, draws its excitement and vitality not from simple pressure on erogenous zones, but by the dramatic play between the visible and the hidden, the available and the withheld, the longing and the revelation"
(S. A. Mitchell)

Introduction

I am interested in the study of sexuality as part of subjectivity, in its most profound and extensive sense, as it intermingles with religion, moral, ethics and ideology. I have always wondered how sexuality, while opening so many worlds of pleasure and satisfaction, can also be a world of frustrations, vulnerabilities, a dark side of identity, eliciting contradictory feelings, and even in many cases becoming the reason for psychic suffering and often the origin of multiple conflictive relationships. I wouldn't suggest with this that sexuality should be approached from a special or different focus than other types of demands in clinical practice, or that it is always the trigger of a diversity of problems, or cause for the strictest psychopathology. At times sex is only sex, with no other explanation or significance.

Clinical practice is usually a faithful reflection of society. When a patient expresses a difficulty or sexual problem, it is frequently the case of an adult who wishes that someone specific explain that what is taking place is an exercise of discovery, as though sexual activity hidden parts of the self appear, some of which resound, while others that they are not attuned to and do not coincide with their self image, distort it. Sexual relations are usually perturbing because they make us face the idea we have of ourselves and show us our vulnerability. Perhaps this is why sexual activity can become the center of problems, conflicts and suffering. It is not rare for two people who practice sex to end up saying phrases like, "you don't give me what I want! Or "you don't give me what I need!" to each other.

Sex is thought about and fantasized and a welcoming and holding environment is necessary for those thoughts to emerge, in which the therapist is not a blank page on which the patient transfers his/her infant conflicts, rather a figure with which to interact recognizing both subjectivities, a close, involved, empathic therapist who does not present himself/herself as an external, neutral and cold observer (Coderch, 2011), as in those cases he/she is perceived as someone with all the solutions creating situations similar to those that Khan criticized *"… we the analysts "infantilize" our most gifted patients through the analytic method. We do not grant them the confidence to think that perhaps at times they are better equipped than we and have achieved more in life than we have"* (1991. p. 31).

Questions arise such as: "Who am I and how am I with my current partner?" "Am I different with each lover?" "What parts of myself do I leave behind in each relationship?" "What do I do and how do I practice sex to avoid being abandoned?" "How can I maintain the pleasure I obtain and that I give my partner?" "Does my sexual behavior coincide with my fantasies?" "What part of myself am I capable of discovering?" "Do I adapt to my partner's demands or am I also capable of demanding?" "When a relationship is over, do I only loose a partner or do I also loose parts of myself that I will never recuperate?"

Some seek contact with others through sex; others seek pleasure; some need it to reaffirm their identity and self-esteem; but in all cases sexuality is the result of the meaning and value each person gives their conduct, to the pleasures known and to those aspired, to fantasies, feelings and dreams and the way in which each one relates with him/herself and is with the other in a spontaneous and mostly unconscious intimacy. Sexuality does not end in orgasm or ejaculation; it goes beyond physical intimacy, reproducing internal operative models – infant relational patterns – and shifting between needs, desires and the love it is often confused with (Crastnopol, 2009).

Sexuality And the Transformation of Intimacy

Since the beginning of the past century, the long and difficult path of intimacy's transformation has been marked by different significant moments.

Ending the 19th century and beginning the 20th, public institutions, schools, doctors and even families began to speak about sex. This enabled a progressive increase in social and medical control over it, at a time when sex was considered a type of danger. The problems the health field referred to as sexual dysfunctions were represented by *scientia sexualis-* [1], created to treat sexuality that was considered the origin of oppression, inequality, violence, alterations and disorders.

During those years, sex gradually left the private domain to become inscribed into the public space, a space already systematically regulated by medicine and pedagogy. The term sexual health began to be used in medical and health institutions. In 1912 in a symposium on masturbation Freud pointed out *I do not consider it necessary to justify the election of the theme in an era such as this, in which at last sexual human life problems are also being subjected to scientific investigation"*.

Psychoanalysis had a great social influence, marking the beginning of a new society was displacing myths and ancient beliefs, evolving into the idea we have today about sexuality as a modern invention, as a result on one hand of scientific discourse (medical, psychological and psychoanalytic) and on the other to the rules and norms dictated by the institutions of power (medical, religious and legal).

Gradually, as of the beginning of the 20th century, psychoanalysis became the new mythology predominating in modern collective imaginary. As of Freud and his discovery of the unconscious, the modern individual began to question

---

1 With reference to *sciencia sexualis,* it is interesting to point out Foucault's description in *The History of Sexuality* (1976) regarding the influence of power over sexuality in modern societies, submitting it to scientific truth and provoking illnesses; submitting the reason of human existence to politics and the health system, which to this day still has great influence and can distance sexuality from the *ars amandi* and erotica.

him/herself, "What don't I know about myself?" "Who am I?" looking at one's body and oneself, towards one's own identity and the manner of desiring in a different way, in constant battle for individuality and living an intimacy that did not correspond to anything known or familiar. Today, popular imaginary still maintains the idea that sex in an adult's life is something degrading and obscure, incestuous in character that must be repressed because the adult experiences the memory of feelings, desires and fantasies experienced during infancy with guilt.

During the second half of the 20th century, three publications regarding sexual investigation were published with great social impact: the two Kinsey Reports about human sexual conduct; the first in 1948 on man and five years later on woman; as well as the studies by Masters and Johnson in 1960. The doubts and concerns society had about sexual behavior are captured on its pages. Words that had been hidden and limited to the bedroom such as masturbation, clitoris, orgasm, vulva, vagina, penis, penetration, pleasure, sexual fantasies or sexual desire became used publicly and began to form part of everyday vocabulary.

The sixties social and sexual revolution and in Europe the events in France in May 1968, were the beginning of profound moral, psychological and social changes that continue to evolve. That sexual revolution was not only in search for pleasure as something fun and desirable, but was also a necessary social phenomenon that coincided with and benefited by:

- The appearance and acceptance of hormone based contraceptives. Sex was no longer only related to reproduction and death; the danger of death by pregnancy and labor that has almost disappeared in our society today.
- The search for equality both socially and privately, in an environment that favored autonomy and the acceptance of the other's individuality; the development of the I as an absolute priority, sharing feelings and desires, frankness and confidence, negotiation, leadership and shared commitment.
- The acceptance of homosexuality[2] as no longer marginal, that began to be part of society giving way to a rise of what Giddens in 1995 called "a plastic sexuality".

So while the postmodern and global[3] society opened its arms to a more spontaneous and free sexuality, divested of its rigid norms and prohibitions, we discovered that sexuality was not as banal as we thought. It is an exchange

---

2 In 1973 the American Psychiatric Association no longer considered homosexuality a disease.
3 The postmodern and global society that are part of the Western society, called the "welfare state".

between two adults in which each offer a mix of childish and mature aspects of their personality; infant and adult experiences that usually activate gender, the attachment style, identity and *self*-cohesion.

Sexuality From A Relational Perspective

Intersubjectivity has been established as the paradigm of the origin and structuring of the psyche, due to attachment research that established the basis of the dyadic structure in the infant mind (Fonagy, 2004) and early relationships (Stern, 1991; Beebe, 1998). These findings demonstrate the importance of the relationship with the adult and the messages the adult transmits. It demonstrates the importance of the other's unconscious, and the role in seduction and narcissism we shall see later. As explained by Lichtemberg it is a way to understand the formation of the psyche and the entrance into the world of desire and subjectivity, in which there are various and different motivational systems in parallel throughout the life cycle and close interactions that generate new dimensions in the psyche.

The relational psychotherapist, as does the classic therapist, recognizes the existence of infant sexuality. From this perspective, physiology and temperament are equally important sexual dynamics, while the significance attached to physiological sensations are also equally important (Mitchell, 1988).

The relational therapist, as did Freud in his time, recognizes the existence of sexuality as something enigmatic, something that does not belong to "everyday knowledge". It is not only related to sexual education and information – although it is interesting to keep this in mind – rather about the conscious and unconscious knowledge of oneself and others.[4]

Gender also became important. This concept was not used explicitly in classic psychoanalysis until Stoller imported it in 1975, along with the concepts of agency and the past, not as hidden beneath the present, rather as the key to why it is configured in this way. The individual is not limited to reliving the past, rather has in some degree the capacity to react to his/her own present experiences – maturity is not the infant in disguise as Freud believed.

---

4 When Freud refers to enigmatic knowledge, he refers to infant curiosity about the origin of life, death, the World and his/her place in the family. He does not refer to an enigma as in a question, riddle or a problem to be solved that one subject presents another, rather that only person who poses the question can respond, as the message is a form of commitment in which the unconscious participates, as explained by Laplanche (Gutiérrez Terrazas, 1999).

Once the family of origin and current contexts of the patient are known, it is important to see how he/she is projected into the future. In the case of sexuality it is interesting to explore the pre and adolescent stages, underlining the importance of identity, a concept that began to be used in psychoanalysis thanks to Erikson. The term identity is a contradiction within itself, as it simultaneously means what is similar and what is different. It arises with the establishment of oneself, as separate from the mother, starting at a crucial experience of symbiosis with her, of total dependence, as Winnicott[5] stated.

The attachment style related to caregivers and primary bonds should also be considered, although other significant figures throughout life are also important. Sexual relationships usually activate attachment – although attachment needs are not the cause of arousal and desire – as, separation anxiety appears in the intimate encounter and plunges its roots into basic anxiety, related to the separation from the attachment object (see Bowlby)[6].

In adult life, sex, eroticism and passion seem to revive the conditions of proximity, intensity and exclusivity that appear in infancy in relation to otherness - with the Other. For the one in love, the Other is not completely different, the type of otherness that sparks erotic passion can be considered as characteristics of the self that are not recognized, like the shadow of the self or the image of the self in a mirror (Mitchell, 2002).

Sexual Pleasure And Erotic Desire

A doubt arises when thinking about erotic pleasure: is desire felt due to arousal, or arousal felt due to desire. The answer is usually complex as, to begin with, we should not study sexual arousal and erotic desire as two separate

---

5 There are two beings in symbiosis – mother and child. However the mother is not half or the complement, as she enters that dyad not only providing physical care but also fundamentally providing her sensuality, her conscious and unconscious fantasies. The infant gradually separates from that otherness – that Other that is not so Other – lacking the subjective distance to see and perceive her as someone different. Otherness as a philosophical concept: E. Lévinas applied it to the discovery of the self towards the Other, that makes a wide range of images of the other arise, of us and multiple images of the self. I will use the Other with a capital to refer to the couple, whether man or woman, as when we speak about emotions and desires with respect to our partner I understand we refer to the real and fantasized other, not so different from ourselves.

6 Attachment theory is being revised after decades of investigation. Some researchers consider it necessary to broaden the attachment concept to any social bond which if lost produces grief, not only limited to the relationship in which the stronger cares for the more dependent.

entities, although for didactic effects, we need to discover them in this way to achieve a better understanding.

Arousal is a physiological reaction with impulses charged with tension, but the relationship between those impulses and desire, between the body and the spirit, will never be a clear irrefutable concept for neither psychology nor psychoanalysis. The biological basis for desire is permanently under study, with constant discoveries regarding brain functioning and the nervous system that for the moment are mainly a mystery, forcing us to use a descriptive model with a basis that is not possible to prove, regarding the link between physical and emotional pleasure.

The human being is a relational animal (Mitchell, 1993) experiencing physical impulses charged with tension since birth, in a broad range of degrees of quality and quantity. The human being has the necessary resources to face the world, however does not actively search for pleasure instead seeks contact, as contact is a necessity.

Pleasure can be actively sought, can be found, or can be felt by absence of pain, as the human being affirms his/her instincts, needs, motivations, emotions and feelings on a basic axis, the most primary one: the pleasure-pain axis, that provokes closeness or contact in the case of pleasure, or aversion and distance – in the case of pain. Nonetheless, we cannot say that the regulation of pleasure and avoidance of displeasure are opposite and constitute the motivational system in itself. In reality from birth and throughout life, humans go where affects are and seeks them knowing that emotions reside in the motivation to seek, avoid or create transactions (Lichtemberg, 2004).

Physical arousal is transformed into sensual and sexual pleasure, at the same time shifting between feelings of security, liberating from fear and preparing for personal relationships, and feelings of plenitude, that are related to feelings of being capable, of being and feeling vital to develop or live with energy (Marina, 1999).

Impulses, arousal and pleasure are transformed into emotions, not only in the body, physiologically, but also subject to language and desire in all hedonic variations, in order to: obtain moral satisfaction, the satisfaction of exploring and knowing, develop curiosity, satisfy power, possess and be possessed and the need to feel needed and to need. Desire can achieve satisfaction in all these fields independently or simultaneously, mixing them, always interpreting them as keys to personal wellbeing or discomfort.

We do not only need pleasure, we also need to give pleasure a meaning, to enjoy possessing and the feeling of being capable; of feeling vital allowing us to chase boredom, anguish and sadness away turning them into interest, excitement, energy and enjoyment at three levels; corporal, personal and social.

This has important implications in psychoanalysis, as we can dismiss sexuality and its repression as the cause of pathologies and disorders, no longer seeking the resolution of the Oedipus complex as the cause of all pathology. Sexuality becomes an aspect of subjectivity, and affects a priority in human motivation, not so much of the unconscious as of the self. Affect regulation – in which pleasure and displeasure are not opposites instead have different nuances – become the principal necessity of the self.

In adult life, although sexual arousal is a physical pleasure, it develops among contrasts such as disquiet and uncertainty, skirting vacuum and vertigo, rather than the principle of constancy proposed by Freud, which is more about routine and boredom; for example, to desire and be desired always implies the vertigo of doubt.

On the other hand, we need to repeat known pleasures while at the same time continue to search for other unknown pleasures. In this sense, sexual pleasure and orgasm have become the link between satisfied desire and the expectation of another yet to be satisfied that maintains us alert and awakens our curiosity and interest, without being compulsive, as there is also pleasure in auto-regulation and in waiting.

A degree of pleasurable anticipation is necessary to maintain physical and mental arousal, making it tolerable and even an enjoyable experience simply because it maintains the mind in the belief of final satisfaction and relief. Additionally, an optimum degree of frustration is necessary to maintain a state of increasing and intense physical and mental arousal through exciting erotic fantasies, as well as the ability to extract pleasure from frustration and/ or arousal while a resolution is anticipated (Davies, 2009).

Pleasure is thought and planned although in appearance is experienced as something spontaneous. Through the intervention of the unconscious, no one escapes from pleasure as even people who say they *feel nothing,* actually erase pleasure and substitute it with something else that represents it. In anorgasmia or psychological impotence, pleasurable feelings are also experienced although orgasm or the expected levels of arousal are not achieved. This absence can be a form of containment of sexual arousal, as a way of maintaining part of one's own individuality, in this way becoming a genuinely significant experience.

Sexual pleasure can occur without the intervention of erotic desire or emotional subjective connection, through the mere stimulation or auto-stim- ulation of genitals, producing liberation of adrenaline, in turn producing the consequent increase in blood flow and the appearance of lubrication or erection; a satisfaction that can be satisfied total or partially by physical orgasm. On the other hand, sexual-erotic pleasure is temporal and relative; there are moments of plenitude although with the paradox that there is never complete satisfaction.

Throughout development, the body becomes the organ of pleasure and desire, with sensations of enjoyment and plenitude located in the whole body in general, with more intense and located sexual arousal in the genital area.

On one hand, the need for sexual enjoyment activates the impulse for tenderness, which is related to affection towards the attachment figures and towards oneself, an impulse that must be expressed and needs to be felt towards others and oneself. As explained by Lichtermberg (2004) this sensual enjoyment can be presented internally as general anguish and irritability as a concrete object in a concrete area, or stimulated externally and the response to this need be in the form of a caress, consoling, rocking in a relaxing and comforting way, or rubbing by oneself or on the other hand reliving of the anguish or irritability and a sensation of pleasure throughout the whole body.

This need is also related to empathy, that pertains to the capacity to put oneself in the other's place without necessarily feeling their emotions and is related to the knowledge of the other, to sharing his/her emotional state, assuming a subjective perspective and responding affectively to the Other (Guimón, 2009).

It is also related to attachment and resilience, the capacity to overcome affective emotional experiences such as abandon, or the stress related to interpersonal relations; and also with the capacity to protect one's own identity and forge a vital positive behavior. In sum the sensual dimension of sexuality is directly related to tenderness, empathy, attachment and resilience.

On the other hand, concrete sexual sensations that increase in a unidirectional way until climax is attained can be felt throughout the whole body although their focal point is the genital area. Sexual arousal actives the feeling of impetus, the impulse for action, the aggressive impulse necessary to approach the Other, an approach that transcends the self and the Other, in the sense of fitting, entering, pressing, penetrating the interior of the Other physically and emotionally; what Freud identified as the active-aggressive-masculine-man and tender-passive-feminine-woman, another of the influences that continue to prevail today, notwithstanding social changes.

The sexual act is also an aggressive encounter in the sense that both seek one another, propelled by intense desires to unite, neither of the two can be passive, the two allow, permit, and incite contact in a – conscious or unconscious – joint decision of mutual penetration in both heterosexual and homosexual relations. This aggressive impulse is also emotional as relation is a predominant part of aggressive behavior, and is in fact usually emotional.

When speaking about aggressiveness and sexuality, there is a degree of fear of confusion between terms such as violence, rape and masculine aggressive conduct in the sense of gender violence – a grave social problem currently of utmost importance – as the sexual dimension is closely related to hormones and neurotransmitters, gender and the self.

Hormones and neurotransmitters have a great influence on sexual desire. Sexual hormones influence arousal and although they are not the only factor responsible for sexual desire activation, they do control the degree of arousal.[7]

These sensual and sexual impulses constitute the evaluation and interpretation of the degree of wellbeing in the physical and psychic sense: *I am – what do I fear – how am I – what shames me – what gives me pleasure – how do I feel with what I do or is done to me.*

I understand that the integration of these two dimensions, sensuality and sexuality, denote the maturity of erotic development and the capacity to express the genital potency – penis and vagina/clitoris – potency that is transformed into vitality and the capacity to survive in erotic play, that is always a game between unequal satisfactions, and that must be integrated to maintain arousal. The developmental capacity to experience eroticism, in a relationship or in solitary, represents a particularly complex challenge to auto-regulation and integration.

Masturbation

Intimacy is nurtured by physical pleasure that serves as a guide, although not as the only stimulus or support. To establish sexual contact demonstrates confidence, autonomy, and security in oneself and the capacity to sustain desires about the Other.

When a patient manifests sexual issues, one of the first questions regards physical pleasure, whether or not there are problems with orgasm in sexual intercourse. In case of an affirmative answer, it is necessary to know if difficulties are also present in masturbation. When this question is posed to women, I frequently find they answer with a surprised, brief and concise

---

7 The brain segregates large quantities of endorphins – the neurotransmitters that generate effects similar to drugs that derive from opium – during orgasm provoking great satisfaction and calmness. Androstenedione also increases considerably, stimulating the cognitive system; oxytocin increases reinforcing empathy patterns and confidence – with oneself and with one's partner – strengthening serotonin that regulates emotional wellbeing and induces pleasure (Basson, 2001, 2006).

"yes" or "no", as if to get it over with quickly. On the other hand, I find that men tend to response with a certain degree of modesty or sometimes shame, but are not so surprised or evasive. This response may have sociological and moral explanations due to the influence of negative connotations the word masturbation has had throughout history. Each period of history has found calming explanations for masturbation, its origins and causes, through fables, legends and religious beliefs.

However, the difficulties in responding to this question are not only due to social influence and education. The question about masturbation from a psychological perspective is very moving for several reasons: it invites us to talk about ourselves, always has a developmental aspect, and can become a symptomatic characteristic.

It invites us to talk about ourselves, referring to pleasure and desire that are always in debt to the body and the unconscious. What one desires and what is pleasurable is not frequently shared, because when we are not in the midst of an erotic experience, this subjectivity can remain hidden to the *self* (Frommer, 2009); and on the other hand, the erotic self can enter in conflict with who we imagine we are. What we find erotic can be strange to the self and in most cases at least in the Western culture we do not have the words to describe the first sensual, sexual corporal and erotic experiences.

Masturbation always has a developmental aspect that is expressed differently at each phase of the developmental process. It could be said that it is a form of speaking with oneself and confronting the world throughout life, not only in adolescence.

It can also have a symptomatic nature when it responds to compulsive activity that can occur in certain situations of emotional tension, crisis or personal stress; using it as an "anxiolytic", as a way to maintain self-cohesion through intense physical perception that triggers a type of emotional anesthesia, triggering the sense of feeling alive.

On the other hand, the absence of masturbation at all developmental stages tends to show the inhibiting influence of serious psychic conflicts rather than manifest a state of personal order.

Sexual Fantasies

Pleasure is felt and thought and also imagined. It's a feeling the covers a complex range from anticipation until consumption and varies in qualities, nuances and intensities (Mora, 2006). Impulse is as important as the motivation to initiate or maintain any sexual encounter, but what role does imagination play in fantasies and the constitution of desire?

In classic psychoanalysis[8], Rodriguez Sutil (2010) explains, fantasies proliferate in the dark, can become impossible to distinguish from memories and find their expression in dreams, symptoms and other unconscious formations. However, from the relational matrix perspective, I consider it is important to underline this same author proposes a similarity between the self and the concept of fantasy that is not situated exclusively in the unconscious, preconscious and conscious, identifying the self with fantasies about oneself, specially unconscious fantasies.

Fantasies in general and sexual fantasies in particular, offer the impression of omnipotent control, and are a space of intimacy in which there are two types of relationships: between the "me with myself" and between the "me with you", a space that drags us into the enigmatic part of sexuality and discovers our bodily self and our erotic self.

Fantasies can appear at the expectation of a relationship; the aroused erotic self co-convokes the other erotic self, and activates a series of desires and anxieties that awaken the idealized image we have of ourselves as sexual and erotic beings, and also activates the beliefs one has about sex in general, that from the beginning determine the form in which contact will be initiated, or not.

The activated erotic self precipitates, firstly, great doses of hopeful anticipation and certain curiosity about the unknown Other, and in more or less degree a feeling of shame and modesty, that does not inhibit behavior, instead is a stimulus...*dare I... shall I do it... no I won't...I am interested...I feel like it... see how it works with this person...I really like him/her...but...* etc.

Fantasies can also be triggered as a consequence of intense states of arousal due to emotional tension from happiness or frustration, or can arise when the erotic self is invoked by an external stimulus that provokes a state of arousal without an existing relationship, for example when we see someone we find attractive, an image, a look, an odor, the scene in a movie, pornography, a book, etc.

Fantasies usually have a perverted counterpart, evoking emotionally charged images that can be experienced as new and unknown but in most cases are recurring images that are not so new or unknown as they activate implicit and explicit relational patterns.

Pleasure and in sum orgasm, is a physiological and physical experience but is also an emotional experience that requires the consciousness of the body

---

8 For Freud fantasy is an activity with the purpose of satisfying desires, as a masked expression and the partial fulfillment of frustrated unconscious desire. He defended that fantasy originates in the unconscious or that it forms part of daydreams that are later repressed.

and of oneself. It can be said to be a voluntary act, a decision that is made and influenced by manifest cultural and gender meanings that this type of experience are charged with.

Gender

Gender is a concept that is impossible to dissociate from the study of sexuality. We can state without qualm that sex is not as private as we think; rather it is an intimate experience that triggers a whole range of emotions within the social group context.

Gender is part of the structure of the self, implanted prematurely from the outside by the Other; it is before sex and sexuality; it precedes symbolization even in the first year of life; it is plural – not dual as has always been thought – and is produced within the attachment relationship and intimacy of the small group of belonging, through the caring of the body, affective language and also through social language (Garriga, 2004, 2010).

Therefore, what is being a woman, being a man? It is a process that begins at birth and entails different dispositions and availabilities for erotic experience (Dio-Bleichmar, 1991, 1998). The vagina and clitoris are eroticized as the girl develops the capacity for impulse and power as receptor and active executor. In the same way the penis is eroticized while the boy not only develops the capacity for impulse and power as active executor, but also as an active receptor. Meanwhile feelings are incorporated and conscious and unconscious moral guidelines pertaining to family and social group are inscribed in the body.

The concept of agency is incorporated from a relational viewpoint, including the capacity to actively incorporate what is socially considered masculine or feminine in the same person, that is, the capacity to incorporate gender actively. The human being knows it is constituted by and dependent on norms and socially implicit and explicit rules, however it is necessary to seek the way to actively adapt to them.

While gender meanings are incorporated, the subject has the basic need to seek and maintain self cohesion, something that is maintained throughout life, needing to feel recognized by the Other, while at the same time needing to recognize that Other as someone equal, although different.

In infancy, this recognition as a subject is produced by thirdness, a quality of the intersubjective relationship that allows mutual recognition and has a correlated internal mental space. The infant must recognize the mother as a different subject with her own world and desires, intentions and experiences; in fact, to recognize the mother as a subject and not a mere object to satisfy his/her own impulses and needs, is a developmental achievement for the infant

(Benjamin, 1997), while the mother also recognizes her baby as a subject with his/her own temperament and particular needs.

"Thirdness" arises in this mutual recognition, a subjective space that is "neither mine, nor yours", a common space that is created and shared by an "us". This "thirdness" is found, it arises spontaneously and invites to mutual entrusting. It is something that happens to us, not forced. It can occur in masochistic form, submissively, in which one feels permanently submissive, ashamed or guilty; or can occur expansively, promoting life, also enclosing subjective shame and guilt as part of the recognition of solitude and otherness, of knowing one is needed by the other but at the same time acknowledging the need for separation.

In adult life this "us" arises in multiple forms, different and unique, depending on each partner. It can nurture or limit the development of erotic sexual desire. It can be defined as: a subjective experience with physiological and physical reactions, within the combination of desires in the individual that activates the search for contact with the Other's desire, generating a connection between the two unconscious desires that become significant in the field of reflexive consciousness that desires union, reciprocity and exclusivity. It is invoked by conscious and unconscious fantasies about oneself and the Other – real or speculative – and is constantly regulated by reality.

Beliefs about one's own identity forms part of the self's structure and develops alongside intimacy, as arousal in sexual experience awakens the conscious and unconscious feelings of vulnerability and risk and/or trust, creating new fantasies and beliefs about one's identity. Freud believed that "identity is behind anatomy" while today fear of loss of sexual gender identity is at the nucleus of sexuality instead of fear of castration or penis envy. All the events related to sexuality have profound significance because they are related to self-esteem and one's own existence.

Eroticism: Relational Concepts

Sexuality is characterized by language and spontaneous gestures as well as by attunement to the Other. A unique emotional experience usually takes place in sexual relationships that is intense, creative and transforming. At the beginning of the relationship the couple learns, in Winnicot's[9], terms, to have

---

9 I am referring to "mutual use" related to the concept of "object use" Winnicott described in 1969. I find the application of this concept to sexuality interesting. This author did not consider sexuality important; he fundamentally studied infancy, however he proposed concepts

sex together, simultaneously experiencing two moments. Firstly by *imitation or docility*, the adult that during infancy began to discover sex, knows there are things learned culturally and makes an intellectual effort to learn them – what a woman does in sex, what does the man do, how to make it more desirable or powerful. And the second, by *mutual use*, both use each other mutually and each one conscious and unconsciously selects what is good or of interest, and usually is also what is most profoundly and remotely idiosyncratic, a mix of personal history and unconscious desires. To enjoy sexuality as something animal, as pointed out by Mitchell, "*To be bestial together can entail a mutual usage of each other, thereby providing a clarity and immediacy which may not be available in the subtle choreography of other dimensions of emotional intimacy*" (1988, p. 143)

Intimacy

All sexual relationships, whether heterosexual or homosexual, show intimacy in two different ways: intimacy with oneself and intimacy with the other. This concept has been specially abused as, in general, it is confused with other concepts such as: identity, privacy, ineffability or solipsism (Pardo, 2004). At times it is considered that every human being sustains him/herself in intimacy and as of that point is a being with a unique natural history to answer to. At other times, intimacy is seen as everything that is private, done at home, and also what is spoken in privacy to a psychotherapist, doctor etc. It is frequently considered that intimacy cannot be explained with words; or that intimacy cannot be shared and can only be genuinely expressed in the most absolute solitude, to save one's own convictions or feelings in secret, guarding oneself from others, in fear of being discovered, thus destroying intimacy.

None of this makes reference to intimacy, which I understand as a refuge where one feels oneself, as someone, with doubts and problems; the place where one can hear oneself – hear and feel one's own voice – a fold in language that allows one to feel flexible and alive, with weaknesses, vulnerable, feel that perhaps we lack firm support, as if one had a double bottom, feel oneself but without the identity of oneself. As La Rochefoucauld (1665) said: "…. *We are*

---

that in clinical practice have helped me understand adult relationships. "Object use" refers to a paradox and the acceptance of that paradox; it requires an intersubjective relationship in which the Other's existence is recognized, it is not mere projection, that is, the pleasure of being used is based greatly on the fact that we were first discovered, recognized in our selfness. This is difference from what occurs in sexual perversions in general, in which the Other is used as a mere object of pleasure not as a subject.

sometimes as different from ourselves as we are from others". To feel oneself is to feel another, but not only another as if a twin, rather as in otherness, where one multiplies oneself in another that is absolutely different, and at the same time oneself; as if to be oneself, one has to divide into two, like the body and its shade, or the voice and its echo.

From the subjective refuge of intimacy with oneself, the individual relates sexually spontaneously and esthetically with the Other, to whom one tries to offer the best image of oneself, which although not false, does not totally respond to how one knows and recognizes oneself in intimacy, which is where one treasures the ultimate and definite truth about oneself.

Intimacy with oneself constitutes a subjective space that allows us to overcome the shame of not being how we have presented and disclosed ourselves in the sexual act, to overcome the fear of being criticized or rejected, or of not being valuable enough for the other. A subjective refuge in which to overcome the battle for power between the desire to destroy the one to whom we have just given ourselves, and the hope that this destruction does not take place; the joy of feeling powerful and at the same time the fear of being destroyed; the fear of being abandoned and the desire to abandon; while the pleasures felt are recreated in the mind and new ones are imagined.

Sexuality puts intimacy of oneself and one's image into play, what is visible and what is hidden; what is available and what is reserved. Perhaps this is why Winnicott insisted that each one of us should remain "incognito" in a certain sense, to recuperate the impression of personal experience and renovate the capacity for intimacy, and feel that we are someone different in each relation with the same person, or with another.

In sex it is possible to feel totally in the hands of the Other, unable to escape. However if sexuality is in service of intimacy, attunement is produced when the partner reacts to vulnerability – inherent to feeling of desire – (Mitchell, 2002), giving the relationship vitality. Sexual relationships usually activate attachment, as mentioned before, although attachment needs are not the cause of arousal and desire, rather the intimate connection of two subjectivities with one another, as Winnicott would say, from the true erotic self of each.

Seduction

The study of seduction in sex allows us to situate the body in the crux of the exchange with the Other, and the crucial role this plays in its eroticizing. It is a concept saturated with negative connotations socially and in psychoanalytic theory. It has become an almost dammed[10] concept because, although Freud abandoned his seduction theory and substituted it by the libido theory, the consequence in clinical practice was the exaltation of therapeutic neutrality, highlighting the therapist's precaution to avoid seducing the patient, whom is always considered in a position of disadvantage, immaturity and passivity, as occurs according to the drive theory, with a child in relation to the adult.

Despite these inherited negative connotations, at both social and psychological levels, the study of seduction is of vital importance for a better understanding of the psychological mechanisms of attraction and arousal in which eroticism is involved. Laplanche speaks of a *general or original seduction*, named this way because it accounts for the necessary confrontation between the infant subject and the adult world, a relationship that no human can avoid and that also constitutes the original fundament of the unconscious.

A significant example of the enigmatic element of seduction is seen when a newborn automatically responds to the mother's facial expressions. It is interesting to observe the mother-baby couple interacting with their entire bodies, looks and gestures. The infant later also responds to these signs and asks, "What does my mother mean with that smile?", "What is she asking me with that look?" As an adult that same question is addressed to one's partner "What is he/she saying with that look or gesture?" It is not a matter of trying to guess the answer or resolve a complex problem, as the enigma is not a question asked between two subjects, the enigma is not directed to the partner as a real and different other, rather to the otherness of the Other, an Other that is not so real or differentiated.

Sexual attraction comes into play in seduction – what I call creative seduction – as a way to transcend the Other, the body of the Other, in an interaction in which needs and complementary desires are exposed through the similarity of gestures, attitudes, verbal and non-verbal communication through half-uttered words and playful appearance. It is not a matter of lies rather of presenting one's most embellished and fun mask. To seduce is perhaps nothing other than turning the Other's deficiencies towards oneself, pushing the button that allows us to awaken that vacuum and absence. What is wanted is that the Other desire and need us. We are not attracted to the Other as such, rather to feeling his/her need and that in spite of ourselves, and precisely for this reason, the Other continues to desire us, in a play of mirrors that is always unequal.

---

10 In 1895 Freud first defended sexuality's exogenous origin, but in 1897 he had to abandon the traumatic seduction theory and substituted it with the concept of drives and the libido theory.

In sum, creative seduction entails the search for the access to the Other and their body, without assuming they are accessible, leaving something of oneself that the Other has no access to, such as the genuine sexual arousal which is characteristic of each person, situated within the real self[11], and whose mere existence can never be totally known by the Other. There is a secret area that is usually preserved, requiring that the erotic self not be totally accessible.

Corporal arousal and sensual pleasures draw the outline and limits of the skin giving sex depth, taste, odor and at the same time, positioning us with respect to the Other - under, over, beside - and positioning the Other with respect to ourselves, as a dialectic of sexes that is yielding; seducing and being seduced; adoring and being adored; idealizing and so on in succession (Mitchell, 2002), transcending beyond oneself and beyond the Other. Therefore looks are the antechamber to eroticism, in a form of dance that occurs within the symbiotic relationship, similar to the mother/infant symbiosis brought to adulthood, however differently from what occurs in infancy, as intimacy is developed uncovering not only needs, but also developed in a relationship in which narcissism is already articulated in form of desires.

Narcissism

From the relational perspective, the newborn is situated in an intersubjective world and narcissism is not innate from birth, rather it develops in the separation and individualization processes, as the symbiotic relationship and total dependence is left behind and the separation and individualization process develops, entering the world of desires and identifications in mirror images.

Narcissism is understood in the intersubjective relationship as *"a confirmation of the self-image and is a protection from the threats to this image, that shift in a play of mirrors of desire that is never-ending."* (Rodriguez Sutil, 2010). It is in effect a never-ending game and therefore is not fixed in early relationships. Although the initial representation of oneself is constructed during those first relationships of family identifications, all significant relationships are unfolded in that game of mirror images and contribute to the transformation of the self throughout life; we are many identities although we are always the same.

---

11 Winnicott defended that the real self could be discovered, as it lets the Other discover it, but is never completely accessible and known by the Other, always leaving a part of the self for oneself.

Eroticism also produces a creative and transforming experience on the basis of self-image and the sexual identity of each one, as man or as woman, independent from the sex one is born with. The impulse that triggers arousal and desire is developed within a common space, in which symbiotic and narcissistic relationships are reproduced and mixed simultaneously, that uncover needs and desires in which the Other is both an opportunity and an obstacle.

The Other's body is an opportunity, mere material support for the preconceived idea of sex. Two people seek each other out because they need each other, but in this sense, the emotions that awaken in these encounters are not mere impulses or instincts, they constitute the selective patterns of evaluations and interpretations for wellbeing: *to what point does he/she alter me, assure me, or make me feel bad.* At the beginning emotions are not very differentiated, such as surprise to see oneself, *who am I when I am nude / before my lover, whom I fear, whom makes me feel what I do and what he/she does to me.* These are encounters are charged with an integration of aggressive and tender impulses that a new couple usually displays spontaneously, and a large part of the unconscious is related to the need for sexual arousal and sensual pleasure.

The Other is an opportunity, but also an obstacle that triggers contradictory and ambivalent emotions in a play of mirrors that is always unequal, between satisfaction of power and the need to have confidence, the capacity to give oneself and discover oneself, and the need to escape and hide. As explained by Mitchell, in that seek-giving-escape sequence, conventional concepts of gender are implied that are central in both heterosexual and homosexual passion: hard/soft, aggressive/tender, independent/dependent, powerful/submissive, etc. However there are many more types of contrasts that reflect those mirror images in which the sexual couple is involved such as: refined/vulgar, sophisticated/simple, expressive/withdrawn etc., in a type of tie that closes in on both but, who is stronger? Who feels more powerful and draws that invisible cord that lights passion, even tighter?

Erotic play undergoes several phases, always beginning with idealization. The desired person is the idealized person, and through imagination we create the image of how we would like the Other to be, situating them in a plane that is distant from us, because we need to provide it with force and magic, making him/her attractive and irresistible. These fantasies about the Other also allow us to imagine ourselves with a more ideal and perfect image, with qualities that in the eyes of the Other are intensified and give us an improved image of what we in reality are.

These idealizations are usually destabilizing, as they tend to separate us from our reality, making the Other and our own self bigger and overrated, discovering parts of oneself in unedited and unknown situations. Additionally, this usually erases limits and causes feelings as if the Other could swallow the self, provoking anxiety about the fear of the self being disintegrated, with states of euphoria and depression, in the incessant search for self-cohesion.

The type of otherness in eroticism, that according to Mitchell lights passion, can be defined as a shadow image of the self, as the unrecognized characteristics largely unknown or even unaccepted of the self, that can also represent what has been crushed, squashed, that has not been allowed within the self. Without these characteristics of the shadow image of the self and without the Other's otherness, it would be difficult to understand the mechanisms that light and maintain eroticism.

Emotional Dependence

Sexual relationships are usually destabilizing because they demand exposing oneself and become conscious of oneself, putting each one's narcissism into play, not as a source of infantilism as explained by Freud, but as a form of vitality, sense and creativity that Kohut and Winnicott indicated, to emotionally connect oneself with the Other.

The inevitable consequence of subjectivity has to do with the development of our own desires, learning to be one, different and unique without feeling strange. The process of separation and individualization in infancy is not undertaken without ambivalences, uncertainties, contrariety, demands, complaints or rejection. These feelings are necessary as the process of identification and recognition entails separation and loss, and therefore, anguish and solitude that arise as a battle between satisfaction, disappointment, pleasure and frustration, love and hate, confidence and distrust, envy and rivalry, power and submission, etc.

In order for this process of separation/individuation to take place one cannot live at the expense of the Other, – the child at the expense of the mother and the mother at the expense of the child. The symbiotic relationship becomes distanced and a subjective space opens, that allows creative seduction to attract the other and bear the shame, envy and guilt that arise as well as the otherness, for not being one with the Other. In adult life these emotions and feelings of shame, envy, and guilt arise conscious and unconsciously and usually impregnate spontaneous expressions of intimate relationships, therefore approaching these feelings in psychotherapy help both patient and therapist to understand the nature of erotic desire.

Shame[12]

The study of shame is another of the fundamental factors in sexuality research, as feeling shame and being ashamed of what one is and does are two different feelings.

The appearance of shame indicates the limits of each one. Shame has its origin in infancy and is tied to the experiences felt by the infant, in relation to others within the family and social context. This feeling does not inhibit the expression of desire, and helps the subject to recognize his/her own existence, recognizing the existence of the other and positioning him/herself with respect to the other and with respect to the other's gaze.

Shame does not suddenly arise and install itself as a consequence of an event, it is prolonged from infancy and becomes consolidated or transformed as the child grows, through crucial stages such as adolescence in which the subject becomes conscious of his/her body's nudeness and the self through the eyes and recognition of attachment figures, as well as those other "special" people for whom he/she feels sexual attraction.

Subjective shame arises consciously and its expression is usually liberating, allowing the constructive revelation of feelings and personal reactions, confirming sexual identity, for example when the partner says *"I am ashamed to feel this or do that, it makes me feel good or bad..."*

On the other hand, to feel ashamed of oneself is an inhibiting feeling that arises in the relationship of the subject with the Other in a family or social context, in which secrets, ambiguity and inconsiderateness are predominant (Gaulejac, 2008). The feeling of being ashamed is usually denied, remaining mainly unconscious and responds to an identity rupture mechanism, as it awakens a feeling of aversion towards oneself, a hateful image of oneself through one's own eyes (Morrison, 1997). To feel ashamed limits spontaneous expression and provokes the predominance of the partners rhythms and pleasure and not one's own pleasure.

Envy[13]

From the relational point of view, unconscious envy is approached in a way that eases the way – between patient and therapist – to better understand the

---

12 For Freud, sexuality is usually something shameful and shame, is the dike of sexuality that originates in the unconscious.

13 Envy socially has negative connotations linked to hate, destruction and enjoying others' downfall. From a classic psychoanalyst perspective, it is related to an instinctive force and matters of gender (see Freud's psychosocial penis envy development theory).

nature of the complaints, fears and in sum the nature of desire. A variety of subtle affective keys, which become integrated mainly outside the field of consciousness and explicit cognition, are necessary to know how to behave in intimate relationships. It is frequent that partner selection of an adolescent, adult, man or woman, is based on a positive or negative copy of the significant attachment figure, with which implicit and explicit relational patterns have been learned.

When there is a failure in the mother-infant couple identification process, and there is no mutual recognition, a common "us" space arises, with a masochistic form, such as submission, in which one feels permanently subjected, ashamed or guilty.

Unconscious envy arises as a consequence of failed emotional efforts to identify with the attachment figure. When this desire to identify lacks response, envy takes its place (Benjamin, 1888). It appears as secondary to an unstable psyche, to insoluble desperation and the masochistic resentment that arises in the face of rejected desire. In general, the infant that feels rejected and not included in the mother's narcissist world finally ends up identifying with the rejected image, awakening feelings of deficiency, of lacking valuable, of resentment together with the omnipotent desire to be like the mother, psychically omnipresent, but unrecognized.

Envy usually gravitates around a combination of primitive order fantasies or the desire that what makes him/her different, from the mother, father and now the partner, does not disappear. It's like consciously saying to his/her partner, terms such as, "I am like this; I am not like the Other!"… but drowning in an unconscious cry, "we are one, we cannot differentiate, I cannot be left alone!"

I use unconscious envy as a common theme in relational psychology as proposed by Benjamin (1988, 2013) and Gerhardt (2010), as the discovery of the desire to be someone valuable and recognized by the Other, directing efforts to feeling unique, different but not strange. Envy appears like an attack of the psyche against itself, the constant feeling of being hurt, of being incapable of thinking and acting effectively in the world. These attacks are a reaction and at the same time a protection of the bonds with the significant Other, because envy destroys all hope for emotional connection, converting the significant relationship, such as the sexual relationship into something so painful that all efforts are made to avoid it. However it is an effort that ends up failing and exposing the self's narcissist injury, with a feeling of not being valuable for the Other.

Guilt

If the caregiver, the significant attachment figure is too controlling, intrusive and is not attuned nor can put him/herself in the place of the innocent[14] infant, there are many probabilities that all subsequent relationships of confidence and intimacy be presided by the loss of spontaneous gesture and dominated by guilt. The real self, as stated by Winnicott will never risk being discovered by the Other, whom is seen as a traitor and tyrant.

In psychoanalysis, subjective guilt [15] is the feeling that arises in the identification process, as well as otherness; what Winnicott named real guilt or the subject's moral code, whose development is linked to the sufficiently good enough raising conditions and is therefore something that cannot be shown, cannot be learned, it is transmitted through the intimate relationship with attachment figures.

However this feeling can be mainly unconscious, when the attempts of recognition fail the feeling of "being ill" arises, an illness as a form of guilt. The child feels ill as separation and individualization is undertaken through absolute bodily dependence that make him/her defenseless with attachment figures, whom are seen as powerful, and that through the cares administered to the body and through the satisfaction of basic needs, transmit their way of loving, their morals and values in the broad sense. This type of guilt that Winnicott calls implanted, is false for the self, it is a failure in constituting the depressive position. Through this type of guilt, psychic suffering becomes installed in the subject, a mental pain[16] that expresses the feeling of being ill, of not being one with the Other and with whom he/she cannot be uncovered as someone different and unique.

Perversion

The systematic study of sexual perversion was in vogue when Freud began to elaborate his sexuality theory; these papers[17] described the combination of sexual perversions in the adult, and Freud's original contribution was the idea that predisposition to perversion is not so rare and special, rather is part

---

14 Innocent, I bring it up here in the sense of the individual that is still acquiring family and group moral values and has not yet separated from childhood significant figures.

15 For Freud, guilt is an unconscious representation linked to neurosis, not an unconscious feeling linked to metapsychology, explaining the theoretic concepts with which psychoanalysis is constituted as a discipline, explaining the development of the psyche.

16 Ávila (2011) distinguishes between mental suffering and mental pain, which clarifies the approach to the patient's "psychological sufferings".

17 Studies before Freud: Krafft-Ebing, 1893, and Havelock Ellis, 1897: *Psychopathia sexualis*; and *Studies in the Psychology of Sex*, have been forgotten, suggesting that the revolution of interpretation of sexuality in Victorian times depends mainly on Freud's contribution.

of the constitution of what is normal sexuality, and confirms and explains the existence of infant sexuality[18].

Perversion has become a controversial term for all, for those who relate it to sin and maliciousness, for those who link it with crime, and for whom it is considered an illness. I therefore clarify.

On one hand, we cannot confuse nor compare concepts such as perversion, disorder or illness. *Perversion refers to basic structures and functioning of human existence, perversion in this sense is a specifically human phenomenon, expression of man to profoundly change the fundaments of man's own existence, in relation to oneself and to other human beings* (Baca, 2011, p.65). In this sense, I find the definition Dimen proposes of perversion as thought provoking, describing it as "the sex that you like and I don't" (2005, 2001, p. 827). She also proposes a challenge in her writings, in which she encourages us as psychotherapists to think about how we "think of perverts" as "they are bad guys", while "I am good", and how in this differentiation one can feel protected from oneself, believing that perverse behavior is something that does not have to do with ourselves, not affecting us as human beings.

On the other hand, our postmodern and global society is not configured around religious beliefs, rather it establishes its basis on ethical norms that defend individual liberty and behavior that is removed from these norms, is not conceptualized as sin rather as behavior that transgresses individual limits. Human experience is therefore substantially the constant experience of limits: on one hand the awareness of what is finite and death, and as Bataille explained in 1957 on the other hand, the awareness of having erased the limits with the Other and the idea of erasing internal and external frontiers in erotic desire as explained by Mitchell (2002, p. 94).

I find it very interesting to apply the concept of transgression to the study of sexuality; it is not a mere opposition to established norms, nor is it a subversion or change in *status quo*. Instead it about deciding to transgress the limits one cannot or chooses not to comply with, not excluding the concept of maliciousness, but making reference to controlling it. All sexual relationships entail a perverse component, in the sense that a minimum capacity to transgress the limits of the Other is always necessary, as an interpenetration of bodies takes place in a dialectic that seeks to dominate, possessing while being possessed

---

18 For classic psychoanalysis perversion does not exist in sexual moral functioning. Normality or perversion is identified according to the genital organization, the capacity to overcome the Oedipus complex, the absence of the castration complex, the acceptance of the prohibition of incest and therefore the adaption to social norms.

and dominated. It also entails a promiscuous component, as an spiritual phenomena that involves something more than what is personal, extending beyond what is familiar. The subject has the feeling of facing something fearful and at the same time admired, a hidden spirituality "in view", waiting to be discovered (Samuel, 2011) and also a characteristic of sexual fantasies that enables the feeling of omnipotent control.

As indicated before, sexual fantasies have a perverse counterpart, and from the relational perspective the biological background of perversions are substituted by a relational matrix, studied as other forms of sexuality are, that is, as behavior that obtains its significance by how it engages with broad relational motivations, not determined by infant sexuality. Perversion can be consented to or not, can be assumed or not by the subject that develops it, without this being a conflict. It can be a conduct that affects the other at a social level, because it can limit individual liberty, be a social reproof, or can also be accepted by society.

Perversion is related to humiliation or abuse, as a challenge to socialization. It is also related to the need to impact the Other because one has the impression that it is not possible to reach him/her without overcoming certain resistance, or with the need to form part of the Other, whether by bearing pain and submission, or by provoking pain in the Other as the only way to be able to feel intense and exclusive intimacy. There is also perversion in the escape from the Other, when only the body is involved in the relationship and arousal is inhibited, so that control is reason for pride and a way to retain a trace of individuality. Other perverse conducts are the avoidance of affective ties and of the person in their totality, with access only to the genitals or specific parts of their body, as occurs in prostitution. Or when sexual relationships are constructed on the reversal of primary structures, as when very dominant people become submissive and passive in sexual relationships.

In view of the above, I ask myself if all sexual acts entail a certain degree of perversion, a transgression, and if sexual arousal always includes perverse factors that are what make it a genuinely significant pleasure; and I agree with Fromm whom affirms that, *I my opinion perversions should be treated only if the person suffers from it, that is to say if the person feels that this is something which disturbs him very much, which splits up his life, which goes against his values, which if he can discover the relationship it has to his character, his relationship to other people. Otherwise I do not consider it something which has to be treated (Fromm, 2007, p. 118).*

251

Conclusion

Psychoanalysis was a great influence in the beginnings of modern society, not only due to the study of sexuality but also to the discovery of the unconscious. As of that moment, the modern individual began to question him/herself, "What don't I know about myself?" "Who am I?" looking at one's body and oneself, towards one's own identity and the manner of desiring in a different way, in constant battle for individuality and living an intimacy that did not correspond to anything known or familiar.

As relational psychoanalysts we begin – as in classic psychoanalysis – with the recognition of infant sexuality and the enigma of adult sexuality. However, we reject that sexuality and its repression are the causes of pathology and disorders. Sexuality becomes part of subjectivity, and affects a priority in human motivation, as a priority of the self, not of the unconscious. Affect regulation – which includes pleasure and displeasure not as opposites rather with different nuances – becomes the self's principle necessity.

The relational psychotherapist prioritizes the integration of physical impulses and needs for sensual enjoyment and sexual arousal that are imbued with relational significance and that are of vital importance in the configuration and development of erotic desire. This capacity to integrate sensual dimensions and sexuality indicate mature erotic development and the capacity to express genital power – penis and vagina/clitoris – a power that is transformed into vitality and capacity for survival in erotic play that is always a game of unequal satisfactions.

Sexuality and eroticism demand the study of concepts such as pleasure, desire, fantasy, intimacy, seduction, narcissism, perversion and emotional dependence, with the affects these provoke, from shame and envy, to the feeling of guilt, as well as gender and agency.

Gender is the essence of oneself; it is not simply a belief, an imaginary extension of sex. It is more than that, it is a reality more fundamental that actual sex. The experiences of gender identity – one's own and in others – are perceived in an invisible way, as gender is ethereal, an exchange of glances, a gesture, an attitude, a taste for something, an interior music, a way of feeling oneself, a combination of lights and shadows as described by Morris[19] (2011)

19 Jean Morris – before James Morris- is a writer and journalist. In her sincere and moving book *The Enigma*, she writes about her change of sex, making her the most known transsexual person in England, offering a clarifying and priceless testimony about the difference between sex and gender.

which although lacking a physical entity is perceived through the body, that is constituted as human, with an identity as a man or a woman.

As expressed by Mitchell, sexual intensity requires the juxtaposition of people with their arousals, fantasies, pleasures, fears, wishes and hopes. The entire range of the mental life enters into play in the sexual act through the interpenetration of bodies as representations of desires, conflicts and negotiations between the self and others.

Summary

For Relational Psychoanalysis the internal world is not something set in stone during the first years of infancy, nor is it something that remains impassive to current experiences, instead the relational context of the internal world co-evolves (co-develops), modifying and recreating each other mutually. This is important as it offers another perspective to the study of sexuality and approach to sexual conduct in psychotherapy.

Both classic and relational psychoanalysis recognize infant sexuality as well as the existence of sexuality as something enigmatic, something that not only has to do with education and sexual information – although it is interesting to not loose sight of these aspects – rather that it belongs to the conscious and unconscious knowledge of oneself and others.

In the approach to adult sexuality, the relational psychoanalyst highlights gender study, the attachment style and identity. Eroticism, sex and passion seem to relive all our proximity conditions again, the intensity and exclusivity that appear in infancy in relation to otherness. For the one in love, the Other is not another, neither completely the same nor completely different.

I ask myself what lights and maintains erotic passion, what aspects influence sexual excitement and sensuality and what characteristics help us understand erotic pleasure. Sexuality is characterized by language and spontaneous gestures and also by the attunement with the Other on two levels: sensually and sexually as well as a whole range of affects, from shame, envy and guilt in a game that develops in intimacy and unfolds narcissism and perversion in its different dimensions.

11

Working From the Relational Perspective With Children And Adolescents

Sandra Toribio Caballero

*'It is life in relationship that heals us,
understanding the experience of being
in relation to others'*
(Ávila, 2013)

PART ONE: THEORY AND TECHNIQUE

What Being A Relational Psychotherapist For Children And Adolescents Means

When a different type of therapist asks me what it is to be a relational psychotherapist, it usually takes me a few seconds to come up with an answer; explaining is no easy task. This may be because it has to do with an attitude learnt through training, rather than a clear conceptualization of what it means. Often, when confronted with this question, I end up explaining what I am *not*:

I am not a psychotherapist with a clear and ready-made set of guidelines telling me which stance to take up with regard to the person who comes to treatment, and when I work with children and adolescents, even less so.

Relational psychoanalysis implied a new way of positioning oneself before the patient (Ávila, 2009), different from the previous model, classical drive theory, in which the person was understood in his or her individuality, and goals and human desires were seen as personal and individual (Velasco, 2009). Many authors cite the book "Object Relations in Psychoanalytic Theory" (1983), by Jay R. Greenberg and Stephen A. Mitchell, as the starting point of this school of thought, which gives us to understand that people are primarily social and that human satisfactions are only attainable within the social context (Velasco, 2009).

But how has this school of thought come to mean adopting a different position vis-à-vis the patient and a different way of understanding work with children and adolescents? That difference is basically related to the following aspects:

Closeness and emotional availability *(where there used to be asymmetry)*.

As relational therapists, we see clearly that the relationship remains asymmetric with respect to ethical responsibility and to the fact that the clinician is still the one who takes care of the patient. But, at the same time, we know that the therapeutic relationship is bi-personal and ethically egalitarian (Ávila, 2016), which gives rise to a greater closeness.

This closeness is in turn related to the relational therapist's emotional availability, probably the most distinctive feature of clinical practitioners working from this approach. We start out from the fact that in everything that happens within the sessions and takes place in treatment, we are *participants* and not simply neutral observers. The patient who comes in is the way he/she is because he/she is with us and not with a different therapist, and vice versa. We take control of (meaning we think about and analyze) our inevitable imprint.

This emotional availability can be understood within the framework of intersubjectivity, which Stern (Delgado et al., 2015) defined as "the capacity to share, know, understand, empathize with, feel, participate in, resonate with, enter into the lived experience of another" and "interpreting overt behaviors such as posture, tone of voice, speech rhythm and facial expression, as well as verbal content... which assumes that [the psychotherapist] can come to share, know and feel what is in the mind of the patient and the sense of what the patient is experiencing" (Stern, 2004, in Delgado et al., 2015).

This brings us to the subject of emotional and affective *attunement* (Stern, 1985), which involves the sharing and alignment of internal states that take place during the mother/father-infant interaction.

In relational clinical practice, this affective attunement refers to the authentic and genuine responses given to the patient; unlike what happens with empathy, the therapist "is not only reflecting on the patient's subjective state but also conveying his or her own internal perspective to the patient" (Delgado et al., 2015, p. 84).

This is especially relevant in child and adolescent therapy: closeness and emotional availability are fundamental for establishing a secure bond of trust, which will lay the foundations for a good therapeutic relationship and a good working alliance. Moreover, when working with children and adolescents, the distance between therapist and patient seems to lessen still more if we compare it to our work with adults.

When we are in a session with a child or an adolescent and we *play* something, we will adopt whatever role they assign us, we will play according to the rules they propose (within the limits and the setting), we will be an *equal* and a *playmate*. Of course, in therapy with adults we will also *let ourselves 'go with the flow'* (inevitably), but the roles tend to blur less. The encounter is more vivid, more spontaneous (on both sides) when we work with children and adolescents.

Mutuality *(where there used to be neutrality).*

From the relational approach, we start out with the assumption that neutrality is not possible, and this is not even considered to be desirable or something that we ought to achieve. We understand that everything we do, say or are transmits something: our consulting room, the way we look, our attitude. And this is because "as analysts (therapists) there is nothing we can say about the other without including ourselves in it, there is nothing we can infer from our experience without considering the relational matrix in which it is generated" (Ávila, 2013, p. 80). Therefore, our subjectivity will remain in sight, and will be part of the relational matrix formed by therapist and patient.

Consequently, from a relational perspective, rather than neutrality we talk about mutuality, understood as the "reciprocal acknowledgment of the experience shared by the clinician and the person asking for help, and of the mutual influence that each one exercises over the other" (Aron, 1996, in Ávila 2013). Patient and therapist are mutually regulated and influenced, consciously and unconsciously, and we start out from the premise that there is no possible neutrality, but "implication and mutuality governed by ethics" (Ávila, 2016).

In our work with children and adolescents, mutuality will be present in a much more powerful way. Children ask a lot of questions, often insistently: they want to know if we see other children, if we have children ourselves, if we live close to where we work. Adolescents will probably want to know if we have ever lost our heads over a boy or a girl or if we have smoked a joint. They want to know if we have gone through those things, if we have had those experiences. It is as if they had a greater interest in knowing who we really are, beyond our therapist's "white coat", or perhaps that interest is made explicit in a blunter, more forceful way. Their dialogue is more direct, more "face to face". Explaining to a child that "this is *your* space and that is why we shouldn't fill it with our stuff" is not always easy and may not always be understood. With adults, such direct questions are less likely: socialization effects have permeated more deeply, and it is (usually) clear to them what is *socially correct* and what is not; there is more self-censorship.

Creativity, spontaneous action and improvisation *(where there used to be abstinence).*

Creativity plays an essential role for the relational therapist, and is key to co-constructing the intermediate space. This space will be composed of the games played together in the session, the tales read together, the videos viewed on YouTube, the short films watched together to deal with certain issues (such as mourning, prevention of drug abuse or the struggle against bullying). Movies can also provide a wonderful opportunity for understanding the patient's subjectivity. For instance, the popular Pixar movie "Inside Out", in which the characters were actually feelings, offered excellent opportunities in the consulting room for sharing and talking about those feelings. With which character did the patient identify? What characters did he or she think were "key"? How did he or she interpret the role of Joy? And of Sadness?

These creative processes which occur in treatment are essential when it comes to vitalizing the experience of the patient. Furthermore, what is done in psychoanalysis is ultimately less important than the effort made and the intentions expressed in that effort (Mitchell (1997), which no doubt helps us when it comes to participating actively in the interaction. But if we are creative, spontaneous and we improvise, does this mean that we have no technique? Not at all. As Ávila (2005) says, "as lax as it may appear, good therapists intuitively know what is therapeutic and what isn't in a certain situation". Obviously, this does not mean that we do not have to take precautions to prevent the way we work clinically from turning into pure, constant spontaneity, but certainly our subjectivity (formed by our experiences, personal history, the books we have read, the seminars we have attended, the hours of supervision, personal analysis and so forth) will be one of our main technical instruments.

Mitchell (1997) says that the analytic clinician necessarily makes clinical judgments all the time, constantly struggling with questions like: What sort of frame should be maintained? Should I express my countertransferential experiences? Should I answer the analysand's inquiries? In response to such questions, most contemporary relational analysts would probably answer, "It depends". In fact, this coincides with Bacal's Specifity Theory (2011), which provides us with a different way of understanding our patients and our work with them, emphasizing the importance of the here and now in the encounters with patients. According to Bacal (2011), each analyst-patient dyad constitutes a unique, reciprocal system, so the therapeutic possibility is co-created in the specificity of the match between that patient's particular therapeutic needs and that therapist's capacity to respond to them, both of which will emerge and change within the unique process of each particular dyad.

With adults the ritual of arrival at the session tends to be more or less the same: you receive them, they greet you, they sit (or lie) down and the session begins. With children and adolescents, arrival is not usually like this. They might sit or not, stand up or not, go to the toilet or not, look at their mobiles or not... and so the idiosyncrasy of each treatment and of each intervention is more evident.

We do not start out from the assumption that each child has to have the exact same standardized box of games, with the same fixed and predetermined elements. We will need more resources, and these we will have to look for along the way with each patient. For instance, the "Emotionary" (Núñez & Romero, 2013), a dictionary of emotions with text and illustrations has become an essential tool for me. Our Jenga, a tower of wooden bricks, has become "the emotions tower". Each brick has the name of an emotion on it: you have to remove it carefully so that the tower does not fall down and consider in which situations you might feel like that (Ponce, p.c.). Then there is Playmobil, a timeless tool that helps to exteriorize what there is inside, used in the therapeutic work itself. In this regard, sharing experiences with other colleagues who work with children and adolescents is enormously enriching.

A more active role *(where there used to be a non-participant observer).*

Despite not having a clear and preconceived set of guidelines telling us which attitude to adopt towards the person who comes to treatment, it is very difficult to see the patient without memory or desire, as Bion suggested. Of course we feel or think that, for a certain patient in a certain situation, doing a certain thing will make them feel better. This is why, when we work with children and adolescents, as Altman (2002) says, the relational therapist will probably have to take the lead in initiating a play exchange (for example). This obviously means the clinician has "to depart from the more usual role of observer and more passive participant, and to incur the risk of actively influencing her patient".

The current pace of life and the economic factor make it difficult for people to find infinite or unlimited time (in the style of the endless analysis of previous eras) to work through every single conflict that might appear. The relational therapist might ask questions and want to know more, suggest doing things, propose doing things together.

We are probably less timid than those using other approaches when it comes to asking questions and participating actively, that is, to revealing who we are and not being mere observers (Ávila, 2009).

As mentioned earlier, if the relational therapist assumes the lead in initiating a play exchange (for example), and departs from the more usual role of observer to incur the risk of actively influencing the patient, it is likely that this therapist may fear that he or she has abandoned all professional responsibility and has simply surrendered to his/her own regressive desire to have fun (Altman et al., 2002). However, we know that is not the case, and that play is definitely something quite serious and which is performed in a highly responsible manner.

Mutual bidirectional influence *(where there used to be transference and countertransference)*.

From the relational approach, we could say that the terms "transference" and "countertransference" have fallen into disuse; they sound outdated. How could we possibly know or separate what is projection or desire in the patient and what belongs to the therapist? From the moment the patient walks through the door, everything that takes place lies within the intersubjective field. The analyst's presence and activity will inevitably pollute the transference (Ávila, 2013), and the same thing occurs with the countertransference, which will be determined and inevitably influenced by the patient's presence. So it makes more sense to talk about "mutual bidirectional influence between therapist and patient, at every level of connection and interaction, and implied by the contexts acting on different phenomena levels (intra, inter and transubjective)" (Ávila, 2016).

Relational work with children and adolescents departs significantly from adult work by moving intersubjectively within and between dyads and triads in the nonlinear dynamic system of the child's relational context (Silber, 2015).

The relational encounter with children and adolescents, as we said, is usually very powerful, and probably the relationship idiosyncrasy will make it unavoidable that various bidirectional influences emerge: we do not only work with the child, or with the adolescent, but also with their father, mother, etc. The relational matrix, already complex in the encounter between two persons, becomes exponentially more complicated when other people's subjectivities come into play.

In sessions with children and with adolescents as well, the corporal shifts into the foreground. We are more aware of our own body because frequently the rhythms of the child or adolescent we see in treatment are very different from our own. Obviously this might be the case with certain adults, but usually they sit in the chair and stay there during the whole session. Children, on the other hand, stand up, go to the toilet... Being aware of how we are feeling physically is very useful for us if mutual regulation is to take place. For instance, if we are with a very restless child that won't keep still, we will have to make an extra effort not to let ourselves be drawn into that state of excitement: if we are controlled and if we are able to regulate ourselves, logically the patient will be able, little by little, to regulate him or herself.

Also related to the corporal theme, it should be noted that with adolescents it is essential to work through what their physical changes mean to them (puberty, first sexual encounters...). We have to work on what the "new body" means for the development of the "new identity". Again, it is likely that we will have to inquire about these issues as, due to embarrassment or shame, it will probably be difficult for them to express their concerns about such things in the sessions.

Interaction and context *(where there used to be individuality).*

When we work with children and teenagers it is vital to get out of the consulting room – literally, I mean. Including facts from the patient's real circumstances will be crucial if we are to understand their history and who they are. Visiting their school is usually a source of tremendously valuable information which will prove very useful for our therapeutic work. Having the chance to meet their form tutor, counsellor and the environment where they spend most of their time offers a new perspective and an opportunity which, if timely and related to the consulting motive, should not be neglected. Moreover, in my experience, visiting the school has a very powerful effect for all the parties involved: for the therapist (as explained above), for the patient (they are usually very pleased to hear we have visited their environment and it usually gives them "real proof" of our involvement), the parents (we are inevitably transmitting involvement) and the school (on many occasions the staff are bewildered or do not know how to manage the situation with their pupil, so having the chance to discuss it with the therapist and gaining an insight into what he/she is going through usually has a calming effect). All of this will have a very positive effect on the relationship and the therapeutic work.

Working with children and adolescents is, due to everything we have said so far, very demanding. Besides the sessions with the patient, we have to see the father, mother, teacher, tutor, school counsellor... respective partners in the case that the parents are divorced. Grandparents and any other main caregivers who might be involved in the patient's upbringing. The therapist could be seen as a juggler trying to balance the different subjectivities (including, of course, his/her own) in a relational matrix which is far more complex than when we deal with an individual treatment, as "the main study object in the relational clinic is the intersubjectivity, the level of phenomena where the intersubjective interchange takes place, decisive for the construction of the subjective experience and the development of the self" (Ávila, 2016).

Evidently, the work alliance too has to be developed not only with the patient: it must also be established with all the other people involved. This is a truly complicated task: often we face resistance to change that might not necessarily come from the patient. It might come from the father or the mother, even though they are the ones who bring their child to therapy. With children and adolescents, we have to "juggle" to understand the motives of each different party involved, trying to comprehend their contexts.

Who wants the patient to change, why and what for? For instance, the father might want his child to change or he might think it is problematic that his son or daughter does a certain thing, but the mother might not agree. If the parents are separated, the situation gets even more complex, as the differences regarding how to raise the child or how to understand or solve certain situations might end up being used as a weapon, on top of the problems that led to separation. Of course, this is not always the case, and might also happen if the parents are not separated, but in my experience when the parents come to treatment and the separation is recent (and much more so if there are unresolved judgments concerning support, custody etc. pending), the disagreement between the parents might end up invading much of the therapeutic space. Children and adolescents often end up bearing the brunt of this; it is as if they had one parent tugging at each of their arms. Clearly, where there is a separation, it is usually because the parents did not agree on many things; the children's education might be one of them. This is probably why we find, in many cases, that one of the parents may seek to form an alliance with us at the expense of the other parent.

On whom does the child's coming to the sessions depend? This has to do with economic factors, related to who assumes the treatment costs, but also with who physically brings the child to the consulting room. It will usually be the same parent, so we have to make a conscious effort to include the one we do not see so often.

Who first expressed the need for consultation? The ideal situation would be that both parents agree and understand the problem in the same way; sometimes just one of them considers it necessary, while the other one raises no objection. There are also many occasions where a child or adolescent comes to consultation because this has been recommended by the education centre. How this situation is experienced by the parents (for instance, with guilt for not having noticed that the problem existed themselves; or with indifference if they do not really agree with what the school suggests) will also be decisive during the process.

But if children and adolescent patients have one thing in common is that, usually, they do not come to see us of their own accord: they are *brought*.

Moreover, it is usual that children quickly find themselves comfortable in the sessions. They come with their defenses lowered, they know they come to play and draw, and they like it. Besides, their mum or dad brings them to the consulting room, which means some moments of exclusiveness and dedication that might not usually be as common as they would like (for instance, if there are other brothers or sisters, of if the parents' work schedules make this difficult). The time spent coming to the consulting room is used to talk about their day, about what goes on in the sessions... thus they obtain a time for intimacy with the father or the mother that would probably be not possible otherwise.

David, 8 years old, was brought by his parents to the consulting room because lately he had not wanted to go to school. Recently there had been many important changes in his life: a little brother was born, he had a new house, a new school. The school advisor recommended that the parents should find the time to talk to David when he asked them to, as he seemed to be very anxious. In the first session, the parents told me they felt David had started abusing that resource, as he asked for time to talk constantly! Without going into the details of the case, the fact that they were able to find some time within the family dynamic (even though the parents thought it excessive) was bringing some relief: David was feeling less anxious.

However, with adolescents it is a different story: they come in better armed, their defenses up... they come because they have to and not because they want to - at least initially. They are more reluctant to talk, to tell us things and to open up, and often they feel us to be an ally of their parents (younger children usually find it easier to think of us as their own allies). It is more difficult to establish the connection and basic trust so that they feel we are on their side. Most probably we will have to ask more questions than when we are working with younger children, but without losing sight of how "dangerous" it can be for the bond if we fall into the *nosy parent* "trap", repeating the pattern that frequently takes place at home when facing this hermeticism.

Consequently, when working with adolescents it is imperative to take the above into account in order to differentiate us, the therapists, from parental figures. Sometimes it seems impossible not to get angry when an adolescent is late for the session (supposing they come unaccompanied), whereas if a child is late, we know the "guilt" lies with the father or mother (responsible for bringing them). In the relational therapist's work with adolescents it is vital to seek, through the interaction, intermediate elements on which to build the bond: we have to enter their world, their context, and try to understand their language and ways of expression (verbal, aesthetic…). Again, this puts us in a more active position so that the relationship can be built: we will have to show genuine interest in their tastes (music, books, TV shows, magazines, leisure…) and ask about them, which will probably take us to new, unknown places, revealing our ignorance of certain issues, but through which we can continue to build the relationship.

Though this might seem obvious to those working with children and adolescents, I cannot stress enough the importance of professional secrecy when it comes to building the bond. We could say that with adult patients this is taken for granted, but with children and adolescents it is necessary to make it explicit, explaining the framework and the way we are going to work with them and with their parents. It is crucial that, after the first session with the parents alone, we ask them to tell the child/adolescent what we have been discussing, advising them we will also be talking about this with the patient the next time we see them. In the first session with the child/adolescent, we must explain to them that whatever happens in the session will be subject to professional secrecy, and that every time we arrange to meet their parents, we will ask them in advance if there is anything they do not want us to repeat.

If the parents are very anxious, it is likely that they will try to reach us by phone, via WhatsApp or by approaching us when they come to pick up their child. Sometimes it can be very complicated to stop them and to emphasize that whatever they tell us will be talked over in the sessions. In my experience, how you deal with these situations will be crucial when it comes to maintaining the trust of all the parties involved, but especially that of the patient.

Mentalization *(where there used to be interpretation)*.

Usually, in child psychotherapy, we know that play is our shared language; with adults, we have words. Teenagers are somewhere in between. But to what extent is what we say, our actual words, so very important? One of the moments I remember most clearly from my own analysis is the first time I heard my analyst laugh out loud. Laughter contains no text, no words, but the emotional impact it had on me was a turning point in my treatment. My analyst was truly human, had emotions! No sentence, no matter how well thought out, studied or full of truth it might have been, could have hit the target as well as that laughter did.

Again, we cannot really understand the interpretation or our intervention without taking into account the relationship, the intersubjective, the context. When working in child and adolescent therapy the basis of our work is probably to put things into words, to narrate and build together. With children we narrate what we do and it is through that narrative, through that shared 'putting into words' that we will be able to shape and integrate the emotional experience, going from what is *done* to what is *felt*, giving more coherence to what has been experienced. This means our work is about how to build the ability to feel the feelings and emotions within the relationship (Munar, p.c.). "Thinking thoughts, or mentalization, becomes the main axis in the therapeutic task, linked to the emotions these carry and address. We, along with the other person, build language and thought, charged with emotion, for the 'experience that could not be formulated'" (Stern, 1997, in Ávila, 2016).

Whether the mirroring function can be good enough will depend on a good enough mentalization capacity on the caregiver's side, which is to say, on how effectively the caregiver can interpret the infant's emotional states. When the caregiver shows the child these (elaborated) emotional states, they will be able to start building their inner emotional world. As Jiménez (2015) says, "To develop an adequate mentalization capacity it is fundamental that the attachment figures try to understand the mental states of their children and let this understanding be reflected in them".

Development of the mentalization capacity will facilitate a better capacity for social relations (the emotional states of others will be more easily recognized) and for relating to oneself (the patient's own/inner emotional states will be more easily recognized), which will inevitably facilitate emotional regulation. Buechler (2008) says that social competence requires the ability to communicate emotions and read them sufficiently accurately when they are expressed by others.

To some extent it is research into attachment and mentalization that has shaped the practices which we find effective in clinical work: putting experiences and emotions into words. To narrate, but to narrate accompanied, in the presence of another.

In my work with Clara, an adolescent who came into treatment when she was fifteen years old and whose case we will look into with more detail later on, there were many occasions on which she asked me to read my session notes to her (the ones she knows I take after each session). This had a calming and soothing effect on her. As she has always had great difficulties in expressing herself, listening to me talking about her emotional experiences had an almost hypnotic effect. Making/drawing a time line of the latest years of her life also helped us integrate parts of her life experience that were disconnected. She asked me several times whether, when she finished her treatment, she might take the session notes with her. "They are like a journal, a diary of all the things I have gone through". Clara was able to develop her mentalization capacity: she went from not knowing what she felt, from having a kind of an "amalgam" of uncontrolled feelings and emotions, to being able to express whatever had happened to her using abstract concepts. This made it easier for her to think of herself and to project herself in the future.

Fundamental human needs for attachment and recognition *(where there used to be drive).*

From birth, we are incorporated in relational matrixes that modulate our personality, and subjectivity is the result of those binding ties. Psychic activity will therefore be derived not from the drive transformations (sexual and aggressive) but from "content of relationship experience that can be thought and represented, arising from the deployment of fundamental human needs (including attachment and recognition)" (Ávila, 2009).

The therapeutic relationship is the setting, a kind of a testing ground, where some of these fundamental needs can be built and deployed.

Frequently, the changes occur without us knowing exactly why. In other words, changes often occur *before* we have been able to formulate what has happened, before we have been able to think about this or put it into words. This is especially intense in sessions with children: perhaps because the changes occur earlier outside consultation than inside, or because the patients themselves find it difficult to recognize them as meaningful and do not "bring them" to the session.

I saw Violeta at a Family Care Center. She was eight years old and had been referred from her school because she did not speak in class, with her classmates or with the teachers. We worked together for three years, on a weekly basis, and Violeta barely spoke in the sessions: it was a terrible ordeal for her to utter a single word and speaking plunged her into an overwhelming, incapacitating shame. She had arrived in Spain two years earlier, along with her mother, her younger sister and grandmother, and her immigrant status (evident by her skin colour and accent) seemed to add to her insecurity when communicating and relating. The sense of uprooting was immense.

Her mother also had considerable difficulties in putting ideas into words and in mentalizing. In my sessions with Violeta, the game was the shared language; the game and myself talking and giving voice to our encounter, narrating what happened in the relationship. The months went by and it seemed that nothing had changed, that everything remained the same. To my professional frustration was added pressure from the City Council which employed me: their service had a maximum time-frame of six months, and only in exceptional cases could the intervention be prolonged. "Three years and the girl is still the same!"

However, in the third year, Violeta's education centre (with which I was in continuous communication), informed me that in the end-of-course theatre play, in front of the entire school, Violeta had chosen the role of *narrator*. At last she had a voice, although that voice had not yet reached the sessions with me. She had a voice in the world, which was the whole point of our work together.

This is to say that theory and technique can be thought out and integrated *later, retrospectively*. In Violeta's case, we might suppose that possibly having a new model (someone who can speak and narrate - and who integrates and "metabolizes" the relational encounter) made it easier for her to choose the role of narrator herself when she had the chance. The staff at Violeta's school and her classmates acknowledged her effort and showed their genuine pleasure (related to the attachment that existed) at seeing that Violeta had begun to join in, to be part of the class. This recognition (to quote Benjamin) would lay the foundations so that Violeta could begin to develop her potentialities.

It is hard to imagine that there could be recognition without attachment, and vice versa. They go hand in hand.

Diagnosis In Relational Clinical Treatment of Children And Adolescents

Working in child and adolescent therapy, it is very common for the patient to arrive with a diagnostic label already attached; possibly other professionals (a neurologist, or a school counsellor, ...) will have already intervened. The fact that the patient arrives with this (or another) diagnosis (often unavoidable) as a "business card", certainly helps us to orient ourselves, since it is a "tag" or summary of the child's or adolescent's functioning. Sometimes it also has a calming effect on parents.

But is this necessary for us? Should it be something we seek? Beyond the inevitable or the information it provides us with, prior diagnoses can make it difficult for us to see beyond them, since we will be "type-casting" the person, fitting them into the "role" that others have considered appropriate. Whereas what really interests us is the intersubjective, the context: who we are, patient and therapist together.

Therefore, rather than diagnostic categories, perhaps we could speak of "relational amalgams-frameworks-matrixes" that define the subjectivity and discomfort of the person who consults. In other words, the person always consults because of their relational difficulties, either with themselves (for example, low self-esteem) or with others (for example, with a father, mother, siblings, teachers, friends, ...). We know that all psychic pathology is relational (Coderch, 2016), therefore we will probably find "categories of relational matrixes" useful, rather than "categories that define the person in a general / generic form". Some of these "categories of relational matrixes" could be: being bullied, witnessing family conflict, or difficulties with learning, as Delgado et al. (2015) state. Also, difficulties in relationships with the main caregivers (attachment), difficulties in the relationship with oneself (self-esteem) or difficulties in social relations. Depending on the person, fears, phobias, sleep disorders or behaviour problems may be understood from any of the above categories.

Let us consider, for example, the most frequent diagnosis in childhood today, the "umbrella diagnosis": Attention Deficit Hyperactivity Disorder (ADHD). If anything about this is clear, it is that the difficulties of self-regulation contained in these labels turn out to be related to difficulties with relationships at school (with classmates and teachers) and at home (with the family). Could we possibly understand ADHD if it did not cause problems with these environments? For example, in a different educational system, where the emphasis was not on doing homework and studying, and the system was more adapted to other types of knowledge, would these children be given a diagnostic label? Are they the problem, or is it the fact that they cause problems in and for the home/ school environment?

Necessarily (and thankfully), we therapists usually receive extensive training before coming face to face with a patient, but I cannot help thinking that when I started working in clinical practice, my experience as a patient/ analysand helped me much more than my training at a technical level. That experience (besides having provided me with a model of "being with" during sessions), helped me to position myself better in relation to the patient. The theory and the technique helped me to integrate the experience later. Again, we do not lose sight of the fact that "technique in the relational perspective is not an instrumental procedure or knowledge, but inevitably subjective "(Ávila, 2013).

Therefore, although it is almost inevitable that we will be presented with diagnostic labels when we work with younger patients, ideally, we should leave these to one side and let the relationship unfold to help us understand the patient's difficulties.

Resources We Use In Session

The technique used by child relational psychotherapists is, as I have stated several times, not a standardized one. The relationship will be built according to the specificity and idiosyncrasy of the person we are working with.

However, in the early sessions, the use of projective techniques is of great value, not so much for the diagnosis, but rather to establish the relationship and to find out a little more about the patient. The graphic tests (the free drawing, the HTP or Draw-a-Person of the Opposite Sex, in the rain, etc.), the Rorschach Test or the storytelling tests (such as the Black Paw Test or the CAT-A) are tools that often help us build the relationship.

Regarding play, which as we said, is the language of childhood, we could add that it is a form of expression which provides an outlet for the inner world, through which this can be "digested", elaborated and reformulated in a way the child can understand. It is through play that we also build the relationship.

The games constructed (such as the tower of emotions), card games (for example, Ikonikus cards, where different icons are used to help us describe how we would feel in certain situations) and shared books (such as the Emocionary, by Núñez & Romero, 2013) will help us to sift the patient's emotional experience.

Other resources will probably have to be included as they become neces- sary, and the new technologies are proving very useful in this sense. For example, in the case of adolescent patients, the mobile phone or smartphone has come to represent a transitional object of particular importance for building the bond. It is through YouTube videos that we can find singers who our patients like, see which songs they choose to show us, ... we can even see their friends, girlfriends, boyfriends, ... and watch them talk on video, which makes them *real people*, flesh and blood people, who enter our consultation. This new variable again places us in the role of a juggler: as they are "real", we will not only be working with the internal image that the patient has of them, but we ourselves can build our own image of these people. Another subjectivity slips into the consultation.

In short: creativity and being open to getting to know the patient's world will help to guide us in sessions with children and adolescents.

Child/Adolescent Relational Psychotherapists In Mediterranean Culture

As Coderch (2016) points out, every psychic pathology is relational pathology, and will inevitably be linked to the cultural contexts in which the person has lived and in which they have learned to develop his or her idea of what it means to be male or female.

Considering the idiosyncrasy of our Mediterranean culture, we could point out some common characteristics shared by the children and adolescents who come to our consultations in Spain:

- Ours is a culture in which relationships with family and friends are central. Generally, leisure time is devoted to relationships, family gatherings, etc. It is assumed that households are primarily responsible for the welfare of their members (Flaquer, 2004).
- We express affection very easily or in obvious ways: we greet with two kisses and we have loud tones of voice that "colour" the way we speak. For example, in the Rorschach test, the indicators that collect "Texture (T)" responses are on average higher in Mediterranean cultures than in Anglo-Saxon cultures.
- I cannot neglect to mention the importance of climate in our way of life: children and adolescents can enjoy playtimes outdoors, which facilitates social games.
- Psychology and the figure of the psychologist have gained importance and visibility: therapy is progressively understood to be the place where emotional difficulties can be solved, and the figure of the advisor/counsellor has facilitated the approach towards what emotional well-being means.

But not all the features that define our culture are positive:

- We live in a sexist society, where deaths caused by gender-based violence continue to increase (INE, 2015) and where gender-based patterns have negative consequences for both sexes. Much remains to be done in terms of equality education.

- There is great overprotection during childhood and adolescence, which hinders and slows down the passage into adulthood. Adolescents are not encouraged to be responsible/independent.

- Schools have high requirements, with long school hours and afternoons occupied by homework and endless extracurricular activities. This makes it difficult to find time to spend with the family.

- The pace of Spanish society, with working hours much longer than in the rest of Europe, also makes it very difficult for parents to be at home at reasonable times.

- Regarding social relations, we tend to gather around food, but also around alcohol, which results in the normalization of its consumption.

Therefore, we have to take into account all the above factors when working with children and adolescents in our context, Spain, and also think about other contexts that may "overlap": living in a big city is not the same as living in a small town, whether the patient was born in Spain or not, etc.

Having completed this "tour" of the distinctive features characterizing the relational psychotherapist treating children and adolescents, in addition to the reflections on diagnosis, resources used in the sessions and the context that our Mediterranean culture implies, we will now turn to some specific cases: one concerning a child and the other a teenager.

PART TWO:
RELATIONAL CLINICAL PRACTICE

We choose to write about certain cases because we have learned from them (based on mutuality and mutual bidirectional influence), because they are representative of our way of working and, of course, because we remember them with affection (thanks to the closeness and emotional availability that unfolds). Samuel and Clara fit well into these three categories.

In both cases I feel that the relationship facilitated the psychic change and the development of their potentialities, probably because the fundamental needs of attachment and recognition were worked on, among others. Creativity, spontaneous action and improvisation facilitated the building of the relationship, and considering that Samuel was a child and Clara a teenager, it was crucial that I should familiarize myself with the devices, applications and social networks that they used. His tablet and her smartphone were almost a part of themselves; being in therapy with them was being in therapy with Samuel plus tablet, with Clara plus smartphone.

In both cases I felt at times that I was juggling the different subjectivities involved: the relationship with the parents of both was also very important. In Samuel's case, it was easier to "team up" because both parents understood that he needed professional help. With Clara, it was more difficult: the parents were divorcing, there was an open war over financial questions and the father did not consider therapy necessary.

I visited both schools in order to see the context firsthand. In the case of Samuel, this was especially important as the reason for consultation was that his parents were worried that he was being bullied. In Clara's case, it was important because her difficulties with language and abstract thinking hindered her emotional development as well as her educational development and learning capacity; in addition, she had problems with social relations, so knowing her daily context helped me to work with her more effectively.

But what did my work with each of them consist of?

Samuel

Samuel's parents consulted us because they were very worried that he might be being bullied at school. He had been going to the school concerned for a year at that point, and had been a victim of bullying at his previous school. Then aged nine, he had been diagnosed with Attention Deficit Hyperactivity Disorder two years previously, and had begun taking medication. He got very good marks, even though he was very scatterbrained and disorganized. He had always found it difficult to make friends: he did not like to play football (the game most children play in breaks: if you do not play, you will almost certainly be excluded), so he spent much of lunchtime and breaks alone, wandering around the playground. He related better to older children, more through words than through games. His parents described him as very insecure and with low self-esteem.

He had many difficulties in processing, expressing, understanding and integrating affections: he misinterpreted the reactions of others, and so he did not manage well in social contexts. "I'm hyperactive and I think hyperactivity makes it difficult for me to relate, I talk nonsense and I talk a lot," Samuel said when he arrived at the consultation. He was very aware of his difficulties, which in turn made him more watchful and insecure when it came to relating and caused him to have a devalued self-image.

In my first sessions with Samuel, I understood why it was probably difficult to relate to him: he was a very serious child, not at all expressive ...

and tremendously dull. Very apathetic too; whenever he came to the session he said that he was "very tired". It had to be me who proposed what to do during the session and which games to play: he felt comfortable playing games with rules, but when he was losing he became so frustrated that he tried to change them, which ended up triggering uncomfortable situations when I did not give in. And when he won, he said that he had been lucky, that he never won at anything more than once.

When sessions with him became dull, to get out of the rut we began to integrate other types of resources. For example, he used to come to the sessions iPad in hand: I was able to approach his inner world through the applications he used to enjoy (one of them for interior decoration, ...). We tried several games, but he got tired of them all (and so did I). "I think we are both getting bored with this game", I would say.

A visit to the school was vital if I was to determine that we were not actually seeing a case of bullying but rather a situation of difficulty in understanding social contexts; several teachers had spent many playtimes watching the dynamics of Samuel and his classmates. Coordination with the school was key for the parents to grasp that calling it "bullying" had been a way of condensing the discomfort that Samuel suffered because he could not relate satisfactorily to his peers. The fact that there were things that bothered him about his companions did not necessarily mean that they were harassing him.

He was able to stop feeling like a victim (for example, if he was losing a game) and started to take control of the way he participated in the interaction (trying to turn the game around). I went on to propose more active games, for example, card games, and I began to narrate and to describe aloud how I felt when I had good cards ("I'm so pleased, I've won this hand!") and when I had poor cards ("I'm furious for having lost!") He began to do the same. It was due to being able to express what happened between us that we could start having fun. We noted the scores of each game, carrying them over to the next session (the first to reach 500 points would win, for example). We had the rules of the game written on a piece of paper on the table (as a "third party"), and when we had doubts we consulted them.

Also, while we were playing, we could talk about other things: the movies he had seen, the things that had happened to him at school ... Being able to talk about them together helped us to understand them better. We had stopped being bored and the sessions became much more enjoyable. In addition, his ability to tolerate frustration had increased: as he felt more involved in the game, he wanted to go on playing - both if he was losing (to try to turn the game around) and if he was winning (to increase his advantage). His self-esteem was also improving. We used several YouTube videos to talk about empathy (short animated films) or grief in children (when his grandfather died).

He began to take part in games with his classmates at school, and the staff there told me that he was daring to do more things and to face situations which he previously did not know how to cope with. He was much more communicative, which had a positive effect on his social relations.

Within a few months of treatment, Samuel had chosen to sign up for "urban dance" as an extracurricular activity (showing an improvement in his body expression), he stood for class representative (and was elected) and had begun to be invited his classmates' birthday parties. The need for recognition and attachment had begun to be fulfilled, and Samuel was much happier. His parents had stopped giving him the medication.

Clara

Clara was 15 years old when her mother first sought therapy for her. Clara's parents had separated a few months earlier. Since then, Clara had been very angry, anxious and unable to sleep. Before that happened, she had been a very open, outgoing, lively and affectionate person, although she had always been a nervous girl and found it difficult to tolerate frustration and accept limits. Her poor language skills – both receptive and expressive - made studying extremely difficult for her, and this in turn had severely undermined her self-esteem. Clara willingly agreed to start treatment and it was very easy to establish contact with her, even though she had great difficulty expressing her thoughts and feelings.

She had a clearly devalued self-image, and showed little concern for her own needs. She exhibited a pessimistic tone in general, expressing views of the future coloured by negative prejudices, even though she was always willing to offer a smile.

During the first year of treatment we focused on working through and elaborating her mourning for what she has lost, but really, we are talking about several losses: her parents' separation, the loss of her idealized image of her father (and in a way that of her mother too, as the mother had to be cared for by the daughters as she felt a victim of the separation), changes of school, the death of the family dog, the desertion of a sister's boyfriend, who had been another member of the family… In short, mourning for the life she used to have and then no longer possessed. "Will I ever be the same again?" she asked herself. A general disillusionment with life started to appear.

Clara found it extremely difficult to put her emotions into words, and also had trouble managing time and organizing daily life: much of our work during the sessions consisted of her trying to narrate her experiences chronologically and elaborate them at an emotional level, so that she could connect her thoughts to her emotions. She needed to "scribble draw" (using Winnicott's term) constantly during our sessions, so as to construct an intermediate space, which seemed to have an anxiolytic effect for Clara: scribbling helped her to calm down, kept her occupied, helped her not to be nervous. She needed to *draw* while she *spoke* (*do* while she *thought*).

She would come into the room and even before taking her jacket off she would ask: "Can I draw?" Words were not enough to co-construct our relationship and work together. Usually, in child psychotherapy, we know that playing is the shared language; with adults, we have words. Teenagers are somewhere in between, but Clara didn't want to play, nor could she express herself well enough to let her inner world emerge.

In our work together, we used the 'Emotionary' referred to previously, the dictionary of emotions I generally use in my work with children, containing illustrations and explanations of the different emotions, and experiences drawn from different movies (e.g. 'Inside Out') as well as music, in order to communicate, elaborate and integrate her vital experiences. This was also essential for me to be able to understand what had happened during the week and how she felt about it.

As Clara was not very good at putting facts and experiences into words, sometimes it seemed all we had were rhythms, voice tones and facial expressions – hers and mine. This led me to be more aware of my own body in the sessions with Clara than with other patients.

Mentalization was fundamental: I had to try to understand her emotional states and "give them back" to her, digested and elaborated. She could then begin to connect what was happening with how she felt about it. Being able to name together what she felt about those situations made her understand the things she was going through.

The second year of the treatment was more complicated: she had left behind her girlhood to rush into adolescence. A classmate lodged a complaint about her (this classmate had sent Clara a private message with a photo of herself without a T-shirt on and Clara had sent it to the WhatApp group of the whole class) and she suffered an alcohol-induced coma (during the town festival in summer). This left her with an enormous sense of guilt on recovering because of the concern she had caused her family.

She started disregarding the therapeutic space (arriving late and even forgetting a few sessions, something she had been very careful about before). She would turn up looking unkempt (she was taking less trouble with her appearance, stopped wearing make-up or combing her hair), more disconnected. She said she couldn't bear herself and she started having problems with everyone (at school, at home, with her friends...). She was more anxious again: she drew less and needed to be constantly pulling things apart with her hands (she used to tear up sheets of paper as we talked). I suggested making collages, so that instead of *destroying* things she could *make* things. She exhibited a greater need to do things (action, the immediate) rather than thinking or reflecting. On many occasions, I had the feeling that I didn't quite know what we were doing there or where our activities (the collages, the music we listened to) would take us, but what I could definitely feel in our relationship was that Clara was more vitalized when she did things.

But what caused her deterioration in this second phase most probably had to do with the dependency relationship she had established with a boy she liked. This relationship contributed to the fact that her self-esteem seemed to have deteriorated further, and her social relations to have suffered.

The subject of gender became particularly relevant: the songs she listened to and the TV shows she liked portrayed young girls who cried over boys that didn't pay attention to them, girls who couldn't seem to find the meaning of life without their "Prince Charming". Here, again, we see the importance of what is visual, musical, and immediate (whatever you want to Google, Google will show you in a few seconds);

During those almost three years of treatment, Clara went through different phases. At the beginning, she used to feel mostly rage and anger, but later on she became more depressed and exhibited a lack of motivation and vitality. She was able to gain in expression and introspection capacity, as well as self-esteem, but later on she was feeling a lot of aggressiveness and generalized demotivation. Over the last months, we were working on self-care behaviours (sleeping, eating), assertiveness and psychoeducation (drugs, sex).

Countertransferentially, I found it a very demanding case: sessions with the mother, father, sisters, meetings at her school... Regarding the bond between Clara and I, trust was a vital factor: she was always fully aware of these communications (in fact, she liked the fact that these contacts existed very much).

Clara gained in introspection and in terms of being able to put into words how she felt. We both understood that she was better when she started using abstract concepts to describe her experience: "We are better at home; my mother gives me more *freedom*." She was able to feel better at home, to relate better to her friends and to distance herself from the boy who had made her suffer so much. She was able to start projecting herself into the future (speaking of her study plans) and even wanted to write a book about her life, including her lifeline, which we had drawn and constructed together.

Conclusions

Samuel could express himself very well on a verbal level; Clara had many difficulties putting into words what was happening to her and how she felt. In both cases the relationship of trust, creativity in working during the sessions and spontaneity (for both of them and for me to be able to express more freely how we felt in a session and the things that happened to us together) was vital so that they could begin to relate better, with others and with themselves. The research on development and mentalization (Fonagy & Bateman, 2016) and taking the cultural aspect and the context into account were also very important for being able to work in the sessions and for achieving a better understanding of who Samuel and Clara were and how they related.

In the cases of Samuel and Clara psychic change was possible thanks to the use of the principles of closeness and emotional availability, as well as taking mutuality into account. Being able to employ creativity, spontaneous action and improvisation, combined with the power to play a more active role and the mutual bidirectional influence allowed me to be more aware of the importance of interaction and context. As a relational psychotherapist of children and adolescents, mentalization and working with the fundamental human needs of attachment and recognition were also key elements.

PART THREE: CHALLENGES AND FUTURE PERSPECTIVES

Despite all the achievements and research that support the foundations of the relational perspective when working with children and adolescents, today's relational psychotherapist inevitably faces constant challenges.

We live in a world which, even as adults, we feel is becoming more and more complex. Our perplexity with regard to certain social developments often proves to be truly difficult to digest (terrorism on a world scale, wars, inequality, innumerable cases of corruption, unemployment, climate change, etc.). It is easy to imagine that if for adults the world we live in is hard to understand, it is even more so for children and teenagers. The world to which children have to adapt is, in the first place, their parents, who are their referents, and if these feel lost, children will inevitably feel the same.

Today child-rearing is decentralized. If, before, the hub was the family, nowadays it is the school: many children spend all day at school, from 7:00 a.m. to 6:00 p.m. (including breakfast, lunch and tea, as well as extracurricular activities), with different caregivers, whereas before there used to be one single form teacher as a reference. In addition, there is now no educational plan that guarantees a minimum level of continuity.

In both the public and private spheres, the primary motive for consultation in childhood and adolescence is related to difficulties with studies: the child does not study, or he/she fails a subject, or daily homework makes the family home a battlefield. Often this is related to the child having a poor relationship with the father/mother and behavioral problems, for example, disobedience. Of course, there are other reasons for consultation (such as difficulties with social relations), but we could almost maintain that as long as the child or adolescent studies, that is, they adapt to what is demanded of them at an educational level, things go smoothly, the parents are satisfied and there is no reason for consultation. This leads us to consider if we may not be witnessing an overmedicalization of childhood, especially in the case of Attention Deficit Hyperactivity Disorder.

Does this mean that any past era was better? Most probably not, but of course we are facing challenges different from those of the past. Relational psychotherapy is particularly valuable in this context, since it emphasizes the idiosyncrasy and specificity of the relationship, which goes against the current tendency to "overdiagnose" or to "label"; children and adolescents are as impressionable as modelling clay. We cannot lose sight of the following points:

1. In order to keep moving forward and to gain further insights into why psychic change is accessed through the relationship (Ávila, 2005), we must continue working towards integrating research and avoid isolating ourselves from scientific advances.

2. It is necessary to continue studying and analyzing the effects that this way of working has on the practitioners: relational psychotherapists. We are involved in the relational patterns of our patients: for us, the therapeutic relationship is undoubtedly a *real relationship*. Are we more exposed, do we suffer more emotional exhaustion? Our focus and our key working tools are the relationship and the bond, and this will always be subjective. To be able to acknowledge us there must be a yielding, there must be an adjustment, and this means that at least one of the parties is open to the possibility of meeting. This means that at some times we will find ourselves doing things that were initially against our principles. We know that in the interactions between patient

and analyst, as noted by Beebe and Lachman (Lachman, 2007), each participant affects the other, so between one point in time and the next, neither the patient nor the analyst will remain the same.

3. We have to think socially, from a macro perspective. We must get out of the consultation room to understand what causes suffering in our patients and to be able to integrate the real circumstances that they live in (at school, at home, etc.). We have to try to understand their context and social environment. The only thing that gives meaning to our patients' experience is the context in which the experience takes place (Nervi, p.c.).

Relational psychotherapy is a way of trying to counteract the negative effects of the crisis, a form of resistance and a response to the challenges of our time. It is fuelled by feminism, by the struggle for the rights of minorities. With mutuality, regulation and recognition as a basis, as well as a deep respect for otherness, we are fighting for the recognition of subjectivity. We are sensitive to the subjectivity of the other.

Among the main advantages of working from this approach is that we can speak more openly about what happens in session, what happens to the patient, the therapist and both together. The relationship built is more genuine, more authentic: it is a real bond, not artificial. And this is important because as psychotherapists we know that the most problematic thing is always what which is not named, so being able to talk about what really happens has been a breath of fresh air for clinical practices. In short, we are freer.

This greater freedom will allow us to connect more authentically with the new generations, whose current way of relating is completely new: social relations are based largely on virtual relationships. On the one hand, with respect to their relationships with themselves, there is much talk about the narcissism of today's teenagers, for whom "selfies" are the natural form of expression and contact with the world. It is through social networks that the constant search for external recognition/approval is channelled (for example, *Likes* on Facebook represent popularity and acceptance of a certain activity). This constant "being connected" represents an over-stimulation and results in a difficulty concentrating on what one is doing, connecting with oneself, and possibly also in a lack of patience and difficulties with working as a team. They have a lower tolerance for frustration and there is less culture of endeavour.

We find ourselves face to face with a new generation that has a lot to teach their elders: in terms of technology, young people have greater knowledge than their parents. Today's children can teach their parents something, and this is something that may not have happened at other times in history. In addition, these days mechanical jobs are disappearing as technologization constantly gains ground. Now, more than ever, we must create, invent. The work of the future will be related to creativity: everything that is repetitive will be done by machines.

Possibly the educational system will also have to change: it is no longer necessary to *know* things, but instead to know how to *look for* them. Today's children and teenagers know that if they want to learn to do something, they do not need to go for a book - there's probably a tutorial on YouTube which explains how to do it.

In short, in order to be able to establish a bond with children and adolescents in order to build a relationship and work with them in therapy, not only will we have to look into their world, but we will need to be taught how to do so by them. At many times we may feel lost, but as we have more freedom we will be able to use more creativity in our work. Of course, we will still have our basic mainstays, common to other approaches (training, self-analysis and supervision), but we will inevitably have to embrace scientific advances and the importance of the context and the cultural facet if we are to continue finding paths which lead us from the relationship to the psychic change, as the relational perspective proposes.

Summary

This chapter will focus on examining how a Relational therapist works in childhood and adolescence. In part one, *Theory and Technique*, we will review fundamental concepts of the Relational approach, comparing them with those that have been used traditionally in Psychoanalysis: closeness and emotional availability (where there used to be asymmetry); mutuality (where there used to be neutrality); creativity, spontaneous action and improvisation (where there used to be abstinence); a more active role of the therapist (where there used to be a non-participant observer); mutual bidirectional influence (where there used to be transference and countertransference); the importance of interaction and context (where there used to be individuality); mentalization (where there used to be interpretation); fundamental human needs for attachment and recognition (where there used to be drive). The relevance of the diagnosis in relational clinical treatment of children and adolescents will also be studied, as well as the resources we use in session and what it means to be a child and adolescent relational psychotherapist in the Mediterranean culture.

In part two, *Relational Clinical Practice*, two clinical cases, one of a child and one of a teenager, will be studied.

And in the third and final part, *Challenges and future perspectives*, we will review the aspects that relational psychoanalysis should continue to take into account and to include in order to be able to continue developing and responding to the demands of patients.

References

Abello Blanco, A. & Liberman, A. (2011). *Una introducción a la obra de Winnicott. Contribuciones al pensamiento relacional.* Madrid: Ágora Relacional [An introduction to Winnicott Works. Contributions to Relational Thinking]

Aburto, M., Ávila Espada, A. et al. (Colectivo GRITA). (1999). La subjetividad en la técnica analítica. Escucha en acción. *Intersubjetivo,* 1(1), 7-55 [The Subjectivity in (Psycho)analytic Technique: Active Healing]

Aburto, M., Ávila Espada, A. et al. (Colectivo Grita). (2007). La terceridad y el cambio según el psicoanálisis relacional. Breve vocabulario. *INTERP-SIQUIS.* 2007 [Thirdness and change in Relational Psychoanalysis]

Allen, J. & Fonagy, P. (2006). *Handbook of Mentalization–Based Treatment.* John Wiley & Sons, Ltd.

Altman, N. (2011). *The Analyst in the Inner City (2nd. Ed.). Race, Class and Culture Through a Psychoanalytic Lens.* New York: Routledge.

Altman, N., Briggs, R., Frankel, J., Gensler, D. & Pantone, P. (2002). *Relational child psychotherapy.* New York: Other Press.

Amery, J. (2001). *Más allá de la culpa y la expiación.* Valencia: Pre-Textos (orig. 1974)

Aristóteles. *Metafísica* (Metaphysics). Madrid: Gredos, 1994.

Armengol, R. y Hernández, V. (1991). La función y el trabajo del analista. Valoración relativa del setting y la interpretación, *Anuario Ibérico de Psicoanálisis,* 2, 21-42.

Aron, L. (1996). *A meeting of minds: Mutuality in psychoanalysis.* Hillsdale, New Jersey: Analytic Press (Spanish version: *Un encuentro de Mentes.* Santiago de Chile: Univ. Alberto Hurtado, 2013).

Aron, L. (2013). Preface to the Spanish edition of *Influencia y Autonomía en Psicoanálisis* (S.A. Mitchell). En Ibid. Madrid. Ágora Relacional (pp. 11-28)

Assoun, P.L. (1981). *Introducción a la epistemología freudiana* (Introduction to Freudian epistemology). México: Siglo XXI.

Astington, J., Harris, P., and Olson, D. (1988). *Developing theories of mind.* New York: Cambridge University Press.

Ávila Espada, A. (2005). Al cambio psíquico se accede por la relación. *Intersubjetivo, 2*, 195-220. [Relation: The path to psychic change]

Ávila Espada, A. (2011). Dolor y sufrimiento psíquico. *Clínica e Investigación Relacional*, Madrid. Vol. 5 (2). febrero 2011. pp 129-145.

Ávila Espada, A. (2013a). Hacernos personas recorriendo el camino del cambio. *Clínica e Investigación Relacional*, 7(1): 79-86. [Becoming persons in the pathway of change]

Ávila Espada, A. (2013b). La relación, contexto determinante de la transformación. Reflexiones en torno al papel de la interpretación, el insight y la experiencia emocional en el cambio psíquico. *Temas de Psicoanálisis* nº 6, Julio 2013. [Relation, a determinant context for transformation. Reflections on the role of interpretation, insight and emotional experience for psychic change]

Ávila Espada, A. (2015a). Psicoterapia psicoanalítica relacional. Lugar de encuentro de la evolución del psicoanálisis. Cap. 3 (pp.41-62 in the compilation by J. Guimón (Coord.) *Un cuarto de siglo de psiquiatría psicodinámica.* Madrid: Eneida/Puntos de Vista 40. [Relational Psychoanalytic Psychotherapy: A meeting point of psychoanalytic evolution]

Ávila Espada, A. (2015b). Del encuadre como factor técnico a la intersubjetividad del vínculo terapéutico. *Clínica e Investigación Relacional*, 9 (2): 394-397. [From setting as technical factor to therapeutic bond intersubjectivity]

Ávila Espada, A. (2016). The intersubjective: A core concept for psychoanalysis. *International Forum of Psychoanalysis*, 25(3), 186-190.

Ávila Espada, A. (Ed.) (2013c). *La tradición interpersonal. Perspectiva social & cultural en Psicoanálisis.* Madrid: Ägora Relacional, Col. Pensamiento Relacional nº 8. [The Interpersonal tradition. Social and Culture Psychoanalytic Perspective]

Ávila Espada, A. et al. (Colectivo GRITA). (2002). Reflexiones sobre la potencialidad transformadora de un psicoanálisis relacional. *Intersubjetivo*, 4(2), 155-192. [Reflections on transformative potential of Relational Psychoanalysis]

Ávila Espada, A. (2009). Artesano de necesidades y tiempos, el psicoterapeuta realiza sus obras con restos de naufragios. *Clínica e Investigación Relacional*, 3(3), 582-592.

Ávila Espada, A. (2009). La psicoterapia psicoanalítica relacional: Conceptos fundamentales y perspectivas. *Interpsiquis*, 1.

Ávila Espada, A. (2016). *La evolución de la clínica relacional: Tendencias y retos*. IV Jornadas de Psicoanálisis Relacional, Salamanca (Spain), 28 & 29 October, 2016.

Baars, B.J. (1986). *The Cognitive Revolution in Psychology*. Nueva York: Guilford.

Baca, E. (2011). Conductas perversas En *Psiquiatría y Ley*. Median, A; Moreno, M.J.; Lillo, R; Guija, J.A.; (editores) Madrid. Fundación Española de Psiquiatría y Salud Mental. Editorial Triacastela.

Bacal, H. & Carlton, L. (2011). *The Power of Specificity in Psychotherapy: When Therapy Works and When It Doesn't*. United Kingdom: Rowman & Littlefield Publishing Group.

Bacal, H.A. (Ed.) (1998). *Optimal responsiveness: How therapists heal their patients*, Northvale, NJ: Jason Aronson.

Balint, M. (1949). Changing therapeutic aims and techniques in psychoanalysis, in *Primary love and psychoanalytic technique*, London: Hogarth Press

Balint, M. (1952). *Primary love and psychoanalytic technique*, London: Hogarth Press

Balint, M. (1968). *The basic fault: Therapeutic Aspects of Regression*. London: Tavistock. (V. castellana: *La falta básica. Aspectos terapéuticos de la regresión*. Barcelona: Paidos, 1979)

Baranger, W. & Baranger, M. (1969). *Problemas del campo psicoanalítico*. B.A: Kargieman [Problems of Psychoanalytic Field]

Baranger, W. (1967). Polémicas actuales acerca del enfoque económico, en *Problemas del campo psicoanalítico*, 1993, Buenos Aires: Ediciones Kargieman.

Baranger, W. y Mom, J. (1984). Corrientes actuantes en el pensamiento psicoanalítico de América Latina, en la Revista de Psicoanálisis, Tomo ILI.

Baron-Cohen, S., Tager-Flusberg, H. and Cohen, D. J. (1993). *Understanding other minds: Perspectives from autism*. Oxford: Oxford University Press.

Basson, R. (2001). Human sex-response cycles *Journal Sexual Marital Ther.* 27 (1) 33-43

Basson, R. (2006). Clinical practice. Sexual desire and arousal disorders in women. *N Eng J Med.*

Bateman, A. W. y Fonagy, P. (2006). *Mentalization-Based Treatment for Borderline Personality Disorder: A Practical Guide*, Oxford: Oxford University Press

Bauman, Z. (1999). *Liquid Modernity.* Cambridge: Polity.

Beebe, B. & Lachmann, F. (2013). *The origins of Attachment: Infant research and adult treatment.* New York, NY: Routledge.

Beebe, B., & Lachmann, F. (2002). *Infant research and adult treatment: Co-constructing interactions.* Hillsdale, NJ. Analytic Press.

Beebe, B; Lachmann, F. (1998). Co-constructing inner and relational processes: Self and mutual regulation in infant research and adult treatment, *Psychoanal. Psychol.* 15: 480-516

Benjamin, J. (1988). *Los lazos de amor. Psicoanálisis, feminismo y el problema de la dominación.* Buenos Aires. Paidos Psicología Profunda. [Original title: *The Bonds of Love: Psychoanalysis, Feminism and the Problems of Domination.* New York: Pantheon books]

Benjamin, J. (1997). Sujetos iguales objetos de amor. Ensayos sobre el reconocimiento y la diferencia sexual. Buenos Aires. Editorial Paidós. (*original title: Like Subjects, love Objects, Essays on Recongnition and Sexual Difference.* Yale University Press, New Haven and London. 1995 by Yale University.

Benjamin, J. (2013). *La sombra del Otro. Intersubjetividad y género en psicoanálisis.* Madrid: Psimática. [original title: *Shadow of the Other: Intersubjectivity and Gender in Psychoanalysis*, Nueva York, Routledge, 1999]

Benjamin, L. (2004). Beyond doer and done to: an intersubjective view of thirdness, *The Psychoanalytic Quarterly, 73 (1)*, 5-46. [Spanish translation in *Intersubjetivo, 2004, 6 (1)*, 7-38].

Benyakar, M. y Lezica, A. (2005). *Lo traumático, clínica y paradoja.* Buenos Aires:Biblos

Berger, L. (2001). *Freud. El genio y sus sombras.* Barcelona: Vergara (orig. 2000)

Bleger, J. (1958). *Psicoanálisis y dialéctica materialista*, Buenos Aires: Nueva Visión.

Bleger, J. (1959). *Psicología de la conducta*. Buenos Aires: Paidos, 1977 [Psychology of Behavior]

Bleiberg, E. (2013) Metalizing-Based Treatment with Adolescents and Families. *Child and Adolescent Psychiatric Clinics of North America*, 2(2), 295-330.

Bohleber, W. (2010). *Destructiveness, Intersubjectivity and Trauma*. London:Karnac

Bolin, A. (2003). La transversalidad de género. Contexto cultural y prácticas de género. En Nieto, J. A. (Ed.), *Antropología de la sexualidad y diversidad cultural* (pp.231-260). Madrid: Talasa ediciones. (Gender transversality. Cultural context and gender practices. In *Anthropology of sexuality and cultural diversity*).

Bollas, C. (1987). *The shadow of the object: psychoanalysis of the unthought known,* Londres: Free Association Books. [Spanish version: *La sombra del objeto*. Buenos Aires: Amorrortu, 1992]

Bollas, C. (1993). *Fuerzas de destino*. Buenos Aires:Amorrortu (orig. 1989)

Bollas, C. (2007). *The Freudian Moment*. London:Karnak

Bonomi, C. (1999). Flight into sanity: Jones´allegation of Ferenczi´s mental deterioration reconsidered, *Int J Psychoanal* 80: 507-542

Boston Change Process Study Group (2002). Explicating the implicit: The local level and the microprocess of change in the analytic situation. *International Journal of Psychoanalysis*, 83: 1051-62.

Boston Change Process Study Group (2005). The something more than interpretation revisited: Sloppiness and co-creativity in the psychoanalytic encounter *Journal of the American Psychoanalytic Association*, 53: 693-729.

Boston Change Process Study Group. (2010). *Change in psychotherapy: A unifying paradigm*. New York, NY: Norton.

Bowlby, J. (1969). *Attachment and Loss. I. Attachment*. Hogarth Press. London

Bowlby, J. (2006). *Vínculos afectivos: Formación, desarrollo y pérdida*; Morata ediciones, 5ª edición 2006 reimpresión de la primera edición, 1986 [The making and breaking of affectional bonds, Taviskock publications, 1979]

Bradshaw, G. A., & Schore, A. N. (2007). How elephants are opening doors: Developmental neuroethology, attachment and social context. *Ethology*, 113, 426-436.

Brandchaft, B., Doctors, S. & Sorter, D. (2010). *Toward an Emancipatory Psychoanalysis. Brandchaft´s Intersubjective Vision*. Psychoanalytic Inquiry Book Series.

Bromberg, P. (1998). *Standing in the spaces: understanding and treating adult on set trauma*. NJ: Analytic press.

Bromberg, P. M. (1995). Resistance, Object-usage, And Human Relatedness. *Contemptemporary Psychoanalysis, 31*, 173-191.

Bromberg, P.M. (1998). *Standing in the Spaces. Essays on Clinical Process, Trauma and Dissociation*. Hillsdale, NJ: The Analytic Press.

Bromberg, P.M. (2009). Truth, human relatedness, and the analytic process: An interpersonal / relational perspective, *Int J Psychoanal* 90: 347-361

Bromberg, P.M. (2011). *The Shadow of the Tsunami and the Growth of the Relational Mind*. New York, NY: Routledge [Spanish versión: *La sombra del Tsunami y el desarrollo de la Mente Relacional*, Madrid; Ágora Relacional, 2017]

Buechler, S. (2008). *Making a difference in patient's lives: Emotional experience in the therapeutic setting*. New York: Routledge. [Spanish versión: *Marcando la diferencia en las vidas de los pacientes. Experiencia emocional en el ámbito terapéutico*. Madrid: Ágora Relacional, 2015]

Busch, F. (2008). *Mentalization*. New York: The Analytic Press.

Castaño, R. (2011). *La terapia sexual. Una mirada relacional*. Madrid: Ágora. (The sexual therapy. A relational look).

Cavell, Marcia (1993). *The Psychoanalytic Mind: From Freud to Philosophy*. Cambridge, MA: Harvard University Press.

Cencillo, L (1977). *Transferencia y sistema de psicoterapia*. Pirámide: Madrid. (Transference and psychotherapy system).

Cencillo, L. (1978). *El hombre. Noción científica*. Madrid: Marova. (Human-being. Scientific notion)

Cencillo, L. (2000). *Lo que Freud no llegó a ver*. Syntagma: Madrid. (What Freud missed to see).

Chacón Fuertes, P. (1994). La Noción de Inconsciente en Psicología (The notion of unconscious in Psychology). In Ávila Espada, A. y Poch i Bullich, J. (eds.) "Manual de Técnicas de Psicoterapia" (cap. 3). Madrid: Siglo XXI.

Chomsky, N. (1980). *Rules and Representations*. New York: Columbia University Press

Cicchetti, D. & Tucker, D. (1999). Development and self-regulatory structures of the mind. *Development and Psychopathology, 6*, 533-549

Coderch de Sans, J. & Codosero Medrano, A. (2015). Entre la razón y la pasión. Algunas reflexiones acerca del espíritu del encuadre en el Psicoanálisis Relacional. *Clínica e Investigación Relacional*, 9 (2): 358-393. [Between passion and reason. Some Reflections on spirit of setting in Relational Psychoanalysis- in this volume, in a shortened version]

Coderch, J. & Plaza, A. (2016). *Emoción y relaciones humanas. El psicoanálisis relacional como terapéutica social.* Madrid: Ágora Relacional. [Human Relations and Emotion. Relational Psychoanalysis as Social Therapy]

Coderch, J. (2001). *La relación paciente-terapeuta. El campo del psicoanálisis & la psicoterapia psicoanalítica.* Barcelona: Paidos-Fundación Vidal i Barraquer. [The therapist-Patient Relationship]

Coderch, J. (2005). Neurociencia y Psicoanálisis. *Revista de psicoterapia,* 16, 62. pp 35-52. (Neuroscience and psychoanalysis)

Coderch, J. (2006). *Pluralidad y Diálogo en Psicoanálisis. Diversidad y vinculaciones interdisciplinares.* Barcelona: Herder. [Plurality and Dialogue in Psychoanalysis. Diversity and interdisciplinary linkages]

Coderch, J. (2010). *La práctica de la psicoterapia relacional. El modelo interactivo en el campo del psicoanálisis* Madrid: Ágora Relacional [The practice of Relational Psychotherapy]

Coderch, J. (2012). *Interacción, Realidad y Cambio Psíquico. La práctica de la psicoterapia relacional-II.* Madrid: Ágora Relacional. [Interaction, Reality and Psychic Change]

Coderch, J. (2016). *Comprendiendo a una sociedad en cambio para comprender a los pacientes.* IV Jornadas de Psicoanálisis Relacional, 28 & 29 October, 2016, Salamanca (Spain).

Coderch, J. (Coord.) (2014). *Avances en Psicoanálisis Relacional. Nuevos campos de exploración para el psicoanálisis.* Madrid: Ágora Relacional. [Advancements in Relational Psychoanalysis]

Cooper, S. H., Levit, D. B. (1998). Old and new objects in Fairbairn an American Relational Theory, *Psychoanalytic Dialogues,* 8 (5), 603-624.

Crabbe, J.C. & Phillips, T.J. (2003). Mother nature meets mother nurture. *Nature Neuroscience.* 6, 440-442

Crastnopol, M. (2009). El frotamiento: el interjuego sexual como un nexo entre el deseo erótico, el amor romántico y el apego emocional. Madrid. *Clínica e Investigación Relacional* Vol. 3 (2) Mayo 2009 pp. 307-325.

Damasio, A.R. (2006). *El error de Descartes. La emoción, la razón y el cerebro humano* – Barcelona: Crítica - Edición Drakontos Bolsillo [Original ed. 1994: Descartes' Error: Emotoon, Reason and the Human Brain, Putnam Pub.]

Daurella, N. (2013). *Falla básica y relación terapéutica.* Madrid: Ágora Relacional [Basic Fault and Therapeutic Relationship]

Davies, J.M. (2007). Sobre la Naturaleza del *Self:* la Multiplicidad, el Conflicto Inconsciente y la Fantasía en el Psicoanálisis Relacional. *Clínica e Investigación Relacional,* 1 (1): 53-62.

Davies, J.M. (2007). Sobre la Naturaleza del *Self*: la Multiplicidad, el Conflicto Inconsciente y la Fantasía en el Psicoanálisis Relacional. *Clínica e Investigación Relacional* 1(1): 53-62

Davies, J.M. (2009). Los momentos en que vibramos y los momentos en que suspiramos: múltiples eróticas de la excitación física, la anticipación y la liberación. *Clínica e Investigación Relacional* Vol. 3(2) mayo 2009 pp. 261-280.

Davies, J.M., Frawley, M.G. (1994). *Treating tue Adult Survivor of Childhood Sexual Abuse.* NY:Basic Books

Delgado, S. V., Strawn, J. R. & Pedapati, E. V. (2015). *Contemporary psychodynamic psychotherapy for children and adolescents. Integrating intersubjectivity and neuroscience.* Berlin: Springer.

Dennet, D. (1987). *The intentional stance.* Cambridge, MA: MIT Press.

Descartes, R. (1641). Objections to the Meditations and Descartes's Replies. Jonathan Bennett: http://www.earlymoderntexts.com/assets/pdfs/descartes1642_3.pdf .

Dimen, M. (2001). Perversion is Us? Eigh Notes. *Psychoanalytic Dialogues.*, 11, 825-860

Dimen, M. (2005). Sexuality and suffering, or the Eew!. *Studies in Gender and Sexuality.* 6, 1-18

Dio Bleichmar, E. (1991). *El feminismo espontáneo de la histeria. Estudios de los trastornos narcisistas de la personalidad.* Madrid: Siglo XXI de España Editores.

Dio Bleichmar, E. (1998). *La sexualidad femenina. de la niña a la mujer.* Paidós: Psicología Profunda.

Dodds, E.R. (1951). *The Greeks and the irrational.* Berkeley, CA: University of California Press, 2004

Eagle, M. N. (2011). *From classical to contemporary psychoanalysis. A critique and integration.* New York: Routledge.

Eagle, M.N. (2013). *Attachment and psychoanalysis: Theory, research and clinical implications.* New York, NY: Guilford.

Edelman, G.M., & Tononi, G. (2000). *Consciousness: how matter becomes imagination.* Penguin Books.

Ehrenberg, D.B. (1992). *The Intimate Edge: Extending the Reach of Psychoanalytic Interaction.* New York: Norton [Spanish versión: *Al filo de la intimidad. Extendiendo el alcance de la interacción psicoanalítica.* Madrid: Ágora Relacional, 2016]

Epstein, S. (1994). Integration of the Cognitive and the Psychodynamic Unconscious. American Psychologist, 49, 8, 709-72.

Erdelyi, M.H. (1985). *Psicoanálisis. La psicología cognitiva de Freud* (Psycho-analysis. Freud's cognitive psychology). Labor: Barcelona, 1987.

Erdelyi, M.H. (2010). The ups and downs of memory. *American Psychologist,* 65, 7, 623-633

Espinosa, S., García-Valdecasas, S., Pinto, J.M., R. Sutil, C., Vivar, P., Aburto, M., Ávila, A. y Bastos, A. (Colectivo GRITA). (2005). Procesos de Mutualidad y Reconocimiento. Un Nuevo contexto para la reconsideración de la transferencial (Mutuality Processes and Recognition. A new context to reconsider transference). *Intersubjetivo, 2, 7,*180-194.

Etchegoyen, H (2002). *Los fundamentos de la Técnica psicoanalítica.* Buenos Aires: Amorrortu

Evans-Pritchard. E E. (1940) *The Nuer: A Description of the Modes of Livelihood and Political Institutions of a Nilotic People.* Oxford: Clarendon Press.

Evans-Pritchard. E. E. (1951). "Kinship and Local Community among the Nuer". in *African Systems of Kinship and Marriage.* A.R. Radcliffe-Brown y D. Forde, (eds). London: Oxford University Press. p. 360-391.

Fabris, Fernando A. (2007). *Pichon-Rivière, un viajero de mil mundos. Génesis e irrupción de un pensamiento nuevo.* Buenos Aires: Polemos [Pichon-Rivière, A traveler of a thousand worlds. Genesis and irruption of a new thought]

Fairbairn, W. R. D. (1958). On the Nature and Aims of Psycho-Analytical Treatment. *Int. J. Psycho-Anal.* 39

Fairbairn, W.R.D. (1940). Schizoid Factors in the Personality. In Ronald D. Fairbairn (1952), *Psychoanalytical Studies of Personality.* Londres : Routledge & Kegan Paul.

Fairbairn, W.R.D. (1952). *Estudio Psicoanalítico de la Personalidad.* Buenos Aires: Hormé, 1978. (*Psychoanalytical Studies of the Personality.* London: Tavistock Press, de 1952, reimpresión en 1994).

Fairbairn, W.R.D. (1958). On the Nature and Aims of Psychoanalytical Treatment. En Selected Papers of W.R.D. Fairbairn. David E. Scharff & Ellinor Fairbairn Birtles (1994) (eds.) N.J.: Jason Aronson (vol. I, Cap. 4). (On the nature and aims of psychoanalytical treatment, International Journal of Psychoanalysis, 39: 374-385).

Fajardo, B. (2000). Where are we going in the field of infant mental health? Comment. *Infant Mental Health* J., 21; 63-66.

Ferenczi, S. (1932). *Sin simpatía no hay curación. Diario Clínico de 1932.* Buenos Aires: Amorrortu, 1996 [*The Clinical Diary of Sandor Ferenczi.* Cambridge, MA: Harvard Univ. Press]

Ferenczi, S. (1928). The elasticity of psychoanalytic technique, *Final contributions to problems and technique of psychoanalysis* Maresfield: London (pp. 156-167)

Ferenczi, S. (1933). The Confusion of Tongues Between Adults and Children: The Language of Tenderness and of Passion. *International Journal of Psycho-Analysis, 30, 4,* 1949 [*Final contributions to problems and technique of psychoanalysis* Maresfield: London (pp. 156-167)]

Ferenczi, S. (1934). Gedanken über das Trauma. *Internationale Zeitschrift für Psychoanalyse.* XX Band Heft 1 5-12

Field, T., Woodson, R., Greenberg, R., & Cohen, D. (1982). Discrimination and imitation of facial expressions by neonatos. *Science,* 218, 179-181.

Fischer, G. & Riedesser, P. (1999). *Lehrbuch del Psychoraumatologie.* Ernst Reinhardt Verlag: München

Flaquer, L. (2004). La articulación entre familia y el Estado de bienestar en los países de la Europa del sur. *Papers, 73,* 27-58.

Fodor, J. A. (1987). *Psychosemantics.* Cambridge, MA. MIT Press.

Fodor, J.A. (1975). *The Language of Thought.* Cambridge: Harvard University Press, 1975.

Fodor, J.A. (1980). Methodological Solipsism Considered as a Research Strategy in Cognitive Psychology. In H.L.Dreyfus (ed.) "Husserl Intentionality and Cognitive Science". Cambridge MA: Massachussetts Institute of Technology.

Fodor, J.A. (1992). A theory of the child´s theory of mind. *Cognition,* 44, 283-296.

Fonagy, P. (1989). On tolerating mental states: Theory of mind in borderline personality. *Bulletin of the Anna Freud Center,* 12: 91-115.

Fonagy, P. (2004). *Teoría del apego y psicoanálisis* Barcelona, Espax. [*Attachment theory and psychonalysis,* 2001]

Fonagy, P. (2013). There is room for more than doublethink: The perilous status of psychoanalytic research. *Psychoanalytic Dialogues,* 23, 116-122.

Fonagy, P. et al. (2002). *Affect regulation, mentalization, and the development of the self.* New York. Other Press.

Fonagy, P. & Bateman, A. W. (2016). Adversity, attachment, and mentalizing. *Comprehensive Psychiatry,* 64, 59-66.

Foucault, M. (2009). *La historia de la sexualidad. vol. 1. La voluntad del saber.* Madrid, siglo XXI editores. [First edition in French 1976. Original title in French *Histoire de la sexualité I:* La volonté de savoir]

Foucault, M. (2009). *La historia de la sexualidad. vol. 2. El uso de los placeres.* Madrid, siglo XXI editores. [First edition in French, 1984, original title. *Histoire de la sexualité.* 2. L´usage des plaisirs]

Frankel, J. (2002). Exploring Ferenczi´s concept of identification with the aggressor. Its role in trauma, everydaylife and the therapeutic relationship, *Psychoanalytic Dialogues,* 12: 101-139

Freud, S. (1887-1902). Los orígenes del psicoanálisis (cartas a W. Fliess). En *Obras completas.* 4ª edición. Madrid: Biblioteca Nueva

Freud, S. (1894). The neuro-psychoses of defence. In J. Strachey (Ed. And Trans.) , *The Standrd Edition of the complete psychological works of Sigmund Freud* (Vol. 3). London: Hogarth Press, 1958.

Freud, S. (1900). La interpretación de los sueños. En *Obras completas.* 4ª edición. Madrid: Biblioteca Nueva

Freud, S. (1905). *Three essays on the theory of sexuality.* In J. Strachey (Ed. And Trans.), The standard edition of the complete psychological works of Sigmund Freud (vol. VII, pp. 123-243). London: Hogarth press, 1955.

Freud, S. (1906). Mis opiniones acerca del rol de la sexualidad en la etiología de las neurosis. En *Obras completas.* 4ª edición. Madrid: Biblioteca Nueva

Freud, S. (1908). La moral sexual cultural y la nerviosidad moderna. . En *Obras completas.* 4ª edición. Madrid: Biblioteca Nueva

Freud, S. (1912). Contribuciones al simposio sobre la masturbación. En *Obras completas.* 4ª edición. Madrid: Biblioteca Nueva, p. 1702 tomo II [Contributions to a discussion on masturbation Vienna Psycho Analytic Society 1912 SE 253-254]

Freud, S. (1912). Sobre la degradación de la vida erótica. En *Obras completas.* 4ª edición. Madrid: Biblioteca Nueva

Freud, S. (1914a) On the History of the Psycho-Analytic Movement. In J. Strachey (Ed. And Trans.) *The Standard Edition of the complete psychological works of Sigmund Freud* (Vol. 14). London: Hogarth Press, 1958.

Freud, S. (1914b). Introducción al Narcisismo. In *Obras Completas* (vol. II). Madrid: Biblioteca Nueva, 1973. Zur Einführung des Narziβmus. En Studienausgabe (vol. III). Frankfurt am Main : S.Fisher, 1975.

Freud, S. (1915). *The Unconscious.* In J. Strachey (Ed. And Trans.) , *The Standard Edition of the complete psychological works of Sigmund Freud* (Vol. 14). London: Hogarth Press, 1958. *Das Unbewu te.* In Studienausgabe (vol. III). Frankfurt am Main: S. Fisher, 1975.

Freud, S. (1916a). La vida sexual humana. Lección XX. En *Obras completas.* 4ª edición. Madrid: Biblioteca Nueva

Freud, S. (1916b). Teoría de la libido y el narcisismo. Lección XXVI. . En *Obras completas.* 4ª edición. Madrid: Biblioteca Nueva

Freud, S. (1920). Beyond the Pleasure Principle. *The Standard Edition of the Complete Psychological Works of Sigmund Freud, Volume XVIII*

(1920-1922): Beyond the Pleasure Principle, Group Psychology and Other Works

Freud, S. (1922-23). Psicoanálisis y teoría de la libido. En *Obras completas*. 4ª edición. Madrid: Biblioteca Nueva

Freud, S. (1923). The ego and the id. In J. Strachey (Ed. And Trans.) , The Standrd Edition of the complete psychological works of Sigmund Freud (Vol. 19). London: Hogarth Press, 1958.

Freud, S. (1924). *The economic problem of masochism*. In J. Strachey (Ed. And Trans.), The standard edition of the complete psychological works of Sigmund Freud (vol. XIX, pp. 155-170). London: Hogarth press, 1955 [El problema económico del masoquismo. En *Obras completas*. 4ª edición. Madrid: Biblioteca Nueva]

Freud, S. (1926). *Inhibitions, Symptoms and Anxiety*. The Standard Edition of the Complete Psychological Works of Sigmund Freud, Volume XX (1925-1926): An Autobiographical Study, Inhibitions, Symptoms and Anxiety, The Question of Lay Analysis and Other Works

Freud, S. (1927). El fetichismo. En *Obras completas*. 4ª edición. Madrid: Biblioteca Nueva

Freud, S. (1939). Moses and Monoteism. In J. Strachey (Ed. And Trans.) , *The Standard Edition of the complete psychological works of Sigmund Freud* (Vol. 23). London: Hogarth Press, 1958.

Freud, S. (1940 [1938]). An Outline of Psycho-Analysis, S. E. XXIII, 144-207. In J. Strachey (Ed. And Trans.) , *The Standard Edition of the complete psychological works of Sigmund Freud* (Vol. 23). London: Hogarth Press, 1958.

Freud, S. (1981). *Obras completas*. 4ª edición. Madrid: Biblioteca Nueva. Traducción del alemán de Luis López Ballesteros y de Torres.

Fromm, E. (1956). *The art of loving*. New York.: Harper and row.

Fromm, E. (2007). *El arte de escuchar.* (original title in Gernan *Von der Kunst des Zuhörens therapeutische Apekte der Psychoanalyse.* Beltz Verlag. Weinheim and Basielea. c 1991 by the Estate of Erich Fromm) [*The Art of Listening,* Bloomsbury Academic; first edition September 1, 1998]

Frommer, M.S. (2009). Sobre la subjetividad de los estados eróticos de la mente. *Clínica e Investigación Relacional*. Vol. 3(2) pp. 241-260.

Gadamer, H-G. (1975). (Subjectivity and intersubjectivity, subject and person). Gadamer, HG. *Continental Philosophy Review,2000, 33,* 275-287.

Gallese, V. (2001). The "shared manifold" hipotesis: from mirror neurons to empathy. *Journal of consciousness Studies.* 8, 33-50.

Gallese, V. (2009). Mirror Neurons, embodied simulation, and the neural basis of social identification. *Psychoanalytic Dialogues, 19,* 519-536.

Garriga, C. (2004). Estudios sobre género y sexualidad. *Aperturas psico-analíticas.* N° 16. *Reseña del artículo Género irónico/sexo auténtico de Virginia Goldner, publicado en Studies in gender and sexuality 4(2) 113-139-2003*

Garriga; C. (2010). Vicisitudes del concepto de género en el psicoanálisis (I). *Clínica e Investigación Relacional,* Vol 4 (1) Febrero 2010

Gaulejac de, V. (2008). *Las Fuentes de la vergüenza.* Buenos Aires. Mármol/ Izquierdo editores. [original edition in French *Les sources de lo honte.* Paris. 1996]

Gehardt, J. (2010). Las raíces de la envidia. La experiencia poco estética del self atormentado desposeído. *Aperturas Psicoanalíticas.* n° 35.

Gerson, S. (2004). The relational unconscious: A core element of intersubjec-tivity, thirdness, and clinical process. *Psychoanalytic Quarterly, LXXIII,* 63-98.

Ghent, E. (1983). Masochism, Submission, Surrender: Masochism as a Perver-sion of surrender, *Contemp. Psychoanal.,* 26 (1), 108- 135.

Ghent, E. (2002). Wish, need, drive: Motive in the light of dynamics system theory and Edelman´s selectionist theory. *Psychoanal. Dial.,* 12, 763-808.

Giddens, A. (1995). *La transformación de la intimidad. Sexualidad, amor y erotismo en las sociedades modernas.* Madrid: Editorial Cátedra. [The transformation of intimacy sexuality, love and eroticism in modern societies, 1992]

Gluckman, P.D. & Adler, H.M. (2004). Living with the past: evolution, develop-ment and patterns of disease. *Science.* 305. 1733-1736

Glymour, C. (1991). Los androides de Freud (Freud's Androids). In Jerome Neu (ed.) *Guía de Freud.* Cambridge: Cambridge University Press, 1996.

Greenberg, J. & Mitchell S.A. (1983). *Object Relations in Psychoanalytic Theory* Cambridge, Mass.: Harvard University Press.

Greenberg, J. (1986). Theoretical models and the analyst's neutrality, Contemp. *Psychoanal.*22, 87-107.

Greenberg, J. (1991). *Oedipus and Beyond. A clinical theory,* Cambridge, Massachusetts: Harvard University Press.

Grossman, D. (1996). *On Killing.* New York:BBBooks

Grossmark, R. (2012). The unobtrusive relational analyst, *Psychoanalytic Dialogues,*22: 629-646

Grossmark, R. (2016). Psychoanalytic Companioning, *Psychoanalytic Dialogues* 26: 698-712

Guerra Cid, L. R. (2006). *Este no es un libro de autoayuda. Tratado de la suerte, el amor y la felicidad.* Bilbao: DDB. (This is not a self-help book. Luck, love and happiness treaty).

Guerra Cid, L. R. (2013). *El clavo ardiendo. Claves de las adicciones amorosas y los conflictos en las relaciones sanas y patológicas.* Barcelona: Octaedro. (Any port in a storm. Love addictions keys and conflicts within healthy and pathological relationships.)

Guerra Cid, L. R. (2016). From virtual reality to the virtualisation of reality: Its impact on our relational world. XIII International Conference of the IARPP. 9-12 June, Roma.

Guerra Cid, L.R. (2001) *Transferir, contratransferir, regredir. Una perspectiva histórica y crítica de la psicoterapia psicoanalítica.* Salamanca: Amarú ediciones. (Transference, contra-transference, regression. A historical and critical perspective of psychoanalytic psychotherapy).

Guerra Cid, L.R. (2012). Why Can Even A Fluttering of a Butterfly's Wings Change Everything: A Chaos Perspective and A Complexity of Therapeutic Relation. X International Conference of the international Association for Relational Psychoanalysis and Psychotherapy (IARPP), March, New York.

Guerra Cid, L.R. (2015). When love becomes a conflict: a relational focus and complexity of love addictions perspective. International XII IARPP conference, Toronto, 25-28 June, 2015.

Guimón, J. (2009). Empatía, intersubjetividad y dialógo tónico: el trabajo pionero de Julian Ajuriaguerra. *Clínica e Investigación Relacional,* Vol. 3 (3) pp. 557-573

Gutiérrez Terrazas, J. (1999). Consecuencia teórico clínicas de la teoría de la seducción originaria. *Revista Aperturas Psicoanalíticas.* Nª 003, 5/11/1999. (sobre Breve tratado del inconsciente de J. Laplance, de la revista de Psicoanálisis de la APA nº 3 1995 pág. 447)

Habermas, J. (1968). La crítica como unidad de conocimiento e interés, en *Conocimiento e interés,* Madrid: Taurus Humanidades, 1990.

Halbwachs, M. (1950/1997). La mémoire collective. Paris: Albin. The collective memory, New York, Harper & Row Colophon Books, 1980.

Hartmann, H. (1939). *Comments on the Psychoanalytic Theory of the Ego,* Nueva York: Inter. Univ. Press,

Heidegger, M. (1927/1962). *Being and Time.* Translated by John Macquarrie & Edward Robinson. Oxford: Basil Blackwell.

Heidegger, M. (1987*). Zollikon Seminars. Protocols-Conversations-Letters.* M. Boss (ed.). R. Askay & F. Mayr (trs.). Northwestern University Press: Evanston, IL, 2001.

Herman, J. (2004). *Trauma y recuperación.* Madrid:Espasa Calpe (Orig. 1997)

Hirsch, I. (1998). The concept of enactment and theoretical convergence, *Psychoanal.Quarterly*, 67, 78-101.

Hirshfeld, L. and Gelman, S. (1994). *Mapping the mind: Domain specificity in cognition and culture.* New York. Cambridge University Press.

Hoffman, I.Z. (2009). Doublethinking our way to "scientific" legitimacy: The desiccation of human experience. *Journal of the American Psychoanalytic Association*, 57 (5): 1043-1069.

Hornstein,G.A. (1992). The Return of the Repressed. Psychology's Problematic Relations With Psychoanalysis. *American Psychologist, 47*, 254-263.

Hyppolite, J. (1974). *Genesis and Structure of Hegel's Phenomenology of Spirit.* Translated by Samuel Cherniak & John Heckman. Evanston, Il: Northwestern University Press.

Instituto Nacional de Estadística (2015). Víctimas mortales por violencia de género. Disponible en: http://www.ine.es. Checked on 15/02/2017.

Jiménez, S. (2011). Transferencia y género, in Guerra Cid, L.R and Jiménez, S. (Eds.). *Psicoterapia psicoanalítica: nuevos caminos para el avance de un método.* Salamanca: Amarú. (Transference and gender, in Psychoanalytic psychotherapy. New ways to development a method).

Jiménez, S. (2015). *Experiencia subjetiva y reconocimiento de múltiples estados del self: cómo poder experimentar ser sujeto.* 6th Annual IARPP-Spain meeting, Valencia, 23 October 2015.

Jones, E. (1958). *The life and work of Sigmund Freud*, New York: Basic Books

Kandel, E. R. (2005). A new intellectual framework for psychiatry. En E. R. Kandel (Ed.). *Psychiatry psychoanalysis and the new biology of mind.* Washington, DC: American Psychiatric Publishing.

Kandel, E.R. (2001a). *Principios de Neurociencia.* Madrid: MacGraw-Hill. (Original of 1981, revised 2012: Kandel, Eric R.; Schwartz, James H.; Jessell, Thomas M.; Siegelbaum, Steven A.; Hudspeth, A. J. *Principles of Neural Science* (5th ed.), New York: McGraw-Hill]

Kandel, E.R. (2007a). *En busca de la memoria. El nacimiento de una nueva ciencia de la mente.* Buenos Aires: Katz [*In Search of Memory: The Emergence of a New Science of Mind*, New York: W. W. Norton & Company, 2006]

Kandel, E.R. et al. (2007b). *Psiquiatría, Psicoanálisis y la Nueva Biología de la Mente*. Barcelona: Ars Médica [Original of 2005]

Kardiner, A. (1941). *The traumatic neuroses of war.* New York: Hoeber

Kenny, A. (1991). The Homunculus Fallacy. En J. Hyman (ed.), *Investigating Psychology. Sciences of the Mind after Wittgenstein*. Londres: Routledge.

Kernberg, O. (1992). *La agresión en las perversiones y en los desórdenes de la personalidad* (Aggression in Personality Disorders and Perversions). Buenos Aires: Paidós, 1994.

Kernberg, O.F. (1984). *Severe personality disorders: Psychotherapeutic strategies.* New Haven, CT: Yale University Press.

Kernberg, O.F. (1995). *Love relations. Normality and pathology*. London: Yale university press.

Khan, M. Masud R. (1979). *Alienation in perversions.* London. Hogarth Press. (Alienación en las perversiones. Buenos Aires, Nueva visión, 1987).

Khan, M. Masud R. (1991). *Cuando llegue la primavera. Tomas de conciencia en el psicoanálisis clásico*. Buenos Aires. Paidós Psicología Profunda. [When spring comes. Awakenings in Clinical Psychoanalysis. Chatto and Windus, 1988]

Killingmo, B. (1989). Conflict and Deficit: implications for technique. International Journal of Psycho-Analysis, 70, 65-79.

Kinsey, A.C. and col. Pomeroy, W.B.; Martin, C.F. (1948). Vol I. Comportamiento sexual en el macho humano [Sexual behaviour in the sexual male] (See also the film *Kinsey, tel's talk about sex* by director Bill Condon, 2004. EE. UU).

Kinsey, A.C. and col. Pomeroy, W.B.; Martin, C. F; Gebhard, P.H. (1953). Vol II. *Comportamiento sexual en la hembra humana. Sexual behaviour in the human Female.* Filadelfia and London, W.B. Saunders y Cia.

Kohut, H. (1966). Forms and Transformations of Narcissism. *Journal of the American Psychoanalytical Association, 14*, 243-272.

Kohut, H. (1971). *The Analysis of the Self: A Systematic Approach to the Psychoanalytic Treatment of Narcissistic Personality Disorders*. New York: Int. Univ. Press. [Spanish version: *Análisis del Self*. Buenos Aires: Amorrortu Ed.]

Kohut, H. (1977). *The Restoration of the Self.* New York: Int. Univ. Press. [Spanish version.: *La restauración del si-mismo*. Buenos Aires: Paidos, 1980]

Kohut, H. (1979). *Los dos análisis del señor Z* [translated and comments by Rogeli Armengol, Ramón Riera & Silvio Sember]. Barcelona:

Herder.2002 [The two analyses of Mr. Z. *The international journal of psychoanalysis,* 60:3]

Kohut, H. (1984). *How Does Analysis Cure?* Ed. A. Goldberg & P. E. Stepansky. Chicago: University of Chicago Press. Traducción castellana *¿Cómo Cura el Análisis?* Buenos Aires: Paidós, 1986.

Krystal, H. (1978). Trauma and Affects. *Psychoanalytic Study of the Child* 33: 81-116

Krystal, H. (2005). Psychoanalytic Approaches to Trauma: A Forty-Year Retrospective. In Figley C.R. (editor), *Mapping Trauma and its Wake* (pp111-118). NY:Routledge

La Rochefoucauld, Francois de. (n.d.). BrainyQuote.com. Retrieved March 20, 2017, from BrainyQuote.com Web site: https://www.brainyquote.com/ quotes/quotes/f/francoisde400129.html

Lacan, J. (1956). Le séminaire sur " La Lettre volée » (*The Purloined Letter*). In Écrits. París: Seuil (vol. I), 1970.

Lacan, Jacques. (1998). *Le séminaire: Les formations de l'inconscient,* 1957-1958 (vol. 5). Paris: Seuil.

Lachmann, F. (2007). El proceso de transformar. *Clínica e Investigación Relacional, 1*(1), 42-52.

Lakoff, G., Johnson, M. (2012). *Metáforas de la vida cotidiana.* Madrid:Cátedra (orig. 1980)

Lancelle, G. (comp.) (1999). *El self en la teoría y en la práctica,* Buenos Aires: Paidós.

Laplanche, J. (1970). *Vie et Mort en Psychanalyse* (Life and Death in Psycho-analysis). París: Falmmarion.

Laplanche, J; Pontalis, J.B. (1987a). *Diccionario de psicoanálisis.* Barcelona, editorial Labor (original title in French *Vocabulaire de la Psychanalyse,* 2ª edition, 1968)

Laub, D. (2012). Traumatic shutdown of narrative and symbolization: a death instinct derivative?. In Fromm, M.G. (editor), *Lost in Transmission.* London:Karnac

Lichtenberg, J, D. (2004). Sistemas motivacionales y escenas modelos con especial referencia a la experiencia corporal. *Aperturas psicoanalíticas* nº 017. 05/07/2004. *Motivational systems and model scenes with special references to bodily experience,* published originally in Psychoanalytic Inquiry, 2001, 21, 3, pp. 430-447.Copyright 2001 of Analytic Press, Inc. Traslated by Marta González Baz and published with authorization of The Analytic Press, Inc.

Lingiardi, V., Holmqvist, R. & Safran, J.D. (2016). Relational Turn and Psycho-therapy Research. *Contemporary Psychoanalysis*, 52 (2): 275-312.

Liszkowski, U., Carpenter, M., Henning, A., Striano, T., and Tomasello, M. (2004). Twelve-month-olds point to share attention and interest. *Developmental Science*, 7, 297-307.

Little, M. I. (1990). *Psychotic and Anxieties. And Containment: a Personal Record of an Analysis with Winnicott*, Londres: Jason Aronson

Lorenz, E. N. (1972). Predictability: does the flap of a Butterfly´s wings in Brazil set off a Tornado in Texas. *American association for the advance-ment of science in Washington*. Washington D.C.

Lothane, Z. (2003). What do Freud say about persons and relations? *Psycho-analytic Psychology, 20, 4*, 609-617.

Lyons-Ruth, K. (1999). The two-person unconscious: Intersubjective dialogue, enactive relational representation, and the emergence of new forms of relational organization. *Psychoanalytic Inquiry* 19:576-617. [Versión castellana en *Aperturas Psicoanalíticas*, nº 4, 2000]

Lyons-Ruth, K. Et al. (1998). Implicit relational knowing: its role in develop-ment and psychoanalytic treatment. *Infant Mental Health Journal*, vol. 19(3)., 282–289

Lyons-Ruth, K.; Zeanah, C. (1993). The family context of infant mental health. Affective development in the primary caregiving relationship. In *Handbook of infant mental health*. Guilford Press. New York.

MacIntyre, A. (1958). *El Concepto de Inconsciente* (The Unconscious. A Conceptual Analysis). Buenos Aires: Amorrortu, 2001.

Main, M. (1995). Discourse, prediction and recent studies in attachment: implications for psychoanalysis. In *Research in Psychoanalysis. Process, Development, Outcome*. ed. Shapiro and Emde, 11, 309 – 244. New York: International Universities Press.

Marina, J.A. (1999). *Diccionario de los sentimientos*. Madrid. Editorial Anagrama.

Marrone, M. (2001). *La Teoría del Apego. Un enfoque actual*. Editorial Psimática. Madrid.

Martín Cabré, L. (1966). "Se ruega cerrar los ojos". Reflexiones sobre el papel del desmentido en la teoría psicoanalítica del trauma, *Revista de Psicoanálisis de Madrid*, Madrid: APM, Extra 1966, 9-59.

Martínez Ibáñez, J.J. (2012). *Las dos edades de la mente. Vicisitudes del funcionamiento mental*. Madrid: Ágora Relacional [The two ages of mind. Vicissitudes of mental functioning]

Martínez Ibáñez, J.J. (2017). *El enigma de la angustia: una conceptualización de la angustia desde el vértice relacional.* Editorial Ágora Relacional. Madrid.

Marty, P. y De M'Uzan, M. (1963). La pensée opératoire, *Revue Française de Psychanalyse* ,27, 345-356.

Masson, Jeffrey Moussaieff *(2003)*. *The Assault On Truth: Freud›s Suppression of the Seduction Theory.* New York: Ballantine Books,

Masters, W. H. y Johnson, V. E. (1978). *Incompatibilidad humana,* Buenos Aires: Editorial Intermédica. [*Human sexual inadequeacy,* 1970]

Meltzoff, A. N. (2007). The 'like me' framework for recognizing and becoming an intentional agent. Acta Psychologica, 124, 26–43.

Meltzoff, A. N., & Gopnik, A. (1993). The role of imitation in understanding persons and developing a theory of mind. En S. Baron-Cohen, H. Tager-Flusberg, & D. J. Cohen, (Eds.)., *Understanding other minds: perspectives from autism.* New York: Oxford University Press.

Meltzoff, A.N. and Moore, M.K. (1977). Imitation of Facial and Manual Gestures by Human Neonates. *Science, 198,* 75-78.

Mills, J. (2005). A critique of relational psychoanalysis. *Psychoanalytic Psychology, 22, 2,* 155-188.

Mitchell, S.A. (1988). *Relational Concepts in Psychoanalysis: An Integration.* Cambridge, MA/London: Harvard Univ. Press (v. castellana: *Conceptos relacionales en psicoanálisis: Una integración.* México: Siglo XXI, 2000)

Mitchell, S.A. (1991). Contemporary perspectives on self toward and integration. *Psychoanalytical dialogues.* 1:121-147.

Mitchell, S.A. (1993). *Hope and Dread in Psychoanalysis.* New York: Basic Books.

Mitchell, S.A. (1997). *Influence and autonomy in psychoanalysis.* New York: The Analytic press. [v. castellana: *Influencia y autonomía en psicoanálisis.* Madrid: Ágora Relacional, 2015]

Mitchell, S.A. (2000). *Relationality: From Attachment to Intersubjectivity.* Hillsdale NJ; Analytic Press.

Mitchell, S.A. (2002). *Can love last? The fate of romance over time.* New York: Norton professional books.

Mitchell, S. A. y Aron, L. (1999). *Relational Psychoanalysis: The Emergence of a Tradition.* Hillsdale, NJ: The Analytic Press

Mitchell, S.A; Black J. M. (2004). *Más allá de Freud, una historia del pensamiento psicoanalítico moderno.* Barcelona. Herder ediciones.

(first edition in English1995, *Freud and beyond. A history of modern psychoanalytic thought*. Basic Books, The Perseus Group. New York)

Mora, F. (2006). *Los laberintos del placer en el cerebro humano*. Madrid: Alianza Editorial.

Moran, M. (1991). Chaos theory and psychoanalysis: the fluidic nature of the mind. *Internat. Rev. Psychoanal.* 18, 211-221.

Morris, J, (2011). *El enigma*. Barcelona. RBA Narrativa (*original title, Comundrum*, 1974)

Morrison, A.P. (2008). Fenómenos Narcisistas y Vergüenza (Narcissistic Phenomena and Shame). *Clínica e Investigación Relacional, 2, 1*, 9-25.

Nietzsche, F. (1883/1954). *Thus Spoke Zarathustra*, Translated by Walter Kaufmann, in "The Portable Nietzsche". New York: The Viking Press.

Núñez, C. & Romero, R. (2013). *Emocionario. Di lo que sientes*. Madrid, Spain: Palabras Aladas.

Orange, D. (2003) Why Language Matters to Psychoanalysis. *Psychoanalytic Dialogues, 13, 1*, 77-103,

Orange, D.M. (2010). *Thinking For Clinicians. Philosophical Resources for Contemporary Psychoanalysis and the Humanistic Psychotherapies*. Nueva York: Routledge. [Spanish version: *Pensar la práctica clínica: Recursos Filosóficos para el Psicoanálisis Contemporáneo & las Psicoterapias Humanistas*, Santiago de Chile: Cuatro Vientos, 2012]

Orange, D.M. (2011). *The Suffering Stranger: Hermeneutics for Everyday Clinical Practice*. Nueva York: Routledge [Spanish version: *El desconocido que sufre*. Santiago de Chile: Cuatro Vientos, 2013]

Orange, D.M. (2016). *Nourishing the Inner Life of Clinicians and Humanitarians; The ethical turn in Psychoanalysis* New York: Routledge.

Orange, D.; Atwood, G. y Stolorow, R. (1997). *Working Intersubjectively*, Hillsdale, The Analytic Press. [Trad. Cast.: *Trabajando intersubjetivamente. Contextualismo en la práctica psicoanalítica*. Madrid: Ágora relacional, 2012]

Orengo, F., Sabbah, D. (2001). Entrevista con Chaim Shatan. *Aperturas Psicoanalíticas* N° 009

Pardo, J. L. (2004). *La intimidad*. Valencia: Editorial Pre-Textos.

Piattelli-Palmarini, M. (1979). *Théories du langage. Théories de l'apprentissage*. (A debate with Jean Piaget and Noam Chomsky, and other authors). París: Seuil.

Pichon Rivière, E. (1985). *Teoría del Vínculo*. Buenos Aires: Ediciones Nueva Visión [Link Theory]

Piers, C. (2005). The mind's multiplicity and continuity. *Psychoanal. Dial.* 15: 229-254.

Racamier, P.C. (1995). *L'inceste et l'incestuel*. París: Les éditions du collège.

Reich, W. (1933/1976). *Análisis del Carácter* (Character Analysis). Madrid: Paidós.

Reik, T. (1944). A Psychologist Looks at Love. In M. Sherman (Ed.). *Of Love and Lust*. (pp. 1–194). New York: Jason Aronson.

Ricoeur, P. (1965). *De l'Interpretation* (About Interpretation). París : Éditions fu Seuil.

Riera, R. (2002). Introducción a la Psicología del Self (pp. 91-126) In H. Kohut: *Los dos análisis del señor Z*. Barcelona: Herder.

Riera, R. (2011). *La conexión emocional*. Barcelona: Octaedro [Original in Catalan, published 2010]

Rizzolatti, G., Gentilucci, R., Camarda, V., Gallese, G., Luppino, M., Matelli, y Fogassi, L. (1990). Neurons related to reaching-grasping arm movement in the rostral part of area 6. Esp. *Brain Res*. 82: 337-350.

Rodríguez Sutil, C. (2007). Epistemología del psicoanálisis relacional, *Clínica e Investigación Relacional* , 1 (1), 9-41.

Rodríguez Sutil, C. (2014). *Psicopatología psicoanalítica relacional. La persona en relación y sus problemas*. Madrid: Ágora Relacional. [Relational Psychoanalytic Psychopathology. Person in Relation and its problems]

Rodríguez Sutil, C. (2010). Narcisismo de piel fina y narcisismo de piel dura. Comentarios adicionales sobre el narcisismo. *Clínica e Investigación Relacional*. Sección "Debate sobre el narcisismo". (www.ceir.org.es)

Rutter, M. (1993). Resilience: Some Conceptual Considerations. *Journal of Adolescent Health*, 1993; 14; 626-631

Safran, J.D. & Kraus, J. (2014). Alliance ruptures, impassess, and enactments: A relational perspective. *Psychotherapy*, 51 (3): 381-387.

Safran, J.D. (2012). Doublethinking or dialectical thinking: A critical appreciation of Hoffman's "double-thinking" critique. *Psychoanalytic Dialogues*, 22, 710-720.

Safran, J.D., Muran, J.C. & Shaker, A. (2014). Research on therapeutic impasses and ruptures in the therapeutic alliance. *Contemporary Psychoanalysis*, 50 (1-2), 211-232.

Sáinz, F. (2002). Winnicott, un psicoanalista intersubjetivo, *Intersubjetivo*, 4, 265-272.

Sáinz, F. (2008). Winnicott, un buen compañero de viaje, en Liberman, A y Abelló, A (comps.), *Winnicott hoy, su presencia en la clínica actual*, Madrid, Psimática, pp. 345-359

Sáinz, F. (2014). *Sentir y pensar con Serrat. Reflexiones de un psicoanalista de hoy a partir de la obra del poeta y músico.* Lleida, Milenio.

Sáinz, F. (2017). Experiencias Transicionales y Mentalización, *Clínica e Investigación Relacional*, 11 (1): 93-100. DOI:10.21110/19882939.20 17.110105

Sainz, F. (2017). *Winnicott y la perspectiva relacional en Psicoanálisis.* Barcelona: Herder-FViB [Winnicott and Relational Perspective in Psychoanalysis]

Sáinz, F. y Cabré, V. (2012). La experiencia terapéutica con un analista suficiente e insuficientemente bueno. Una contribución de Winnicott al psicoanálisis relacional, *Clínica e Investigación Relacional*, 6 (3), 570-586.

Samuel, A. (2011). Promiscuites: Psychology, Politics, Spirituality and hypocrisy. IX Annual Conference of the International Association for Relational Psychoanalysis and Psychotherapy Changing Psychonalysis for a Changing Society. Relational Perspectives.

Sartre, J.P. (1943). *L'Être et le Néant. Essai D'Ontologie Phénoménologique* (Being and Nothingness). París: Gallimard.Schore, A. (1994). *Affect regulation and the origin of the self.* New Jersey. Hillsdale. Lawrence Erlbaum Associates, Publishers.

Schore, A. (1996). The experience-dependent maturation of a regulatory system in the orbital prefrontal cortex and the origin of developmental psychopatology. *Development and psychopatology*, 8, 59-87

Schore, A.N. (2000). Attachment and the regulation of the right brain. *Attachment and Human Development*, 2, 23-47.

Seligman, S. (2014). Paying attention and feeling puzzled: the analytic mindset as an agent of therapeutic change. *Psychoanalytic dialogues.* Vol.24 No 6, 648-662.

Seligman, S. (2005). Dynamic Systems Theories as a Metaframework for Psychoanalysis. *Psychoanal. Dial.*, 15(2):285-319

Shay, J. (1994). *Achilles in Vietnam. Combat Trauma and the Undoing of Character.* New York:Scribner

Shevrin, H. y Dickman, S. (1980). The Psychological Unconscious. A Necessary Assumption for all Psychological theory? American Psychologist, 35, 432.

Siegel, D.J. (1999). *The Developing Mind*, Nueva York: The Guilford Press (V. castellana: *La mente en desarrollo. Cómo interactúan las relaciones y el cerebro para modelar nuestro ser.* Bilbao: Desclée de Brouwer, 2007)

Siegel, D.J. (2012). *The developing mind.* (2nd. Edition). The Guilford Press. New York.

Siegel, D.J. & Hartzell, M. (2005). *Ser padres conscientes. Un mejor conocimiento & comprensión de nosotros mismos contribuye a un desarrollo integral & sano de nuestros hijos.* Vitoria: La Llave [Original ed. 2003]

Silber, L. M. (2015). A view from the margins: Children in Relational Psychoanalysis. *Journal of Infant, Child and Adolescent Psychotherapy, 14,* 345-362.

Slavin, M. O. (1996). Is one self enough? Multiplicity in self organisation and the capacity to negotiate relational conflict. *Contemporary psychoanalysis, 32,* 615-625.

Slavin, M.O. & Kriegman, D. (1992). *The adaptative design of the human psyche: Psychoanalysis, Evolutionary Biology and the Therapeutic Process.* New York: Guilford Press.

Sroufe, L. A. (1979). Socioemotional development. En J. Osofsky (Ed.). *Handbook of infant development.* New York. Wiley.

Sroufe, L. A. (1996). *Emotional development: the organization of emotional life in the early years.* New York. Cambridge University Press.

Stephens, W. N. (1963). *The family in cross-cultural perspective.* Holt: Rinehart and Winston.

Stern, D.B. (1997). *Unformulated Experience. From Dissociation to Imagination in Psychoanalysis.* Hillsdale, NJ: The Analytic Press.

Stern, D. B. (2007). El ojo que se ve a sí mismo: Disociación, *enactment* y el éxito en el conflicto. *Clínica e Investigación Relacional, 1* (2): 329-358. [Original of 2004: The Eye Sees Itself. *Contemp. Psychoanal.,* 40(2):197-237]

Stern, D. B. (2010). *Partners in thought, working with unformulated experience, dissociation and enactment.* New York: Routledge.

Stern, D.N. (1983)., The early development of schemas of self, other, and 'self with other'. En J.D. Lichtenberg y S. Kaplan (comps.), Reflections on Self Psychology, Hillsdale, N.J. : The Analytic Press, pp. 49-84.

Stern, D.N. (1985). *The interpersonal World of the Infant.* Nueva York: Basic Books. [Spanish translation: *El mundo interpersonal del infante. Una perspectiva desde el psicoanalisis y la psicologia evolutiva.* Buenos Aires: Paidós, 1991]

Stern, D.N. (1991). *El mundo interpersonal del infante.* Barcelona, Paidós. (original title *The interpersonal world of the infant. A view from Psycho-analysis and Developmental Psychology.* Basis Book, New York. 1985.

Stern, D. N. (1997). *La constelación maternal. La psicoterapia en las relaciones entre padres e hijos.* Barcelona: Paidós.

Stern, D.N. (2004). *The present moment in psychotherapy and everyday life.* NY: Norton & Co. [version castellana: *El momento presente en la psicoterapia y en la vida cotidiana.* Santiago de Chile; Cuatrovientos, 2017]

Stoller, R. J. (1976). *The structure of sexual perversity.* London: Harverter Press.

Stolorow, R.D. & Atwood, G. (1989). The unconscious and unconscious fantasy: An intersubjective-developmental perspective. *Psychoanalytic Inquiry*, 9:364-374.

Stolorow, R.D. & Atwood, G.E. (1997). Deconstructing the Myth of the Neutral Analyst: An Alternative from Intersubjective Systems Theory. *Psychoanal. Q.*, 66:431-449 (Versión castellana en CeIR, 7 (1), 2013.)

Stolorow, R.D. & Atwood, G.E. (2004). *Los contextos del ser. Las bases intersubjetivas de la vida psíquica.* Barcelona: Herder. [Original *Contexts of Being: The Intersubjective Foundations of Psychological Life.* Hillsdale, NJ: The Analytic Press. 1992] Translation by Ángels Córcoles, M. Josep Estruch, Maite Jordán, Marta Lleonart, Núria Mata, Teresa Mas, Ramon Riera & Montse Ventura.

Stolorow, R.D., Atwood, G. E., & Orange, D. M. (2002). *Worlds of experience: Interweaving philosophical and clinical dimensions in psychoanalysis.* New York: Basic Books.

Stolorow, R.D., Atwood, G.E. & Brandchaft , B. (Eds.) (1994). *The Intersubjective Perspective.* Northvale, NJ/London: Jason Aronson, Inc. 220 pp.

Stolorow, R.D., Brandchaft , B. & Atwood, G.E. (1987). *Psychoanalytic Treatment. An Intersubjective Approach.* Hillsdale, NJ: The Analytic Press. 1987. Pp. 187 pp.

Stolorow, R.D., Orange, D.M., y Atwood, G.E. (2001). Cartesian and post-Cartesian trends in relational psychoanalysis. Psychoanalytic Psychology, 18, 468-484.

Strawson, P.F. (1959). *Individuals. An Essay in Descriptive Metaphysics.* London : Methuen & Co Ltd.

Sullivan, H. S. (1956). *The Interpersonal Theory of Psychiatry*, New York: Norton

Sullivan, H.S. (1963). *Estudios Clínicos de Psiquiatría.* Buenos Aires: Ed. Psique [*Clinical Studies of Psychiatry*, Ed. de Helen Swick, Mary Ladd y Marta Gibbon. New York: Norton, 1956]

Sullivan, H.S. (1964). *La teoría interpersonal de la Psiquiatría*, Buenos Aires: Horme, [*Interpersonal theory of Psychiatry*: edition commissioned by H. S. Perry & M. L. Gawel. N. Y: w. w. Norton & Co., 1953]

Suomi, S. (2004). How gene-enviroment interaction shape biobehavioral development. Lessons from studies with Rhesus monkeys. *Research in human development.* 1 (3) 205-222.

Talarn, A.; Sáinz, F. y Rigat, A. (2013). *Relaciones, vivencias y psicopatología*, Barcelona: Herder.

Taylor, M., Esbensen, B. M., & Bennet, R. T. (1994). Children´s understanding of knowledge acquisition: the tendency for children to report that they have always known what they have just learned. *Child Development*, 65 (5) 1581-1604.

Tomasello, M. (2007). *Los orígenes culturales de la cognición humana.* Buenos Aires: Amorrortu [Original ed. 1999: *The Cultural Origins of Human Cognition.* Cambridge, MA: Harvard University Press]

Tomasello, M. (2009). *Why we cooperate?* The MIT Press.

Trevarthen, C. (1979). Communication and cooperation in early infancy: A description of primary intersubjectivity. En M. M. Bullowa (Ed.). *Before speech: the beginning of interpersonal Communications.* New York: Cambridge University Press.

Trevarthen, C. (1990). Growth and education of the hemispheres. En C. Trevarthen (Ed.). *Brain circuits and functions of the mind.* Cambridge, England: Cambridge University Press.

Trevarthen, C. (1993). The self born in intersubjectivity: an infant communicating. En U. Neissser (ed.) *The perceived self: Ecological and interpersonal sources of self-knowledge* (pp. 121-173). Cambridge: Cambridge University Press.

On Contributors

Manuel Aburto Baselga (Madrid) is Clinical Psychologist and Psycho-analytic psychotherapist. Member of IARPP and IARPP-Spain. Training and Faculty member of the Institute of Relational Psychotherapy. Member of the Research Group for the Advancement of Analytic Technique (GRITA) in Madrid (Spain). Specialist in Relational Psychotherapy and Trauma and author of several papers on Trauma´s work develops his Private practice in Madrid. Contact: aburtobaselga@gmail.com

Alejandro Ávila Espada (Madrid) Ph.D. Clinical Psychologist & Psychoanalytic Psychotherapist. Full Professor & Chair of Psychotherapy at Madrid Complutense University (1984-1990 / 2004-present) and University of Salamanca (1990-2004), both in Spain. Founder and Honor President of IARPP-Spain chapter. Member of the IARPP Board of Directors (2011-2018). Honor President and Training-Faculty Member of the Instituto de Psicoterapia Relacional (Madrid, Spain). Editor of the e-journal *Clínica e Investigación Relacional*, founded 2007. Author of many books, the last: *La tradición interpersonal. Perspectiva social y cultural del psicoanálisis* (Ágora Relacional, Madrid, 2013) [The Interpersonal Tradition. A Social and Cultural Perspective of Psychoanalysis] Contact: avilaespada@psicoterapiarelacional.es; More info and selected papers can be retrieved at: www.psicoterapiarelacional.es/paginaspersonales/AlejandroAvilaEspada.aspx

Rosario Castaño Catalá (Madrid) MA in Psychology from University Complutense (U.Complutense, 1980), Specialist in clinical psychology and Sexologist. Currently heads the Clinical Psychology Department and coordinates the Sexology Unit at the Palacios Institute of Women's Health. Vice-president of the Board of the Institute for Relational Psychotherapy, Madrid; part of the teaching team for the Master in Relational Psychotherapy; and President of the Psychoanalytic Psychotherapist's Section in the Spanish Federation of Psychotherapy. Member of the Spanish Association of Professional Sexology, founding member of the Governing Board of the Spanish Foundation for Women and Health and participant in national and international conferences. Author of a book: Sex Therapy: A relational view (2010) and many papers.

Joan Coderch de Sans (Barcelona) holds a M.D. in Psychiatry. Training Analyst and member of the Spanish Society of Psychoanalysis (SEP) and the International Psychoanalytic Association. He has been dedicated to teaching through the Fundació Vidal i Barraquer and the SEP, and is an honorary member of the Institute of Relational Psychotherapy (IPR, Madrid). Since 2008, he is a professor emeritus of Ramon Llull University. Through his classes, seminars and publications he has examined the links between psychoanalysis and psychiatry, neuroscience, cognitive psychology, philosophy of language and science in general. He has also deepened, in the field of psychoanalysis, in the concepts of the psychology of two people, the interaction, transference and countertransference, interpretation and analyst patient relationship. Author of ten books and more than 200 papers on psychoanalysis and mental health. More info and selected papers can be retrieved at the web page: http://www.psicoterapiarelacional.es/documentacion/AutoresDestacados/JoanCoderch/Publicaciones.aspx

Angels Codosero Medrano (Barcelona) is a Clinical Psychologist and Psychoanalytic Psychotherapist. Member of the Catalonian Association of Psychoanalytic Psychotherapy (ACPP). She has papers on clinical psychoanalysis. Private practice in Barcelona.

Neri Daurella (Barcelona) is a Ph.D. and psychologist specialized in Clinical Psychology; Psychoanalyst, member of the SEP (the Sociedad Española de Psicoanálisis that is part of the IPA) and the Spanish Section of the IARPP (International Association for Psychotherapy and Relational Psychoanalysis). She has been a professor for 30 years at the Faculty of Medicine of the UB (University of Barcelona). She is currently a professor and supervisor in the Psychoanalytic Psychotherapy Master of the Universitary Institute of Mental Health (Vidal i Barraquer Foundation) of the Ramón Llull University and Honor member of Institute of Relational Psychoanalysis (Madrid). Expert in Balint groups, which she has coordinated in many primary care centers of the Catalan Institute of Health. Together with her clinical activity as a psychotherapist and psychoanalyst of adolescents and adults, she has contributed her reflection on the relationship between psychology, psychoanalysis and medicine in papers, articles and book chapters. She is the author of the book Falla Básica y relación terapéutica. La aportación de Michael Balint a la concepción Relacional del Psicoanálisis (Basic Fault and Therapeutic Relationship: The Contribution of Michael Balint to the Relational Concept of Psychoanalysis) (edited by Agora Relacional).

Luis Raimundo Guerra Cid (Valencia) holds a Ph.D. in Psychology (University of Salamanca) and a Degree in Social Anthropology and Culture (UNED). Lecturer at Master's Degree of the University of Salamanca. Author and co-author of eleven books on clinical psychology, psychopathology and psychotherapy, and articles in scientific journals. Member of the Board and Treasury of IARPP-Spain. Full member of Institute of Relational Psychotherapy (Madrid). Former President and psychotherapist member of the SEPPI; member of IARPP and Honorary member of the Spanish Society of Psychosomatic Medicine and Medical Psychology.

Ariel Liberman Isod (Madrid) holds a Ph.D. in Psychology. Clinical Psychologist and Psychoanalyst is a member of Madrid Psychoanalytic Association (APM, IPA). Author/Editor of two books and many papers and chapters on Winnicott, Fairbairn, Mitchell, Levenson, as well as different articles on psychoanalytic clinical matters. Now, it carries out teaching activity in different Masters and groups-studies. He does his clinical private practice in Madrid.

Juan José Martínez Ibáñez (Sevilla) is a clinical psychologist, psychoanalyst and relational psychotherapist. He is a member of the Spanish Society of Psychoanalysis, the British Psychoanalytic Society and the International Psychoanalytic Association. He has created the Giralda Psychotherapy Centre in Seville, an associate center of the Institute of Relational Psychotherapy and IARPP (International Association for Relational Psychotherapy and Psychoanalysis). He is Professor of the Master in Relational Psychotherapy / Specialist in Relational Psychoanalytic Psychotherapy. He has presented papers in different international psychoanalytic congresses and has published articles in different psychoanalytic journals. The evolution of his thinking comes from the mainstream of psychoanalysis towards relational psychoanalysis, integrating the contributions of Bion, Bowlby, Fonagy, Stern and Siegel, and developing a therapeutic method that is practiced at the Giralda Psychotherapy Centre.

Spyros D. Orfanos (New York) Ph.D., ABPP, Clinic Director of New York University Postdoctoral Program in Psychotherapy & Psychoanalysis and Senior Research Fellow, Center of Byzantine & Modern Greek Studies, Queens College, CUNY. He has held numerous leadership positions in major contemporary psychoanalytic organizations, including President of the *International Association for Relational Psychoanalysis and Psychotherapy*; Board of Directors, The Stephen Mitchell Center for Relational Studies; Former President of the Division of Psychoanalysis (39) of the APA; the Academy of Psychoanalysis; and the American Board of Professional Psychology. Author of numerous publications on clinical process, creativity, and culture and arts, he is in independent practice in NYC and Montclair, NJ, treating infants, children, adolescents, and adults.

Carlos Rodríguez Sutil (Madrid) holds a PhD in Psychology from the Universidad Complutense, Madrid (1990), with a thesis on the philosophy of psychology (Wittgenstein and the problem of the mind in contemporary psychology) and a degree in Philosophy and Educational Sciences (Psychology). He has published four books and more than 80 papers about psychopathology, assessment, psychoanalytical psychotherapy and philosophy of psychology during the last 35 years. President of the Institute of Relational Psyhcotheraoy (Madrid) and Editor in chief of the on-line journal Clinica e Investigación Relacional, from 2007 onward. (http://www.psicoterapiarelacional.es/CeIRREVISTAOnline/).Blog: http://crsutil56.blogspot.com.es/

Francecs Sáinz Bermejo (Barcelona) Ph.D., Psychologist. Member of the Spanish Psychoanalytical Society and International Psychoanalytical Association. Psychotherapist ACPP / FEAP. Member of the Relational Psychotherapy Institute (IPR, Madrid. Professor at the University of Barcelona and at Fundació Vidal i Barraquer (Ramón Llull University). Supervisor in public healthcare services of Mental Health and Social Services (Barcelona). Psychoanalyst and psychotherapist, with private practice in Barcelona. President of the Winnicott Barcelona Association. One of the introducers of the work of Winnicott for psychotherapists' training. Author and co-author of various books and articles on psychoanalysis' subjects.

Sandra Toribio Caballero (Madrid) is a Psychologist and Child, adolescent and adult psychotherapist. Specialist in Relational Psychotherapy. Member of the Institute for Relational Psychotherapy (Madrid) and of the International Association for Relational Psychoanalysis and Psychotherapy (IARPP). She works in private practice and as Education coordinator at Ágora Relacional/ Institute for Relational Psychotherapy (Madrid).